Consumer Reports®

Best Buys
for your
H◎ME
2004

FROM THE EDITORS OF CONSUMER REPORTS

Published by Consumer Reports ■ A Division of Consumers Union ■ Yonkers, New York

A Special Publication from Consumer Reports

Group Managing Editor Nancy Crowfoot
Coordinating Editor Merideth Mergel
Contributing Editors Sue Byrne, Bette LaGow
Design Manager Rosemary Simmons
Contributing Art Director Trish Gogarty
Illustrations Trevor Johnston
Technology Specialist Jennifer Dixon
Page Composition Charlene Bianculli

Consumer Reports Technical Division

Vice President and Technical Director Jeffrey A. Asher
Associate Technical Director Alan Lefkow
Director, Product Research Frank Iacopelli
Director, Appliances, Recreation & Home Improvement Mark Connelly
Director, Consumer Sciences Geoffrey Martin
Senior Director, Electronics Evon Beckford
Testing Director, Recreation & Home Improvement John Galeotafiore
Manager, Electronics Gerard Catapano
Manager, Home Improvement James Nanni
Director, Product & Market Information Julie Levine
Manager, Product & Market Information Celeste Monte
Products Director, Technical Information Strategy Carolyn Clifford-Ferrara

Consumer Reports

Editor, CR/Senior Director Margot Slade
Director, Production Operations/Acting Director, Editorial Operations David Fox
Design Director, Consumers Union George Arthur
Creative Director, CR Tim LaPalme
Products Director Paul Reynolds
Vice President, Publishing John Sateja
Senior Director/General Manager, Consumer Reports Information Products Jerry Steinbrink
Senior Director/General Manager, Product and Market Development Paige Amidon
Product Manager, Special Publications Carol Lappin
Director, Survey Research Charles Daviet
Associate Director, Survey Research Mark Kotkin
Manufacturing/Distribution Ann Urban

Consumers Union

President James A. Guest
Executive Vice President Joel Gurin
Senior Vice President, Technical Policy R. David Pittle

Table of Contents

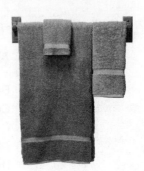

Part Two: Nuts & Bolts

Chapter 6 | **Hassle-Free Remodeling**

Chapter 8 | **Heating, Cooling, Filtering**

Part Three: Reference Section

Best Buys for Your Home covers, in a convenient format, the latest buying tips and product Ratings from CONSUMER REPORTS. Published by the nonprofit Consumers Union, CONSUMER REPORTS is a comprehensive source of unbiased advice about products and services, personal finance, health and nutrition, and other consumer concerns. Since 1936, the mission of Consumers Union has been to test products, inform the public, and protect consumers. Our income is derived solely from the sale of CONSUMER REPORTS magazine and our other publications and services, and from nonrestrictive, noncommercial contributions, grants, and fees. We buy all the products we test. We accept no ads from companies, nor do we let any outside entity use our reports or Ratings for commercial purposes.

Other Buying Guides from Consumer Reports

- Digital Buying Guide
- New Car Buying Guide
- Used Car Buying Guide
- Consumer Reports Buying Guide

Other Publications from Consumer Reports

- Sport-Utility Special
- New Car Preview
- Used Car Yearbook
- Road Tests
- Consumer Drug Reference
- Guide to Baby Products
- How to Clean and Care for Practically Anything

All Around the House

Home centers, mass merchandisers, department stores, kitchen and bath boutiques—all of these retailers and more have been enjoying the ripple effects of the recent boom in the housing market. Whether people are having houses built or are moving into existing construction, they're buying all the trappings that make a house a home, from appliances and wood flooring to wallpaper and replacement windows.

For those folks who are staying where they are, more and more are undertaking home-improvement projects, which could be as minor as painting the living room or as major as remodeling the kitchen. And once the necessities are taken care of, it's time to look for the fun stuff like new video components or labor-saving equipment for working in the yard.

No matter where you fit in this picture, this book is designed to give you an in-depth look at the home-products marketplace so you can get the most for your investment, whether you're buying new products or upgrading existing ones. Generally, what you'll find is that appliance manufacturers are working to satisfy a consumer's desire for kitchen and laundry equipment that is quick, convenient, and "smart," with sensors and other controls—with varying degrees of success—for easier and more precise operation. The home-entertainment industry continues its race toward making everything digital, which can greatly enhance audio and video performance. Out in the yard, equipment is getting safer, quieter, and friendlier to the environment.

Despite the excitement over the Internet and the popularity of catalog sales, the principal shopping arena is still the retail store, from the neighborhood hardware purveyor to Home Depot and Wal-Mart. One thing that hasn't changed is the need for informed decision making. CONSUMER REPORTS provides an invaluable service in that regard, delivering information that can help consumers shop smart in today's world.

Using this book

"Best Buys for Your Home" is designed to help you sort through the myriad choices faced by shoppers for home products. It's divided into three parts. In "Feathering Your Nest," the chapters focus on how a home can be equipped in a way that is functional and often fun, from a step-by-step guide to setting up a home theater and choosing key components such as TV sets and DVD players to advice on appliances for the kitchen and laundry, equipment and tools for the yard, gear that keeps your home clean or safe such as vacuums and smoke detectors, and home "software" such as bedding and carpeting.

In "Nuts & Bolts," you'll find information on home-remodeling, followed by chapters on decorative products, such as paint and wallpaper; building components, such as countertops and windows; and important home equipment, such as air conditioning.

In the back of the book you'll find a comprehensive 98-page reference section that includes CONSUMER REPORTS Ratings of more than 750 brand-name products, as well brand-repair histories for many product categories.

How Consumer Reports tests

For nearly 70 years, CONSUMER REPORTS has bought products and tested them so consumers can make informed decisions. From methodical, scientific tests of products that we buy at retail, we develop our Ratings. (Reliability information for key products, such as TV sets, lawn mowers, and washing machines, comes from surveys of readers of CONSUMER REPORTS magazine, who report their actual experience with specific brands.)

To determine what to test, our engineers, market analysts, and editors attend trade shows, read trade publications, and look at what's in the stores to spot the latest products and trends. They also pay attention to letters from readers. Our market analysts query manufacturers about product lines and update in-house databases listing thousands of models. Eventually, staff shoppers anonymously visit dozens of stores or go online to buy the selected models. A test plan is then prepared to evaluate performance and other aspects of the product, such as safety, energy and water consumption, noise, and convenience. For every product tested, the technical staff records a "pedigree," a thorough accounting of all features and idiosyncrasies.

Measurements are made by computers and by various sensitive instruments, including the most important instruments of all—human eyes, ears, noses, and hands. Much of the work we do in our labs mimics how a product would be used at home, albeit more systematically. Testers read and try out the buttons on the controls. They turn the knobs on the receivers and washing machines and flip through channels on the TV sets. A panel of testers systematically compares everything from TV pictures to vacuum-cleaner handling, sewing-machine ease of use, and more.

For some products, we have to test away from our headquarters in Yonkers, N.Y. We test lawn mowers, for instance, in Florida, where a large lawn of winter rye is specially prepared for five to six weeks of tests every January through March in order to have results by spring. Sometimes our tests are supplemented by the real-life experiences of engineers and volunteers who use the products in their homes.

HOW HOT? For ranges, we determine heating speed by bringing measured amounts of water to a near boil, over and over, model after model. Cooking performance is gauged in various ways: by melting chocolate in a saucepan, by baking cakes and broiling burgers in an oven, and by reheating food in a microwave. To evaluate a range's self-cleaning feature, we bake on and then remove our own special blend of gunk, consisting of cherry pie, tomato puree, egg yolk, mozzarella, cheese spread, tapioca, and lard. To help us evaluate whether irons heat uniformly or have hot spots, we use a thermal camera, which represents different temperatures on the soleplate of each iron as different colors.

HOW COLD? We test refrigerators and room air conditioners in an environmental chamber—a large, heavily insulated room that allows us to control temperature and humidity. To see how readily refrigerators respond to changes in room temperature, we heat up the test chamber from 70° F to 90°, cool it back down to 70°, and then take it down further to 55°. To measure the reserve power a refrigerator might need for torrid weather, we set the room at 110°. Sensors inside each refrigerator monitor how evenly the unit keeps cold.

To test room air conditioners, we mount them in a room within the environmental chamber to create an "outside" and an "inside." Can they maintain a comfortable temperature and humidity level in the room when the outside temperature is 95°? How level do they keep humidity? The chamber's instruments tell the tale.

HOW CLEAN? We feed vacuum cleaners measured amounts of fine sand and talcum powder that we sprinkle onto and then grind into a medium-pile carpet. After a vacuum is passed back and forth over the carpet eight times, we weigh and measure what's left on the carpet and what's inside the machine. To see how much dust spews back into the air, we vacuum fine sawdust from carpeting and use instruments to detect dust in the air.

With dishwashers, we wash dozens of place settings, all systematically soiled with tenacious foods such as chili, spaghetti, mashed potatoes, egg yolk, peanut butter, raspberry jam, cheese spread, cornflakes and milk, oatmeal, stewed tomatoes, and coffee. With washing machines, we assess performance by washing several specially soiled fabric swatches in a load of bedsheets, dress shirts, pillowcases, T-shirts, towels, boxer shorts, and a washcloth.

HOW GREEN? Environmental factors are taken into consideration. For big energy users such as refrigerators, we measure electricity consumption. For washing machines and dishwashers, we measure usage of hot water—typically more costly than the electricity used to run the machine. For room air conditioners, we note energy efficiency. Noise is an important concern when it comes to equipment such as power blowers and wet/dry vacs. It's also a consideration for items that might be located near a living area, such as washing machines, dishwashers, clothes dryers, toilets, room air cleaners, and room air conditioners.

HOW EASY TO USE? No matter how well a product performs its task, if it isn't convenient to use and live with, it isn't a useful product. Small inconveniences on a product that is used every day—the shelf arrangement in a refrigerator, the design of the loading racks in a dishwasher, the arrangement of buttons on a remote control—can become annoying. We carefully examine every product to see how thoughtfully it was designed. We also try out all the built-in menus and prompts to make sure they're logical and not irksome. And we read and evaluate all product instructions.

For updates on the products in this book, check out monthly issues of CONSUMER REPORTS or our Web site, *Consumer Reports.org*.

Kitchen & Laundry

Today's appliances are smarter, more capable, and more energy-efficient than ever before. New technologies and tightened government energy standards have sparked the change. A bonus is that today's appliances, large and small, are likely to be more stylish than the appliances you own now. Here's a rundown on some of the current trends:

ADDED INTELLIGENCE. Everything from dishwashers to mixers has been embellished with electronic sensors, controls, and monitors. "Smart" products are supposed to minimize the guesswork of knowing when the clothes are dry, the food is cooked, the dishes are washed, or the toast is browned.

New technology uses water and energy more efficiently, as with a washer that automatically fills to the water level the load requires, or a refrigerator that defrosts only as necessary, rather than at set intervals.

But such advances are only the first wave. In the pipeline: microwave ovens that scan bar codes on packaged-food labels and automatically set the precise cooking time and power level; Internet-connected refrigerators that scan labels and automatically reorder provisions when you're running low; and self-diagnosing appliances that can convey information to a repair center by computer, allowing a technician to make a preliminary diagnosis before a service call. Whether these products will truly fill a consumer need—or merely serve a manufacturer's need to spark sales—remains to be seen.

FASTER COOKING. Consumers seem to want food cooked ever faster, or at least manufacturers say they do. Titans such as GE and Whirlpool have introduced appliances that claim to reduce cooking times by as much as 60 percent over conventional means by combining various methods—microwave, convection, and halogen or quartz light bulbs. Such hybrid devices may offer another advantage: no preheating.

Longing for a barbecued burger without the hassle of firing up the grill? Some of the increasingly popular electric grills designed for indoor use can cook up to eight burgers in just 3 to 6 minutes.

IMPROVED EFFICIENCY. As of January 1, 2004, the U.S. Department of Energy (DOE) mandated that new washing machines be about 35 percent more efficient than previously required. Based on recent CONSUMER REPORTS tests, many top-loading models now on the market won't pass muster, so expect innovative designs in the future.

Perhaps in anticipation of DOE regulations, manufacturers have introduced more front-loading machines, inherently more frugal because they tumble clothes through water instead of submerging them, as a top-loader does. Front-loaders consume about two-thirds less water than most top-loaders, though newly designed top-loaders are narrowing the gap.

One challenge during this transition period is making sure to pay attention to the yellow EnergyGuide label to determine whether it's the new or old sticker. Newer labels do have slightly revised wording, with a black band across the top that reads: "This model has been tested using the 2004 test procedure. Compare only with models displaying this statement." Be sure to heed that advice. Old and new models were tested to different standards, so the old and new labels are not directly comparable.

Refrigerators, which typically devour more electricity than any other kitchen appliance, are now required to be less gluttonous. In general, side-by-side units are less space- and energy-efficient than either top- or bottom-freezer models. Over the long run, a pricier model with a low annual energy cost may be less expensive than a cheaper model that uses more electricity.

EASIER CLEANING. More products are designed with flat, seamless surfaces, fewer buttons, and touchpad controls, making them easier to clean. Smoothtop electric ranges continue to rise in popularity. And more manufacturers are offering the stainless-steel look-alike finish known as VCM that hides the smudges and fingerprints that seem to multiply on stainless steel.

Gas ranges are cleaning up their act, too, as companies such as GE unveil gas smoothtops: Burners and grates sit atop a solid-glass surface, eliminating pesky nooks, crannies, and dripbowls—although you do have to use a special cleansing cream. Nearly all refrigerators now feature movable glass shelves bound by a lip to retain spills.

SLEEKER STYLING. Just about every major appliance maker now offers stylish kitchen appliances with curved doors, sleek-looking hardware and controls, and a flashy logo or nameplate. Such equipment can cost twice as much as mainstream products, but extra features can help justify the price tag.

Some dishwashers relocate controls from the front panel to the top lip of the door, where they're out of sight and out of reach of little fingers. With a front panel that matches kitchen cabinets, this design can help the dishwasher blend in with its surroundings.

Color choices are proliferating as well. "Pro-style" stainless steel is available on more mainstream models for those who want that look. At the other end of the spectrum, appliances that blend so well with cabinetry you can hardly tell you're in a kitchen. Brushed aluminum finishes are also widely available in mass-marketed products. Biscuit, bisque, and linen have replaced almond. Splashier colors—such as cobalt blue—are available from premium brands such as Jenn-Air, KitchenAid, and Viking.

FAMILY-FRIENDLY FEATURES. Manufacturers are using child lockouts or removable knobs to keep curious fingers out of potentially hazardous places. Some microwaves let you

---

THE APPLIANCE NAME GAME

Who makes what? Despite all the nameplates, only a handful of companies actually make refrigerators, ranges, washers, dryers, and dishwashers. The companies typically sell products under their own brand and also produce specific models for other manufacturers. For example, we know from our laboratory inspections that GE's front-loading washer comes off Frigidaire's assembly line. Sears' Kenmore brand, the biggest name in appliances, isn't made by Sears at all. Kenmore products are made entirely by other companies. Here's a rundown of the key players and the familiar names they sell, listed alphabetically:

FRIGIDAIRE The company, owned by Sweden's Electrolux, also makes Gibson, Kelvinator, and Tappan appliances. The Frigidaire line is typically higher priced, especially in the tony Frigidaire Gallery and Gallery Professional series. Tappan is a significant force in gas ranges. Kelvinator and Gibson are harder to find; products sold under those names are generally less expensive, with fewer features.

GENERAL ELECTRIC One of the two biggest U.S. appliance makers (along with Whirlpool), GE is particularly strong in the cooking categories. The GE name is considered a midrange brand; GE Profile is geared toward people who want to spend more. GE Monogram, focusing on high style and a commercial look with both freestanding and built-in products, competes with boutique names and is distributed separately. Hotpoint is GE's value brand.

KENMORE The nation's biggest source of major appliances, Sears has its store-brand Kenmore models made to order by companies such as Whirlpool, long a manufacturer of many Kenmore laundry machines. Kenmore washing machines and dryers are also made by Frigidaire. Kenmore Elite is Sears' high-end brand of kitchen and laundry products.

MAYTAG The company that made its name in washers and dryers cultivates a premium image, with many of its products bearing the flagship name. Maytag Neptune is a line of premium laundry machines. Performa is the company's value-priced line. Jenn-Air, best known for modular cooktops and ranges, is Maytag's upscale kitchen brand. Admiral and Magic Chef are budget brands. Maytag purchased Amana in 2001 and continues to market appliances under the Amana brand name.

WHIRLPOOL Also strongly positioned in the laundry room, the nation's other major appliance maker sells products under its corporate name in a wide variety of prices. Whirlpool Gold products are a notch up from the mainstream Whirlpool line; KitchenAid is the company's upscale brand; Roper is the bargain brand.

EUROPEAN AND BOUTIQUE BRANDS Small in market share but often leaders in design and styling, brands such as Asko, Bosch, and Miele were among the first to showcase water-efficient engineering and clean-looking controls for dishwashers and washing machines. Viking is the leading manufacturer of pro-style kitchen appliances and outdoor grills. Sub-Zero is gaining market share with products sold under its own name and the Wolf brand. KitchenAid sells pro-style appliances under the KitchenAid Architect moniker. Other makers of pro-style ranges include DCS, Dacor, and Dynasty.

punch in a code to prevent accidental activation. A lockout button disables the knobs on a gas range or keeps the dishwasher from shutting down midcycle if little Nolan starts poking at the keypad. Such niceties are still relatively new and not yet found on many products.

MORE POWER. Sales of powerful commercial-style, stainless-steel ranges—with four or more high-output burners rated at maximum outputs of 15,000 British thermal units per hour, or Btu/hr.—continue to rise. More typical upscale stoves come with an assortment of burners with maximum outputs from 5,000 to 14,000 Btu/hr. Microwaves continue to get more powerful, too, with 1,300 watts the benchmark, up from around 800 a few years ago.

MORE SHOPPING OPTIONS. Frigidaire, GE, Maytag, Sears, and Whirlpool sell almost three-fourths of all major appliances. In some categories, Sears alone sells more than several of its biggest competitors combined, and the company is trying to strengthen its position by selling white goods online.

But the competitive landscape is changing. Deep-discount warehouse membership clubs such as Costco have expanded their selection of refrigerators, ranges, and the like. Home Depot and Lowe's, the nation's biggest home-center chains, have publicly announced they want to dethrone Sears as the leading appliance marketer.

While the Internet has become a popular way to purchase books and get travel deals, it's not much of a factor in the appliance category.

BRAND BATTLES IN SMALL APPLIANCES. Coffeemakers, toasters, and blenders rule the kitchen countertop, with consumers purchasing more of them every year than any other countertop appliance. Three brands account for nearly three-quarters of small-appliance sales: Black & Decker, Hamilton Beach/Proctor-Silex, and Sunbeam/Oster.

Major mass retailers, where most of the products are sold, are trying to grab an even larger share of the business by gaining exclusive rights to established national brands. Hamilton Beach/Proctor-Silex, for example, makes products under the GE name (via a licensing agreement) for sale at Wal-Mart. Philips markets a line under its own name through Target. Black & Decker has partnered with chains such as Kmart. Sears sells small appliances under its Kenmore name.

Breadmakers

Machines costing $50 or less can turn out white bread and raisin bread that is comparable in texture, color, and taste to loaves kneaded by hand and baked in a conventional oven.

Breadmakers allow virtually anyone to bake bread with just minutes of effort and few skills beyond the ability to measure ingredients and push some buttons. What's more, they produce bread that is more than respectable in quality. And they allow you to control what goes into your bread, which might appeal to people with food allergies or gluten intolerance.

What's available

There are fewer brands today than there were 10 years ago, when this product was introduced. Salton, owner of the Breadman and Toastmaster brands, dominates the market. Breadmakers can be found everywhere from specialty kitchen shops to Wal-Mart. You can also find many models through online retailers such as Amazon.

Breadmakers typically take up a lot of room. Most are 12 to 13 inches high and 10 to 11 inches deep; they vary in width from 10 to 19 inches. Most make one 2-pound traditionally shaped loaf, which typically measures about 7x5 inches and yields 13 half-inch-thick slices.

Price range: $40 to $200.

Key features

Most of the machines have a rectangular bread **pan,** which produces a more customary-looking loaf than did the tall, squarish pan common in the past. Typically, you place the ingredients in the pan, insert the pan in the machine, close the cover, and push buttons to select the right cycle.

A **paddle** fitted on a shaft in the pan's base mixes the ingredients and kneads the dough, stopping at programmed times to allow for rising before kneading again. An electric **heating coil** in the machine's base then bakes the bread. The time required for each step depends on the type of bread. Whole-wheat dough, for example, needs more time to rise and bake than does white.

The typical breadmaker has **cycles** for basic white bread, whole-wheat, sweet, or fruit-and-nut bread, plus "dough" (to be used when you want to finish the dough by hand and bake it in the oven—for challah or other shaped breads, for example).

Most models also have specialty cycles for, say, French bread and pizza dough. On their regular white-bread cycle, breadmakers can take as long as 3½ hours. Most have one or two rapid cycles, which increase heat during mixing to prepare loaves in as little as an hour. Recipes for rapid bread often call for more yeast than recipes for regular bread.

Convenience features let you bake without constantly having to hover. A **delay-start timer,** available on most models, lets you postpone when your bread is done—typically 13 hours from the time you press the button—nice if you'd like to wake up to a just-baked loaf of bread.

A **temperature-warning signal** lets you know when the kitchen temperature isn't optimal for yeast growth. An **add-in signal** tells you when to add fruit, nuts, or other extras so they don't get chopped during kneading.

Crust control adjusts baking time so you get the crust color of your choice. A **keep-warm/cool-down function** keeps the bread from getting soggy for at least an hour if you aren't there to take it out right away.

Power-outage protection ensures that the breadmaker will pick up where it left off after an outage. Some machines can withstand an hour-long outage; others can handle only a few seconds.

How to choose

PERFORMANCE DIFFERENCES. Very good bread is symmetrical and evenly baked, with an interior that's somewhat soft, moist, and airy and a crust that's crisp but not too thick or hard. All the breadmakers we tested made very good white bread on their regular cycle (at a cost of about 90 cents per loaf). And all made very good raisin bread as well. Tests did turn up differences, however, in the quality of whole-wheat bread. We also found that most machines produced short, dense loaves when set on the rapid cycle.

RECOMMENDATIONS. If you're looking for a breadmaker that will turn out very good white or raisin bread, opt for the least expensive model. The largest selection can be found at mass-merchandiser outlets, discount stores, and online. Don't base your decision on the availability or speed of a rapid cycle or you're likely to be disappointed in the results.

Should you need to replace a bread pan or dough blade after the warranty expires, it might make more sense to buy a new machine. We found that replacing those parts could cost up to 65 percent of the original purchase price.

Coffeemakers

Most models make a good cup of coffee. Higher-priced coffeemakers usually have more convenience features and fancier styling.

The popularity of Starbucks and other specialty coffee shops seems to be driving the demand for a new generation of coffeemakers that replicates the coffeehouse experience at home. Customized brewing, water filtration, and thermal carafes are a few of the features manufacturers are hoping will encourage consumers to trade up. Truth is, virtually any model can make a good cup as long as you use decent coffee.

What's available

While manual-drip systems, coffee presses, and percolators are available, consumers buy more automatic-drip coffeemakers than any other small kitchen appliance: 17 million per year. Mr. Coffee and Black & Decker are the two largest brands, along with well-known names such as Braun, Cuisinart, Delonghi, Krups, Melitta, and Proctor Silex.

Coffeemakers come in sizes from single-cup models to machines capable of brewing up to 12 cups at a time. Ten- and 12-cup machines account for more than 80 percent of the market, although manufacturers are trying to expand sales by pushing fully featured 4-cup models.

At the low end are bare-bones coffeemakers with a single switch to start the brewing process and a plain metal hotplate; pricier models can have programmable start and stop times, a water filter, frothing capability, and a thermal carafe. Most consumers opt for the more basic models. Black and white remain the standard colors, but some brands have added other hues.

Price range: $15 to more than $90.

Key features

A **removable filter basket** is the easiest for loading and for removing the used filter; baskets that sit inside a pullout drawer can be messy. **Paper filters**—usually "cupcake" or cone-shaped—absorb oil and keep coffee sediment from creeping through. Models with a **permanent mesh filter** need to be cleaned after each use, but they can save you money over time.

Neither type of filter detracted from coffee flavor in our tests. The simplest type of water **reservoir** is one with a big flip-top lid and lines that mark the number of cups in large, clearly visible numbers. Some reservoirs are removable—so you can fill up at the sink—and dishwasher safe. **Transparent fill tubes** with **cup markings** let you check the water level while pouring.

A **thermal carafe** helps retain flavor and aroma longer than a glass pot on a hotplate. Other niceties: a **small-batch setting** to adjust brew time when you make fewer than 5 cups; **temperature** and **brew-strength controls;** and a **drip-stop feature** that lets you pour a cup before the whole pot's done.

A **programmable timer** lets you add ground coffee and water the night before, so you can wake up to a freshly brewed pot. A **clock-timer** automatically turns off the hotplate at a specified or programmed time after brewing.

New models frequently have a more **compact footprint** and flat, **electronic-touchpad controls.** Some high-end models feature a **built-in bean grinder. A built-in water filter** may cut chlorine and, sometimes, mineral buildup (but a filter can harbor bacteria if you don't change it regularly).

How to choose

PERFORMANCE DIFFERENCES. In our tests, just about any drip coffeemaker made good-tasting coffee. The differences among machines mostly pertain to convenience. Some models have hard-to-clean nooks and crannies or unclear markings; some easily show stains.

Some programmable models were much tougher to set than others. Brewing time for a full pot took from 9 to 11 minutes; models designated as "restaurant" type—which keep a full reservoir of hot water at the ready—brewed 8 cups in less than 4 minutes.

RECOMMENDATIONS. If all you want is a good cup of java, there are plenty of coffeemakers from which to choose, starting at around $15. A few dollars more buys a machine that's easier to fill and a carafe that's easier to pour from.

At higher prices, you get luxuries such as programmability, sculptural style, and extras such as a drip-stop feature or a grinder.

Ratings: page 216

Cookware

Nonstick pots and pans are easy to clean. Uncoated cookware is often more durable. Your best bet might be some of each.

Is boiling water the extent of your kitchen prowess or do you routinely take on much more challenging tasks? Could you work in the kitchen of a five-star restaurant or are you a culinary klutz? How you answer those questions is a good gauge of the price range for the cookware you need.

A basic set of seven to 10 pieces, typically one or two pots, a skillet, a stockpot, and lids, can be had for $50. At the other end of the spectrum, you can get a set of stylish and sturdy commercial-style cookware for as much as $600. And there are lots of choices in between.

What's available

Farberware, Mirro/Wearever, Revere, and T-Fal are the most widely sold brands. Commercial-style brands include All-Clad and Calphalon. TV's celebrity chef Emeril Lagasse is mixing it up in the cookware market with Emerilware (made by All-Clad). Other more recent entrants in the cookware field include the appliance maker KitchenAid and the knife maker Henckels.

Choices abound. You can find aluminum, stainless steel, copper, cast iron, tempered glass, or porcelain on carbon steel; nonstick, porcelain-coated, or uncoated; lightweight or heavy-duty commercial-style; handles of metal, plastic, or wood.

Commercial-style cookware is typically made of aluminum or stainless steel. Cooking enthusiasts will appreciate the fact that these sturdy pots and pans are built to conduct heat evenly up the sides and that their riveted metal handles can be put to hard use. A stovetop grill pan often has raised ridges that sear meat and vegetables. Basic sets of cookware can be supplemented with individual pieces from open stock.

Price range: $50 or less for a low-end set; $50 to $100 for midlevel; $200 and up for high-end or commercial-style.

Key features

The most versatile materials for pots and pans are the most common ones: aluminum and stainless steel. **Aluminum,** when it's sufficiently heavy-gauge, heats quickly and evenly. On the other hand, thin-gauge aluminum, besides heating unevenly, is prone to denting and warping. **Anodized aluminum** is an excellent conductor of heat and is relatively lightweight; it's durable, but easily stained and not dishwasher-safe. **Enamel-coated aluminum,** typically found in low-end lines, can chip easily.

Stainless steel can go in the dishwasher, but it conducts and retains heat poorly. It's usually layered over aluminum. Some stainless-steel pots have a bottom with a copper or aluminum core.

Copper heats and cools quickly, ideal when temperature control is important. It's good for, say, making caramel sauce. Provided that it's kept polished, copper looks great hanging on a kitchen wall or from the ceiling. Because copper reacts with acidic foods such as tomatoes, it's usually lined with stainless steel or tin, which may blister and wear out over time. Solid-copper cookware, thin-gauge or heavy-gauge, is expensive. As such, you might want to purchase a few choice pieces rather than an entire set.

Consider some **cast-iron** or **tempered-glass** pieces. Cast iron is slow to heat and cool, but it handles high temperatures well, and it's great for stews or Cajun-style blackening. Be careful when using cast-iron cookware on a glass smoothtop stove since its weight could damage the surface. Tempered glass cookware breaks easily and cooks unevenly on the stove, but it can go directly from the freezer to the stove, oven, broiler, or microwave—and then on to the table.

Most Americans opt for **nonstick** pots and pans to reduce the need for elbow grease when cleaning up. Introduced on cookware more than 30 years ago, the first nonstick coatings were thin and easily scratched. Nonsticks have greatly improved, but still shouldn't be used with metal utensils or very high heat.

To improve durability, some manufacturers use a thicker nonstick coating or create a gritty or textured surface before applying the nonstick finish. Many nonstick pots and pans aren't meant for the dishwasher, but they're easy to wash by hand.

There are some advantages to **uncoated** cookware. It's dishwasher-safe, it can handle metal utensils, and it's good for browning. Uncoated cookware is also better when you want food to stick a little—say, when you want particles of meat left behind in a pan after sautéing so you can make a flavorful pan sauce. **Porcelain coatings** are easy to maintain and they're tough (although they can be chipped).

Handles are typically made from tubular stainless steel, cast stainless steel, heat-resistant plastic, or wood. **Solid metal handles** are unwieldy but sturdy. Solid or **hollow metal handles** can get hot but can go from stovetop to broiler without damage. (Check the label first; some can warp or discolor when used that way.)

Lightweight plastic handles won't get as hot as metal ones, but they can't go in ovens above 350° F—and they occasionally break. While **wooden handles** stay cool, they can't go in the oven or dishwasher. And they may deteriorate over time. Handles are either welded, screwed, or riveted onto cookware. **Riveted handles** are the strongest. Some sets have removable handles that are used with different pieces, but we've found that the handles may fit with some pieces better than others.

Cookware with a specific shape simplifies certain cooking tasks. A skillet with **flared sides** aids sautéing or flipping omelets. **Straight sides** are better for frying. **Flat bottoms** work well on an electric range, especially a smoothtop.

How to choose

PERFORMANCE DIFFERENCES. Most people now opt for nonstick pots and pans, which require little or no oil and clean easily. But uncoated cookware is better for browning and can stand up to metal utensils. While commercial-style sets are sturdy, they're also relatively heavy and their metal handles get hot. "Hand weigh" pieces as you shop, and

Bird-watch
Pet birds should be kept out of the kitchen. They can die from fumes produced by accidentally heating nonstick coatings above 500° F. DuPont, maker of Teflon, notes on its Web site that the fumes from polytetrafluoroethylene (PTFE), a nonstick coating, are dangerous to the delicate lungs of birds.

imagine how they will feel when full. You might be happier using lightweight pots and pans with comfortable plastic handles that stay better insulated from the heat. Cast iron and copper are great for making certain dishes, but they may not be practical as basic cookware.

RECOMMENDATIONS. Choose a set with pots and pans that best match your cooking style. Over time, you can supplement your set by buying from open stock. Some people prefer individual pieces in different styles—a nonstick frying pan, say, and an uncoated stockpot.

Ratings: page 220

Dishwashers

Models selling for as little as $350 or so can excel at washing dishes. But they may not measure up to pricier models in quietness, water and energy efficiency, or features.

Spend $300 to $400 and you can get a dishwasher that's a little noisy but still does a good job cleaning dirty dishes without prerinsing. To get the best of everything—cleaning prowess plus quieter operation, more convenience features, efficiency with water and energy, even designer styling—you'll have to spend $600 or more.

A dirt sensor, once a premium feature, has made its way down to lower-priced models. That's not necessarily a plus. Sensors are designed to adjust water level to the amount of soil on dishes, but we've found them to be of marginal use in our tests. And they're not as energy efficient as the federal government's EnergyGuide stickers and Energy Star designations suggest: Those labels are based on water and energy usage with completely clean loads, not the soiled dishes you'll be washing in normal use.

What's available

Frigidaire (owned by Electrolux), GE, Maytag, and Whirlpool make most dishwashers and sell them under their own names, the names of associated brands, and sometimes the Sears Kenmore label. Whirlpool makes high-end KitchenAid, low-end Roper, and most Kenmore models.

Maytag makes the high-end Jenn-Air, midpriced Amana, and low-priced Admiral dishwashers. GE offers a wide range of choices under the GE label and also makes the value-priced Hotpoint. Asko, Bosch, and Miele are high-end European brands; Viking dishwashers are made by Asko.

Most models fit into a 24-inch-wide space under a kitchen countertop and are attached to a hot-water pipe, drain, and an electrical line. Compact models fit into narrower spaces. If you've got the room, it's now possible to get a wider, 30-inch dishwasher. Portable models in a finished cabinet can be rolled over to the sink and connected to the faucet.

A "dishwasher in a drawer" design from Fisher & Paykel, a New Zealand–based company, has two stacked drawers that can be used simultaneously or individually, depending upon the number of dishes you need to wash.

Price range: $250 to $1,300 (domestic brands); $500 to $1,800 (foreign-made brands).

Key features

Most models offer a choice of at least three **wash cycles**—Light, Normal, and Heavy—which should be enough for typical dishwashing jobs. **Rinse/Hold** lets you rinse dirty dishes before using the dishwasher on a full cycle. Other cycles offered on many models include **Pot Scrubber, Soak/Scrub,** and **China/Crystal,** none of which we consider crucial. Dishwashers often spray water from multiple places, or "levels," in the machine. Most models typically offer a choice of **drying** with or without heat.

Some dishwashers use two **filters** to keep wash water free of food that can be redistributed on clean dishes. A coarse outer filter captures large bits and a fine inner filter removes smaller particles. Most such models are self-cleaning: A spray arm cleans residue from the coarse filter during the rinse cycle, and a food-disposal **grinder** cuts up large food particles.

Some of the more expensive dishwashers have a filter that you must pull out and clean manually; these are usually quieter than those with grinders. If noise is a concern, see if better **soundproofing**—often in the form of hard, rubbery insulation surrounded by a thick fiberglass blanket—is available as a step-up feature.

Sensors determine how dirty the dishes are, or how large the load is, and provide the appropriate amount of water. But in our tests with very dirty dishes, models with dirt sensors didn't clean noticeably better than those without. Sensors that determined load size did reduce water used on small loads, however, particularly when the dishes weren't very dirty.

A sanitizing wash or rinse option that raises the water temperature above the typical 140° F doesn't necessarily mean improved cleaning. Remember, the moment you touch a dish while taking it out of the dishwasher, it's no longer sanitized.

Most dishwashers have **electronic touchpad controls.** On more expensive ones, the controls may be fully or partially hidden, or integrated, in the top edge of the door. The least expensive models have **mechanical controls,** usually operated by a dial and push buttons. Touchpads are the easiest to clean. Dials indicate progress through a cycle. Some electronic models digitally display time left in the wash cycle. Others merely show a "clean" signal. A **delayed-start** control lets you run the dishwasher at night, when utility rates may be lower. Some models offer **child-safety features,** such as locks for the door and controls.

GET THE MOST FROM YOUR DISHWASHER

With any dishwasher, you'll get better performance if you load the dishes correctly, use a dishwasher detergent with enzymes, and use a rinse aid. A few tips:

• **Consult the user manual for guidelines on loading your machine most efficiently. Place the heavily soiled side of dishes toward the center of the machine for better exposure to the spray. Keep large items at the sides and back so they don't prevent the water spray from reaching the detergent dispenser.**

• **Don't let dishes or utensils nest, or rest side by side, which can prevent water from reaching all surfaces. To prevent chipping, make sure that china, crystal, and stemware don't touch other items. Don't machine-wash brass, bronze, cast iron, disposable plastics, gold-colored flatware, gold-leaf china, hollow-handle knives, pewter, tin, or anything made of wood (including handles).**

• **Most machines do a fine job if you don't prerinse dishes, so skip the sink. You'll save about 6,500 gallons of water a year (based on average household usage). You can also save water by running full loads. If you don't like leaving dirty dishes unwashed, run the rinse-and-hold cycle, which uses about 2 gallons of water—much less than used by hand-rinsing under running water.**

• **Use a rinse aid such as Jet-Dry to help minimize spotting and a detergent with enzymes to dissolve starches and proteins. Among the enzyme-based products that performed well in our detergent tests: Great Value (sold at Wal-Mart stores), Cascade Pure Rinse Formula, and Electrasol Dual Action Tabs with Baking Soda.**

Most dishwashers hold cups and glasses on top, plates on the bottom, and silverware in a basket. **Racks** can sometimes be adjusted to better fit your dishes. On some models, the top rack can be adjusted enough to let you put 10-inch dinner plates on both top and bottom racks simultaneously. Maytag manufactures a model with three racks instead of the usual two: The shelf-like third rack below the others can hold large, shallow items such as platters.

Other features that enhance flexibility include **adjustable** and **removable tines,** which flatten areas to accept bigger dishes, pots, and pans; **slots for silverware** that prevent nesting; **removable racks,** which enable loading and unloading outside the dishwasher; **stemware holders,** which steady wine glasses; **clips** to keep light plastic cups from over-turning; and **fold-down shelves,** which stack cups in a double-tiered arrangement

Stainless-steel **tubs** may last virtually forever, whereas plastic ones can discolor. But plastic tubs usually have a warranty of 20 years, much longer than most people keep a dishwasher. In our tests, stainless-steel-lined models had a slightly shorter drying time but didn't wash dishes any better.

If you want a front panel that matches your cabinets, you can buy a kit compatible with many dishwashers. Some higher-priced models are designed to be customized; they come without a front panel so you can choose your own, usually at a cost of several hundred dollars.

How to choose

PERFORMANCE DIFFERENCES. Most dishwashers we tested did an excellent or very good job, with little or no spotting or redepositing of food. Manufacturers typically make a few different wash systems, with different "levels" and filters.

According to our tests, the main differences among dishwashers are in water and energy use and in noise level. The quietest models are so unobtrusive you might hear them only if you're really listening. Cycle times vary from about 1½ hours to 2½ hours. Several machines that did an excellent job at washing dishes have cycle times of less than 2 hours.

While a dishwasher uses some electricity to run its motor and its drying heater or fan, about 80 percent of the energy is used to heat water, both in the home's water heater and in the machine itself.

Long-term water efficiency differences can noticeably affect the cost of the machine over its life cycle. Dishwashers in recent tests used between 5 and 12 gallons in a normal cycle. The annual cost of operation might range from about $28 to $52 with a gas water heater, $48 to $85 with an electric water heater.

Dishwashers with dirt sensors aren't as efficient as you might think. If you run very dirty loads—especially without prerinsing—these dishwashers will use much more hot water, and require more energy to heat that water, than the labels indicate. To reduce energy costs with any dishwasher, don't prerinse, wait until you have a full load, and choose the lightest cycle that experience tells you will get your dishes clean.

RECOMMENDATIONS. The best-performing dishwashers aren't always the most expensive. You can get fine performance at a low price if you don't insist on the quietest operation and the most flexible loading. High-priced models, including foreign brands, offer styling and soundproofing that appeal to some buyers. Foreign brands are also often more energy efficient.

Compare prices of delivery and installation. Installation can run $100 to $200 or more; removing your old dishwasher may cost an extra $25 to $50.

Ratings: page 222 Reliability: page 290

Dryers

On the whole, all clothes dryers do a good job. The more sophisticated models do it with greater finesse.

Dryers are relatively simple. Their major differences are how they heat the air (gas or electricity) and how they're programmed to shut off once the load is dry (thermostat or moisture sensor). Gas models typically cost about $50 more than electric ones, but they're cheaper to operate.

CONSUMER REPORTS has found that dryers with a moisture sensor tend to recognize when laundry is dry more quickly than machines that use a traditional thermostat. Because they don't subject clothing to unnecessary heat, moisture-sensor models are easier on fabrics. And since they shut themselves off sooner, they use less energy. Sensors are now offered on many dryers, including some relatively low-cost ones. In our most recent tests, some $350 models had sensors.

What's available

The top four brands—GE, Maytag, Kenmore (Sears), and Whirlpool—account for just over 80 percent of dryer sales. Other brands include Amana (owned by Maytag), Frigidaire (owned by Electrolux), Hotpoint (made by GE), and KitchenAid and Roper (both made by Whirlpool).

You may also run across smaller brands such as Crosley, Gibson, and White-Westinghouse, all of which are made by the larger brands. Asko, Bosch, and Miele are European brands. Fisher-Paykel is imported from New Zealand, LG from Korea, and Haier from China.

FULL-SIZED MODELS. These models generally measure between 27 and 29 inches in width—the critical dimension for fitting into cabinetry and closets. Front-mounted controls on some models let you stack the dryer atop a front-loading washer.

Full-sized models vary in drum capacity from about 5 to 7½ cubic feet. Most dryers have ample capacity for typical wash loads. A larger drum can more easily handle bulky items such as queen-sized comforters.

Price range: $200 to $800 (electric); $250 to $850 (gas). Buying a more expensive model may get you more capacity and a few extra conveniences.

SPACE-SAVING MODELS. Compacts, exclusively electric, are typically 24 inches wide, with a drum capacity roughly half that of full-sized models—

about 3½ cubic feet. Aside from their smaller capacity, they perform much like full-sized machines. They can be stacked atop a companion washer, but shorter people may find it difficult to reach the dryer controls or the inside of the drum. Some dryers operate on 120 volts, while others operate on 240 volts.

Price range: $380 to about $1,400.

Another space-saving option is a laundry center, which combines a washer and dryer in a single unit. Laundry centers come with either gas or electric dryers.

There are full-sized (27 inches wide) or compact (24 inches wide) models available. The dryer component of a laundry center typically has a somewhat smaller capacity than a full-sized dryer. Models with electric dryers require a dedicated 240-volt power source.

Price range: $700 to $1,900.

SWEAT THE SMALL STUFF

You may not give a second thought to the ducts that funnel the moist, hot air and lint from your dryer to the outdoors, but you should. The Consumer Product Safety Commission reports that there were 15,600 fires associated with clothes dryers in 1998 (the most recent year for which data are available), accounting for about 20 deaths, 370 injuries, and more than $75.4 million in property damage. Gas dryers pose another potential hazard to consumers: If they are not properly vented, carbon monoxide can be forced back into the home, causing illness or even death. Heed these simple precautions to make sure that you don't become a statistic:

• **Follow the manufacturer's instructions on how to vent your dryer properly.**

• **If you have a choice of where to install your dryer, position it so that the ductwork is short and free of twists and turns. That will minimize the risk of lint buildup inside the ductwork.**

• **No matter what the setup, use metal dryer ductwork. Rigid ducts are best, but flexible metal ductwork can be used where needed for turns. Never use foil or plastic ducts, which tend to kink and sag, creating pockets where lint or condensation can accumulate. Make sure the exhaust opening on the exterior of your house isn't blocked. If airflow from the dryer is blocked either in the duct or at the opening, the dryer can overheat and cause a fire.**

• **Clean the dryer's lint filter after every use and have the ducts cleaned once a year—more often if the dryer is heavily used. You should find the instructions in the user's manual, or you can hire a professional to do the job for you. If you do the job yourself, accessories such as long brushes and blowers can make it easier.**

Key features

Full-sized dryers often have two or three **auto-dry cycles,** which shut them off when clothes reach the desired dryness. Each cycle might have a **More Dry** setting to dry clothes completely, and a **Less Dry** setting to leave clothes damp and ready for ironing. Setting the dryer in between those two extremes is a good idea.

Manufacturers have refined the way dryers shut themselves off. As clothes tumble past a **moisture sensor,** electrical contacts in the drum sample their conductivity for surface dampness and relay signals to electronic controls. Dryers with a **thermostat** measure moisture indirectly by taking the temperature of exhaust air from the drum (the temperature rises as moisture evaporates).

Moisture-sensor models are more accurate than those with a thermostat, sparing your laundry unnecessary drying and sparing you from needlessly high energy bills. Once found only on higher-priced models, sensors are now available on about half the dryers on the market, including some lower-cost models.

Most dryers have a separate **temperature control** that lets you choose a lower heat for delicate fabrics, among other things. An **extended tumble** setting, sometimes called Press Care or Finish Guard, helps to prevent wrinkling when you don't remove clothes from the dryer immediately.

Some models continue to tumble without heat; others cycle on and off. An **express-dry cycle** is meant for drying small loads at high heat in less than a half hour. Large loads will take longer. Higher-priced dryers may offer a dozen or so choices, including specialty cycles such as "dry cleaning." We've found that specialty cycles can usually be replicated with standard settings. A choice of heat level, timed or auto-dry, and a few fabric types (regular/cotton and permanent press/delicate) is generally adequate.

Touchpad electronic controls found in higher-end models tend to be more versatile and convenient than mechanical dials and buttons—once you figure them out, that is. Some models let you save favorite settings. High-end dryers have a video display with a progression of menus that let you program specific settings for recall at any time.

A **top-mounted lint filter** may be somewhat easier to clean than one that resides inside the drum. Some models have a **warning light** that reminds you to clean the lint filter. It's important to clean the lint filter regularly to minimize any fire hazard. It's also advisable to use metal ducting (either rigid or flexible) instead of plastic or flexible foil, which can create a fire hazard by trapping lint.

Most full-sized models have a **drum light,** making it easy for you to spot stray items that may be clinging to the top of the drum or hiding in the back. Some models let you raise or lower the volume of an **end-of-cycle signal** or shut it off.

A **rack** included with many machines attaches inside the drum and is intended to hold sneakers or other bulky items. Models with a **drop-down door** in front may fit better against a side wall, but a **side-opening door** may make it easier to access the inside of the drum.

How to choose

PERFORMANCE DIFFERENCES. We've found that nearly all machines dry ordinary laundry loads well. Models with a moisture sensor don't overdry clothes as much as models using a thermostat, saving energy as well as sparing fabric wear and tear.

Think twice about pricey extras. Electronic touchpads or push buttons and displays look impressive and may allow you to save custom programs. But they don't offer any performance advantage over mechanical push buttons or dials, and they can be confusing.

If you plan on putting the dryer near the kitchen or a bedroom, pay attention to the noise level. Some models are loud enough to drown out normal conversation. Virtually all dryers can accommodate the load from a typical washer, so capacity isn't an issue unless you want to dry bulky items such as comforters.

RECOMMENDATIONS. It's worthwhile to spend the $30 to $50 extra for a moisture-sensor model. More efficient drying will eventually pay for the extra cost.

Purchase a gas dryer if you can. Although priced about $50 more than an electric model, a gas dryer usually costs about 25 cents less per load to operate, making up the price difference in a year or two of typical use. The extra hardware of a gas dryer, however, often makes it more expensive to repair.

Ratings: page 226 Reliability: page 291

Freezers

Chest freezers cost the least to buy and run, but self-defrost uprights are the winners for convenience.

If you buy box loads of burgers at a warehouse club or like to keep a few weeks' worth of dinner fixings on hand, the 4- to 6-cubic-foot freezer compartment in most refrigerators may seem positively Lilliputian. A separate freezer might be a good investment.

What's available

Most freezers sold in the U.S. are from one of two companies: Frigidaire, which makes models sold under the Frigidaire, GE, and Kenmore labels; and W.C. Wood, which makes models sold under its own name as well as Amana, Magic Chef, Maytag, and Whirlpool.

There are two types of freezer: chests—essentially horizontal boxes, with a door that opens upward—need to be defrosted manually; and uprights, which resemble a single-door refrigerator and come in self-defrost and manual-defrost versions.

CHESTS. These freezers vary most in capacity, ranging from 4 to 25 cubic feet. Aside from a hanging basket or two, chests are wide open, letting you put in even large, bulky items. Nearly all the claimed cubic-foot space is usable. The design makes chests more energy efficient and cheaper to operate than uprights. Cooling coils are built into the walls, so no fan is required to circulate the cold air. Because the door opens from the top, virtually no cold air escapes when you put in or take out food.

But a chest's open design does make it hard to organize the contents. Finding something can require bending and, often, moving around piles of frozen goods. If you're short, you may find it difficult to extricate an item buried at the bottom (assuming you can remember it's stashed there). A chest also takes up more floor space than an upright. A 15-cubic-foot model is about 4 feet wide by 2½ feet deep; a comparable upright is just as deep but only 2 to 2½ feet wide.

Defrosting a chest can be a hassle, especially if it's fully loaded or has a thick coating of ice. Since all chests are manual-defrost, you have to unload the food, keep it frozen somewhere until the ice encrusting the walls has melted, remove the water that accumulates at the drain, then put back the food.

Price range: $140 to $550.

SELF-DEFROST UPRIGHTS. These models (sometimes called frost-free) have from 11 to 25 cubic feet of space. Like a refrigerator, they have shelves in the main compartment and on the door; some have pullout bins. This arrangement lets you organize and access contents, but reduces usable space by about 20 percent. Interior shelves can be removed or adjusted to fit large items.

When you open the door of an upright, cold air spills out from the bottom while warm, humid air sneaks in at the top. That makes the freezer work harder and use more energy to stay cold, and temperatures may fluctuate a bit. These models compensate by using a fan to circulate cold air from the cooling coils, which are located in the back wall.

Self-defrosting involves heaters that turn on periodically to remove excess ice buildup, eliminating a tedious, messy chore but using extra energy: A self-defrost model costs about $20 a year more to run than a similar-sized chest. For many people, the convenience may be worth the extra cost. Self-defrosting models are a bit noisier than other types, an issue only if they're located near a living area rather than in the basement or garage. While freezers of old weren't recommended for use in areas that got very hot or cold, current self-defrost models should work fine within a wide ambient temperature range—typically 32° F to 110° F.

Price range: $350 to $750.

MANUAL-DEFROST UPRIGHTS. These freezers have a capacity of 5 to 25 cubic feet, of which some 15 percent isn't usable. They cost less to buy and run than self-defrost models but aren't as economical as chests. Unlike their self-defrost counterparts, they don't have a fan to circulate cold air, which can result in uneven temperatures.

Defrosting is quite a chore with some. The metal shelves in the main space are filled with coolant, so if you're not careful scraping off the ice you can damage the shelves. What's more, ice tends to cling to the shelves, so defrosting can take up to 24 hours. Other models have a "flash" defrost system that heats the cooling coils to quickly melt any frost. There's no need to scrape, but, as with any freezer, you must empty the contents before defrosting. Because a manual-defrost upright's shelves contain coolant, they can't be adjusted or removed to hold large items.

Price range: $160 to $600.

Key features

While freezers are simpler than some other major appliances, there are several features worth looking for. **Interior lighting** makes it easier to find things, especially if you place the freezer in a dimly lit area. A **power-on light,** indicating that the freezer has power, is helpful. A **temperature alarm** lets you know when the freezer is too warm inside, such as after a prolonged power outage. (If you lose power, don't open the freezer door; food should remain frozen for about 24 to 48 hours.)

A **quick-freeze** feature brings the freezer to its coldest setting faster by making it run continuously instead of cycling on and off; that's handy when you're adding a lot of food. The **flash-defrost** feature on some manual-defrost upright freezers can make defrosting easier and faster.

How to choose

PERFORMANCE DIFFERENCES. We've found that most freezers of a type are similar in terms of performance, efficiency, and convenience. The usable capacity of chest freezers is generally the same as the labeled capacity; the capacity of some manual-defrost and self-defrost uprights is somewhat less than what's claimed. Operating a new 15-cubic-foot freezer costs $30 to $55 a year at typical electric rates, depending on the type. That's in the same ballpark as a new refrigerator's annual energy cost.

RECOMMENDATIONS. A chest freezer gives you the most space and the best performance for the lowest purchase price and operating cost. But you'll have to defrost it periodically, which is a real chore. For freedom from defrosting and ease of access, go with a self-defrost upright. It will cost a little more to buy and operate than a chest, but the convenience may be worth it. We don't see a compelling reason to buy a manual-defrost upright when

Ice cold

Use a freezer thermometer, which costs less than $10 at hardware and houseware outlets, to see whether your freezer is maintaining the optimum temperature of 0° F.

comparable self-defrosting models perform better and cost about the same. Manual models, however, do offer more usable space for the money than self-defrost models.

Irons

Many new irons are bigger, more colorful, more feature-laden, and more expensive. But you can still get a fine performer for $25 or so.

Casual Fridays at work have meant fewer trips to the dry cleaner and more ironing at home—of chinos, cotton shirts, and such. Manufacturers are trying to make ironing seem like less of a chore, with features galore on pricey new models. You'll find many models to choose from—including budget models that should do just fine on those chinos.

What's available

GE, Kenmore, and Toastmaster have started selling irons, joining familiar names such as Black & Decker and Proctor-Silex, which together account for more than half of all iron sales. More consumers are springing for a higher-priced iron than in years past, but three out of four still spend less than $40.

But budget-priced doesn't necessarily mean bare bones. Features such as automatic shutoff, burst of steam, and self-clean are now standard on most $25 to $40 models. Irons priced at $40 and up tend to be larger, with innovations such as vertical steaming, antidrip steam vents, and even anticalcium systems designed to prevent mineral buildup.

Price range: $10 for plain vanilla to $150 for top of the line models.

Key features

Steam makes a fabric more pliable, allowing the heat and pressure of the iron to press it flat. Many new irons release more steam than did earlier models. Most produce the best steaming during the first 10 minutes of use and then gradually taper off as the water is used up. You can usually adjust the amount of steam or turn it off, but models with **automatic steam** produce more steam at higher temperature settings. A few models won't allow you to use steam at low settings, since the water doesn't get hot enough and simply drips out. An **antidrip feature,** usually on higher-priced irons, is designed to prevent leaks when using steam at lower settings.

Burst of steam, available on most new irons, lets you push a button for an extra blast to tame stubborn wrinkles. If steam isn't enough for something such as a wrinkled linen napkin, dampen it using the **spray function,** available on virtually all irons today. On some models, burst of steam can be used for vertical steaming to remove wrinkles from hanging items.

An iron should have an easy-to-see **fabric guide** with a list of settings for common fabrics. A **temperature control** that's clearly marked and easily accessible, preferably on the front of the handle, is a plus. Most irons have an **indicator light** to show that the power is on; a few also indicate when the iron reaches or exceeds the set temperature.

Automatic shutoff has become standard on most irons, but a few still lack this must-have feature. Some irons shut off only when they're left motionless in a horizontal or vertical position. Those with three-way shutoff also turn off when tipped on their side. Shutoff times vary from 30 seconds to 60 minutes.

Water reservoirs in general are getting larger. Some are a small, vertical tube; others are a large chamber that spans the saddle area under the handle. Transparent chambers, some brightly colored, make it easy to see the water level.

A growing number of irons have a **hinged** or **sliding cover** on the water-fill hole. The idea is to prevent leaking, but it doesn't always work. Also, the cover may get in the way during filling, or can be awkward to open and close. Most convenient is a **removable tank.** Some irons come with a handy plastic **fill cup.** Nearly all new irons can use tap water, unless the water is very hard. More expensive irons may offer an **anticalcium system,** which is designed to reduce calcium deposits.

Several models now offer a **self-cleaning feature** to flush deposits from vents, but it's not always effective with prolonged use of very hard water. The **burst of steam** feature also cleans vents to some extent.

Many irons have a nonstick **soleplate.** Some more expensive models have a stainless-steel soleplate, while some budget models have an aluminum one. We didn't find any difference in glide among the various types of soleplates when ironing with steam. Nonstick soleplates are generally easier to keep clean, but they may be scratched by something such as a zipper, and a scratch could create drag over time. You should clean the soleplate occasionally to remove residue, especially if you use starch; follow the manufacturer's directions for cleaning.

The **power cord** on many irons pivots down or to the side during use, which keeps it out of the way. A retractable cord can be convenient, as long as it doesn't whip around when retracted. Cordless irons eliminate fumbling with the cord but must be reheated on the base for 90 seconds or so every couple of minutes, which can be inconvenient and time-consuming.

Weight is more critical to comfort than performance. Managing a heavy iron can be an arm workout you might prefer to have at the gym. Some handles might be too thick for smaller hands; others provide too little clearance for larger hands.

How to choose

PERFORMANCE DIFFERENCES. Many of the irons on the market will do a fine job of removing wrinkles. The most significant differences come in ease of use. Some controls are easier to see and use, for example. For everyday pressing, a $20 or $25 iron should have the performance and basic features to do the job. Models selling for $10 or $15 are less likely to satisfy. A $30 to $50 model will generally have more bells and whistles but won't necessarily offer better performance. Spending more than that is likely to get you the most (and the newest) features but may not result in better ironing.

RECOMMENDATIONS. Features differ from model to model, so determine what is important to you—and be sure to include automatic shutoff on your must-have list. Try handling an iron that's on display in a store to see if its size and shape feel right to you.

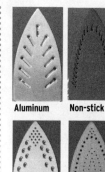

Aluminum   Non-stick

Stainless   Enamel
steel   coated

Soleplates

Soleplates of steam irons are made of different materials, all of which performed well in CONSUMER REPORTS tests.

Kitchen knives

Expensive forged knives generally cut the best. But some moderately priced alternatives do a fine job.

Whether you routinely whip up gourmet meals or rarely rise above making sandwiches, good knives are essential kitchen equipment. With them, you can work more efficiently and safely. Without them, even slicing a tomato can be tricky. While top-notch kitchen knives can cost hundreds, there are less expensive options that can be good choices for most home cooks.

What's available

Ekco, Farberware, and Oxo are among the less expensive brands. High-end brands include Calphalon, Cuisinart, Emerilware, Henckels, KitchenAid, and Wüsthof. Starter sets of kitchen knives typically cost less than the same knives sold individually. There are often seven or nine pieces in a set that includes a storage block, a sharpening steel, and the following four basic knives:

CHEF'S KNIFE. Perhaps the most versatile, it's used for chopping, dicing, slicing, and mincing, often with a rocking motion. The blade is wide for extra heft. Typical blade length: 8 to 10 inches.

SLICING KNIFE. The thin, flexible blade of this knife is especially appropriate for carving beef, poultry, and pork. Typical blade length: 8 to 10 inches.

UTILITY KNIFE. Probably second to the chef's knife in usefulness, it's good for similar but smaller cutting tasks. The blade is narrower than the blade of a chef's knife. Typical blade length: 5 to 6 inches.

PARING KNIFE. Handy for peeling, coring, paring, cleaning (shrimp, say), and slicing. It's also good for creating garnishes and fine work. Like a utility knife, it has a thin blade, but it's even shorter. Typical blade length: 3 to 4 inches.

Price range for sets: $10 to $200 or more.

Key features

Most expensive knives are forged from stain-resistant and rust-resistant high-carbon steel. Forged blades are created by pounding a steel slab into shape with a mechanical hammer that exerts tons of force. They demand regular honing, but the payoff is a razor-sharp edge.

Many cheaper kitchen knives, and a few expensive ones, are stamped from a single sheet of steel, creating a relatively thin, light blade. Some require regular honing; some don't.

There are three main types of knife blades: **fine-edged blades** that require sharpening; fine-edged blades that don't require sharpening; and **serrated blades,** with teeth along part or all of the edge. These latter don't require sharpening and are especially good at cutting through bread and tomatoes.

Most knives have a hard-plastic **handle.** Restaurants favor plastic for sanitary reasons and because it stands up to hot water and the dishwasher. A bare-wood handle may be vulnerable, although a waterproof coating can help it resist moisture. Riveted handles

Hone sweet hone

Fine-edged knives that require maintenance should be honed before or after each use, and sharpened periodically. Honing smooths and realigns the edge, helping it stay sharp longer. Hold the sharpening steel in front of you or stand it on its tip, then sweep the blade across it from heel to tip, keeping a 20° angle between blade and steel. Repeat several times on each side of the blade.

might appeal to traditionalists, but CONSUMER REPORTS tests uncovered no drawbacks to molded handles. A **sharpening steel,** used to keep a fine-edged knife in top shape, is a good addition to your kitchen.

How to choose

PERFORMANCE DIFFERENCES. Knives that need routine sharpening generally cost more but do perform best, according to our tests. While stamping can produce a top-notch blade, stamped knives generally don't perform as well as forged ones. Blades that don't require sharpening typically cut unexceptionally, but they're usually cheaper and require little upkeep.

RECOMMENDATIONS. You generally get what you pay for. But there are some decent sets for $60 or less. When shopping, hold a knife in your hand. It should feel balanced, neither too heavy nor too light. Check to ensure that the handle is attached securely, without gaps that can trap food residue.

We advise that kitchen knives be hand-washed, since dishwasher detergent can pit the blades. And always hand-wash knives with wooden handles.

Ratings: page 240

Microwave ovens

You'll see larger capacity, more power, sensors that detect doneness, and stylish designs. You can get a countertop model for less than $40.

Microwave ovens, which built their reputation on speed, are also showing some smarts. Many automatically shut off when a sensor determines that the food is cooked or sufficiently heated. The sensor is also used to automate an array of cooking chores, with buttons labeled for frozen entrées, baked potatoes, popcorn, beverages, and other common items. Design touches include softer edges for less boxy styling, hidden controls for a sleeker look, stainless steel, and, for a few, a translucent finish.

What's available

GE leads the countertop microwave-oven market with almost 25 percent of sales, followed by Sharp, Panasonic, Emerson, and Kenmore. GE sells the most over-the-range models.

Microwaves come in a variety of sizes, from compact to large. Most sit on the countertop, but a growing number sold—about 25 percent—mount over the range. Several brands offer speed-cooking via halogen bulbs or convection. Speed-cook models promise grilling and browning, though results can vary significantly depending on the food. Manufacturers are working to boost capacity without taking up more space by moving controls to the door and using recessed turntables and smaller electronic components. Be warned: To gauge capacity, manufacturers tend to tally every cubic inch, including corner spaces, where food on the turntable can't rotate. In fact, the diameter of the turntable is a more realistic measurement, and we base our calculation of usable capacity on that dimension.

Microwave ovens vary in the power of the magnetron, which generates the microwaves. Midsized and large ovens are rated at 900 to 1,350 watts, compact ovens at 600 to 800 watts. A higher wattage may heat food more quickly, but differences of 100 watts are probably inconsequential. Some microwave ovens have a convection feature—a fan and, often, a heating element—that lets you roast and bake, something you don't generally do in a regular microwave.

Price range: $40 to $200 (countertop models); $300 to $500 (over-the-range); $350 to $700 (convection or halogen-bulb countertop or over-the-range).

Key features

On most microwaves, a **turntable** rotates the food so it will heat more uniformly, but the center of the dish still tends to be cooler than the rest. Most turntables are removable for cleaning. With some models, you can turn off the rotation when, for instance, you're using a dish that's too large to rotate. The results won't be as good, however. Some models have replaced the turntable with a **rectangular tray** that slides from side to side to accept larger dishes.

You'll find similarities in controls from model to model. A **numeric keypad** is used to

---

COUNTERTOP OR OVER-THE-RANGE?

Decide which type of microwave oven meets your needs. Start by determining whether you want the easier reach and lower price of a countertop oven or the added style and counter space of an over-the-range model. Think carefully about speed-cook models; we've found them pricey for what they offer.

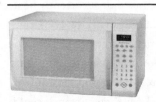

COUNTERTOP Best for kitchens with lots of counter space. Small models cost the least; larger ones have space and features comparable to over-the-range models. Even compact models steal counter space, however. And most lack the built-in style of over-the-range models.

OVER THE RANGE (OTR) Best for stretching counter space as part of a kitchen remodel. They fit over a 30-inch range or cooktop and include an exhaust vent. But installation can be costly and often requires an electrician. The exhaust vent isn't as effective as a range hood.

SPEED-COOK (OTR) Best for mostly routine microwave cooking, with light browning on chicken breasts, salmon steaks, and the like. But you pay a lot more for relatively little benefit. Some foods we prepared in our tests weren't roasted, baked, or grilled as well as by a conventional oven.

OTHER BUILT-INS Best for freeing up counter space with easier installation than OTR models. Many can be built into a wall or offer kits for below-cabinet mounting. But under-cabinet mounting requires short cabinets, otherwise you'll get little usable space below the oven.

set cooking times and power levels. Most ovens have **shortcut keys** for particular foods, and for reheating or defrosting; some start immediately when you hit the shortcut key, others make you enter the food quantity or weight. Some models have an **automatic popcorn feature** that takes just one press of a button.

Pressing a **1-minute** or **30-second key** runs the oven at full power or extends the current cooking time. Microwave ovens typically have a number of **power levels.** We've found six to be more than adequate.

A **moisture sensor** gauges the steam that food emits when heated and uses that information to determine when the food is cooked. The small premium you pay for a sensor (about $10 to $30) is worth it. A few ovens have a **crisper pan** for making bacon or crisping pizza, since microwave cooking without the special pan leaves food hot but not browned or crispy.

Over-the-range ovens vent themselves and the range with a **fan** that usually turns on when heat is sensed from the range below. The exhaust can go outside or into the kitchen; if you want the oven to vent inside, you'll need a **charcoal filter** (sometimes included). An over-the-range microwave generally doesn't handle ventilation as well as a hood-and-blower ventilation system because it doesn't extend over the front burners.

How to choose

PERFORMANCE DIFFERENCES. Most microwave ovens are easy to use and competent at their main tasks of heating and defrosting. Nearly all the ones we've tested heated a baking dish full of cold mashed potatoes to a fairly uniform temperature. We found a few ovens that left large icy chunks while defrosting ground beef, however. Be skeptical about special technologies claimed to improve cooking evenness.

RECOMMENDATIONS. A large or midsized countertop model is a good choice. Compact models, though less expensive, typically have lower power ratings and don't heat as fast. Your kitchen layout may dictate an over-the-range microwave, but these models cost about twice as much as large countertop models, are heavy, and may take two people—or sometimes even an electrician—to install.

Ratings: page 242 Reliability: page 292

Mixing appliances
**Choosing the right machine for the way you prepare foods is the trick.
You may find you need more than one.**

Which food-prep appliance best suits your style and the foods you prepare? Blenders usually excel at mixing icy drinks. Stick-shaped immersion blenders are handy mostly for stirring powdered drinks or puréeing vegetables in a saucepan. Food processors are versatile machines that can chop, slice, shred, and purée many different foods. Mini-choppers are good for small jobs such as mincing garlic and chopping nuts. Hand mixers can handle light chores such as whipping cream or mixing cake batter. And powerful stand mixers are ideal for cooks who make bread and cookies from scratch.

What's available

BLENDERS. Rugged construction and increased power are driving blender sales. Ice-crushing ability is one of the key attributes that shoppers look for in a blender, according to manufacturers.

But appearance matters as well, since a blender is one of the appliances consumers are more likely to leave on the countertop than store in a cupboard. As a result, you'll see more colors and metallic finishes, and styling that ranges from retro to ultramodern.

Hamilton Beach and Oster account for more than 40 percent of countertop-blender sales. Other brands include Black & Decker, Braun, Cuisinart, GE, KitchenAid, Krups, Proctor-Silex, Sharp, Sunbeam, Vita-Mix, and Waring, a product pioneer.

Price range: $10 to $400.

IMMERSION BLENDERS. These stick-shaped handhelds with a swirling blade at the bottom are on a power trip, with models juiced up to 200 watts or more. With these devices, power seems to make more of a difference than with countertop blenders. An immersion blender in the 100-watt range didn't even have the energy to mince onions in our tests. Immersion blenders are popular for stirring soups and puréeing and chopping vegetables. Increasingly, they're being paired with accessories such as beaters, whisks, and attachments to clean baby bottles. Braun controls the handheld segment of the market.

Price range: $30 to $100.

FOOD PROCESSORS. Several brands have introduced multifunction models designed to do the job of two or more machines. Cuisinart's Smart Power Duet comes with an interchangeable food-processor container and a glass blender jar and blade. Either attachment fits on the motorized base. Another design trend is a minibowl insert that fits inside the main container for preparing smaller quantities. Newer designs tend to be sleek, with rounded corners. Dominant brands are Black & Decker, Cuisinart, and Hamilton Beach.

Price range: $30 to $300.

MINI-CHOPPERS. These are essentially little food processors. They work best for small jobs, like mincing onions or garlic, or chopping a cup of nuts. Black & Decker is the foremost name here.

Price range: $10 to $20.

STAND AND HAND MIXERS. As with blenders, the big push in mixers is for more power, which is useful for handling heavy dough. You'll find everything from heavy-duty models offering the most power and the largest mixing bowls to light-service machines that are essentially detachable hand mixers resting on a stand. Models vary in power from about 200 to 700 watts. Sales of light-duty, convenient hand mixers have held their own in recent years.

KitchenAid owns about half the stand-mixer market; Hamilton Beach and Sunbeam are the next best-selling brands. Black & Decker, Hamilton Beach, and Sunbeam are the dominant brands among hand mixers.

Price range: $40 to $250 (stand mixers); $10 to $75 (hand mixers).

Key features

WITH BLENDERS: Three to 16 **speeds** are the norm; power ratings range from about 300 to 500 or so watts. Manufacturers claim that higher wattage translates into better performance, but in our recent tests, lower-wattage models often outperformed beefier ones, turning out icy drinks faster and leaving them smoother in consistency. Three well-differentiated speeds are adequate; a dozen or more that are hard to distinguish from one another are overkill.

Containers are made of glass, plastic, or stainless steel, and have a capacity of about 5 to 8 cups. A glass container is heavier and more stable. In tests, the blenders with glass jugs tended to perform better because they didn't shake.

Glass is also easier to keep clean. Plastic may scratch and is likely to absorb the smell of whatever is inside. Stainless steel looks good, but prevents you from seeing how the blending is going.

A wide mouth container makes loading food and washing easier; big and easy-to-read markings help you measure more accurately.

A **pulse setting** lets you fine-tune blending time. **Touchpad controls** are easy to wipe clean. A **blade** that's permanently attached to the container (typical of the Warings) is harder to clean than a removable blade.

WITH FOOD PROCESSORS: All have a clear plastic **mixing bowl** and lid, an S-shaped metal **chopping blade** (and sometimes a duller version for kneading dough), and a **plastic food pusher** to safely prod food through the feed tube. Some models have a wider tube so you don't have to cut up vegetables—such as potatoes—to fit the opening. One speed is the norm, plus a **pulse setting** to control processing precisely. Bowl capacity ranges from around 3 cups to 14 cups (dry), with most models holding 6 to 11 cups.

A **minibowl insert,** which has its own chopping blade, essentially allows you to convert to a minichopper. This saves you from having to wash the large bowl if all you need is to chop a small amount of onions or herbs, for example. A **shredding/slicing disk** is standard on full-sized processors. Some come with a **juicer** attachment. **Touchpad controls** are becoming more commonplace, too.

Mini-choppers look like little food processors, with a capacity of 2 to 3 cups, but they're for small jobs only, like chopping small quantities of nuts or a few shallots.

WITH MIXERS: Stand mixers generally come with one **bowl,** a **beater** or two, and a **dough hook.** Some mixers offer options such as **splash guards** (also called pouring shields) to prevent flour from spewing out of the bowl, plus **attachments** to make pasta, grind meat, and stuff sausage.

Stand mixers generally have 5 to 16 speeds; we think three well-differentiated settings

---

MIX AND MATCH

Choose machines that excel at the tasks you do most.

BLENDERS Best for making smoothies; crushing ice; puréeing vegetables for soup. Handheld immersion models, more delicate than hand mixers, can mix or purée in a saucepan.

FOOD PROCESSORS Best for chopping, slicing, shredding; grating hard cheese; making peanut butter. Many mix cookie dough well; some knead bread dough.

CHOPPERS Best for mincing garlic; chopping herbs, onions, or nuts; grating a bit of Parmesan. In a pinch, they can purée small quantities of vegetables.

STAND MIXERS Best for whipping cream or egg whites; mixing cake batter and cookie dough; kneading bread dough.

HAND MIXERS Best for whipping cream or egg whites; mixing cake batter; mashing potatoes.

is enough. You should be able to lock a mixer's power head in the Up position so it won't crash into the bowl when the beaters are weighed down with dough. Conversely, it should lock in the Down position to keep the beaters from kicking back when tackling stiff dough.

Just about any hand mixer is good for nontaxing jobs such as beating egg whites, mashing potatoes, or whipping cream. The **slow-start** feature on some mixers prevents ingredients from spattering when you start up, but you can achieve the same result by manually stepping through three or so speeds. An indentation on the underside of the motor housing allows the mixer to sit on the edge of a bowl without taking the beaters out of the batter.

How to choose

PERFORMANCE DIFFERENCES. With blenders, power, performance, and price don't always go hand in hand. In our recent tests, some modestly powered, inexpensive blenders turned out smooth-as-silk mixtures, while some bigger and fancier blenders left food pulpy or lumpy.

Most food processors we've tested can shred cheese, purée baby food, and slice tough, fibrous produce such as ginger and celery without missing a beat. Kneading dough takes power, and large models handled the job with aplomb. Smaller machines force you to split the dough into batches, and, even after we did so, some labored while performing the task.

Heavy-duty stand mixers can tackle tough tasks such as kneading large quantities of dense dough. In tests, light-duty, less powerful models strained and overheated under a heavy load.

RECOMMENDATIONS. Choose the right machine for your cooking tasks. Blenders excel at puréeing soup, crushing ice, and making fruit smoothies. A food processor is better at grating cheddar cheese and chopping meat, vegetables, and nuts. A processor can also slice and shred. Neither machine, however, can match a mixer's prowess at mashing potatoes or whipping cream to a light, velvety consistency. For those kinds of tasks, you can buy a perfectly adequate hand mixer for as little as $10.

Most blenders we tested are convenient and competent at various tasks; most have the oomph to crush ice. Choose a blender by noting the specific strengths of the various models we tested.

A midsized food processor is probably the best choice for basic tasks. Bigger models are geared toward cooking enthusiasts who want to create picture-perfect salads and knead large quantities of pasta dough. Mini-choppers save space but aren't too versatile.

Not everyone needs a stand mixer. But if you're a dedicated baker, a stand mixer is useful and convenient. Some weigh more than 20 pounds or so, however; keep that in mind if you're planning to store your mixer in a cabinet and haul it out as needed.

Spending more for any of these appliances will typically get you touchpad controls, extra speeds and power, and perhaps designer styling or colors to match your kitchen's décor. You'll pay more for a blender with a stainless-steel or other metallic jar than you will for one with a plastic or glass container. You'll also pay more for a stand mixer with lots of power and extra-sturdy construction.

Ratings: page 208, 235, 244

Ranges, cooktops, and wall ovens

Choices can be confusing, but you don't have to spend top dollar for impressive performance with high-end touches.

If you're in the market for cooking appliances, it pays to decide whether you want a freestanding range (with a built-in oven) or a separate cooktop and wall oven. A cooktop/wall oven combo may offer you more flexibility with your kitchen design, although ranges can be less expensive than components. You may also need to make a decision regarding gas, electricity, or both; gas, of course, is only possible if you have access to a gas hookup.

Electric ranges include the traditional coil-element type and smoothtop models, in which a sheet of ceramic glass covers the heating elements. Both types of cooktop elements offer quick heating and the ability to maintain low heat levels.

Gas ranges use burners. Burners—even the high-power variety—tend to heat more slowly than the fastest electric coil elements because the heavy cast-iron grates sometimes slow the process by absorbing heat. On the other hand, an advantage to burners is being able to see how high or low you are adjusting the flame. Many high-end gas stoves are "professional-style" models with beefy knobs, heavy cast-iron grates, stainless-steel construction, and four or more high-powered burners. These high-heat behemoths can cost thousands, and typically require a special range hood and blower system. They may also need special shielding and a reinforced floor.

You'll find more and more shared characteristics between electric and gas ranges. For example, some gas models have electric warming zones, and "gas-on-glass" versions blend the visual response of a flame with a smoothtop's easier cleaning by placing the burners over a smooth ceramic surface. What's more, a growing number of high-end gas ranges pair gas cooktop burners with an electric oven. Fortunately, you don't have to spend top dollar for top cooking performance.

What's available

GE and Whirlpool are the leading makers of ranges, cooktops, and wall ovens. Other major brands include Frigidaire, Jenn-Air, Kenmore (Sears), KitchenAid, and Maytag. Mainstream brands have established high-end offshoots, such as GE Profile, Kenmore Elite, and Whirlpool Gold. High-end, pro-style brands include Bosch, Dacor, DCS, GE Monogram, Thermador, Viking, and Wolf.

FREESTANDING, SLIDE-IN, AND DROP-IN RANGES. Freestanding ranges can fit in the middle of a kitchen counter or at the end. Widths are usually 20 to 40 inches, although most are 30 inches wide. They typically have oven controls on the vertical backguard. Slide-in models eliminate the side panels to blend into the countertop, with their controls up front, below the cooktop surface. Drop-in ranges are similar, but they rest atop a toe-kick-level cabinet and typically lack a storage drawer. Ovens can be self-cleaning or require manual cleaning, although most mainstream ranges and a growing number of

Smoke-free kitchen

Several brands of ranges offer matching hood-and-blower ventilation systems to whisk heat, smoke, odor, and combustion gases out of the kitchen. An alternative is an over-the-range microwave oven, which also handles ventilation when vented outside, but not as well. Manufacturers of pro-style ranges and cooktops recommend a hood-and-blower system capable of moving at least 1,000 cubic feet of air per minute.

pro-style models now come with a self-cleaning feature.

Price range: $400 to $1,500.

PRO-STYLE RANGES. Larger than freestanding ranges, these can be anywhere from 30 to 60 inches wide. The biggest include six or eight burners, a grill or griddle, and a double oven. Many have a convection feature, and some have an infrared gas broiler. You usually don't get a storage drawer, and some lack sealed burners, which keep crumbs from falling beneath the cooktop.

Price range: $2,500 to $8,000.

COOKTOPS. You can install a cooktop on a kitchen island or anywhere else counter space allows. As with freestanding ranges, cooktops can be electric coil, electric smoothtop, or gas. Paired with a wall oven, a cooktop adds flexibility, since it can be located in another part of the kitchen. Most cooktops are 30 inches wide and are made of porcelain-coated steel or ceramic glass, with four elements or burners. Some are 36 or 48 inches wide and have space for an extra burner or two.

Modular cooktops let you mix and match parts any time you choose—removing burners and adding a grill, say—although you'll pay more for that added flexibility. Preconfigured cooktops are less expensive.

Price range: $200 to $1,300 (electric); $300 to $1,800 (gas).

WALL OVENS. These are mostly electric and usually offer a convection setting (this usually adds $300 to the price). Width is typically 24, 27, or 30 inches. Best of all, you can eliminate having to bend to put things in or take things out by installing the oven at waist or eye level—although you can also nest it under a countertop if that suits your needs.

Price range: $400 to more than $3,500 for double-oven models.

Key features

ON ALL RANGES: Look for easy-cleaning features such as a **glass** or **porcelain back-guard** instead of a painted one; **seamless corners** and **edges,** especially where the cooktop joins the backguard; and a **raised edge** around the cooktop to contain spills.

ON ELECTRIC RANGES AND COOKTOPS: Freestanding ranges typically locate **controls** on the backguard, with burner controls to the left and right, and oven controls in between, giving you a quick sense of which control operates which element. Backguard controls clustered in the center offer the advantage of being visible when tall pots sit on the rear heating elements. On most electric cooktops, controls take up room on the surface; some models, however, have electronic touchpads that allow the entire cooktop to be flush with the counter.

Coil elements, the most common and least expensive electric option, are easy to replace if they break. On an electric range with coil elements, look for a **prop-up top** for easier cleaning. Deep **drip pans** made of porcelain can better contain spills and ease cleaning.

Smoothtop models generally use radiant heat, although some halogen units are available. **Radiant elements** take about six seconds to redden when first turned on; **halogen elements** redden immediately. Some smoothtops have **expandable elements,** which let you switch between a large, high-power element and a small, low-power element contained within it. Some smoothtops also include a **low-wattage element** for warming plates or keeping just-cooked food at the optimal temperature. An elongated **"bridge" element** spans two burners—a nicety for accommodating rectangular or odd-shaped cookware, such as a large roasting pan or a fish poacher. Many have at least one **hot-surface light**—a key safety feature, since the surface can remain hot long after the elements have been turned off. The safest setup includes a dedicated, prominently placed "hot" light for each element.

Most electric ranges and cooktops have one large **higher-wattage burner** in front and one in back. An **expanded simmer setting** in some electric models lets you fine-tune the simmer setting on one burner for, say, melting chocolate or keeping a sauce from getting too hot.

ON GAS RANGES AND COOKTOPS: Most gas ranges have four **burners** in three sizes, measured in British thermal units per hour (Btu/hr.): one or two medium-power burners (about 9,000 Btu/hr.), a small burner (about 5,000 Btu/hr.), and one or two large ones (about 12,000 Btu/hr.). We recommend a model with one or more burners of about 12,000 Btu/hr. for quick heating. On a few models, the burners automatically reignite if the flame goes out for any reason.

For easier cleaning, look for **sealed burners** and **removable burner pans** and **caps.** Gas ranges typically have **knob controls;** the best rotate 180 degrees or more for flame

---

── SIZZLING CHOICES ──

Once an infomercial novelty, indoor grills have come into their own, with more models, larger sizes, and more features. There are two basic styles available: contact grills and open grills. Of the former variety, George Foreman's Lean Mean Grilling Machine—and more than a dozen variations made by Salton—have pretty much KO'd the competition, winning nearly 80 percent of sales. Hamilton Beach also markets several contact grill models. Open grills made by DeLonghi and T-Fal are also available.

CONTACT GRILLS sandwich the food between two hot surfaces or grids, like a waffle iron. A drip pan in front or beneath catches any grease. Speed is the key to the cooking clout of this type of grill, which can cook burgers in just 3 to 6 minutes (after a 3- to 10-minute warm-up period). While basic black or white are the predominant colors, the George Foreman line now has grills in translucent colors and even a Michael Graves-designed stainless steel version. One drawback of contact grills is that they have trouble with items more than an inch thick. Because the food won't fit properly between the grids, cooking will be uneven. Price range: $25 to $100

OPEN GRILLS come closer to cooking food in the manner of their outdoor cousins, by grilling meat or other items one side at a time on an open broiler plate. The result is quickly seared food and clearer grill marks, a real draw for some cooks. Grease and juices fall into a drip pan underneath the cooking surface. Not surprisingly, open grills cook more slowly than contact grills, but they are more adept at handling thicker items such as steaks. Price range: $65 to $90.

Indoor grills heat only to 200° to 400°, as opposed to an oven broiler, which should exceed 600°. As a result, grilled foods will turn out much less crispy than what you'd get by putting something under a broiler. Most grills' nonstick surfaces make them easy to clean, though the slotted grates on some open grills are a little tough to get at. What's more, our tests found that the nonstick finish on most grills stood up well to intense scrubbing. Almost all grills are large enough to cook four burgers at a time; some can handle as many as eight. The bigger the cooking surface (they range from 38 to 192 square inches), the more counter or storage space you'll need to house it. Timers and temperature controls are available on some models. Don't pay extra for these features, however, since the grills don't heat to much more than 400° and food cooks best at the higher temperature anyway. As for a timer, the kitchen timer you likely have sitting around serves the same purpose.

adjustment. Try to avoid knobs that have adjacent "off" and "low" settings and those that rotate no more than 90 degrees between High and Low.

Spending more on a gas stove or cooktop gets you heavier **grates** made of porcelain-coated cast iron, multiple high-power burners, and **stainless-steel accents.**

ON PRO-STYLE RANGES: These models have **brass** or **cast-iron burners,** all of which offer very high output (usually about 15,000 Btu/hr.). The burners are sometimes non-sealed, with hard-to-clean crevices, though sealed burners are appearing on some models. **Large knobs** are another typical pro-style feature, as are **continuous grates** designed for heavy-duty use. The latter, however, can be unwieldy to remove for cleaning.

ON OVENS: Electric-range ovens used to have an edge over gas ovens in roominess, but we've recently found roomy ovens among both types. Note, though, that an oven's usable **capacity** may be less than what manufacturers claim, because they don't take protruding broiler elements and other features into account.

A **self-cleaning cycle** uses high heat to burn off spills and splatters. Most ranges have it, although some pro-style gas models still don't. An **automatic door lock** on most self-cleaning models is activated during the cleaning cycle, then unlocks when the oven has cooled. Also useful is a **self-cleaning countdown** display, which shows the time left in the cycle.

Higher-priced ranges and wall ovens often include a **convection mode,** which uses a fan and, sometimes, an electric element to circulate heated air. In our tests, the convection mode usually shaved cooking time for a large roast and, in some cases, baked large cookie batches more evenly because of the circulating air. But the fan can take up valuable oven space. Another cooking technology, found in the GE Advantium over-the-range oven, uses a **halogen heating bulb** as well as microwaves. Some models have **covered elements,** which make for easier cleaning.

A **variable-broil** feature in most electric ovens offers adjustable settings for foods such as fish or thick steaks that need slower or faster cooking. Ovens with **12-hour shutoff** turn off automatically if you leave the oven on for that long; most models allow you to disable this feature. A **child lockout** lets you disable oven controls.

Manufacturers are updating oven controls across the price spectrum. **Electronic touchpad controls** are a high-end feature now showing up in more lower-priced ranges. A **digital display** makes it easier to set the temperature and keep track of it. A **cook time/delay start** lets you set a time for the oven to start and stop cooking; remember, however, that you shouldn't leave most foods in a cold oven very long. An **automatic oven light** comes on when the door opens, although some ovens have a switch-operated light. A **temperature probe,** to be inserted into meat or poultry, indicates when you've obtained a precise internal temperature.

Oven **windows** come in various sizes. Those without a decorative grid usually offer the clearest view, although some cooks may welcome the grid to hide pots, pans, and other cooking utensils sometimes stored inside the oven.

How to choose

PERFORMANCE DIFFERENCES. Almost every range, cooktop, or wall oven we've tested cooks well. Differences are in the details. An electric range may boil a pot of water a bit more quickly than a gas range, while a gas model can sometimes be adjusted with more precision. Our tests have also shown that the powerful burners on some pro-style gas ranges may not be able to simmer some foods without scorching them. Among electric ranges, smoothtops are displacing coil-tops, but they aren't necessarily better or more reliable. A smoothtop's glass surface can ease cleaning. However, you need to wipe up sugary spills immediately to avoid pitting the surface. Be aware that the doors and windows of some ovens can become fairly hot during self-cleaning, while others are left with a permanent residue.

RECOMMENDATIONS. Decide on the type you want, then consider the features, price, and brand reliability. You must also factor in your cabinetry and floor plan, and whether or not you have access to a gas hookup. A freestanding range generally offers the best value; a very basic electric or gas model costs $400 or less. Smoothtop electric ranges cost $100 to $200 more than those with coil elements. Spending more than $1,000 buys lots of extras, including electronic controls and pro-style touches such as stainless-steel trim. Expect to pay thousands for a real pro-style model. In wall ovens, the convection feature adds hundreds of dollars to the price.

Ratings: page 218, 250, 280 Reliability: page 293

Refrigerators

Top-freezer and bottom-freezer fridges generally give you more for your money than their side-by-side siblings—and cost less to run.

If you're shopping for a new refrigerator, you're probably considering models that are fancier than your current fridge. The trend is toward spacious models with flexible, more efficiently used storage space. Useful features such as spillproof, slide-out glass shelves and temperature-controlled compartments, once only found in expensive refrigerators, are now practically standard in midpriced models. Stainless-steel doors are a stylish but costly extra. Built-in refrigerators appeal to people who want to customize their kitchens, but they're expensive. Some mainstream models offer a built-in-style look for less.

Replacing an aging refrigerator may save you in electric bills, since refrigerators are more energy efficient now than they were a decade ago. The Department of Energy toughened its rules in the early 1990s and imposed even stricter requirements in July 2001 for this appliance, which is among the top electricity users in the house.

What's available

Only a handful of companies actually manufacture refrigerators. The same or very similar units may be sold under several brand names. Frigidaire, General Electric, Kenmore, and Whirlpool account for about three-quarters of top-freezer sales. For side-by-side models, these brands and Maytag account for more than 80 percent of sales. Brands offering bottom-freezers include Amana, GE, Jenn-Air, Kenmore, KitchenAid, LG, Maytag, Samsung, and Whirlpool. Mainstream manufacturers have introduced high-end sub-brands such as GE Profile and Kenmore Elite. Five brands specialize in built-ins: Sub-Zero, Viking, GE Monogram, Jenn-Air, and KitchenAid. Amana, GE, Jenn-Air, KitchenAid, LG, and Whirlpool offer built-in-style, or "cabinet depth" models. LG and Samsung, brands new to the U.S. market, offer side-by-side, top-freezer, and bottom-freezer types.

TOP-FREEZER MODELS. Accounting for almost two-thirds of models sold, these are generally less expensive to buy and run—and more space efficient—than comparably sized side-by-side models. Width ranges from about 24 to 36 inches. The eye-level freezer offers easy access. Fairly wide refrigerator shelves make it easy to reach the back, but you have to bend to reach the bottom shelves. Nominal labeled capacity ranges from about 10 to almost 27 cubic feet. (Our measurements show that a refrigerator's usable capacity is typically about 60 to 80 percent of its nominal capacity.)

Price range: $450 to more than $1,200, depending on size and features.

SIDE-BY-SIDE MODELS. These are by far the most fully featured fridges, and are where you'll most often find through-the-door ice and water dispensers—among the most requested consumer feature—as well as temperature-controlled bins and rapid ice-making cycles. Their narrow doors are handy in tight spaces. High, narrow compartments make finding stray items easy in front (harder in the back); they may not hold such items as a sheet cake or a large turkey.

Compared with top- and bottom-freezer models, a higher proportion of capacity goes to freezer space. Side-by-sides are typically large—30 to 36 inches wide, with nominal capacity of 19 to 30 cubic feet. They're much more expensive than similar-sized top-freezer models and are less efficient in terms of space and energy use.

Price range: $800 to more than $2,400.

BOTTOM-FREEZER MODELS. A small but growing part of the market, these allow you to store frequently used items at eye level. Fairly wide refrigerator shelves provide easy access. Though you must bend to locate items in the freezer, even with models that have a pull-out basket, you will probably do less bending overall because the refrigerator is at eye level. Bottom-freezers are a bit pricier than top-freezers and offer less capacity (up to 25 cubic feet) relative to their external dimensions because of the inefficiency of the pull-out bin.

Price range: $700 to $1,800.

BUILT-IN MODELS. These are generally side-by-side and bottom-freezer models. They show their commercial heritage, often having fewer standard amenities and less sound-proofing than lower-priced "home" models. Usually 25 to 26 inches front to back, they fit nearly flush with cabinets and counters. Their compressor is on top, making them about a foot taller than regular refrigerators. Most can accept a front panel that matches the kitchen's décor. Side-by-side models in this style are available in 42-inch and 48-inch widths (versus the more typical 36-inch width). You can even obtain a built-in pair: a separate refrigerator and freezer mounted together in a 72-inch opening.

Price range: $4,000 to over $6,000.

BUILT-IN-STYLE, OR CABINET-DEPTH MODELS. These freestanding refrigerators offer the look of a built-in for less money. These are available mostly in side-by-side and bottom-freezer styles, with a few top-freezers. Many accept front panels for a custom look.

Price range: $1,500 to $2,500.

Key features

Interiors are ever more flexible. Adjustable door **bins** and **shelves** can be moved to fit tall items. Some shelves can be cranked up and down without removing the contents. Some split shelves can be adjusted to different heights independently. With other shelves, the front half of the shelf slides under the rear portion to provide clearance.

Shelf snuggers are sliding brackets on door shelves that secure bottles and jars. A few models have a **wine rack** that stores a bottle horizontally.

Glass shelves are easier to clean than **wire racks.** Most glass shelves have a raised, sealed rim to keep spills from dripping over. Some slide out. Pull-out freezer shelves or bins give easier access. An alternative is a bottom-freezer with a sliding drawer.

FREEZER CHOICES

Pick where you want the freezer. Then pick depth.

**TOP-FREEZER MODELS Generally least expensive and in a range of sizes, they're economical to run and offer a lot of storage space for their dimensions. Some have stylish curved doors with smooth, stainless-look surfaces. Best for small spaces, and people looking for value above all. On the downside, they're not generally full-featured. You must bend for frequently used items in the fridge. Doors swing wide.
Cost to run, about $36 to $44 a year.**

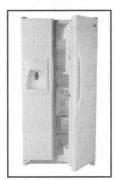

SIDE-BY-SIDE MODELS While more expensive to buy and run, they do have more features. They're large on the outside but not very efficient with space inside. Best for spaces where you can't have a wide-swinging door. For households wanting a custom look, some models accommodate cabinet-matching panels, or offer a stainless or stainless-look finish. On the downside, no room for wide items like pizza boxes. Moving items within the narrow space can be tedious. Cost to run, about $49 to $60 a year.

BOTTOM-FREEZER MODELS More expensive than top-freezer types, they also have less usable freezer space. One plus: they put things you use most at eye level. Best for people who don't like to bend for frequently used items. On the downside, not generally as full-featured as side-by-side models. You must bend or squat for items at the back of the deep freezer drawers. Cost to run, about $42 to $46 a year.

A **temperature-controlled drawer** can be set to be several degrees cooler than the rest of the interior, useful for storing meat or fish. Crispers have controls to maintain humidity. Our tests have shown that, in general, temperature-controlled drawers work better than plain drawers; results for humidity controls are less clear-cut. See-through drawers let you see at a glance what's inside.

Refrigerators with **curved doors** offer a distinctive profile and retro look. Most manufacturers have at least one curved-door model in their lineups.

Step-up features include a variety of **finishes** and **colors.** Every major manufacturer has a stainless-steel model that typically costs significantly more than one with a standard pebbled finish. Another alternative is a smooth, glasslike finish.

Color choices include biscuit, bisque, or linen instead of almond. Several lines include black models, and KitchenAid has a cobalt-blue finish to match its small appliances. Kenmore, LG, Samsung, and Whirlpool have models with a stainless-steel look that, unlike stainless, resists fingerprints and accepts magnets.

Most models have an **icemaker** in the freezer (or give you the option of installing one yourself). Typically producing 3 or 4 pounds of ice per day, an icemaker reduces freezer space by about a cubic foot. The ice bin is generally located below the icemaker, but some new models have it on the inside of the freezer door, providing a bit more usable volume.

A through-the-door **ice-and-water dispenser** is common in side-by-side refrigerators. Top- and bottom-freezer refrigerators don't offer through-the-door ice-and-water dispensers, but as an alternative, some models have water dispensers inside the main compartment.

With many models, the icemaker and/or water dispenser includes a **water filter,** designed to reduce lead, chlorine, and other impurities, a capability you may or may not need. An icemaker or water dispenser will work without one. You can also have a filter installed in the tubing that supplies water to the refrigerator.

Once a refrigerator's controls are set, there should be little need to adjust temperature. Still, accessible controls are an added convenience.

How to choose

PERFORMANCE DIFFERENCES. Most refrigerators—even the least expensive—keep things cold very well. Many models are fairly quiet, and some are very quiet. But configurations and convenience features vary considerably. Less expensive models usually lack spillproof glass shelves, large bins, and easily arrangeable shelves.

Some refrigerators can be placed flush against a side wall; others need space for doors to swing open. Top- and bottom-freezer models usually have reversible hinges so they can open to either side. The doors on side-by-side models require the least amount of front clearance space.

Energy efficiency does vary, according to our tests. An efficient model that costs more may be a better buy in the long run than a cheaper but less-efficient model.

Refrigerators made as of July 2001 are required to meet efficiency standards up to 30 percent more stringent than those in place before. Some models on the market have an Energy Star designation; that means they're at least 10 percent more efficient than what the 2001 regulations require. (Products manufactured after Jan. 1, 2004 are at least 15 percent more efficient than mandated.)

Yellow EnergyGuide stickers, which include information on energy usage, are required on all refrigerators. As of 2003, new models must be made without hydrochlorofluorocarbons, which can harm the Earth's ozone layer.

RECOMMENDATIONS. Top-freezer models give you the most refrigerator for the money. But kitchen layout or personal preference may necessitate another type. Most built-in models offer no performance or efficiency advantages. In general, larger refrigerators have more features.

An icemaker adds $50 to $75 to the price; a through-the-door water dispenser adds about $100. Models with an interior water dispenser are increasingly common, as are models with a built-in filtration system.

CONSUMER REPORTS surveys show that the presence of an icemaker or a water dispenser tends to increase the chances of needing a repair. A recent survey of refrigerators found that almost 25 percent of five-year-old side-by-side models with an icemaker and a water dispenser had needed a repair, compared with around 15 percent for top-freezer models of the same age with an icemaker, and just 10 percent for top-freezer models without an icemaker.

Considering cost of repair, cost of replacement, and technology improvements, you'll probably want to fix a broken top-freezer that's less than five years old or a side-by-side that's less than six years old.

You may want to consider repairing a model up to eight years old if you're satisfied with its performance. You'll probably want to replace an older model that's broken to take advantage of a new model's features and reduced energy costs.

Ratings: page 257 Reliability: page 294

Toasting appliances

Some people like the straightforwardness of a basic toaster. Others prefer an appliance that toasts, bakes, and more. Either way, you can get good performance without spending a lot.

Piggybacking on the popularity of bagels, toaster pastries, and frozen ready-to-heat omelets, manufacturers are redesigning the basic toaster for improved functionality. What's more, new models have styling and cachet that can make them the sharpest-looking appliance on the counter.

Developments in toaster functionality include a setting for bagels, which browns only a single side; a cancel mode to interrupt the toast cycle; and nonstick slots. "Smart" toasters with microchips and heat sensors promise perfect doneness from first batch to last (they don't always deliver, we've found). Some models incorporate an LED indicator to show the darkness selection and to count down the time remaining in a particular cycle.

You'll see more toasters with rounded sides and that retro look, and more extra-wide and long-slot models. Black & Decker has introduced a toaster with clear glass sides that let you watch the browning.

West Bend has the unorthodox Slide Thru toaster: You insert the bread in the slot and remove it through a door at the base. The door doubles as a "dressing table" for spreading butter or jam.

You don't need a $100 or $200 toaster to get perfectly browned bread. For $20 or less, you can buy a competent product that will make decent toast, two slices at a time, with all the basics: a darkness control to adjust doneness, a push-down lever to raise or lower the bread, and cool-touch housing to keep you from burning your fingers.

And of course there's life beyond the toaster. With increased demand for multifunction appliances—and the space savings that result from having one machine that can do the work of two—many people opt for a hybrid appliance that can not only toast but also bake muffins, heat frozen entrées, or broil a small batch of burgers or a small chicken.

What's available

Toastmaster invented the pop-up toaster in the 1920s and now shares shelf space with other venerable brands of toasters and toaster ovens such as Black & Decker, Hamilton Beach, and Sunbeam, plus players such as Cuisinart, DeLonghi, Kenmore (Sears), KitchenAid, Krups, Rival, T-Fal, and West Bend. Dualit makes old-fashioned, commercial-style, heavy-gauge stainless-steel toasters.

Toasters come in a variety of exterior finishes, such as chrome and brushed metal. Of the 12 million toasters sold annually, two-slice models outsell four-slicers 4 to 1. Nearly three-quarters of toaster ovens sold are equipped with a broiler function. Most toaster ovens are countertop models, though a few under-the-cabinet models are sold.

Price range: $20 to $100 and up (toasters); $30 to $100 and up (toaster ovens and broilers).

Key features

For all the bells and whistles on today's toasters, a simple **dial** or **lever** to set for darkness is sufficient. **Electronic controls** regulate shadings and settings with a touchpad instead. A **pop-up control** lets you eject a slice early if you think it's done.

A **toast boost,** or **manual lift,** lets you raise smaller items such as English muffins above the slots so there's no need to fish around with a fork, a potentially dangerous exercise if you don't unplug the toaster. Another safety note: Underwriters Laboratory (UL) now requires that toasters shut off at the end of the toasting cycle even if a piece of bread is still in the carriage.

A few models offer an astounding (and unnecessary) 63 time and temperature toasting options. Recent toaster-oven innovations include a **liner** that can be removed for cleaning, and various ways to speed up the cooking process, including use of a **convection fan** or **infrared heat.**

A **removable crumb tray** facilitates cleaning. **Nonstick slots** also make it easy to remove baked-on goop left by toaster pastries. More and more models incorporate a control that automatically defrosts and toasts in a single step, nice if you regularly prepare items such as frozen hash-brown patties. With toaster ovens, a **removable cooking cavity** makes cleaning easier.

How to choose

PERFORMANCE DIFFERENCES. Most toasters make respectable toast. But few models, including those with microchips and heat sensors, toast to perfection. In our tests, problems included toast that came out darker on one side than the other and successive batches that were inconsistently browned.

As in the past, toaster ovens as a group were not as good as their plainer cousins at making toast—though they do let you keep an eye on the browning process. Their ability to bake and broil does make them more versatile than toasters. Elegant styling and a sleek design can carry a high price tag, but may offer little else.

RECOMMENDATIONS. If all you want is toast, a $20 toaster will do the job just fine. Toaster ovens and broilers offer versatility so you needn't, for example, heat up your big oven to warm leftovers or use the stove to melt a grilled-cheese sandwich.

Washing machines

Nearly all do a fine job of washing. Top-loaders are usually less expensive, but front-loaders cost less to operate because they use less water and energy.

Virtually any washing machine will get your clothing clean. Front-loaders do the job using less water, including hot water, and thus less energy than most top-loaders. But top-loading washing machines are becoming more energy efficient.

New, stricter Department of Energy standards regarding energy and hot-water use and water extraction became effective January 2004, and standards will become even more stringent in 2007. (Front-loaders already meet the tougher requirements, as do some top-loaders.)

Several manufacturers have introduced high-efficiency top-loading washers that work somewhat like front-loaders. They fill partially with water and spray clothes with a concentrated detergent solution. They outscored other top-loaders in our tests of water and energy efficiency.

In the past few years, front-loading washers, which you load the same way you would a dryer, have gained in popularity. Today about 15 percent of newly purchased washing machines are front-loaders, up from less than 5 percent several years ago.

What's available

The top four brands—GE, Maytag, Kenmore, and Whirlpool—account for just over 80 percent of washing machine sales. Other brands include Amana (owned by Maytag), Frigidaire (owned by Electrolux), Hotpoint (made by GE), and KitchenAid and Roper (both made by Whirlpool).

You may also run across smaller brands such as Crosley, Gibson, and White-Westinghouse, all of which are made by the larger brands. Asko, Bosch, and Miele are European brands. Fisher-Paykel is imported from New Zealand, LG from Korea, and Haier from China.

TOP-LOADERS. Most top-loaders fill the tub with enough water to cover the clothing, then agitate it. Because they need to move the laundry around to ensure thorough cleaning, these machines have a smaller effective load capacity than front-loaders—generally about 12 to 16 pounds. Models from GE, Kenmore, Maytag, and Whirlpool are unusual in that they don't use an agitator to move clothes around. This frees up the center of the machine and enables them to hold larger loads than conventional top-loaders.

It's easier to load laundry and to add items midcycle to a top-loader. But top-loaders are also noisier than front-loaders. Top-loaders are generally 27 to 29 inches wide.

Price range: $200 to $1,000.

FRONT-LOADERS. Front-loaders get clothes clean by tumbling them in the water. Clothes are lifted to the top of the tub, then dropped into the water below. The design usually makes front-loaders gentler on clothing and more adept at handling unbalanced loads.

They can typically handle 12 to 20 pounds of laundry. Front-loading washing machines perform best with front-loader detergent, which doesn't produce as many suds as detergent intended for top-loaders. Like top-loaders, they're typically 27 to 29 inches wide.

Price range: $600 to $1,500.

SPACE-SAVING OPTIONS. Compact models are typically 24 inches wide or less and wash 8 to 12 pounds of laundry. A compact front-loader can be stacked with a compact dryer. (Many full-sized front-loaders can also be stacked with a matching dryer.) Some compact models can be stored in a closet and rolled out to be hooked up to the kitchen sink.

Price range: $450 to $1,700.

Washer-dryer laundry centers combine a washer and dryer in one unit, with the dryer located above the washer. These can be full-sized (27 inches wide) or compact (24 inches

---

— WASHING MACHINE CHOICES —

Decide whether you want to pay a higher price for better performance.

Top-loaders

HOW THEY WORK Most top-loaders fill the tub with enough water to cover clothing, then churn it with an agitator. (A few higher-priced models have flat wash plates instead of agitators and use less water.)

PROS Value. For $400 or so, you can get excellent washing performance, very good capacity, and quiet operation. You have a wide selection of models from many different brands.

CONS They use more water and energy than front-loaders and generally aren't as gentle on clothing. Some are noisier and hold a little less laundry than front-loaders.

Front-loaders

HOW THEY WORK Front-loaders fill partially with water and tumble clothing around.

PROS The best washing performance. They use considerably less water and energy than top-loaders, and their high spin speeds reduce drying time. They're gentle on clothing, and most hold very large loads. Most are extremely quiet.

CONS Price. Many cost $1,000 or more, but you may find one for $600 or so. There are fewer brands and models from which to choose. Cycle times are generally a bit longer. You can't soak laundry as in a top-loader. There are few high-efficiency detergents, which are recommended for best results.

wide). The full-sized models hold about 12 to 14 pounds, the compacts a few pounds less. Performance is generally comparable to that of full-sized machines.

Price range: $700 to $1,900.

Key features

Stainless-steel or plastic tubs won't rust. A porcelain top/lid resists scratching better than a painted one.

High-end models often have **touchpad controls;** others have traditional **dials.** Controls should be legible, easy to push or turn, and logically arranged. A plus: **lights** or **signals** that indicate the cycle.

On some top-loaders, an **automatic lock** during the spin cycle keeps children from opening the lid. Front-loaders lock at the beginning of a cycle but can usually be opened by interrupting the cycle, although some doors remain shut briefly after the machine stops.

Front-loaders automatically set wash speed according to the fabric cycle selected, and some also automatically set the spin speed.

Top-loaders typically provide wash/spin speed combinations, such as Regular, Permanent Press, and Delicate (or Gentle). A few models also allow an **extra rinse** or **extended spin.** They also allow you to adjust water temperature if desired.

Front-loaders and some top-loaders set water levels automatically, ensuring efficient use of water. Some top-loaders can be set for four or more levels; three or four are probably as many as you would need.

Most machines establish wash and rinse temperatures by mixing hot and cold water in preset proportions. For incoming cold water that's especially cold, an **automatic temperature control** adjusts the flow for the correct wash temperature.

A **time-delay feature** lets you program the washer to start at a later time, such as at night, when your utility rates are low. **Automatic bleach, detergent,** and **fabric-softener dispensers** release powder or liquid at the appropriate time. Bleach dispensers also prevent spattering. Some machines offer a **hand-washing cycle.**

How to choose

PERFORMANCE DIFFERENCES. All washing machines get clothes clean. In our tests, differences in washing ability tended to be slight. Differences were more apparent in water and energy efficiency and in noisiness. Front-loaders have the edge on all counts.

WASHING WISDOM

Getting good results from your washer isn't too hard if you use common sense and follow basic guidelines about sorting, reading care labels, and following the manufacturer's instructions. Here are less obvious steps from our experts to help you get better washing results.

DELAY ADDING BLEACH. Chlorine bleach loses effectiveness if added to the wash too soon, so wait 5 minutes or so into the wash cycle. Consider a washer with an automatic bleach dispenser that will release the bleach at the proper time.

DON'T USE FRIGID WATER. If water is too cold, liquid detergent may not work well and powdered detergent may not dissolve. Get a washer with automatic temperature control to prevent this. Otherwise, if the water feels too cold, run a warm wash.

MAXIMIZE COLOR, MINIMIZE LINT. To preserve the like-new appearance of colored fabric, use cool water on the delicate cycle and liquid detergent. Wash towels and sweatshirts separately from fabrics that attract lint, such as corduroy, and from permanent-press items likely to pill. Turn any garment you want to protect inside out, and use net bags for delicate items.

WATCH OUT FOR BLEEDING. Bright colors, especially red, may bleed. To test for color-fastness, wet a garment and blot it with an old white cloth. If color bleeds, wash the item on its own or have it dry-cleaned.

DON'T OVERSTUFF THE WASHER. Clothing needs room to move so it can be properly cleaned and rinsed, especially in a top-loader. You can fill the tub of a front-loader, but don't jam clothes in.

The water efficiency of any washing machine rises with larger loads, but overall, front-loaders use far less water per pound of laundry and excel in energy efficiency.

Using electricity to heat the water, and using an electric dryer, the most energy-efficient front-loaders can save you about $60 worth of electricity annually compared with the least efficient top-loader. (Costs are based on 2003 national average utility prices; differences would narrow with a gas water heater, gas dryer, full loads, or carefully set water levels.) Front-loaders are generally quieter than top-loaders except when draining or spinning, and they are usually gentler on your laundry.

RECOMMENDATIONS. Top-loaders generally cost less than front-loaders and do a fine job. Best values: midpriced top-loaders with few features, which you can usually find for less than $500. Bells and whistles such as extra wash/spin options or time delay don't necessarily improve performance.

While front-loaders are usually more expensive to buy, they can cost significantly less to operate, especially in areas where water or energy rates are very high. In general, though, the savings are not likely to make up the price difference over a washer's typical life span.

Buying one of the more expensive top-loading or front-loading models can get you larger capacity and features that give you more flexibility, such as programming frequently used settings.

Ratings: page 281 Reliability: page 296

Home Entertainment

I n recent years, digital entertainment products such as DVD players, digital video recorders (DVRs), and satellite-TV receivers have transformed the marketplace. Camcorders, cameras, receivers, cable boxes, and many TV sets have moved from analog to digital and, in the process, have made leaps in what they promise and often can deliver.

CONSUMER REPORTS tests show that digital capability often results in giant steps in performance. Audio CD players consistently reproduce sound better than turntables did. The typical digital camcorder provides much clearer video than the best of their older, analog cousins. Receivers supporting digital audio can provide more realism when you're watching movies at home than those using earlier, analog-audio standards. High-definition TV shows off not just the football game but the sweat glistening on the players' arms.

But despite digital's superiority over the analog ways of cassette tape, videotape, and traditional NTSC-standard TV, analog products will still be sold for some time to come. And if industry infighting and consumer confusion are any indication, it will be years before we see the last of the analog breed. Here's what you can see in today's home-entertainment products:

DIGITAL MOVIES, ANALOG TVS. DVDs, with their capacity for extra features such as director-commentary chapters, are replacing videotapes as the preferred home-movie choice among consumers. Meanwhile, DVD players have quickly become almost a commodity, with excellent performance the norm and prices well below $100 for an increasing number of models.

Despite the record pace of DVD adoption, however, analog TVs and VCRs are still by far the most-sold home-entertainment products, and the best of them are fine performers despite their "nondigitized" nature. VCRs are still a mainstay, though digital recorders—sold under TiVo, Replay, and other names—can record with greater speed and finesse.

The popularity of recordable DVDs has grown more slowly than predicted because of high cost, technical difficulties, and wrangles over copy-protection concerns. But DVD recorders priced as low as $500 are winning new fans in the quest for more-permanent storage of home movies. And TiVo, Replay, and similar digital video recorders (DVRs) still require you to transfer material to videotape for long-term storage.

THE DIGITAL REVOLUTION IN AUDIO KEEPS ROLLING. It turns out that the introduction of CD players in 1982 was just part one of the digital revolution in consumer audio—the playback part. Part two: the current boom in digital recording options. Audio component CD player/recorders, which let you "burn" your own CDs for a dollar or two each, have been dropping in price; you can now buy one for a few hundred dollars. (The same process can also be done, often more easily, using computers.) Newer MP3 players offer huge capacity, 5 to 80 GB, in very small packages. Digital-music options make music "liquid"—you can pour out what you want to hear, in the order you want, in the format you choose—at home, in the car, or while jetting to Bermuda.

Improvements in digital audio technology, such as DVD-Audio and Super Audio CD (SACD), take full advantage of surround-sound speaker systems developed for movies. Such capability has worked its way into an increasing number of DVD players.

SURROUND SOUND MARCHES ON. One of the biggest attractions of DVD is its digital surround sound, most commonly represented by the Dolby Digital format. To take full advantage, you need up to six speakers (potentially more) and a Dolby Digital receiver to manage them—in addition to your TV and DVD player.

You can buy those components completely à la carte, as a receiver plus a separate matched set of six speakers, or as a "home theater in a box," which combines six speakers plus a receiver (possibly with a built-in DVD player as well). See "Setting Up a Home Theater" page 54.

PRODUCTS GET SMALLER...YET AGAIN. Manufacturers continue to shrink hard drives, batteries, and other parts of audio and video components. MP3 players can be as small as an ink pen. Portable CD and DVD players can be as thin as an inch. Many capable speakers for home theater are as small as those intended for computer use. "Executive sound systems" have shrunk minisystems into microsystems that fit readily on a desk or into flat systems that hang on a wall.

MORE OPTIONS BUT FEWER PROVIDERS. Even as consumers' ability to control how they view and listen to content continues to expand, corporate mergers are further shrinking the number of companies that control the flow of content. Content providers now own media organizations and vice versa, with Internet service in the mix as well. General Electric owns NBC; Viacom owns CBS, MTV, VH1, Paramount Pictures, Showtime, and Blockbuster; Walt Disney owns ABC; Sony owns Columbia and TriStar; Time Warner includes AOL, HBO, Warner Brothers, New Line Cinema, Time Warner Cable, and Turner Broadcasting; and Vivendi Universal Net owns MP3.com and Rollingstone.com, among others. One result of these conglomerations is that, more than ever, what's available is affected by forces other than viewer preference.

COPYRIGHTS AND WRONGS. At the same time, copyright issues are limiting control of content—and possibly increasing prices. The creators and publishers of content such as movies and music have legitimate claims to legal protection of what belongs to them. But copyright concerns have led to the use of hardware that blocks you from copying a DVD title you've purchased onto a VHS tape for your personal use. (Expect similar roadblocks when DVD recorders go mainstream.)

Some recent releases of music CDs include copy protection that may distort the sound if you try to play the disc in your computer's CD-ROM drive—or even freeze up the PC altogether. And blank CDs for recording music include a surcharge to cover royalties the music industry believes would otherwise be denied to musicians.

LESS PRIVACY. Every company with which you contract for your home entertainment seems to have gone full-throttle into data mining. Rent a videotape or DVD from Blockbuster or order pay-per-view on cable, and the transaction is recorded in some way. Ditto when you buy a CD off the Web, choose a channel on your cable or satellite setup, or fill out a warranty card.

You might expect the original company to use that information to offer related products and services to you. But it's another thing to be bombarded with phone calls, letters, e-mail, and other offers from companies you've never heard of, simply because they have purchased data about you.

MORE COMPLEX CHOICES ALL AROUND. One more effect of the so-called digital revolution is that it's even harder to be an informed consumer. Products are more complicated, requiring you to study to make a smart choice.

More products involve a service provider, not just for Web access and cell phones but now some video equipment. Not only must you choose among competing services, but once you've chosen and bought the hardware, you're committed to that provider. Switching can involve paying hundreds of dollars more to buy new, provider-specific gear, as with satellite-TV equipment or DVRs.

More and more, electronics components need to connect with one another, requiring compatible video and audio connections for best results. And competing formats mean that early adopters cannot be sure that the format they choose will be the one that prevails, as manufacturers conjure up newer media formats, music-encoding schemes, and connection specifications.

All this, of course, means a greater challenge for consumers shopping for home-entertainment products. That's where CONSUMER REPORTS can help.

Setting up a home theater

Adding surround sound to a TV can transform the viewing and listening experience even more than buying a bigger set.

Most TV sound can be improved by adding external speakers; a pair of self-powered speakers is a simple, easy way to do that. But for a real home-theater experience, you need a big TV, a video source (hi-fi stereo VCR or DVD player), a surround-decoding receiver/amplifier, and five speakers plus a subwoofer. Following is an overview of the whole system.

How surround sound works

Surround sound adds more channels to familiar two-channel stereophonic sound for stronger movie-theater realism, allowing additional speakers to carry the multichannel sound found on movies.

What you'll hear depends on three things: the format used for the source (a TV show or DVD, for instance), the software decoder (on the receiver or DVD player) used to decipher the format, and the number of speakers you have. If your gear lacks the latest, most sophisticated decoder, it can still handle a TV broadcast or DVD, but it will do so with fewer audio channels and less dramatic effect. Conversely, state-of-the-art hardware can play older material only because new decoders are generally backward-compatible with early formats. Again, you'll hear fewer channels.

The following is a rundown on the major formats:

Dolby Surround, an early version of surround sound, is an analog encoding scheme used mostly for VHS movies and TV shows. It combines four channels into stereo soundtracks. With no decoder—say, on a TV—you'll hear stereo.

With a **Dolby Pro Logic** decoder, you'll hear four channels: left, right, center (unlike Dolby Surround), and one limited-range surround channel. A newer version, **Pro Logic II,** has the same left, right, and center channels, but also has two discrete, full-range surround channels for a total of five channels. Most new receivers have Pro Logic II; older models may have only Pro Logic. You'll need four or five speakers for optimal sound.

The next step up is **Dolby Digital,** a digital encoding scheme that's also called Dolby Digital 5.1. Like Pro Logic II, it has full-range left and right channels in front and rear plus a center channel; it adds a subwoofer channel for deep bass (called ".1" because it's limited to low-frequency effects). Dolby Digital is used on digital media, such as DVDs, digital cable, digital broadcast TV, and satellite transmissions. It can also decode material that uses Dolby Surround. Virtually all new receivers and some DVD players have Dolby Digital decoders. You'll need five full-range speakers and a subwoofer for optimal sound.

DTS (Digital Theater Systems) is a rival to Dolby Digital, also with six channels. It's offered on most new receivers and on some DVD players. It calls for the same speaker setup as Dolby Digital.

Dolby Digital EX and **DTS-ES** are "extended surround" formats that add either a center-rear surround channel or an extra pair of rear-surround speakers that go behind the listener. With Dolby Digital EX, the two flavors are referred to, respectively, as Dolby Digital 6.1 (with three surround speakers) and 7.1 (with four surround speakers). Both

Arranging your home theater components

FINDING THE SWEET SPOT

The trick to setting up a home theater is arranging components in a way that maximizes their capabilities. The room you choose has a fundamental bearing on sound quality. For the best sound, try to strike a balance between acoustically "live" (bare floor and walls) and "dead" (carpeted floor and curtained walls) areas.

Upholstered furniture, wall hangings, and stocked bookshelves can help deaden the front of a room, where the TV is. The back of the room, where the rear-channel speakers are, should be live. The size and shape of room also matter. A 17-foot by 11-foot room with an 8-foot ceiling is good. A square room can make bass sound boomy or uneven. The diagrams here show "sweet spots" for various shapes of rooms.

HOOKING IT ALL UP

When hooking up components, go from left to right across the back of the receiver. Here are steps to follow:

1. Connect the receiver to the audio devices with stereo patch cords.

2. Connect the video devices, using the best video signal that your TV set, receiver, and DVD player have—component video, if you have that; S-video, if you have that; or composite, available in all video equipment.

3. With speakers, start as close to the ideal as you can. The main speakers should approximately form an equilateral triangle with you, the listener, and should be at the same height as your ears. The center speaker should be atop or below the TV and aligned with, or only slightly behind, the main speakers. The best place for your surround speakers will depend on the room's acoustics. You may have to experiment with their positions and directions. The surround speakers may be placed alongside the seating position, facing each other or facing the back wall. The subwoofer can go anywhere convenient, for starters.

4. Connect the speakers, observing polarity; connect the power cords.

5. Experiment with the speaker locations and tweak the tone controls. Moving the subwoofer out of the corner or away from the wall may make it sound less boomy.

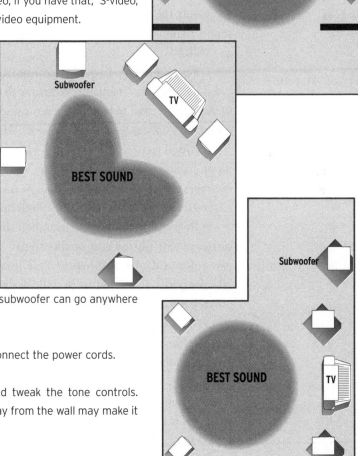

formats are still relatively new and not widely used on either equipment or programming. At this stage, they are mostly for video enthusiasts. With them, you'll need seven or eight speakers to achieve the full effect.

THX is a certification that indicates that a multichannel audio product has passed certain performance and ergonomic tests and can process sound to simulate movie-theater acoustics.

Connecting the components

The way you connect your video and audio equipment can affect the quality of the sound and images you receive. Here's what you need to know about each.

VIDEO CONNECTIONS. Even the best TV set won't live up to its potential without a high-quality video source and a high-quality connection. As described below, TV sets can have four different types of inputs, each of which accepts a specific kind of signal. Most sets 27 inches and larger have an RF antenna/cable, composite-video, and S-video input; a component-video input is found mostly on higher-end models.

Antenna/cable input, sometimes called a VHF/UHF input, is the most common connection. It's the easiest connection to use because it's the only one that carries both sound and picture on one cable—in this case, the familiar coaxial cable. (The other video inputs carry only the picture, requiring the use of a separate pair of audio inputs to carry the sound.) The antenna/cable input is used with video sources such as antennas, cable boxes, and VCRs.

Offering a step up in quality, **composite-video input** uses a single standard RCA-style jack—a round jack (frequently yellow) with a single pin—to pass video signals. Two separate RCA jacks are used to pass the stereo audio signals. Most video sources—including cable boxes and VCRs, as well as DVD players—have a composite video connection.

A round jack with four pins, **S-video input** accepts even better-quality signals. This input separates the signal into two—color and luminance (black and white)—which improves the image quality. This can be used to connect your TV to DVD players, satellite receivers, and digital-cable boxes, as well as digital, S-VHS, or Hi8 camcorders.

A three-cable connection found on some higher-end TVs, **component-video input** carries potentially the best-quality signals. It separates the video signal into three signals, two color and one luminance. This input is used primarily with DVD players. On HD-ready sets, this input is specially designed to handle signals from HDTV tuners and progressive-scan DVD players.

Some TVs come with more than one S-video, composite-video, or component-video input, letting you connect several devices. On many TVs, a composite-video or S-video input is on the front of the set for easy access.

AUDIO CONNECTIONS. The picture is obviously only half the story. You will also need to hook up your sound equipment. To obtain the audio from a device such as a VCR, DVD player, cable or satellite receiver, or camcorder, you generally connect one or a pair of **audio inputs** to your receiver, which routes sound to the speakers. Stereo analog audio inputs are labeled L and R for left and right. Newer multichannel receivers will also have **coaxial** or **optical digital-audio inputs** for providing surround sound; some have both. These are

Home theater setup

Here's one example of how to set up a home theater. This receiver-based system uses an audio/video receiver as the nexus for TV signals from a cable box (it could also be a satellite box or an antenna), along with video and audio signals coming from the DVD player, VCR (or DVR), and CD player. Sound is handled by the receiver, not the TV set. You use five speakers plus a subwoofer in a typical surround-sound setup. See page 55 for more on placing speakers.

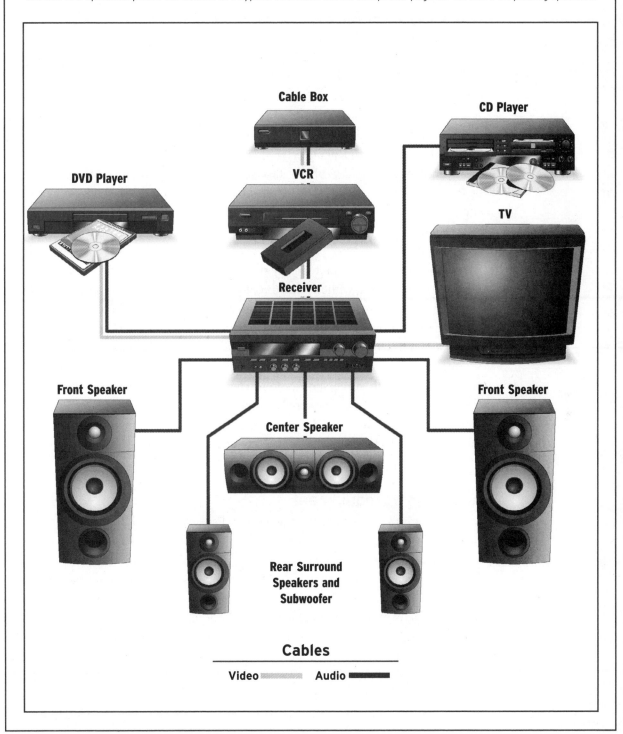

Cable Box

CD Player

DVD Player

VCR

TV

Receiver

Front Speaker

Center Speaker

Front Speaker

Rear Surround Speakers and Subwoofer

Cables

Video ▨▨▨▨   Audio ▰▰▰▰

used for connecting a DVD player and some digital-cable and satellite receivers. Be sure that the receiver's input matches the output of any device you want to connect—in other words, to use an optical output on the DVD player, you will need to have an optical input on the receiver. After-market converter boxes are also available.

To output the sound, every multichannel receiver will have at least six speaker terminals so it can accommodate a surround-sound system with six speakers. You don't have to use all six terminals—you can use only two for a stereo setup, for instance. Most receivers also have a **subwoofer pre-amp out,** an output that carries unamplified low-frequency signals to an active (powered) subwoofer.

Some receivers come with **5.1 inputs,** six connectors that accept multichannel analog audio signals that another device—such as a DVD player that has a built-in Dolby Digital or DTS decoder, or that plays DVD-Audio or SACD discs—has already decoded through a process that splits a signal into six or more audio channels. The inputs are typically marked Front L and R, Rear (or Surround) L and R, Center, and Subwoofer (which also may be labeled LFE, for low-frequency effects).

User manuals should be able to take you through much of the setup process. Hang on to these for future reference. First, give yourself easy access to the back of the receiver and other components. You will need good lighting to read the labeling on the back panels, so have a flashlight ready. Connect audio devices first, using the cables that came with each component.

To connect speakers, you typically strip off enough insulation from the ends of the wires to connect them, without shorting, to adjacent wires. Observe proper polarity; a speaker, like a battery, has "+" and "−" terminals. (The insulation of one wire in each pair should have a distinguishing feature, such as color or striping.) Reversing polarity will cause a loss of bass or other frequencies.

You can plug almost all of your components into a two-prong AC power strip—preferably one with surge suppression. The exceptions are the three high-powered devices: the TV, receiver, and powered subwoofer. Plug those directly into the wall or into a three-prong AC power strip. Or you can plug all of your components into a power control center, which handles the entire system and can include surge suppression.

Arranging the equipment

Make sure your room has enough distance between you and the TV for comfortable viewing. The ideal for viewing a conventional, 30- to 40-inch set is 8 to 12 feet, which gives your eyes enough distance to knit the scan lines into a unified picture. But a high-definition TV screen has no visible scan lines, so you can sit closer. For analog sets larger than 40 inches—flat-panel or projection sets—figure on sitting more than 10 feet away. Another way of looking at it: The bigger the room, the bigger the TV can be.

Receivers generate more heat than other audio and video components, so they need to go on the top of the stack or on their own shelf, with at least a couple of inches of head space and a path for the heat to escape. If a receiver's surface becomes hot to the touch, try one of the following: turn down the volume; provide more cooling, perhaps with a small fan; use speakers with a higher impedance; or play only one set of speakers at a time.

Matching speakers and receiver

Speakers and the receiver must match in two ways: power and impedance.

POWER. Generally, the more power (measured in watts) that a receiver delivers, the louder you can play music, with less distortion. Each doubling of loudness uses about 10 times as much power. Most models these days provide plenty of power—at least 60 watts per channel.

Here's a quick guide to power requirements for various room sizes: 80 to 100 watts per channel for a large living room (15x25 feet or more with an 8-foot ceiling); 40 to 80 for an average living room (12x20 feet); 20 to 40 for a bedroom (12x14 feet). A "live" (echoey) room will need less power than a "dead" (muffled-sounding) room.

IMPEDANCE. Materials that conduct electrical current also resist the current's travel to varying degrees. This resistance, or impedance, is measured in ohms. Standard speaker impedance is 8 ohms, which all receivers can handle. Many speakers have an impedance as low as 4 ohms, according to CONSUMER REPORTS tests. All else being equal, 4-ohm speakers demand more current than 8-ohm speakers. The use of the former generally doesn't pose a problem at normal listening levels but may eventually cause a receiver to overheat or trip its internal overload switch when music is played very loud. Before buying 4-ohm speakers to regularly play loud music, check the manual or back panel of your receiver to confirm that it's compatible.

Some speakers overemphasize various frequencies when placed against the wall or tucked in a bookshelf. Manufacturers' recommendations can help you decide on the optimal placement in your particular room.

The best position for the main front speakers is roughly an equilateral triangle whose points are the left speaker, the right speaker, and you, the listener. Try to place them at about the same height as your ears as you sit. The center speaker should be atop or below the TV and aligned with, or only slightly behind, the main speakers. The left and right surround speakers can be placed alongside the seating, facing each other or the back wall. The subwoofer can go anywhere convenient—under a table, behind the sofa. Watch out for corners, though. They accentuate the bass, often making it unacceptably boomy.

The fine-tuning

You can optimize the system by properly setting audio levels and taking advantage of some of your components' features.

DVD AUDIO SETTINGS. A DVD player can output each disc's audio signal in a number of ways. The raw "bitstream" signal is undecoded; use this setting if your receiver decodes Dolby Digital and DTS audio. If you have only a digital-ready (or DVD-ready) receiver and your DVD player has a built-in Dolby Digital or DTS decoder, use the "analog 6-channel output" setting, which outputs decoded audio to the receiver. And if you have only a stereo receiver or TV (or just stereo speakers), set the DVD player for "analog 2-channel;" this downmixes the multiple channels into two.

SUBWOOFER ADJUSTMENTS. Most powered subwoofers have two controls: cutoff frequency and volume level. The former is the frequency above which the subwoofer won't reproduce sound. If your main speakers are regular, full-range types (not satellites), set the subwoofer to the lowest setting, typically 80 hertz. If they're satellite speakers with no woofers, see the manual regarding setup of the satellite and subwoofer combination. Adjust the subwoofer's volume so its contribution is noticeable but subtle.

RECEIVER SETTINGS. With your user manual as a guide, adjust the receiver speaker by speaker, according to each speaker's size, distance from the listener, and sound level relative to the other speakers. With most audio systems, you should be able to sit where you will be listening and make the proper adjustments by using the receiver's remote control.

Camcorders

Fine picture quality and easy editing have improved the functionality of these moviemakers. That's especially true for digital models, which are replacing analog.

Those grainy, jumpy home movies of yesteryear are long gone—replaced by home movies shot on digital or analog camcorders. You can edit and embellish the footage with music using your computer, then play it back on your VCR; you can even turn it into video shorts to send via e-mail.

Digital camcorders generally offer very good to excellent picture quality, along with very good sound capability, compactness, and ease of handling. Making copies of a digital recording won't result in a loss of picture or sound quality.

Analog camcorders generally have good picture and sound quality and are less expensive. Some analog units are about as compact and easy to handle as digital models, while others are a bit bigger and bulkier.

What's available

Sony dominates the camcorder market, with multiple models in a number of formats. Other top brands include Canon, JVC, Panasonic, Samsung, and Sharp.

Most digital models come in the MiniDV format. New formats such as the disc-based DVD-RAM and DVD-R and tape-based MicroMV have also appeared. Some digital models weigh as little as one pound.

MINIDV. Don't let their small size deceive you. Although some models can be slipped into a large pocket, MiniDV camcorders can record very high-quality images. They use a unique tape cassette, and the typical recording time is 60 minutes at standard play (SP) speed. Expect to pay $6 for a 60-minute tape. You'll need to use the camcorder for play-back—it converts its recording to an analog signal, so it can be played directly into a TV or VCR. If the TV or VCR has an S-video input jack, use it to get a high-quality picture.

Price range: $400 to more than $2,000.

DIGITAL 8. Also known as D8, this format gives you digital quality on Hi8 or 8mm cassettes, which cost $6.50 and $3.50, respectively. The Digital 8 format records with a faster tape speed, so a "120-minute" cassette lasts only 60 minutes at SP. Most models can also play your old analog Hi8 or 8mm tapes.

Price range: $400 to $800.

DISC-BASED. Capitalizing on the explosive growth and capabilities of DVD movie discs, these formats offer benefits tape can't provide: long-term durability, a compact medium, and random access to scenes as with a DVD. The 3¼-inch discs record standard MPEG-2 video, the same format used in commercial DVD videos. The amount of recording time varies according to the quality level you select: from 20 minutes per side at the highest-quality setting for DVD-RAM up to about 60 minutes per side at the lowest setting. DVD-RAM discs are not compatible with DVD players, but the discs can be reused. DVD-R is supposed to be compatible with most DVD players and computer DVD drives, but the discs are write-once. We paid about $25 at a local retailer for a blank DVD-RW.

Most analog camcorders come in one of three formats: VHS-C, Super VHS-C, and Hi8. They usually weigh around 2 pounds. Picture quality is generally good, though a notch below that of digital.

VHS-C. This format uses an adapter to play in any VHS VCR. Cassettes most commonly hold 30 minutes on SP and cost $3.50.

Price range: $225 to $500.

SUPER VHS-C. This high-band variation of VHS-C uses special S-VHS-C tapes. (A slightly different format, S-VHS/ET-C, can use standard VHS-C tapes.) One S-VHS-C tape yields 40 minutes at SP and costs $6.50. JVC is the only brand that offers camcorders in this format.

Price range: $250 to $500.

HI8. This premium variant of 8mm (an analog format that is virtually extinct) promises a sharper picture. For full benefits, you need to use Hi8 tape and watch on a TV set that has an S-video input. A 120-minute cassette tape costs about $6.50.

Price range: $200 to $400.

Key features

A flip-out **liquid-crystal-display (LCD) viewer** is becoming commonplace on all but the lowest-priced camcorders. You'll find it useful for reviewing footage you've shot and easier to use than the eyepiece viewfinder for certain shooting poses. Some LCD viewers are hard to use in sunlight, a drawback on models that have only a viewer and no eyepiece.

Screens vary from 2½ to 4 inches measured diagonally, with a larger screen offered as a step-up feature on higher-priced models. Because an LCD viewer uses batteries faster than an eyepiece viewfinder does, you don't have as much recording time with it.

An **image stabilizer** automatically reduces most of the shaking that occurs from holding the camcorder as you record a scene. Most stabilizers are electronic; a few are optical. Either type can be effective, though mounting the camcorder on a tripod is the surest way to get steady images. If you're not using a tripod, you can try holding the camcorder with both hands and propping both elbows against your chest.

Full auto switch essentially lets you point and shoot. The camcorder automatically adjusts the color balance, shutter speed, focus, and aperture (also called the "iris" or f-stop with camcorders).

Autofocus adjusts for maximum sharpness; **manual focus override** may be needed for problem situations, such as low light. (With some newer camcorders, you may have to tap buttons repeatedly to get the focus just right.) With many models, you can also control exposure, shutter speed, and white balance.

The **zoom** is typically a finger control—press one way to zoom in, the other way to widen the view. The rate at which the zoom changes will depend on how hard you press the switch. Typical optical zoom ratios range from 10:1 to 26:1. The zoom relies on optical lenses, just like a film camera (hence the term "optical zoom"). Many camcorders offer a digital zoom to extend the range to 400:1 or more, but at a lower picture quality.

Regardless of format, analog or digital, every camcorder displays **tape speeds** the same way a VCR does. Every model, for example, includes an SP (standard play) speed. Digitals have a slower, LP (long play) speed, which adds 50 percent to the recording time. A few 8mm and Hi8 models have an LP speed that doubles the recording time. All VHS-C and S-VHS-C camcorders have an even slower EP (extended play) speed that triples the recording time. With analog camcorders, slower speeds worsen picture quality. Slow speed doesn't reduce picture quality on digital camcorders. Using slow speed, however, means sacrificing some seldom-used editing options and may restrict playback on other camcorders.

Quick review lets you view the last few seconds of a scene without having to press a lot of buttons. For special lighting situations, preset **auto-exposure settings** can be helpful. A "snow & sand" setting, for example, adjusts shutter speed or aperture to accommodate high reflectivity.

A **light** provides some illumination for close shots when the image would otherwise be too dark. **Backlight compensation** increases the exposure slightly when your subject is lit from behind and silhouetted. An **infrared-sensitive recording mode** (also known as night vision, zero lux, or MagicVu) allows shooting in very dim or dark situations, using infrared emitters. You can use it for nighttime shots, although colors won't register accurately in this mode.

Audio/video inputs let you record material from another camcorder or from a VCR, useful for copying part of another video onto your own. (A digital camcorder must have such an input jack if you want to record analog material digitally.) Unlike a built-in microphone, an external microphone that is plugged into a microphone jack won't pick up noises from the camcorder itself, and it typically improves audio performance.

A camcorder with **digital still** capability lets you take snapshots, which can be downloaded to your computer. The photo quality is generally inferior to that of a still camera.

Features that may aid editing include a **built-in title generator,** a **time-and-date stamp,** and a **time code,** which is a frame reference of exactly where you are on a tape—the hour, minute, second, and frame. A **remote control** helps when you're using the camcorder as a playback device or when you're using a tripod. **Programmed recording** (a self-timer) starts the camcorder recording at a preset time.

How to choose

PERFORMANCE DIFFERENCES. Digital camcorders got high marks in our picture-quality tests. Top-performing models yielded pictures that were sharp and free of streaks and other visual "noise" and had accurate color. Audio quality wasn't quite as impressive, at least using the built-in microphone. Still, digitals recorded pleasing sound devoid of audio flutter, a wavering in pitch that can make sounds seem thin and watery.

Typically, the best analog models we tested were good—on a par with the lowest-scoring digitals. The lowest-scoring analog models delivered soft images that contained noticeable video noise and jitter, and they reproduced colors less accurately than any digital model. And while sound for 8mm and Hi8 analog camcorders was practically free of audio flutter, all the VHS-C analog camcorders suffered from some degree of that audio-signal problem.

RECOMMENDATIONS. If you don't want to spend a lot, an analog camcorder is a good value—many are now priced at $300 or less. Analog models may also appeal if you have little interest in video editing. If you want to upgrade, however, choose a digital model. Prices are as low as $400 and are continuing to fall.

Try before you buy. Make sure a camcorder fits comfortably in your hand and has controls that are easy to reach.

Ratings: page 210 Reliability: page 290

CD players

Delivering superb performance at an affordable price, the CD is the music medium of the moment.

But regular console CD players are losing ground to digital video disk players, which can play both CDs and DVDs, and to dual-function devices that can both record and play CDs. Niche CD players are thriving. Jukebox models can hold hundreds of discs. Portable players are now incorporating MP3 capabilities.

What's available

Sony dominates the CD-player category, making nearly one out of three CD players sold. Other big sellers are RCA and Technics.

CONSOLE MODELS. Single-disc models have virtually disappeared. Multiple-disc changers, typically holding five or six discs, can play hours of music nonstop. A magazine changer holds discs in a slide-in cartridge the size of a small, thick book; cartridges double as disc storage boxes. Magazine changers aren't as easy to load and unload as carousel-type changers, which have taken over the market. Carousel changers usually let you change discs not currently in use without interrupting the music.

Price range: $100 to $250.

MEGACHANGERS. Also known as CD jukeboxes, these typically store 100 to 400 discs. Marketed as a way to manage and store an entire music collection, most let you segment a collection by music genre, composer, artist, and so forth. They flash album titles as you hunt through the discs. Inputting all the necessary data can be a tedious task (made easier on models that connect to a computer keyboard), but it's worth the effort because you can then set a jukebox to shuffle and play random selections all night or play discs only from a chosen genre. To fit all those CDs, megachangers can be quite large. In fact, some may not fit the typical stereo rack. And some are inconvenient to load, or noisy and slow in selecting CDs.

Price range: $200 to $450.

PORTABLE PLAYERS. Small, sporty, and designed for a single disc, these have simple controls. A growing number of models also play CDs you record yourself, using both the CD-R and CD-RW formats (see CD player/recorders for more on these formats) and digital file formats such as MP3 and WMA. Early portables often skipped or had poor-quality headphones. Today's players skip less, and many have good headphones that will convey decent sound. Some still have mediocre headphones, however, and you'll enjoy better listening if you replace them.

Battery life is improving, but it varies considerably from model to model. In our latest tests, battery life was typically 16 to 30 hours, but went as long as 40 hours. Some have an AC adapter, and some have a built-in battery charger. Most portables can connect to other audio gear and in that case can often play music as well as any console unit. Using a car kit, you can attach a portable player to your car's speakers.

Price range: $30 to $160.

Key features

Console models come with more features than portables. Their **controls** should be easy to see in dim light. A **calendar display** shows a block of numbers indicating the tracks on the active disc and highlights the current track. As play continues, previous track numbers disappear, so you can quickly see how many selections are left. A **numeric keypad** on the remote takes you to a particular track more quickly than pressing Up or Down buttons.

A **remote control** is convenient and now fairly standard. The best have buttons that are grouped by function or are color-coded; they should be visible in dim light. Most CD remotes operate the player only.

Some changers and jukeboxes have a handy **single-play drawer** or slot so you can play a single disc without disturbing any already loaded. **Cataloging** capability offers various ways to keep track of the many CDs stored inside a jukebox, such as categorizing by genre.

Memory features that make track selection easy include **delete track,** which lets you skip specified tracks but otherwise play a disc from start to finish, and **favorite track** program memory, which lets you mark your preferences. **Music sampling** (or **track scan**) plays a few seconds of each selection. Most models can be programmed to play tracks in sequence, to shuffle play (look for "nonrepeat shuffle"), or to repeat a track. A **volume-limiter switch** on portable players lets you hear softer passages without having other sounds at ear-splitting levels.

People who do a lot of taping will appreciate **auto edit** (also called "time fit for recording"). You enter the cassette's recording time, and the player lays out the disc's tracks, usually in sequence, to fill both sides of your tape. With **comprehensive time display,** you check time elapsed and time remaining for the current track and for the entire disc. **Running-time total** lets you total the time of tracks to be recorded to fit the maximum on a tape. **Music-peak finder** scans for the loudest passage in a track you're going to record, allowing you to adjust the tape deck's recording level correctly and quickly. **Fade out/fade in** performs the audio equivalent of a movie fade for less abrupt starts and endings. **Auto spacing** inserts a few seconds of silence between tracks.

With a **synchronizing jack,** you can connect a cable to a tape deck of the same brand so you can run both machines simultaneously. Those recording digitally to a MiniDisc recorder or a digital tape deck need a **digital output jack** in order to attach a fiber-optic or coaxial cable.

Portable CD player features focus on sound-quality enhancement and power management. Most portables have a **bass-boost control** to compensate for the thin bass of poorer headphones. Some have a **digital signal processor** (DSP), which electronically simulates the ambience of a concert hall or other venue. Skip-free performance depends on a good **buffer**—a memory feature that scans the disc, continuously storing upcoming music (typically from 10 to 45 seconds, sometimes more) so the player won't cause audio dropouts.

Most portables have a **liquid crystal display** (LCD) that shows which track is playing, and a **battery-level indicator** that warns of low batteries. (The best indicators show a shrinking scale to reflect power remaining.) An **AC adapter** runs the player on house current and enables some models to charge rechargeable cells. Rechargeable batteries may cost extra.

Colorful "sports" models tend to be pricier than the rest of the portable pack and differ in a few other respects. Their lid is secured with a **latch** and sealed with a **rubber gasket,** and they have **rubberized plugs** covering jacks for an AC adapter and headphones. The latch keeps the lid closed so successfully that some sports models are a bit hard to open. The gasket and plugs help resist sand, dirt, and moisture, though you'll need to wipe off a dusty or wet player before you open it. Keep in mind that these players are **water-resistant,** not waterproof—the difference between a splash and total immersion.

A **car kit,** standard with some portables, consists of an adapter that powers the unit through a car's cigarette lighter and a cassette adapter that pipes the player's sound through the car's tape player and speakers. (You can buy aftermarket kits at electronics or auto-supply stores.) Some adapters added noise to the sound or otherwise compromised performance in our tests. A line-out jack is a better choice than the headphone jack for connecting a portable to a component receiver or other gear.

How to choose

PERFORMANCE DIFFERENCES. Many CD players can produce excellent sound, with accurate tonal balance and no coloration or distortion. However, not all CD players are equally convenient to use. Better console models have an uncluttered front-panel display with clearly labeled main buttons grouped together by function. They also include features that make it easy to produce tapes from CDs.

For portable players, a good buffer is key for smooth, skip-free performance. Some models skipped with just a mild jouncing, others only when jolted hard. Battery life in recent tests varied from 5 to 40 hours of continuous play.

Headphones that come with portable players differ in comfort and performance. In our tests, they ranged from decent to mediocre. Comfort is very subjective, of course. Sometimes you can improve sound by buying replacement headphones. A decent set costs about $10 to $30.

RECOMMENDATIONS. If you're looking to play CDs in a home-theater setup, consider getting a DVD player instead of a CD player. Some are nearly as cheap as CD players these days. The price of CD player/recorders has also dropped enough to make them a reasonable alternative, with the premium for the recording functionality perhaps $100.

If you want to play only CDs, a multidisc changer will save you from having to swap discs in and out. Shoppers for portable players should weigh battery life heavily if they're frequent listeners. They should also pay particular attention to antiskip performance if they listen on the go.

CD player/recorders
They make it easy to copy the music you want onto compact discs, with no loss of quality.

Audio CD player/recorders let you make your own recordings and play back pre-recorded material. They cost more than CD players without recording capability, but prices are dropping. They sell as stand-alone units and as components of some minisystems.

There's another way to make your own music CDs: Record them using a computer. CD drives that burn CDs are now standard on many computers and can be as adept as component CD player/recorders, often performing the task faster.

Both CD player/recorders and computer CD burners let you copy entire discs or dub selected tracks to create your own CD compilations. There's no quality lost in high-speed CD-to-CD dubbing. Recording speeds usually are real-time or 4x, which records four times faster. (Computer CD burners can be as fast as 16x.)

With either approach, you can record to CD-Rs (discs that can be recorded on only once) or to CD-RWs (rewritable discs that can be erased and rerecorded). The CD-R format plays on almost any CD player, whereas CD-RWs generally play only on newer disc players that are configured to accept them. Be aware that some older DVD players will have problems reading CD-R and CD-RW discs.

What's available

Audio CD player/recorders are sold by audio-component companies such as Denon, Harman-Kardon, JVC, Philips, Pioneer, and Sony.

DUAL-TRAY MODELS. One tray is for play/record, another for play. Price range: $250 to $600.

CHANGER MODELS. These hold four or five discs and let you change a disc while another is playing. Price range: $350 to $600.

Key features

With CD recorders, you program your selections from up to three discs installed in the changer; the steps will be familiar to anyone who has programmed a CD changer. Most recorders give you a running total of the accumulated time of the tracks as you are programming them. The computer approach to burning CDs makes compiling "mix" discs easier than it used to be. Once a blank CD is inserted into a computer CD drive, the accompanying software displays a track list from the source disc and lets you "drag" the desired tracks into the lower panel. As you insert successive CDs, you can see the **playlist** for your CD-to-be and even change the order of the tracks, combine two or more tracks or files into one, or split a track or file into two or more.

With both the CD player/recorder and the computer option, you must program the selections from each disc in succession. **Defining tracks** on the CD onto which you're recording is accomplished with varying degrees of flexibility. How many track numbers a given player/recorder can add per disc, for example, differs from one model to another. Additionally, assigning track numbers when you're recording from cassette tapes may be automatic or manual. (Such track numbers are inserted automatically when recording from CDs.)

Text labeling, available on some models, lets you type in short text passages, such as artist and song names. This is a much easier procedure with a computer keyboard than with a console's remote control. The number of **delete-track modes** grants you flexibility, whether you need to delete one track or the entire disc. One-track, Multitrack, and All-disc are three common modes. An audio CD player/recorder typically has three playback modes: **Program,** which plays tracks in a specific order; **Repeat;** and **Random Play** (or **Shuffle**), which plays tracks randomly.

Connection types can affect which external sources you're able to use to make a CD. A **digital input jack** may be optical or coaxial. An **analog input jack** lets you record your tapes and LPs. A **microphone input** offers a low-cost way for home musicians to make digital recordings of their performances. A **record-level control** helps you control loudness while recording digitally from analog sources—a problem you don't face when recording from digital sources.

How to choose

PERFORMANCE DIFFERENCES. Either method of burning a CD—using an audio CD player/recorder or a computer—makes a recording that's audibly (even electronically) indistinguishable from the original CD.

Audio CD player/recorders excel in versatility; you can record from CDs, LPs, cassettes, radio, and even TV (anything, in fact, that you can connect to a sound system's receiver). This method is the clear standout for recording LPs, since connecting a turntable to a computer requires additional equipment.

The computer method has advantages. Because it affords a connection to the Internet, the computer option lets you burn downloaded MP3-encoded files onto CDs. A computer offers more setup choices when you're assembling a CD from several prerecorded discs. And, when you're recording from analog sources, the computer's CD-burning software often includes sound processing that will reduce the snap and crackle of a vinyl LP or the hiss of a cassette tape.

RECOMMENDATIONS. The relatively low cost of burning high-quality CDs makes CD recording a good alternative to making cassette tapes. If you're buying a CD player/recorder, first consider a changer model; its multidisc magazine or carousel will make it easy to record compilation CDs or to play uninterrupted music.

The computer-based CD-recording option allows you to record music from both CDs and from the Internet. If you don't already have a CD-burning drive in your computer, you can buy one and the necessary software for about $100 to $150. If you're buying a new computer, you'll find that a CD-RW drive is standard equipment on many models. Based on our test experience, we would expect any CD-burner drive to perform competently.

Digital video recorders
DVRs outperform VCRs in many ways, but you'll still need a VCR to archive recordings.

Digital video recorders combine the easy navigation of a DVD player with the recording capability of a VCR and the convenience of a program guide. These set-top receivers have a hard drive much like the one in a computer, generally with space for 20 to 60 hours of programming, although some can hold up to 320 hours. You can get a stand-alone DVR or one that's integrated into a satellite-TV receiver, digital TV decoder, or DVD player/recorder.

Depending on which provider and plan you choose, you may pay for the service as well as the equipment—either a one-time activation charge or a monthly fee on top of your current cable or satellite-TV bill. Newer devices with built-in DVRs offer basic functions for no fee.

Because they can record and play at the same time, DVRs allow you to pause (and rewind or fast-forward) the current show you're watching, picking up where you left off. Should you pause a one-hour show for 10 or 15 minutes at the beginning, you can resume watching it, skip past all the commercials, and catch up to the actual "live" broadcast by the end of the show. Dual-tuner models can record two programs at once, even as you're watching a third recorded program.

A DVR does not replace your usual programming source. You must still get broadcasts via cable, satellite service, or antenna. Program guides are downloaded via your phone line, generally late at night to avoid tying up the line. These guides are customized according to which broadcast channels are available in your area and to which cable or satellite service you subscribe.

What's available

There are only two service providers for stand-alone DVRs: TiVo and ReplayTV. Hardware prices depend mostly on how many hours of programming you can store; service charges vary. The DVRs intended for use with one provider will not work with the other. You can buy TiVo equipment directly from TiVo or AT&T Broadband, or from Hughes or Sony under their brand names.

Price range: $250 to $500.

TiVo service requires a paid subscription of $13 per month, or $299 for the life of the DVR (transferable if you sell it). You can also get a DirecTV satellite receiver that incorporates TiVo capability (TiVo service charges still apply).

ReplayTV offers some models bundled with lifetime service included in the equipment price. With other models, service is separate; you can pay a one-time activation fee of $299 or a monthly charge of $13. In either case, you must buy equipment directly from the company.

Price range: $300 to $1,400.

Key features

Most DVRs resemble VCRs in size and shape but don't have a slot for a tape or disc. (The internal hard drive is not removable.) They connect to your television like a cable or satellite receiver, using composite, S-video, or RF antenna outputs to match the input of your TV set.

A recorder's **hard-drive capacity** varies in actual usage. Like digital cameras, DVRs record at different **compression settings** and thus at different quality levels. For the best image quality, you have to record programming at the DVR's lowest level of compression. To get the maximum capacity advertised, you have to use the highest level of compression, which gives the lowest quality. For example, a model that advertises a 30-hour maximum capacity will fit only about 9 hours at its best-quality setting.

The **program guide** is an interactive list of the programs that can be recorded by the DVR for the next 7 to 10 days. You can use it to select the show currently being broadcast to watch or record—or you can search it by title, artist, or show type for programs you want to record automatically in the future.

Custom channels, available with some models, are individualized groupings of programs that interest you. The feature allows you to set up your own "channel" of your favorite shows, such as crime dramas or appearances by William Shatner, whether on "Star Trek," a talk show, or any other program. A DVR can also record a specified show every time it runs.

A **remote control** is standard. Common features include instant replay, fast-forward, rewind, and pause of either recorded or live programs.

How to choose

PERFORMANCE DIFFERENCES. At the highest-quality settings, the picture quality of DVRs in our tests fell below that of most DVD players and was on a par with that of high-quality S-VHS VCRs. At the lowest-quality setting, picture quality matched run-of-the-mill VHS VCRs at their standard play (SP) speed. Audio quality is a notch below CD quality.

Ultimately, the DVR's picture quality, like the VCR's, depends on the quality of the signal coming in via your cable or satellite provider. A noisy or mediocre signal will produce mediocre digital recordings.

RECOMMENDATIONS. TiVo and ReplayTV represent an intriguing interactive technology, but the market is still developing. Avid TV watchers are prime candidates for these devices, as are those who'd like to sort programming according to their individual viewing preferences. DVRs are also a good bet for those people who hate sitting through commercials.

If a satellite dish is an option, consider one that includes a DVR. Keep in mind that you may have to pay a separate fee for the DVR service. Satellite DVRs work only with satellite programming and won't record from cable or an antenna.

Today's DVR can't replace a VCR, which you'll need if you want to make a permanent copy of what you record. Consider a DVR as a companion product, not a replacement, for your VCR.

DVD players

These devices play high-quality videos as well as CDs. You can get a basic model for less than $100.

As the fastest-growing consumer-electronics product in history, digital video disc players offer picture and sound quality that clearly surpasses what you get with a VCR. DVDs are CD-sized discs that can contain a complete two-hour-plus movie with a six-channel (5.1) Dolby Digital or DTS soundtrack, plus extra material such as multiple languages, interviews, additional camera angles for chosen scenes, behind-the-scenes documentaries, and even entire replays of the movie with commentary by the director or some of the actors.

DVD players also play standard audio CDs. Prices on multidisc models are low enough for a DVD player to serve as a practical stand-in for a CD player. There is a catch if you record your own CDs: Some models may still have problems reading the CD-R and CD-RW discs that you record yourself.

The DVD player is still a product in transition. New capabilities include being able to play DVD-Audio or SACD, two competing high-resolution audio formats designed to offer two- to six-channel sound. Meanwhile, DVD recorder prices are soon expected to drop, to a starting point of about $500. And, despite a DVD's superior sound and picture quality, VCRs remain the least expensive alternative for recording your favorite TV programs.

What's available

Apex, Panasonic, Sony, and Toshiba are among the biggest-selling brands. DVD players

---

┌─────────────────────────────────────┐

MOVIES *AND* MUSIC

Single-disc, multidisc, or combo DVD-VCR player?

SINGLE-DISC PLAYERS Cheaper than comparable multidisc DVD models. Slightly smaller and easier to fit on a shelf. Fine if you play mostly movies. But you have to swap CDs in and out to get continuous music.

MULTIDISC PLAYERS Good if you want to have continuous music play. Jukeboxes let you store your music collection in an easy-to-play way. These cost more than single-disc players, however, and they're bigger, especially those few jukeboxes with 300-disc capacity.

DVD-VCR COMBINATIONS These space-efficient units allow you to combine DVD and VCR in a space little bigger than a stand-alone unit of either type. They eliminate hooking up an extra device. They're fairly basic and lack the features of the better stand-alone units of either type. (As with stand-alone models, you won't be able to record most DVD movies on videotape because of copy restrictions on DVDs.)

└─────────────────────────────────────┘

are evolving as manufacturers seek to differentiate their products and come up with a winning combination of features. You can choose from a console or portable model. Many consoles offer built-in karaoke features and MP3 and Windows Media playback.

STANDARD SINGLE-DISC CONSOLES. Console models can be connected directly to your TV for viewing movies or routed through your receiver to play movies and audio CDs on your home-entertainment system. Even low-end models usually include all the video-output jacks you might want.

Price range: less than $100 to more than $800.

STANDARD MULTIDISC CONSOLES. Like CD changers, these players accommodate two to five or even seven discs. DVD jukeboxes that hold 400 or so discs are also available.

Price range: $150 to $1,000.

PROGRESSIVE-SCAN SINGLE AND MULTIDISC PLAYERS. These provide HD-ready TVs with a slightly sharper image by letting the set redraw 480 consecutive lines of the image 60 times per second. (By comparison, a conventional TV typically redraws every other line at that rate.) You can use a progressive-scan DVD player with a conventional TV, but you'll see the added benefit only with a set that supports the player's progressive-scan mode (480p), such as a high-definition or HD-ready set.

Price range: $150 to $1,000.

PORTABLE PLAYERS. These models generally come with a small wide-screen-format LCD screen and batteries that claim to provide three hours or more of playback—OK for a car trip or plane ride. Some low-priced models don't come with a screen; they're intended for users who plan to connect the device to a TV set. You pay extra for the portability either way.

Price range: $200 to $1,000.

Key features

DVD-based movies often come in various formats. **Aspect-ratio control** lets you choose between the 4:3 viewing format of conventional TVs (4 inches wide for every 3 inches high) and the 16:9 ratio of newer, wide-screen sets.

A DVD player gives you all sorts of control over the picture—control you may never have known you needed. **Picture zoom** lets you zoom in on a specific frame. **Reverse frame-by-frame** gives you backward incremental movement in addition to the **forward frame-by-frame** and **slow motion** that most players provide.

Black-level adjustment brings out the detail in dark parts of the screen image. If you've ever wanted to see certain action scenes from different angles, **multi-angle capability** gives you that opportunity. Note that this feature and some others work only with certain discs. Digital video discs, unlike VHS tapes, are sectioned for easy navigation. **Chapter preview** lets you scan the opening seconds of each section or chapter until you find what you want. **Go-to by time** lets you enter how many hours and minutes into the disc you'd like to skip to. Marker functions allow easy indexing of specific sections.

A **composite-video connection** to the TV can produce a very good picture, but with some loss of detail, and some color artifacts such as adjacent colors bleeding into each other. Using the **S-video output** can improve picture quality. It keeps the black-and-white

Auto show

Built-in DVD players for your car, which let kids (or anybody) watch movies from the backseat, are being offered as $1,200-plus options with new minivans, SUVs, and some cars. Similar fold-down roof players can be installed by an electronics dealer, but usually for $1,500 and up. Both offer an OK picture and very good sound.

and the color portions of the signal separated, producing more picture detail and fewer color defects than standard composite video.

Component video, the best connection you can currently get on a DVD player (but possibly lacking on the lowest-end models), improves on S-video by splitting the color signal, resulting in a wider range of color. If you use a DVD player attached with an S-video or component connection, don't be surprised if you have to adjust the TV-picture setup when you switch to a picture coming from a VCR or a cable box that uses a radio-frequency (RF, also called antenna/cable) connection or a composite connection.

One selling point of DVDs is the ability to enjoy movies with **multichannel surround sound.** To reap the full benefits of the audio encoded into DVD titles, you'll need a Dolby Digital receiver and six speakers, including a subwoofer. **Dolby Digital decoding built-in** refers to circuitry that lets a DVD player decode the six-channel audio encoded into DVD discs; without the built-in circuitry, you'd need to have the decoder built into the receiver or use a separate decoder box to take advantage of six-channel audio. (A Dolby Digital receiver will decode an older format, Dolby Pro Logic, as well.) Some players also may support **Digital Theater System (DTS) decoding** for titles using the six-channel encoding format. When you're watching DVD-based movies, **dynamic audio-range control** helps keep explosions and other noisy sound effects from seeming too loud.

DVD players also provide features such as **multilingual support,** which lets you choose dialog or subtitles in different languages for a given movie. Parental control lets parents "lock out" films by their rating code.

How to choose

PERFORMANCE DIFFERENCES. In CONSUMER REPORTS tests, most DVD players delivered excellent picture quality, all but eliminating the noise, jitters, and other aberrations typical of pictures from a VCR. They also offered CD-quality sound and, depending on the program material, multichannel capability. Some models may be more convenient to use than others. Remote controls vary considerably, so it's worth checking them out before making a purchase.

RECOMMENDATIONS. A DVD player offers better picture quality for movies than does a VCR. Provided you have the receiver and speakers to back it up, the sound is also superior to that of a VCR. You'll need a VCR, DVD recorder, or digital video recorder (DVR) to record, however.

Even a low-end DVD player will provide excellent video and audio. A single-disc model is the least expensive option, and should do the job if you mostly watch movies. A multidisc console makes more sense if you also plan to play music CDs.

If your audio/video setup includes a receiver with built-in Dolby Digital and DTS decoding, you don't need to pay a premium to get these decoders on your DVD player. Even a low-end player will let you enjoy six-channel surround sound, assuming you have the required audio system.

If you plan to buy an HD-ready TV, it may be worthwhile getting a progressive-scan DVD player. It will work with your conventional TV now and let you take advantage of the superior video quality when you get the HD-ready set.

Ratings: page 229, 232

Home theater-in-a-box

No inclination to mix and match speakers and receiver? All-in-one systems that you hook up to your TV and VCR or DVD player can minimize the hassle.

Good speakers and the components for a home theater system cost less than ever. But selecting all those components can be time consuming, and connecting them is a challenge even for audiophiles. You can save some hassle by buying an all-in-one product that combines a receiver with a six-speaker set and wirings. Unless your needs are very demanding, you'll compromise little on quality.

A "home theater in a box" includes a receiver that can decode digital-audio soundtracks and a set of six compact, matched speakers—two front, one center, two surround, and a subwoofer. You also get all the cables and wiring you need, usually labeled and color-coded for easy setup. Generally, the presumption is that you already own a TV and a VCR or DVD player, although many systems come with a separate DVD player or have one built into the receiver.

What's available

Kenwood, Pioneer, Sony, and Yamaha account for more than half of sales, with Sony on its own commanding almost a third of the market. The cheapest models usually don't include a DVD player.

Price range: $300 (for a basic system without a DVD player); $400 to $750 (for a system that has a DVD player and a powered subwoofer); and $2,000 or more (for systems aimed at audiophiles).

Key features

The receivers in home-theater-in-a-box systems tend to be on the simple side. They usually include both Dolby Digital and DTS decoders. Controls should be easy to use. Look for a front panel with displays and controls grouped by function and labeled clearly. **Onscreen display** lets you control the receiver via a TV screen.

Switched AC outlets let you plug in other components and turn on the whole system with one button. The receivers offer about 20 or more presets you can use for AM and FM stations. Some receivers also offer a **sleep timer,** which turns them on or off at a preset time. **Remote controls** are most useful when they have clear labels and different-shaped and color-coded buttons grouped by function. A universal remote can control a number of devices.

A **component-video output** on the receiver that can connect to a relatively high-end TV allows for the best picture quality; however, not many receivers have such an output. Instead, most have the next-best option, **S-video output,** which is better than a composite-video or RF (antenna) connection.

Look also for an **S-video input,** which lets you connect an external DVD player, digital camcorder, or certain cable or satellite boxes. Any player you might want to connect will need the same digital-audio connections, either optical or coaxial, as those of the

Ins and outs

Home-theater-in-a-box systems typically have fewer connections than you'll find on a stand-alone receiver. That reduces flexibility somewhat, but it can also simplify setup.

included receiver. And if you want to make occasional connections at the front—perhaps for a camcorder or an MP3 player—you'll need **front-panel inputs.**

DSP (for digital signal processor) modes use digital circuitry to duplicate the sound measurements of, say, a concert hall. Each mode represents a different listening environment. A **bass-boost** switch amplifies the deepest sounds.

A **subwoofer** may be powered or unpowered. Either type will do the job, but a powered subwoofer requires fewer wires, provides more control over bass, and lets a powered receiver drive the other speakers.

An integrated DVD player, available with some models, typically has fewer features than does a stand-alone DVD player. Features to expect are **track programmability** (more useful for playing CDs than DVDs), **track repeat,** and **disc repeat.** If you want more features, a stand-alone DVD player may be the wiser choice.

How to choose

PERFORMANCE DIFFERENCES. Performance doesn't always depend on price, we found in recent tests of these boxed sets. The receivers generally have a very good FM tuner and adequate power, and do a fine job switching signals. Overall, however, the boxed systems don't perform as well as component systems, and their features are a notch below those of component receivers, particularly in how easy their remote controls and onscreen menus are to use.

RECOMMENDATIONS. Home theaters in a box offer convenience and decent sound, better than you'd get from a typical minisystem with home-theater capability. The trade-off for that convenience is that you'll generally have to settle for less than the best in receiver and speaker technology.

Ratings: page 238

Minisystems

These all-in-one sound systems offer decent sound in an economical, convenient package.

A minisystem can be just the ticket if you're cramped for space or don't have the time or inclination to search out individual components and set them up. Minisystems typically include a receiver, an AM/FM tuner, a CD changer, and a dual-cassette tape deck in a bookshelf-sized box with two separate speakers. While the sound on the better models is quite good, even the best won't match the sound quality you can get from a component-based system. Still, a minisystem costs considerably less than the $1,000 or so you'd pay for a full complement of decent components, so it can be a good value for many listeners.

What's available

The top-selling brands include Aiwa, Panasonic, Philips, RCA, and Sony. Most of the models sold are two-channel stereo systems. You'll also find surround-sound systems that come with multichannel decoders such as Dolby Digital on the receiver. Such systems complement the usual two speakers with additional speakers for center- and surround-channel sound.

Models with a CD player/recorder instead of a playback-only CD changer are becoming more common. Some systems eliminate the tape deck for maximum compactness.

Most minisystems integrate everything but the speakers into a console that's more or less a 12-inch cube with a black or silver chassis and blinking displays. More compact minisystems, also called microsystems, are as narrow as 6½ inches—considerably smaller than a 17-inch standard-sized component. Lower-priced minisystems may have limited power and anemic bass. Buying one of the more expensive models may get you more amplifier power, CD recording capability, Dolby B noise reduction, or more speakers.

Price range: $100 to $500.

Key features

Minisystems have some of the same features of full-sized components, but controls are more integrated, and displays are often more vivid, even hyperactive.

Minisystems vary in how much power their **amplifiers** deliver to the speakers—from 15 to 70 watts per channel. In tests, we found that regardless of claimed wattage, all the systems tested produced enough sound to fill the typical office, dorm room, or bedroom, but would probably have a hard time in a large room or noisy party. Power ratings in minisystem ads are calculated in so many different ways that the claims are of little use when you're comparing brands.

Among worthwhile CD-player features is **play exchange,** which lets you change the CDs that aren't currently being played without interrupting the one that is. **Direct-track access** lets you go straight to a specific track. A display of the **time remaining** on either the track or the disc is useful when you're taping off a CD.

Music peak finder sets the recording level for the highest sound level on the disc, and **digital output** lets you record onto a CD or MiniDisc using a separate recorder. Some models can play CD-R or CD-RW discs you've recorded yourself.

Dual-cassette tape decks are becoming a less important feature and somewhat less common, given the predominance of CDs. If you are a tape listener, however, one feature we consider important for basic tape use is **auto reverse,** so you don't have to flip the tape over to play the second side. An **auto tape counter** helps find a particular location on a tape.

High-speed dubbing doubles the speed when you're copying from one tape onto another, though with some loss of quality. If you're likely to play the tapes on a good car stereo or component system, look for the ability to record and play **Type II tapes** and for **Dolby B Noise Reduction,** which reduces background hiss.

Full-logic controls are soft-touch electronic buttons on the minisystem's chassis. The **remote control** may group two or more functions on one button, which can sometimes be confusing, although remotes for the latest models have improved. A few models have a **microphone input** jack, along with **karaoke capability**.

A **subwoofer output** lets you connect a separately powered subwoofer, helpful for maximizing the lowest bass tones. Instead of bass and treble tone controls, some minisystems provide a three- or five-band **equalizer,** which gives you slightly more control over the full audio spectrum and is a bit easier to use. Some models have only **tone settings** such as Pop, Jazz, and Classical, which automatically determine the bass/treble mix, often over-boosting the bass in the process.

A **clock** lets you program the system to turn on at a predetermined time; an accompanying **timer** lets you make timed recordings. Some systems permit you to set the cassette deck to record from the radio in a fashion similar to using a VCR to tape a TV.

How to choose

PERFORMANCE DIFFERENCES. Overall sound quality varies, largely depending on the quality of the speakers. Minisystems in the last round of our tests were judged anywhere from fair to very good for sound quality. Most systems had adequate power for their speakers, although a few distorted the sound when played at very high volumes.

We've found that the FM tuners on most minisystems were fine. The AM tuners were mediocre, but that's true of component receivers, too. The sound quality on the CD players was typically excellent across the board. Tape deck performance was adequate for both playing and recording cassettes.

RECOMMENDATIONS. By bundling all the major audio functions in one package, a minisystem can save you the trouble of choosing separate components—and several hundred dollars in the bargain. While these units would disappoint a demanding listener, the quality of the better minisystems is surprisingly good considering the price. Don't expect top sound quality much below $150, however.

Take along a few familiar CD recordings to play when you go to the store. If you expect to play tapes much, consider trying out a few cassettes as well. Adjust the tone controls to see if you like the sound. Check out the controls and the appearance, which can be anything from sedate to high-tech. Ask about return or exchange policies in case the sound of the minisystem isn't to your liking when you get it home.

Receivers

For a home-theater surround-sound system, look for a receiver that can decode Dolby Digital and DTS soundtracks.

The receiver is the brain of an audio/video system. It provides AM and FM tuners, amplifiers, surround sound, and switching capabilities. It's also the heart—most of the players in a home-entertainment system connect to it, including audio components such as speakers, a CD player, cassette deck, and turntable, as well as video sources such as a TV, DVD player, VCR, and cable and satellite boxes.

Even as receivers take on a bigger role in home entertainment, they're losing some audio-related features that were common years back, such as tape monitors and phono inputs. Manufacturers say they must eliminate those less-used features to make room for other, newer features.

What's available

Sony is by far the biggest-selling brand. Other top-selling brands include Denon, JVC, Kenwood, Onkyo, Panasonic, Pioneer, RCA, and Yamaha. Most models now are digital, designed for the six-channel surround-sound formats encoded in most DVDs and some TV fare. Here are the types you'll see, from least to most expensive:

STEREO. Basic receivers accept the analog stereo signals from a tape deck, CD player, or turntable. They provide two channels that power a pair of stereo speakers. For a simple music setup, add a cassette deck or a CD player. For rudimentary home theater, add a TV and VCR. Power typically runs 50 to 100 watts per channel.

Price range: $125 to $250.

DOLBY PRO LOGIC. Dolby Pro Logic and Pro Logic II are the fading analog home-theater surround-sound standard. Receivers that support it can take three front channels and one surround channel from your TV or hi-fi VCR and output them to four or five speakers—three in front, and one or two in back. Most receivers supporting the Dolby Pro Logic standard are "digital-ready," which means they have the capability to send six channels of predecoded sound to the speakers. "Ready" means you must use a DVD player with a built-in digital decoder. (You won't be able to decode other digital audio sources such as satellite TV.) Power for Dolby Pro Logic models is typically 60 to 100 watts per channel.

Price range: $150 to $250.

DOLBY DIGITAL. Now representing the prevailing digital surround-sound standard, a Dolby Digital 5.1 receiver has a built-in decoder for six-channel audio capability—front left and right, front center, two rear with discrete wide-band signals, and a powered sub-woofer for bass effects (that's where the ".1" comes in). Dolby Digital is the sound format for most DVDs, high-definition TV (HDTV), digital cable TV, and some satellite-TV broadcast systems.

Newer versions of Dolby Digital, 6.1 and 7.1, add one or two rear channels for a total of seven-channel and eight-channel sound, respectively. To take advantage of true surround-sound capability, you'll need speakers that do a good job of reproducing full-spectrum sound.

Receivers with digital decoding capability can also accept a signal that has been digitized, or sampled, at a given rate per second and converted to digital form. Dolby Digital is backward-compatible and supports earlier versions of Dolby such as Pro Logic and Pro Logic II. Power for Dolby Digital receivers is typically 80 to 120 watts per channel.

Price range: $200 to $500 or more.

DTS. A rival to Dolby Digital 5.1, Digital Theater

Systems also offers six channels. It's a less common form of digital surround sound that is used in some movie tracks. Both DTS and Dolby Digital are often found on the same receivers. Power for DTS models is typically 80 to 120 watts per channel.

Price range: $200 to $500 or more.

THX-CERTIFIED. The high-end receivers that meet this quality standard include full support for Dolby Pro Logic, Dolby Digital, and DTS. THX Select is the standard for components designed for small and average-sized rooms; THX Ultra is for larger rooms. Power for THX models is typically 80 to 120 watts per channel.

Price range: $500 to $2,500 and up.

Key features

Controls should be easy to use. Look for a front panel with displays and controls clearly labeled and grouped by function. **Onscreen display** lets you control the receiver via a TV screen, a squint-free alternative to using the receiver's tiny LED or LCD display. **Switched AC outlets** (expect one or two) let you plug in other components and turn the whole system on and off with one button.

Remote controls are most useful when they have clear labels and buttons that light up for use in dimly lit rooms. It's best if the buttons have different shapes and are color-coded and grouped by function—a goal that is seldom achieved in receiver remotes. A **learning remote** can receive programming data for other devices via their remote's infrared signal; on some remotes, the necessary codes on other manufacturers' devices are built in.

Input/output jacks matter more on a receiver than on perhaps any other component of your home theater. Clear labeling, color-coding, and logical groupings of the many jacks on the rear panel can help avert glitches during setup such as reversed speaker polarities and mixed-up inputs and outputs. Input jacks on the front panel make for easy connections to camcorders, video games, MP3 players, digital cameras, MiniDisc players, and PDAs.

A stereo receiver will give you a few audio inputs but no video jacks. Digital-ready receivers with Dolby Pro Logic will have several types of video inputs, including composite and S-video and sometimes component-video. **S-video** and **component video jacks** let you route signals from DVD players and other high-quality video sources through the receiver to the TV.

Digital-ready receivers also have **audio 5.1 inputs** that accept input from a DVD player with its own built-in Dolby Digital decoder, an outboard decoder, or other components with multichannel analog signals. Dolby Digital and DTS receivers have the most complete array of audio and video inputs, often with several of a given type to accommodate multiple components.

Tone controls adjust bass and treble. A **graphic equalizer** breaks the sound spectrum into three or more sections, giving you slightly more control over the full audio spectrum. Instead of tone controls, some receivers come with tone styles such as Jazz, Classical, or Rock, each accentuating a different frequency pattern; often you can craft your own styles. But tone controls work best for correcting room acoustics and satisfying listening preferences, not enhancing a musical genre.

DSP (digital signal processor) modes use a computer chip to duplicate the sound characteristics of a concert hall and other listening environments. A **bass-boost switch** amplifies the deepest sounds, and **midnight mode** reduces loud sounds and amplifies quiet ones in music or soundtracks.

Sometimes called "one touch," a **settings memory** lets you store settings for each source to minimize differences in volume, tone, and other settings when switching between sources. A similar feature, **loudness memory,** is limited to volume settings alone.

Tape monitor lets you either listen to one source as you record a second on a tape deck or listen to the recording as it's being made. **Automatic radio tuning** includes such features as **seek** (automatic searching for the next in-range station) and 20 to 40 **presets** to call up your favorite stations.

To catch stations too weak for the seek mode, most receivers also have a **manual stepping knob** or buttons, best in one-channel increments. But most models creep in half- or quarter-steps, meaning unnecessary button tapping to find the frequency you want. **Direct tuning** of frequencies lets you tune a radio station by entering its frequency on a keypad.

How to choose

PERFORMANCE DIFFERENCES. The most recent CONSUMER REPORTS tests of receivers show that you don't need to spend more than $200 to $300 to get a fine performer (unless you want a THX model; those begin at $500). Most models are very good at amplifying and tuning in FM stations, but only good for AM stations. Ease of use is often somewhat disappointing.

RECOMMENDATIONS. Don't buy more receiver than you need. The size of the room you're using, how loudly you play music, and the impedance of the speakers you'll use all determine how much power is appropriate. Generally, 50 watts or more per channel should be fine for a typical system in a typical 12x20 foot room. Then it becomes a question of features and usability.

Virtually all new receivers support Dolby Digital 5.1 and DTS, and we strongly recommend you buy a model that supports those formats. A few receivers may support newer versions of Dolby (6.1, 7.1) that have seven or eight channels; they'd be good choices if you want the latest surround-sound capabilities.

Make sure a model you're considering has all the connection types you need, preferably in a clear, logical grouping. Explore the layout of the front panel and remote control to see how easy they'll be to use.

To compare receivers at the store, have the salesperson feed the same CD or DVD soundtrack to each one, adjust each receiver's volume to be equally loud, then select between each receiver's speaker output using the same set of speakers. Compare two receivers at a time. Stop the CD and listen for background hiss.

Ratings: page 254

Satellite TV

Before you opt for satellite TV, make sure a dish can be mounted on your property with a clear view of the satellite. Then choose the service provider and the hardware.

Frustration with cable companies has fueled the growth of satellite-TV broadcast systems. Some 20 million homes now sport a saucer-shaped dish antenna.

Satellite TV offers something most cable subscribers don't get—a choice of provider. DirecTV and EchoStar's Dish Network operate nationwide. Once renowned for offering hundreds of channels but no local stations, both DirecTV and Dish Network now provide local service in many cities and outlying areas. That's the result of a 1999 federal law allowing satellite companies to offer so-called local-into-local service. In January 2002, the FCC ruled that if a satellite company offered one local channel, it had to carry all local channels in the markets where local service was offered.

People in an "unserved" household—in rural areas where an acceptable signal cannot be received via a rooftop antenna—can pick up local stations (regional affiliates of major networks) from a satellite provider. According to the FCC, you should be able to confirm your status through your satellite provider. For much of the country, however, cable remains the only way to receive all local programming, including community and school channels.

What's available

DirecTV and EchoStar's Dish Network have comparable programming fare, with packages offering up to several hundred channels. Movie and sports programming is strong, and foreign-language programming is available. In addition to television, both providers carry 30 to 40 commercial-free music services in many genres.

Typically, the dish and receiver are sold together and will only work with the signal of the chosen provider. Hughes, RCA, and Sony are among the companies that offer DirecTV equipment; EchoStar and JVC offer Dish Network equipment. You can also buy the hardware directly from the service provider.

Satellite dishes typically measure 18 or 24 inches. The larger dishes offer increased programming options, such as more channels, pay-per-view movies, high-definition TV (HDTV) reception, and international programming. Sometimes a second 18-inch dish may be required to receive some of those services.

Receivers accept the signal from the dish, decode it, and send it to your TV. To be able to watch different programs on different TVs at once, you'll need one receiver for each TV. To facilitate this, you need a dish with multiple low-noise block converters (LNBs). Alternatively, the receiver's RF-output jack or an inexpensive splitter may be used to send the same channel to multiple TVs.

For pay-per-view ordering and other provider contact, satellite-TV receivers must be connected to a telephone line. Typically, you use your existing line. Limited high-definition programming is available from both providers.

Price range for programming: $25 to $35 per month for basic packages with 50 or

100 channels (local-channel service adds about $5 per month); $30 to $45 for midrange packages with 100 to 150 channels; $75 to $85 a month for high-end packages with several hundred channels. Pay-per-view movies cost about $5; special sports packages are available separately.

Price range for a dish-receiver package: $100 to more than $800 for a receiver with more features. Extra receivers cost about $100 each and add about $5 apiece to the monthly bill. Some equipment may be free or offered at reduced prices as part of a special promotion.

Key features

On the receiver, the number and type of **audio** and **video output jacks** make a difference in the quality of your picture and in the equipment you can connect. The lowest-quality connection is **radio-frequency (RF)**—the typical antenna-type connector. Better is a **composite-video output;** better still are **S-video outputs,** provided your TV is appropriately equipped, which can take advantage of the higher visual resolution of the digital video source.

An **on-screen signal-strength meter** lets you monitor how well the satellite signal is coming in. Satellite receivers with **Dolby Digital audio** capability may have optical or coaxial output for a direct digital connection to a Dolby Digital audio receiver.

Some remote controls accompanying the receiver are infrared, like TV or VCR remotes, requiring a direct line of sight to the receiver. Others use a radio-frequency signal, which can pass through walls, allowing the receiver to be placed in an unobtrusive, central location and controlled from anywhere in the house.

Remotes typically include a **program-description button,** which activates an on-screen **program-description banner.** The program guide helps you sort through the hundreds of channels.

A **program guide with picture** lets you continue to watch one program while you scan the onscreen channel guide for another. Some receivers have a **keyword search:** You can enter the full or partial name of a program or performer and search automatically through the listings.

How to choose

PERFORMANCE DIFFERENCES. The differences between the two satellite providers are subtle. Our testers saw some small defects when they viewed pictures from both satellite providers. You may notice minor visual impairments, mostly in fast-moving scenes (the most bandwidth-hungry screen content), which may be caused by expanded channel offerings at the expense of bandwidth.

RECOMMENDATIONS. Find out what the program offerings are in your area, including whether digital cable is available (or when it will be) and if local channels are available via satellite. It can be a major inconvenience if they're not available in your market. Choose the service, then the hardware. You need a clear view of the southern horizon and a place to mount the dish. Satellite dealers and installers will come out to assess your location. Be aware that if you switch providers, you'll need to pay for everything all over again.

Speakers

Speakers can make or break your audio or video setup. Try to listen to them in a store before buying. And if you can splurge on only part of your system, splurge here.

The best array of audio or video components will let you down if matched with poor-quality speakers. Good speakers don't have to cost a bundle, though it is easy to spend a lot. For a home-theater system, you can start with two or three speakers and add others as need and budget allows. Size is no indication of quality.

What's available

Among the hundreds of speaker brands available, the major names include Boston Acoustics, Bose, Cambridge Soundworks, Infinity, JBL, Pioneer, Polk, RCA, and Sony. Speakers are sold through mass merchandisers, audio/video stores, and "boutique" retailers. You can also buy them online, but may pay up to $100 for shipping.

Speakers are sold as pairs for traditional stereo setups, and singly or in sets of three to six for equipping a home theater. To keep a balanced system, buy left and right speakers in pairs, rather than individually. The center-channel speaker should be matched to the front (or main) speakers. For the best sound, the rear speakers should also have a sound similar to the front speakers. The front speakers supply the stereo effect and carry most of the sound to the listener's ears. The center (or center-channel) speaker chiefly delivers dialog and is usually placed on top of or beneath the TV in a home-theater setup. Rear speakers, sometimes called surround or satellite speakers, deliver ambient effects such as crowd noise. A subwoofer carries the lowest tones.

Price range: under $300 to over $1,000.

BOOKSHELF SPEAKERS. These are among the smallest, but, at 12 to 18 inches tall, many are still too large to fit on a typical bookshelf. A pair of these can serve as the sole speakers in a stereo system or as the front or rear duo in a home-theater setup. One can serve as the center-channel unit, provided it's magnetically shielded so it won't interfere with the TV. Small speakers like these have made strides in their ability to handle deep bass without buzzing or distortion. Any bass-handling limitations would be less of a concern in a multispeaker system that uses a subwoofer for the deep bass.

Price range: $200 to more than $600.

FLOOR-STANDING SPEAKERS. Typically about 3 to 4 feet tall, these can also serve as the sole speakers in a stereo system or as the front pair in a home-theater system. Their big cabinets have the potential to do more justice to deep bass than smaller speakers, but we believe many listeners would be satisfied with smaller speakers that scored well for bass handling in our tests. Even if floor models do a bit better, their size and cost may steer buyers toward smaller, cheaper bookshelf models.

Price range: $300 to more than $1,000.

CENTER-CHANNEL SPEAKER. In a multichannel setup, the center-channel speaker sits on or below the TV. Because it primarily handles dialog, its range doesn't have to be as full as that of the front pair, but its sound should be similar so all three blend well. Dedicated center-channel speakers are short and wide (6 inches high by 20 inches wide, for instance) so they perch neatly atop a TV.

Price range: $100 to over $500.

REAR-SURROUND SPEAKERS. Rear speakers in a multichannel setup carry mostly background sound such as crowd noise. Newer multichannel formats such as Dolby Digital, DTS, DVD-Audio, and SACD make fuller use of these speakers than did earlier formats. You'll get the best blend if the rear pair sounds similar to the front pair. Rear speakers tend to be small and light (often 5 to 10 inches high and 3 to 6 pounds) so they can be wall mounted or placed on a shelf.

Price range: $100 to over $400.

THREE-PIECE SETS. Designed to be used as a stand-alone system or integrated with other speakers, these sets combine two bookshelf or satellite speakers for midrange and higher tones with either a center-channel speaker or a subwoofer for bass.

Price range: $300 to $800.

SIX-PIECE SETS. These systems have four satellites (used for both the front and rear pairs), one center-channel speaker, and a subwoofer. Six-piece sets save you the trouble of matching the distinctive sounds of six speakers. That can be a daunting task at home, and even more of a challenge amidst the din of a store that doesn't have a decent listening room.

Price range: $400 to more than $1,000.

OTHER SHAPES AND SIZES. A "powertower" is a tower speaker, usually priced above $1,000, with a side-firing, powered subwoofer in its base. Flat-panel speakers save space and cost $500 and up per pair.

Key features

Lovers of loud sound should pay attention to a speaker's measured **impedance,** which affects how well the speaker and receiver get along. **Power range** refers to the advertised watts per channel. The **wattage** within a matched pair, front or rear, should be identical. Additionally, a speaker's power range should exceed the watts per channel supplied by your receiver or amplifier. Speakers sold to be near a TV set typically have magnetic shielding so they won't distort the picture with their core magnets.

How to choose

PERFORMANCE DIFFERENCES. What distinguishes the best from the rest is the accuracy with which speakers reproduce the original signals fed to them. Most models we've tested have been capable of reasonable accuracy. You can adjust the receiver's tone controls to compensate for a speaker's shortcomings. Making those adjustments is usually a minor, one-time inconvenience.

No speaker is perfect. Every speaker we've tested alters music to some degree, overemphasizing some sounds and underemphasizing others. Some speakers "roll off" entirely at extremes of bass and treble, meaning they can't reproduce some low or high sounds at all. Some speakers buzz, distort, or otherwise complain when playing low notes at window-rattling volume.

RECOMMENDATIONS. Look for the size and configuration that fit your listening space. Models of equal accuracy will sound different, so try to audition before you buy, using a familiar piece of music. Especially demanding: music with wide dynamics and frequencies—such as classical symphonies—and the other end of the scale, simple music, such as a solo piano performance.

Listen to the music soft and loud, for clarity and lack of harshness in the high range and a lack of boominess in the low. Start in the best position, in an equilateral triangle with the speakers, and move off-center until you find the angle at which the high frequencies become muffled. The farther you can go, the better the speakers. Sharpen your listening skills by first comparing each store's top performer with its low-priced entry-level model.

Ratings: page 260

TV sets

Conventional TVs, high-definition TVs (HDTV), flat screens, projection sets— you have more (and better) viewing choices than before, at ever-lower prices.

Conventional direct-view TVs—the picture-tube models you've been watching for years—are still what most buyers choose, and many offer outstanding performance at low prices. But of course there are other options. Want a big picture? Projection TVs have a screen measuring up to 73 inches or so, diagonally. If you'd love a screen that's only a few inches thick, you can get an LCD or plasma TV. All those TV types come in digital versions that can display high-definition (HD) signals, which offer sharper, more detailed picture quality than with an analog set. You can opt for the familiar squarish screen or a wide-screen model that simulates the movie-theater experience, better suiting much HD programming.

What's available

Among the brands selling TVs are JVC, Panasonic, Philips, RCA, Samsung, Sanyo, Sharp, Sony, Toshiba, and Zenith.

CONVENTIONAL ANALOG SETS. Direct-view TV sets typically have a screen ranging in size from 13 inches up to 36 inches. Analog sets are usually squarish, with an aspect ratio of 4:3, meaning they're four units wide for every three units high. A 27-inch screen, once thought large, is now the norm, and these sets are among the best values among TVs. Models with 27-inch or larger screen frequently offer many features, including picture-in-picture (PIP), S-video input, simulated surround-sound effects, a universal remote control, and a comb filter. A 32-inch screen, the entry level for big-screen TV, adds two-tuner PIP and more input jacks. The largest direct-view sets have a 36-inch screen (with an occasional 40-inch set) and usually the most features and inputs.

Price range: $75 and up (13-inch sets); $250 and up (27-inch sets); $400 and up (32-inch sets); $600 and up (36-inch sets).

PROJECTION TVS. Measuring 42 to 73 inches diagonally, rear-projection sets are the most affordable jumbo-screen TVs on the market. You can get either a 4:3 screen or a widescreen model with a 16:9 aspect ratio. Most rear-projection sets use three CRTs that have to be aligned periodically to converge their image. Picture quality is usually good and sometimes very good, but doesn't equal that of a conventional set. Viewing angle can be a drawback: The image appears dimmer as your position angles away from the center of the screen. Projection sets have plenty of features, such as two-tuner PIP and custom settings. HD-capable digital sets are becoming the norm as analog models are being phased out. Note that readers have reported that parts can be hard to get and repairers hard to find.

Price range: $1,000 and up (analog sets); $1,500 and up (HD-capable sets).

LCD FLAT PANELS. With a screen measuring about 10 to 40 inches diagonally, LCD TVs are only a few inches thick. They come in both 4:3 and 16:9 screen shapes and in conventional and HD models. These sets use the same technology as flat-panel computer monitors. A bright, smooth image is created by a white backlight and thousands of pixels that open and close like shutters. Slow pixel response may make fast-moving images appear fuzzy.

Price range: $600 and up.

PLASMA FLAT PANELS. Renowned for their thin profile, plasma displays tend to be bigger than LCD models, ranging from about 32 to 63 inches, measured diagonally. Most are widescreen models; both conventional and HD versions are available. With plasma technology, an image is created by a huge array of tiny fluorescent lights. Plasma displays may not include a TV tuner or speakers. Sets are often wall-mounted.

Price range: $3,000 and up.

HD-CAPABLE SETS. HDTV sets can provide the best at-home viewing experience currently available. When you're watching specially formatted HD programming, the picture has more resolution and more detail than a conventional TV can display. You can get HD programming via an antenna, HD cable box, or HD satellite receiver. Even with standard (non-HD) signals from a good cable connection, a satellite signal, or a DVD player, the picture quality is often better than a conventional set's.

Two types of TV sets can display HD images. By far the more common of the two types, HD-ready sets, also known as HD monitors, can display standard-definition

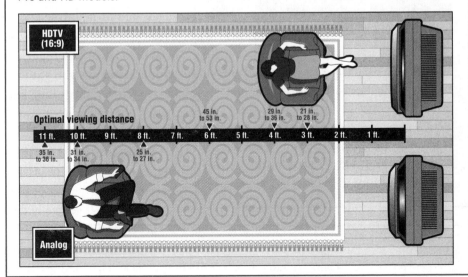

─── **PULL UP A CHAIR** ───

Bigger screens mean you need to sit farther from the TV for comfortable viewing, but HD sets cut the distance roughly in half. Shown are distances that offer the ideal compromise between image size and picture quality for both conventional analog TVs and HD models.

HDTV (16:9)

Optimal viewing distance

45 in. to 53 in.   29 in. to 36 in.   21 in. to 28 in.

11 ft.   10 ft.   9 ft.   8 ft.   7 ft.   6 ft.   5 ft.   4 ft.   3 ft.   2 ft.   1 ft.

35 in. to 36 in.   31 in. to 34 in.   25 in. to 27 in.

Analog

▲4:3

▲16:9

▲16:9

A digital set with a conventional 4:3 shape displays most programming well, but can't use the screen's full height to display wider images (top). Since a wider, 16:9 set can't use the screen's full width when displaying a standard-sized image, it must either fit it into a narrow portion of the screen (center), crop it, or distort it (bottom).

programs (most TV broadcasts) on their own. To display HD programs, they require a box to decode the signals—such as a digital cable box or satellite receiver specifically designed for HD programming. To get HD signals from a rooftop antenna, you'll need a separate digital-TV receiver, which costs several hundred dollars. You don't have to pay to receive the signals, however, as you do with cable and satellite. (To receive HD via antenna, you must be fairly close to a transmitter, with an unobstructed view.)

Integrated HD sets, also called HDTVs, have a built-in digital tuner that lets them display HD with only a roof antenna and no additional equipment. You may be able to receive the major networks' HD offerings, but not the premium channels available on satellite and cable. Although a digital tuner is built in, HDTV sets require an HD-capable cable box or satellite receiver to get HD via cable or satellite. Integrated sets typically cost more than HD-ready sets. Many HD sets are widescreen models because the 16:9 shape is better suited for displaying movies and other HD programming.

Price range: Depends on size and technology. $700 and up (27-inch direct-view set); $10,000 or more (high-end plasma set).

Key features

The **flat screen,** a departure from the decades-old curved TV tube, reduces off-angle reflections and glare, but doesn't necessarily improve picture quality. A **comb filter,** found on most sets, minimizes minor color flaws at edges within the image and increases picture clarity. An **auto-color control** can be set to automatically adjust color balance to make flesh tones look natural. **Adjustable color temperature** lets you shade the picture toward the blue range ("cooler," better for images with outdoor light) or toward the red range ("warmer," preferred for movie-theater-like realism).

Picture-in-picture (PIP) shows two channels at once, one on a small picture inserted in the full-screen image. **Stereo sound** is virtually universal on sets 27 inches or larger, but you'll generally discern little stereo separation from a set's built-in speakers. For a better stereo effect, route the signals to a sound system. A few larger TV sets have an **audio amplifier** that can power regular (unpowered) speakers connected to the set's audio output jacks, eliminating the need for a receiver. **Ambience**

sound is often termed "surround sound" or the like, but this is not true surround, like that from a multispeaker Dolby Digital or Pro Logic home-theater system; rather, it's accomplished through special audio processing. Some people find the wider "soundstage" pleasing; others find it distracting. **Automatic volume control** compensates for the jarring volume jumps that often accompany commercials or changes in channel.

Virtually all TV sets come with a **remote control** to change channels and adjust sound volume and picture. A **universal remote** will control all or most of your video (and some audio) devices once you program it by entering codes. (Aftermarket universal remotes typically cost $10 to $40.) **Active-channel scan** automatically detects and memorizes active channels, eliminating the need to scan manually.

Last-channel recall lets you jump to the previously viewed channel. With channel labeling, you enter channels' names (ESPN, CNN, AMC, for example) so you'll know where you are as you change channels. Some models offer an **Extended Data Services (XDS) decoder,** which displays channel and programming information on the show you're watching (if the station transmits that information). **Guide Plus,** offered by several manufacturers, displays program listings; the set receives program information when it's off but still in "standby."

Some features are important to specific users: **Separate audio program (SAP)** lets you receive a second soundtrack, typically in another language. **Multilingual menus** are also common. **Parental controls** include the V-chip, which blocks specific shows based on their content rating; for access, you must enter a code. A TV with **channel block-out** will block specific channels and may also prevent use of the audio/video inputs to which video games are connected.

Cable/antenna, or **RF** inputs are the most basic type; the next step up is **composite video. S-video input** lets you take advantage of the superior picture quality from a satellite-dish system, a DVD player, or a digital camcorder. **Component-video input** offers even better quality, useful with equipment that comes with component outputs, such as some DVD players, high-definition satellite receivers, and cable boxes. For a camcorder or video game, **front-mounted A/V jacks** are helpful. Audio output jacks, essential for a home-theater setup, let you direct a stereo TV's audio signal to a receiver or self-powered speakers. A **headphone jack** lets you watch (and listen) without disturbing others.

Sets that are **1080i/720p capable** can display digital signals in those two high-definition specifications. **VGA/SVGA input** allows the TV to accept signals from a computer.

Some features are most often found on HD sets and projection TVs. **Motion compensation** can improve the smoothness of movies played on standard (not progressive-scan) DVD players. This feature is sometimes referred to as 3:2 pulldown compensation or by brand-specific names such as CineMotion. On 16:9 sets, **stretch and zoom modes** will expand or compress an image to better fill the screen shape. This helps to reduce the dark bands that can appear above, below, or on the sides of the image if you watch content formatted for one screen shape on a TV that has the other shape. (The picture may be distorted or cut off a bit in the process of stretching and zooming.) Those bars make the picture slightly smaller and use the cathode-ray tubes' (CRT) phosphors unevenly, which can leave residual images on the screen over time. This "burn-in" is also a risk with any images left on the screen for long periods.

On CRT-based projection sets, **auto convergence** provides a one-touch adjustment to automatically align the three CRTs for a sharp, accurate image. It's much more convenient than manual convergence, which can require many time-consuming mechanical adjustments.

How to choose

PERFORMANCE DIFFERENCES. Most TV sets we've tested do at least a good job, many very good. HD sets generally have the best picture quality, even with conventional programming. Some of the biggest differences show up in sound quality. On most sets, the audio quality is sufficient for the usual TV fare, but for watching movies you can improve the audio by running the TV sound through a receiver to external speakers.

RECOMMENDATIONS. Before you start shopping, decide whether you want to stick with a direct-view set or go with a big-screen projection set or a flat panel, and whether you want a conventional analog TV or one that can handle HD signals. For the most part, CONSUMER REPORTS thinks HD-ready sets make more sense for most buyers than integrated HDTVs.

Size is another key consideration. For a fine picture plus many useful features, a 27-inch model may be the best deal. But if you have the space, you may prefer a 32-inch or 36-inch set, which are becoming more affordable. A big-screen TV is best viewed in a larger room that allows adequate viewing distance from the screen. Flat-panel LCDs and plasma sets are still fairly expensive; prices are likely to drop, as they have on other electronic gear, as these technologies mature and more sets are manufactured.

Also take into consideration how your TV will fit in with the other components of your home theater. If you plan to output sound to external speakers, you'll want audio outputs. DVD players, digital camcorders, and other devices require S-video inputs; for DVD players, a component-video input is better. Check with your cable-service provider regarding availability of digital cable service. Even if you watch mostly conventional programming now, buying an HD-capable set will give you superior picture quality now and the option of watching HD programming down the road. But you'll pay a premium for this type of TV.

Ratings: page 270, 274 Reliability: page 295

VCRs

Video cassette recorders don't match the picture and sound quality of DVD players, but they're still the most inexpensive way to play, record, and archive videos.

Today's VCRs are more of a bargain than ever. Hi-fi models, which cost about $150 to $300 when we tested them in November 1998, now have list prices as low as $80—and may sell for as little as $50.

What's available

Panasonic, RCA, Emerson, JVC, and Sony are among the biggest-selling brands. Most VCRs are standard VHS models; S-VHS, or super VHS, models can record in higher resolution.

Monophonic models, starting at about $50, record sound adequately for playback through a small TV speaker. Hi-fi VCRs cost a little more but offer sound of near CD quality. They're much better for larger TVs with stereo sound or for connecting to a receiver that supports the basic surround-sound formats (Dolby ProLogic or ProLogic II) used on some VHS tapes. Dual-deck models, which hold two cassettes at once, let you copy tapes easily. There are also a few digital VCRs that can record digital satellite-TV content.

Price range: $80 to $250 (hi-fi); $200 and up (S-VHS); $200 to $350 (dual-deck); $750 and up (digital).

Key features

Hi-fi models record **high-fidelity sound,** a desirable feature for a home-theater setup. **S-VHS** records more information onto a special tape for better picture detail. A newer variation, **S-VHS ET,** uses standard VHS tape.

Cable/satellite-box control, also referred to as C3 (for "cable-channel changer"), lets the VCR change the channel when you tape a program. **VCR Plus,** now quite common, lets you set the VCR to tape a program simply by punching in a code number from your local TV listings. **Memory backup** saves programming information if the VCR temporarily loses power; depending on the model, you may have a few minutes or less before the program settings are gone.

There are various "skip" features on VCRs. **Automatic commercial advance** lets the VCR bypass all commercials during playback by fast-forwarding past such cues as fade-to-black and changes in sound level. **Movie advance** lets you fly over previews at the beginning of a rented tape. **One-button skip** lets you fast-forward 30 to 60 seconds with each button press. There are also different kinds of searches: A **go-to search** skips to a section according to the time on the counter, while a **zero search** finds the place on the tape where the counter was set to zero. An **index search** forwards the tape to a specific index point set by the machine each time you begin a recording.

Editing features include **shuttle** and **jog controls,** which let you scan large segments or move forward or backward one frame at a time to find the exact spot you want. **Audio dub,** a higher-end feature, lets you add music or narration to existing recordings. A **flying erase head** lets you insert segments without noticeable video glitches.

Plug and play eases setup; you connect the VCR to the cable system or an antenna, then plug it in. The VCR reads signals from broadcasters to automatically program the channels and the clock. The latter feature is also known as **auto clock set.** Some VCRs can automatically switch from SP to EP speed, a feature called **auto speed-switching** that extends recording time and helps ensure that you don't miss a climactic scene because you ran out of tape.

A **universal remote** lets you control other devices along with your VCR. If the kids misplace it, a **remote locator** will page the remote, causing it to beep from its hiding place. **Child lock** disables the VCR's controls to keep programming from being changed.

How to choose

PERFORMANCE DIFFERENCES. Because DVD players have redefined excellence in picture quality for inexpensive video gear, none of the VCRs that we tested produced what we now consider an excellent picture. Still, most models performed very well—and the best picture you can get from a VCR is almost as good as what you'd get from a typical DVD player.

RECOMMENDATIONS. For basic recording of movies and TV shows, VCRs offer great value. Even inexpensive models now offer hi-fi sound and some level of VCR Plus programming. If you have an S-VHS-C, a Hi8, or a digital camcorder, you'll want a VCR that supports S-VHS to view the improved video quality. If you're hooking a VCR into a home-theater system that includes a DVD player, note that built-in encryption contained in many DVD discs typically won't let you copy DVD movies onto videotape. Such copying is a copyright violation in most cases.

Many VCRs have four or more recording heads, but that doesn't necessarily translate into better performance than you get with a dual-head model. For the best assurance of quality, try to get a side-by-side demonstration of the models before you buy.

VCR/DVD combos

These save space and reduce the need for connections. For many buyers, the compromise is worth it.

At a time when many consumers want both a VCR and a DVD player, these combo units may appeal. Their main advantage is that they fit in about the same space as a VCR, can involve less wiring than two separate devices, and can be operated with just one remote. VCR/DVD combos can play either form of media; a few models let you record non-copy-protected DVDs onto videotapes. The combos may simplify cabling; if you're not fussy about picture or sound quality, you can connect one to your TV through a single cable. Such convenience and simplicity exact a price: a combo can cost as much as or more than a stand-alone VCR and DVD player together.

What's available

The top manufacturers of VCR/DVD combos are also major players among makers of stand-alone units; they include Panasonic, Samsung, and Toshiba. As with stand-alone units, combos are rapidly evolving as manufacturers seek to differentiate their products and come up with a winning combination of features. The key differences relate to their DVD-playback capability:

STANDARD DVD MODELS. These perform with typically excellent DVD quality when connected to any TV made within the past few years. VHS picture quality is comparable to that of a stand-alone VCR.

Price range: $120 to $300.

PROGRESSIVE-SCAN DVD MODELS. This newer generation of combos, when connected to a regular TV, delivers the same high-quality picture as a standard player. But, when paired with an HDTV, a progressive-scan player delivers a cleaner image—the next best thing to true HD. VHS picture quality is the same as for models with standard DVD.

Price range: $150 to $350.

Key features

What you'll find in a combo VCR/DVD player is mostly a subset of what you get with stand-alone VCRs and DVD players, plus a few features that play off the integration of the two functions.

The DVD-player side of these units lets you take advantage of **multichannel surround sound** by routing the movie's digitally encoded soundtrack to a receiver through the **coaxial** or **optical digital-audio output.** (The receiver must have built-in decoding capability—Dolby Digital, DTS, or better—that lets it decode the multichannel audio encoded into DVD discs.) Should you want to connect the DVD's digital-audio output to a receiver, make sure its output (coaxial or optical) matches the receiver's input.

One capability affecting both primary functions of the combos is that aside from their digital-audio features they also let you take advantage of **Dolby Pro Logic** analog multi-channel surround sound. This may be encoded onto DVDs, VHS tapes, and even some TV programming. Again, you'll need a receiver with Dolby Pro Logic decoding; you connect it to the combo unit's stereo audio outputs.

If you don't have the full multispeaker setup, **virtual surround sound** mimics the effects of a full surround-sound system. It sounds pleasing to some people but artificial to others. **Dynamic audio-range** control helps keep a movie's explosions and other noisy sound effects from seeming too loud.

Besides playing standard DVDs, combos (as with stand-alone DVD players) can often play discs of numerous other formats. These include **CD-Recordable (CD-R)** and **CD-Rewritable (CD-RW),** along with—depending on the model—discs in the recordable **DVD+R, DVD-R, DVD+RW,** and **DVD-RW formats.** Many models can play **MP3** music files burned onto a CD, and all can play commercial audio CDs. With some new combos, a **memory-card slot** lets you insert removable media on which you've stored MP3 music files or photos shot with a digital camera.

Some models can record a non-copy-protected DVD onto videotape. But since most movies on DVD are copy-protected, you probably won't be able to use this feature often.

The VCR side of the combo player usually offers **index search,** which fast-forwards or rewinds the tape to a specific index point set by the machine at the start of a recorded segment. Some models can automatically switch tapes from SP to EP speed, a feature called **auto speed-switching,** to extend recording time and help ensure that you don't miss a climactic scene because you ran out of tape. Also helpful on some is the ability to play S-VHS tapes at VHS quality.

What's typically missing is any form of VCR Plus, which eases the process of programming **time-shift recording** (taping a program for later viewing) by letting you enter numerical codes from TV listings instead of the program's date, time, duration, and channel.

For connecting to the TV set, VCR/DVD combos offer radio-frequency (RF) output for either DVD or VHS signals, a major advantage if you have an old TV with only that form of input. (The downside is mediocre image quality.) A composite-video connection can produce a very good picture, but there will be some loss of detail and some color artifacts, such as adjacent colors bleeding into each other. S-video output, on some models, can improve DVD picture quality. It keeps the black-and-white and the color portions of the signal separated, producing more picture detail and fewer color defects than standard composite video. Component video, the best connection these combos offer (for DVD output), improves on S-video by splitting the color signal, resulting in a wider range of color. Component video also supports a progressive-scan signal for those DVD players that provide it.

Among other features, a **screen saver** is a moving image that kicks in after a set duration of inactivity to prevent still images from burning into your TV screen. It won't, however, prevent long-term burn-in of the dark bands displayed while you're watching letterbox-format programming. With a **lighted remote,** buttons are illuminated so you can see them more easily in a darkened room.

How to choose

PERFORMANCE DIFFERENCES. Picture quality from a VCR/DVD combo is comparable to what you'd get from stand-alone devices—excellent for DVD and so-so for VHS, depending on tape speed. Owing to the number of features, both the VCR and DVD functions of combo players make them slightly more complicated to use than stand-alone units.

RECOMMENDATIONS. If convenience and saving space are paramount, choose from among the models that require the fewest compromises. And if space is especially cramped, consider a newer combination product that marries a TV, VCR, and DVD player to offer portability and capabilities similar to those of a TV/VCR combo. Also worth weighing into your decision: If one combo function breaks, you'll be without both until the player comes back from the repair shop.

Ratings: page 234

Yard & Garden

Innovations, often prompted by tougher state and federal regulations, are making home and yard gear easier and safer to use, as well as friendlier to the environment. So buying a new piece of equipment rather than nursing along an old one may be a good move. Here are continuing trends in this segment of the marketplace.

"GREENER" PRODUCTS. Government rules for emissions by lawn mowers and other gasoline-powered yard tools are designed to reduce emissions by hundreds of thousands of tons per year. Emissions aren't the only type of pollutant: dozens of towns and cities have also been enacting laws designed to quiet gasoline-powered leaf blowers.

FRIENDLIER, SAFER CONTROLS. Clutchless hydrostatic transmissions on a growing number of ride-on mowers and tractors make mowing go more smoothly. All these machines stop the engine and blade when you leave the seat. Some higher-priced models stop the blade but not the engine, eliminating the need to restart the mower. All chain saws are now equipped with anti-kickback safety features.

MORE CAPABILITY–AND MORE LUXURY. Lawn and garden tractors can power accessories that allow you to plow and tow, as well as throw snow. Many models have become the backyard equivalent of sport-utility vehicles with their large engines and ever-wider cutting swaths. You'll also find a growing number of "zero-turn-radius" mowers and tractors that can turn 360° in one spot to better maneuver around obstacles.

Built-in gas barbecue grills with stainless-steel finishes now rival professional-style kitchen ranges in size and price. You'll also find stainless-steel stand-alone grills priced at $1,000 and beyond—though increasingly, you can get grills with a thousand-dollar look for about $500.

MORE SHOPPING OPTIONS. Yard and garden products are sold over the Internet through sites such as Amazon.com, HomeDepot.com, Lowes.com, and Sears.com. Such online sites can be useful, especially as research tools, but there's still a lot to be said for the local hardware store or home center. Large chains such as Sears and Wal-Mart usually have the best selection of lower-priced brands. Home centers such as Home Depot and Lowe's offer a mix of low-priced, midpriced, and upscale brands. Local hardware stores and other independent dealers tend to carry midpriced and upscale brands. Such stores often offer service that mass merchandisers and home centers don't provide.

Chain saws

They're still noisy, but many of the latest are safer and cleaner. Gasoline-powered saws still outperform electrics, although plug-ins can be fine for light-duty use.

Chain saws are inherently dangerous and noisy, though modern designs attempt to improve usability on both counts. Nearly all chain saws now have multiple features aimed at minimizing "kickback," which occurs when the saw snaps up and back toward the operator.

Electric models are quieter and cleaner than gasoline-powered ones. Gasoline-powered saws are cleaning up their act, however, as tougher federal standards reduce allowable emissions for these machines.

What's available

You'll find gasoline- and electric-powered chain saws at home centers, discount stores, and lawn-and-garden shops. Major brands include Craftsman (Sears), Homelite, Husqvarna, Poulan, Remington, and Stihl. Gas-powered saws use a small two-stroke engine that requires a mixture of gasoline and oil. Nearly all electric saws plug into an outlet and run off an electric motor. A few rechargeable, battery-powered chain saws are available, but they tend to be underpowered for most jobs.

As with most outdoor tools, the gas-powered versions tend to offer the most power and mobility. But plug-in electrics compensate somewhat with lighter weight, less noise, and trigger starting. They also emit no exhaust, don't need engine tune-ups, and typically cost less.

Price range: $100 to $300 (gas); less than $100 (electric).

Key features

Chain saws are typically marketed by the size of the **bar** (the metal extension that supports the chain—usually between 14 and 20 inches long) as well as the **engine** or

motor (measured in cubic centimeters for gas saws, amps for electrics). Usually, the larger the saw, the more you'll pay, though smaller models from high-end brands such as Husqvarna and Stihl can cost more than larger ones from Craftsman, Homelite, and other lower-priced brands.

Other features are aimed mainly at safety and convenience. Major kickback-reducing devices include a **reduced-kickback chain** with added guard links to keep the cutters from taking too large a bite, along with a narrow-tipped, **reduced-kickback bar** that limits the contact area where kickback occurs. All saws also have a **chain catcher**—an extension under the guide bar that keeps a broken chain from flying rearward. Some saws have a **chain brake,** which stops the chain almost instantly when activated, or a **bar-tip guard,** which prevents kickback by covering the bar's tip, or "nose."

Other safety features for most chain saws include a **trigger lockout switch** that must be pressed for the throttle trigger to operate and, for gas saws, a **shielded muffler** designed to prevent burns from accidental contact.

Common labor-saving features include an **automatic chain oiler,** which eliminates the need to periodically push a plunger to lubricate the chain and bar. Metal **bucking spikes** act as a pivot point when cutting larger logs. Some saws have a **chain-adjuster screw** mounted on the side of the bar. A few models feature a **tools-free adjuster** that lets you loosen or tighten the chain by turning a wheel.

Visible bar-oil and **fuel levels** are also convenient, as is a **wide rear handle** that eases gas-saw starts by allowing room for the toe of a boot to secure the saw on the ground. Also look for **antivibration bushings** or **springs** between the handles and the engine, bar, and chain, along with a combined **choke/on-off switch** that activates a gas saw's ignition while closing off air to its carburetor for easier starting.

How to choose

PERFORMANCE DIFFERENCES. Our tests confirm that gas-powered saws cut faster than electric models. More saws now have useful and important safety features—but any chain saw should still be handled with care. And even quieter electric saws remain noisy enough for us to recommend ear protection.

RECOMMENDATIONS. Buy a gasoline-powered saw if you need go-anywhere mobility. The best electric models, which cost less than $100, are fine for small branches and other light-duty cutting. In either case, you'll find a light saw (less than 14 pounds for gas models, less than 10 pounds for electrics) easier to use for longer periods of time. Unless you're felling large trees, a 14- or 16-inch bar should be more than adequate.

Chain-saw basics

1. **Reduced-kickback chain**
2. **Reduced-kickback bar**
3. **Chain brake**
4. **Bar-tip guard**
5. **Trigger lockout**
6. **Shielded muffler**
7. **Chain adjuster**
8. **Bucking spikes**
9. **Front handle**
10. **Visible bar-oil level**
11. **Visible fuel level**
12. **Rear handle**

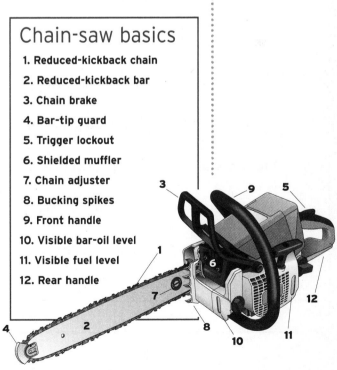

9 Essential garden tools

Tools for digging in the earth and harvesting its bounty are as old as civilization, with classic shapes honed through the centuries. But if you haven't looked at the tool section of your local hardware store in a while, you might be surprised at the new designs aimed at making digging, raking, pruning, and harvesting easier.

Here are nine garden tools that every homeowner should have, with tips on how to choose them. You'll find them at home centers, mass merchandisers, hardware stores, and through online retailers such as Toolsforless.com and Amazon.com, and catalogs such as A.M. Leonard and Smith & Hawken.

1. Trowel

Look for a trowel with a forged-steel head, which is thicker and sturdier than stamped steel, or one made of aluminum. Stainless steel and aluminum resist corrosion. The connection between head and handle is a trowel's weak spot. Look for a model with a strong "throat." Models with one-piece construction eliminate weak connections between the head and handle.

2. Cultivator

A cultivator breaks up compacted surface soil and loosens weeds with the sharp tines of its three- or four-pronged metal claw. The handle is often hardwood or fiberglass, although some short-handled cultivators are made entirely of aluminum. Wood provides shock absorption that may be welcome when working hard soil. Aluminum and fiberglass are lighter weight and may be less tiring to use. The claw is typically made of steel. You'll want a sturdy shank connecting the handle to the claw.

3. & 4. Spade & Shovel

A sharp-edged spade is a versatile digging tool for planting, edging, digging perennials, and lots of other chores short of moving soil. That's where a scoop-shaped shovel comes in. Spade and shovel handles may be hard wood or fiberglass. Both are sturdy, so choose what's comfortable. Shovels usually have a long, straight handle. Choose one that reaches to about shoulder level. Spade handles are shorter to give you good control in tight spaces. For best durability, look for features such as a long, fully welded shank joining the head to the handle. Forged steel will hold up better against rocks and other obstacles. Stainless steel is relatively easy to maintain, but you pay a premium for it. Forged carbon steel is sturdy, but beware of rust. Don't skimp on a cheap stamped-steel spade or shovel. It may not be up to the work required.

5. Pruner

There are two basic types of this indispensible garden tool. Bypass pruners are better for shaping shrubs, removing spent blooms, and taming overgrown vines. Their blades pass each other like scissors and provide close, clean cuts in live wood.

Anvil pruners crush branches between a sharp blade and a flat "anvil," a design that allows the pruner to cut through larger objects. They're better for dead wood. Handles are typically an integral part of the tool, and range in length from 6 to 9 inches. When shopping, hold the tool to make sure it's comfortable in your hand. Try the blade-locking mechanism to make sure it operates easily, reliably, and conveniently. With pruners, you get what you pay for. Pricier models have rotating handles that reduce the pressure on hands and fingers, along with removable blades that can be sharpened or replaced.

6. Lopper

Loppers are essentially long-handled pruners used to trim tall shrubs or to tidy short trees while you stand firmly on the ground. As with pruners, the blade design is either bypass or anvil. Handles are often made of wood. Longer handles give you more leverage as you cut thick branches. Pricier models may sport lighter fiberglass handles, telescoping aluminum handles that can extend your reach by 2 to 3 feet, or a rotating or swiveling head that allows

you to angle the blades for a precise cut without having to be a contortionist.

7. Hedge clippers

Manual hedge clippers are the tool of choice for precisely shaping an ornamental shrub or trimming a few foundation shrubs. Basic models typically have a wooden handle and 9½-inch blades, which are fine for most needs. Check for weight and balance. Clippers that are blade heavy or heavy overall will tire extended arms quickly. So will clippers that are hard to open and close; be sure there is a tension-adjustment knob. Also look for a limb notch located close to the handles on one of the blades. It's designed to snag thicker branches that may elude an unnotched blade's grip.

8. Leaf rake

Rake tines are made of bamboo, steel, or plastic. Bamboo tines can dry out and snap off over time. (An occasional soaking can reduce brittleness.) Steel tines are sturdy; plastic tines can snap in cold weather. Look for closely spaced tines, which will better contain leaves and other yard debris. Some rakes have an adjustable fan that can be widened for raking large areas

and narrowed for getting between closely spaced plants or shrubs. Handles may be wood or fiberglass, some with rubber cushioning.

9. Garden cart

A garden cart eases some of the more backbreaking gardening chores. Unlike wheelbarrows, which typically have one wheel up front, carts have two widely spaced wheels beneath their container or tray. The added support means that the wheels, rather than your arms, help keep the load from tipping sideways. Small carts can hold as much as 250 pounds, while medium- and large-capacity models typically hold 300 to 400 pounds. But because most people can comfortably handle no more than about 150 pounds of cargo at a time, a cart's maximum volume is more important than its weight capacity. Large 20- to 26-inch wheels help a cart roll more easily in and out of ditches and over ruts. Bicycle-style pneumatic tires and ball bearings also ease pushing.

Grills

Many people are choosing models that do more than just grill. Go high-end, and you can pay as much as you would for a pro-style kitchen range.

A $15 charcoal hibachi is all it takes to give burgers that outdoorsy barbecue taste. But a gas or electric grill offers flexible controls and spares you the hassle of starting the fire and getting rid of the ashes when you're done. Most grills have extras such as a warming rack for rolls; some have an accessory burner for, say, boiling corn on the cob. Shoppers looking for a backyard statement will find models that cost thousands of dollars and have stainless-steel exteriors and grates, porcelain-coated steel and aluminum lids, separately controlled burners, utensil holders, and other perks. You'll also find more modest grills that can serve up flavor and convenience for $200 or so.

What's available

Char-Broil, Coleman, Kenmore (Sears), and Weber account for more than 60 percent of gas-grill sales. Char-Broil is a mass-market brand, with both gas and electric models available. Weber is a high-end brand that also markets its classic dome-top charcoal grills. Sears covers the entire spectrum under its Kenmore name.

GAS. These grills are easy to start, warm up quickly, and usually cook predictably, giving meat a full, grilled flavor. Step-up features include shelves and side burners. Better models offer added sturdiness and more even cooking.

Price range: $100 to more than $3,000.

ELECTRIC. Easy to start, these offer precise temperature control and let you grill with nonstick cookware. But they take a bit longer than gas models to warm up.

Price range: about $100 to $300.

CHARCOAL. These provide an intense, smoky flavor prized by many. But they don't always light easily (using a chimney-style starter can help remedy that). They also burn less cleanly than gas, their heat is harder to regulate, and cleanup can be messy—major reasons why charcoal models are no longer the top-selling type.

Price range: usually $100 or less.

Key features

Most cooking **grates** are made of porcelain-coated steel, with others made of the somewhat sturdier porcelain-coated cast iron, bare cast iron, or stainless steel. A porcelain-coated grate is rustproof and easy to clean, but it can eventually chip. Bare cast iron is sturdy and sears beautifully, but you have to season it with cooking oil to fend off rust.

The best of both worlds: stainless steel, which is sturdy, heats quickly, and resists rust without a porcelain coating. Cooking grates with wide, closely spaced bars tend to provide better searing than grates with thin, round rods, which may allow more food to fall to the bottom of the grill.

Both gas and electric grills are mounted on a **cart**, usually made of painted steel tubing assembled with nuts and bolts. Higher-priced grills have welded joints, and some have a cart made of stainless steel. Carts with two wheels and two feet must be lifted at one end to move; better are two large wheels and two casters or four casters, which make moving easier. Wheels with a full axle are better than those bolted to the frame, which can bend over time.

Gas and electric grills generally have one or more **exterior shelves,** which flip up from the front or side or are fixed on the side. Shelves are usually made of plastic, though some are made of cast aluminum or stainless steel, which is more durable. (Wood shelves are the least sturdy and tend to deteriorate over time.) Most grills have **interior racks** for keeping food warm without further cooking. Another plus for gas or electric grills is a **lid** and **firebox** made of stainless steel or porcelain-coated steel, both of which are more durable than cast aluminum.

Still other features help a gas grill start more easily and cook more evenly. An example is the **igniter,** which works via a knob or a push button. Knobs emit two or three sparks per turn, while push buttons emit a single spark per push. Better are **battery-powered electronic igniters,** which produce continuous sparks as long as the button is held down. Also look for **lighting holes** on the side of or beneath the grill, which are handy if the igniter fails and you need to use a wooden match to start the fire.

Most gas grills have steel **burners,** though some are stainless steel, cast iron, or cast brass. Those premium burners typically last longer and carry warranties of 10 years or more. Most grills have two burners, or one with two independent halves. A few have three or four, which can add cooking flexibility. A **side burner,** which resembles a gas-stove burner and has its own heat control, is handy for cooking vegetables or sauce without leaving the grill. Other step-up features include an **electric rotisserie,** a **fuel gauge,** a s**moker drawer**, a **wok**, a **griddle pan**, a steamer pan, a deep fryer, a **nonstick grill basket,** and one or more high-heat **infrared burners** in lieu of the conventional type.

Most gas grills also use a **cooking medium**—a metal plate or metal bars, ceramic or charcoal-like briquettes, or lava rocks—between the burner and grates to distribute heat and vaporize juices, flavoring the food. Our tests have shown that no one type is better at ensuring even heating. But grills with nothing between the burner and the cooking grates typically cook less evenly.

Gas grills sometimes include a **propane tank**; buying a tank separately costs about $25. Some grills can be converted to run on natural gas or come in a natural-gas version. Tanks usually sit next to or on the base of the grill and attach to its gas line with a

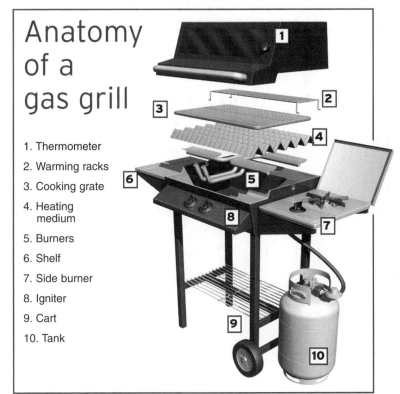

Anatomy of a gas grill

1. Thermometer
2. Warming racks
3. Cooking grate
4. Heating medium
5. Burners
6. Shelf
7. Side burner
8. Igniter
9. Cart
10. Tank

handwheel. All tanks must now comply with upgraded National Fire Protection Association standards for overfill protection. Noncompliant tanks have a circular or five-lobed valve and aren't refillable, although they can be retrofitted with a three-lobed valve or swapped for a new tank at a hardware store or other refilling facility.

How to choose

PERFORMANCE DIFFERENCES. Most gas or electric grills do a good job at hot, even grilling. Salespeople might tell you that more Btus (British thermal units) mean faster warm-up, but that's not always true.

Assembling one of these grills can take anywhere from 30 minutes to 3 hours; some stores include assembly and delivery in the price, while others charge for that service. Some minor safety problems have turned up in our tests. Typically they involved handles, knobs, or thermometers that got too hot to handle without pot holders. Also, grills without a grease cup or another means of catching and draining grease from the burners can flare up if the grease catches fire.

RECOMMENDATIONS. Consider how often you cook outdoors and how many people you typically feed. While price and performance don't track precisely, our tests have shown that some lower-priced gas grills ($275 or less) are particularly good values. Gas models priced at $350 to $600 have more features—grates with wide bars, ample warming shelves, stainless-steel burners and grates, electronic igniters, longer warranties, and sturdier carts. Spending thousands of dollars gets you many or all of those features plus more burners and mostly stainless-steel construction, but few consumers spend that much on a grill.

An electric grill can be a good, inexpensive option for places where gas grills aren't allowed. Charcoal grills cost the least overall, but they require the most preparation and cleanup work.

Hedge trimmers

A good electric trimmer is all most people need to shape and trim greenery. Gasoline- or battery-powered models free you from a cord, but you pay for that convenience.

A gas or electric hedge trimmer can be a useful addition to your tool shed if your property includes lots of shrubs. Either type of trimmer can save you some of the physical effort hand clippers require, since an engine or motor—rather than elbow grease—powers their blades. But using any powered hedge trimmer can still be hard work, since you're holding the device in midair for extended periods. That can make a trimmer's weight, balance, and vibration as important as its cutting power.

What's available

Black & Decker makes electric-powered models and sells more than half of all hedge trimmers. Craftsman (Sears) is Black & Decker's largest competitor, and sells electric plug-in and battery-powered trimmers as well as gas-powered models. Other brands include Echo, Homelite, Husqvarna, Little Wonder, Stihl, Ryobi, Toro, and Weed Eater.

ELECTRIC CORDED HEDGE TRIMMERS. Most consumers prefer plug-in electric trimmers, which are relatively light and quiet, start with the push of a button, produce no exhaust, and require little maintenance. The best electrics can also perform comparably to gasoline-powered models—provided you're within 100 feet of a power outlet.

Price range: $30 to $100.

GASOLINE-POWERED HEDGE TRIMMERS. Commercial landscapers usually favor gas-powered models for their power and mobility. Indeed, a gas-powered, long-reach trimmer can provide access to remote spots a corded electric trimmer can't reach. But their two-stroke engines entail the fuel-mixing, pull-starting, noisiness, maintenance, and exhaust emissions of other gas-powered, handheld yard tools. Gas trimmers can also be expensive.

Price range: $120 to $450.

ELECTRIC BATTERY-POWERED HEDGE TRIMMERS. Cordless trimmers combine the mobility of gas models with the convenience, clean running, and easy maintenance of plug-in electrics, courtesy of an onboard battery. On the downside, battery-powered trimmers offer relatively little cutting power, along with a short running time before the battery must be recharged. They can also cost as much as some gas-powered models.

Price range: $80 to $120.

Key features

A hedge trimmer's **blades** are simply two flat metal plates with tooth-lined edges. Blade length typically ranges from 13 to 30 inches, although most are between 16 and 24 inches long. **Blade gap**—the distance between teeth—is also important, since it helps determine how large a branch the trimmer can cut. In general, the wider the gap, the larger the branch a trimmer can handle and the easier it is to push the machine through a hedge.

Gasoline-powered, professional-grade trimmers have blade gaps of 1 inch or more, while homeowner-grade models typically have ⅜- to ¾-inch gaps—narrow enough to help keep fingers safe.

Still other factors make some blades more effective than others. **Double-sided blades** allow cutting in both directions, letting you stand in one position longer than you can with **single-sided blades**, which cut in one direction only. Pricier trimmers also tend to use **dual-action blades**, where both the top and bottom blade plates move back and forth, reducing vibration. With **single-action blades,** only the top blade moves.

Handle designs also vary. Trimmers with a wrap-around front handle let you keep your hands in a comfortable position as you pivot the trimmer to cut vertically or at odd angles. Safety features include tooth extensions, which are designed to prevent thighs and other body parts from contacting the blades' teeth. Some tooth extensions are part of the blades and move with them; we think separate, stationary tooth extensions provide better protection. Trimmers also have a front-handle shield designed to prevent your forward hand from touching the blade.

How to choose

PERFORMANCE DIFFERENCES. Any powered hedge trimmer should be up to light-duty tidying. The best can cut branches just shy of ⅝ inches in diameter, while dense, ¼-inch-thick branches were enough to stop the battery-powered trimmers we tested.

RECOMMENDATIONS. Begin by deciding which type of trimmer matches the chores you do. Electric corded models are relatively quiet and inexpensive. They also deliver the best combination of cutting power, maneuverability, and ease—provided you stay within range of a power outlet. Battery-powered trimmers offer cord-free convenience, but their lack of cutting power and limited running time between charges make them best suited to touchups and other light-duty work. In either case, look for an Underwriters Laboratories (UL) seal, which requires trimmers to have crucial safety features. Gasoline-powered models are best for heavier-duty trimming beyond the range of a cord. Wear hearing protection when using a gas-powered trimmer, and wear protective work gloves, safety glasses or goggles, and nonskid shoes when using any powered trimmer. Also be sure to do your trimming on firm footing or on a steady ladder. And if you're using an electric model, make sure the cord trails away from the blades.

Lawn mowers and tractors

Practically any mower—even an inexpensive one—will cut your grass. But you can get better results with less effort by choosing a machine based on your lawn size and shape and your mowing preferences.

Mowing options range anywhere from $100 manual-reel mowers to tractors that can cost $4,000 and beyond. Manual-reel and electric walk-behind mowers are appropriate for people with a small yard, while gasoline-powered walk-behind mowers are fine for most lawns up to about a half-acre. Those with lawns larger than that will appreciate the ease and speed of a riding mower or a lawn tractor.

Gasoline-powered mowers produce a disproportionate amount of air pollution compared with cars. Federal regulations aimed at reducing smog-producing lawn-mower emissions by 390,000 tons annually are being phased in over the next few years.

What's available

Manual-reel mowers are still made by a few companies, such as Great States and Scotts, while major electric-mower brands include Black & Decker and Craftsman (Sears). Craftsman is also the largest-selling brand of gasoline-powered walk-behind mowers, riding mowers, and lawn tractors. Other less expensive, mass-market brands of gas-powered mowers and tractors include Bolens, Murray, Troy-Bilt, Yard Machines, and Yard-Man. Pricier brands, traditionally sold at outdoor power-equipment dealers, include Ariens, Cub Cadet, Honda, Husqvarna, John Deere, Kubota, Lawn Boy, Poulan, Simplicity, Snapper, and Toro, although models from several of these brands are now available at large retailers.

Which type is best for your lawn? Here's what to consider:

MANUAL-REEL MOWERS. Pushing these simple mowers rotates a series of curved blades that spin in conjunction with the wheels. Reel mowers are quiet, inexpensive, and nonpolluting. They're also relatively safe to operate and require little maintenance other than periodic blade adjustment and sharpening. On the downside, our tests have shown that most can't cut grass higher than 1½ inches or trim closer than 3 inches around obstacles. Cutting swaths of just 14 to 18 inches wide are also a drawback if you have a decent-sized yard. Consider a manual mower for a small, flat lawn of one-quarter acre or less.

Price range: $100 to about $250.

ELECTRIC MOWERS. These push-type walk-behind mowers use an electric motor to drive a rotating blade. Both corded and cordless versions start with the push of a button, produce no exhaust, and, like reel mowers, require little maintenance aside from sharpening. Most offer a side or rear grass catcher, and many can mulch—a process in which clippings are recut until they're small enough to hide unobtrusively within the lawn. But electrics tend to be less powerful than gas mowers and less adept at tackling tall or thick grass and weeds. What's more, their narrow, 18- to 19-inch swaths take a smaller bite than most gas-powered mowers.

Both corded and cordless electrics have other significant drawbacks. Corded mowers limit your mowing to within 100 feet of a power outlet—the typical maximum length for an extension cord. Cordless versions, while more versatile, weigh up to 30 pounds more than corded models and typically mow just one-quarter to one-third acre before their sealed lead-acid batteries need recharging. That makes both types of electrics suitable mainly for small, flat lawns of one-quarter acre or less.

Price range: $125 to $250 (corded); $300 to $400 (cordless).

GASOLINE-POWERED WALK-BEHIND MOWERS. These include push as well as self-propelled models. Most have a 3.5- to 6.5-hp four-stroke engine and a cutting swath 20 to 22 inches wide, allowing them to do more work with each pass and handle long or thick grass and weeds. And all can keep mowing as long as there's fuel in the tank. But gas mowers are relatively noisy and require regular maintenance.

Most gas mowers provide three cutting modes: bagging, which gathers clippings in a removable catcher; side-discharging, which dispenses clippings onto the lawn; and mulching (see electric mower description above). Consider a push-type model for relatively flat one-quarter acre lawns or for trimming larger lawns, and a self-propelled model for lawns of a half-acre or more or those that are hilly.

Price range: $100 to more than $400 (push-type); $250 to $900 (self-propelled).

RIDING MOWERS AND TRACTORS. These are suitable for lawns of a half-acre or larger. Riding mowers have their engine in back and tend to be smaller, simpler, and easier to maneuver than tractors. While their 28- to 33-inch mowing swath is larger than a walk-behind mower's, it's far smaller than the 38 to 48 inches offered by lawn tractors and the 60 inches available with some larger garden tractors.

Lawn and garden tractors have a large engine mounted in front for better weight distribution. Both can also accept attachments that let them plow and tow a cart as well as clear snow; garden tractors accept soil-tilling equipment. Lawn tractors have become far more popular than garden tractors, although even these usually can't mulch or bag without accessories. Figure on another $25 to $150 for a mulching kit and $200 to $450 for a bagging system.

Zero-turn-radius ride-ons and tractors are also gaining ground in the marketplace. With most, you steer by pushing or pulling control levers, each controlling a driven rear wheel, although John Deere manufactures a zero-turn lawn tractor that uses a conventional steering wheel. The payoff for these tight-turning machines is added maneuverability in tight spots and around obstacles, but you can experience less steering control on hills. You pay a premium for the agility of a zero-turning-radius mower.

Price range: $700 to $2,000 (riding mowers); $800 to $3,500 (lawn tractors); $2,000 to $6,000 (garden tractors); $3,000 to $7,000 (zero-turning-radius mowers).

Key features

FOR ELECTRIC MOWERS: A sliding clip helps ease turns with corded mowers by letting the cord move from side to side. Some mowers have a flip-over handle you move from one end of the machine to the other as you reverse direction, say, at the end of a row.

FOR GAS-POWERED MOWERS: Some high-end models have a blade-brake clutch system that stops the blade but lets the engine keep running when you release the handlebar safety bail. This is more convenient than the usual engine-kill system, which stops the engine and blade and requires you to restart the engine. A four-stroke engine, which burns gasoline alone, runs more cleanly than a two-stroke engine, which runs on a mixture of oil and gasoline. An overhead-valve four-stroke engine tends to pollute less than a traditional side-valve four-stroke engine.

Replacing the traditional choke on most gas mowers is a small rubber bulb called a primer, which you press to supply extra fuel for cold starting. An electric starter is easier to use than a pull starter, though it typically adds $50 to $100 to the price. Most mowers with a recoil starter are easier to start than they once were, however. Some models from MTD-made Cub Cadet, White, and Yard-Man now have a spring-powered self-starter, which uses energy generated as the engine is shut off to provide push-button starts without a battery or outlet. CONSUMER REPORTS tests have found the device effective, provided you don't attempt starts in thick grass.

Some self-propelled mowers have just one speed, usually about 2½ mph; others have **several speeds** or a **continuous range,** typically from 1 to 3½ mph. Self-propelled mowers also include front-drive and rear-drive models. Front-drive mowers tend to be easier to maneuver and turn, although rear-wheel-drive models generally have better traction on hills and can maintain traction even with a full grass bag. Mowers with **swivel front wheels** offer the most maneuverability by allowing easy 180-degree turns. But, on many models, each front casterlike wheel must be removed to adjust cutting height.

You'll also find several different **deck** choices. Most decks are **steel,** although some mowers have an **aluminum** or **plastic deck,** which is rustproof; plastic also resists dents and cracks. Even many lower-priced mowers now have **tools-free cutting-height adjusters,** which raise and lower the deck with one or two levers. Most models also let you change mowing modes without tools, although a few still require tools and, sometimes, a blade change. Some mowers use a **side-bagging deck design,** in which a side-exit chute routes clippings into a side-mounted bag or out onto the lawn—or is blocked with a plate or plug for mulching.

Mowers with a **rear-bagging deck** tend to cost more, but their rear-mounted bag holds more than side bags and eases maneuvering by hanging beneath the handlebar, rather than out to the side. The rearward opening is fitted with a chute for side discharging or a plug for mulching. Some **"hybrid" rear-baggers** have a discharge port for clippings on the side of the deck as well as one for the bag in back.

FOR RIDING MOWERS AND TRACTORS: Some are gear-driven and require a lever and combination brake/clutch to change speed. Some gear-drive models use foot pedals with a pulley that allows continuously variable speed changes without the usual shifting. Spending more will buy you a model with a clutchless hydrostatic drive, which allows even more convenient continuously variable speed changes. Most models have a translucent fuel tank, making it easy to check the fuel level. Some have a fuel gauge. Still others let you remove the collection bag without flipping the seat forward.

How to choose

PERFORMANCE DIFFERENCES. Nearly all gas-powered push and self-propelled walk-behind mowers now handle mulching, bagging, and side discharging. In our tests, we've found that most do at least a good

---

BASIC MOWER MAINTENANCE

Prolong the life of your mower by performing regular checks and tune-ups.

Gas-powered mowers

CLEAN THE DECK According to manufacturers, built-up clippings interfere with airflow and hurt performance. Disconnect the spark-plug wire and remove the clippings with a plastic scraper—especially important in damp conditions and at the end of the mowing season.

SHARPEN THE BLADE A dull blade tears grass rather than cutting it, promoting disease. Remove the blade and sharpen it with a file, about $10, or pay a mower shop to do it. Sharpen the blade at least once each mowing season.

CHANGE THE OIL Once each mowing season, drain a four-stroke engine's crankcase and refill it with the oil recommended in the owner's manual. Check the level before each mowing and add more if needed. Two-stroke engines require no oil changes.

CLEAN OR REPLACE THE AIR FILTER Some mowers have a sponge filter you can clean and reoil, though most now use a disposable paper filter. Service when dirty–as often as once per mowing season. Replace the spark plug when the inner tip has heavy deposits, which can occur as often as once per mowing season. A new plug makes for easier starts and cleaner running.

STORE THE MOWER PROPERLY At the end of the mowing season, clean the deck thoroughly. Manufacturers suggest filling the gas tank and adding a stabilizer to prevent deposits that can clog the fuel passages, then briefly running the engine to circulate the mixture.

Electric mowers

CLEAN BENEATH THE DECK First disconnect the mower's cord or, on cordless models, remove the safety key.

KEEP THE BLADE SHARP Follow the procedure for gas mowers, above.

SAVE THE CELL With cordless models, stop mowing and plug in the charger when the battery starts running down. Draining a battery completely shortens its life. New ones cost about $100. Manufacturers also suggest leaving the battery on "charge" whenever you're not using the mower.

---

job at mulching, which is the fastest and easiest way to dispose of clippings. All but the best mulchers leave a few visible clippings on the lawn, while the worst leave enough clippings to require raking. Even the best mulchers won't work well if the grass is too tall or wet, however.

Our tests also found that a mower's horsepower rating tends to have little bearing on mowing performance. Rear-bagging mowers, whether gas or electric, tend to perform better than side-baggers. Electric models do a decent job at mulching, bagging, and side discharging, but they struggle with tall grass or weeds. And they take a relatively narrow bite with each pass.

Virtually all riding mowers and tractors can handle all three mowing modes. In tests, most did a thorough job of vacuuming up clippings when bagging, although some clogged before their bags were full. The best held more than twice as many clippings as the best push mowers.

RECOMMENDATIONS. Balance the size of your yard with how much you want to spend. Gas-powered push and self-propelled mowers are appropriate for many lawns. Electric mowers offer cleaner, quieter running and easy maintenance—but they're limited by a cord or, for cordless models, the relatively short mowing time between battery charges.

Homeowners with a small lawn can also consider a manual-reel mower. Just be sure that your lawn isn't too thick and that you don't skip a week. If you decide to ride, you'll probably want a lawn tractor unless your lawn has lots of tight areas and obstacles; then the smaller size of a riding mower is an advantage. You can also opt for a zero-turn-radius mower or tractor, which combines a wide deck with tight turning. But, at $3,000 and beyond, it's an expensive option.

Reliability: page 291, 292

Power blowers

The best electric handheld blowers outperform their gas counterparts and cost less. But they aren't any quieter, and the power cord can be a hassle.

These miniature wind machines take some of the effort out of sweeping and cleaning fallen leaves and other small yard and driveway debris. Many can also vacuum and shred what they pick up. But practically all available models still make enough noise to annoy the neighbors. Indeed, some localities have ordinances restricting or forbidding their use.

What's available

Mainstream brands include Black & Decker, Craftsman (Sears), Homelite, Ryobi, Toro, and Weed Eater. Pricier brands of gas-powered blowers include Echo, Husqvarna, John Deere, and Stihl. As with other outdoor power tools, gas and electric blowers have their pros and cons. You'll also find variations among gas-powered models. Here are your choices:

ELECTRIC HANDHELD BLOWERS. Designed for one-handed maneuvering, these are light (about 7 pounds or less). Many are also relatively quiet, produce no exhaust emissions, and can vacuum and shred. Some perform better than handheld gas-powered models, although mobility and range are limited by the power cord.

Price range: $30 to $100.

GASOLINE HANDHELD BLOWERS. These perform like the best electrics but can go anywhere. As with other gas-powered equipment, tougher regulations have reduced allowable emissions. Manufacturers have also quieted some of models in response to new noise ordinances. Most blowers, however, are still loud enough to warrant hearing protection. Other drawbacks include added weight (most weigh 7 to 12 pounds) and the fuel-and-oil mixing that is required by the two-stroke engines most models use. A few blowers, notably from Ryobi, have a four-stroke engine that burns gasoline only.

Price range: $75 to $225.

GASOLINE BACKPACK BLOWERS. At 16 to 25 pounds, these are double the weight of handheld blowers, which is why you wear them instead of carry them. But the payoff with most is added power and ease of use for extended periods, since your shoulders support their weight. Hearing protection is recommended. Backpack blowers don't vacuum. And they can be expensive.

Price range: $300 to $420.

GASOLINE WHEELED BLOWERS. These offer enough oomph to sweep sizable areas quickly. All use a four-stroke engine that requires no fuel mixing. But these machines are large and heavy, requiring some effort to push them around. They also cost the most and tend to be hard to maneuver, which can make it difficult to precisely direct leaves and other yard waste. Count on using hearing protection.

Price range: $400 to $600.

Key features

Look for an easy-to-use **on-off switch** on electric blowers, a **variable throttle** you can preset on electric and gasoline-powered models, and a convenient **choke** on gas-powered units. Some handhelds have **variable speeds,** which can provide maximum force for sweeping and minimum force around plants. Blowers that excel at cleaning usually have **round-nozzle blower tubes; oblong** and **rectangular nozzles** are better for moving leaves. A bottom-mounted **air intake** is less likely to pull at clothing.

A **control stalk** attached to the blower tube of backpack models improves handling, while an **auxiliary handle** on the engine or motor housing of a handheld blower makes it easier to use—provided the handle is comfortable. Other useful features on gas-powered models include a **wide fuel fill** and a **translucent fuel tank,** which shows the level inside. An **adjustable air deflector,** found on most wheeled blowers, lets you direct airflow forward or to the side.

How to choose

PERFORMANCE DIFFERENCES. In our tests, the strongest blowers could push leaves into piles 20 inches high, while the weakest had trouble building 12-inch piles. The best

BLOWHARDS

Which blower fits your yard and locale?

ELECTRIC HANDHELD Best for small to medium-sized properties where work takes place near an outlet and for those with less arm strength. The electric motor's cord can be a hassle to maneuver, however, and typically limits use to within 100 feet of an outlet.

GAS HANDHELD Best for small to medium-sized properties with obstacles or where some of the cleanup work is far from an outlet. But higher price and weight, more maintenance, harder starting, and more noise are drawbacks.

GAS BACKPACK Best for properties one-half acre and larger with lots of trees and other obstacles; good for those with less arm strength. These have the same drawbacks as gas handheld, plus they have no vacuum mode.

GAS WHEELED Best for properties one-half acre and larger without major obstacles or steep hills where ultimate blowing power is needed. But they're pricey, hard to maneuver, and noisy, and take lots of storage space. And there's no vacuum mode.

electric blowers are better than most gasoline-powered models and tend to be lighter and easier to handle. Backpack blowers, while heavy, tend to be easiest to use for extended periods, since the blower tube is all you hold in your hands.

RECOMMENDATIONS. Begin by matching the blower to your needs. The smaller the leaf-clearing job, the less blowing power you'll require. You can also get by with less power if you'll be clearing mostly hard surfaces such as a driveway—jobs for which relatively quiet, light, and inexpensive handheld electric machines may suffice. Models that vacuum can be handy for sucking leaves out of corners and from beneath shrubs. Whichever power blower you're considering, find out about any local noise restrictions before buying.

Ratings: page 246

String trimmers

An electric model can do a good job for many trimming tasks. But for strong all-around performance, you'll need a gasoline-powered string trimmer.

A string trimmer can pick up where a lawn mower leaves off. It provides the finishing touches, slicing through tufts of grass around trees and flower beds, straightening uneven edges along a driveway, and trimming stretches of lawn your mower or tractor can't reach. Gasoline-powered models can also whisk away tall grass and weeds.

Thanks to their flexible plastic lines, all string trimmers can venture into rock-strewn areas that would destroy a mower's metal blades. Some, however, are less capable and convenient at their intended tasks.

What's available

Black & Decker, Craftsman (Sears), Homelite, Ryobi, Toro, and Weed Eater are the major mainstream brands, with Weed Eater selling the most. Leading high-end brands include Echo, Husqvarna, and Stihl.

Gasoline-powered trimmers. These are better than electrics at cutting heavy weeds and brush, and are often better at edging—turning the trimmer so its spinning line cuts vertically along a walk or garden border. They also go anywhere and cut relatively large swaths, up to 18 inches wide. Some accept a metal blade (usually an option) that can cut branches up to about ¾-inch thick. On the downside, gas trimmers can be heavy, weighing about 10 to 16 pounds. Most have a two-stroke engine that requires a mixture of gas and oil. These tend to pollute more than a four-stroke engine that uses gasoline only, and entail pull-starting and regular maintenance.

Price range: less than $100 to more than $300. Most models, however, cost from $100 to $200.

Electric-corded trimmers. These are the least expensive and lightest; many weigh only about 5 pounds. Some work nearly as well as gas trimmers for most trimming. All are quieter and easier to start than gas trimmers—you simply pull a trigger rather than a starter cord. The power cord does limit your range to about 100 feet from an outlet. Many electrics have the motor at the bottom of the shaft, rather than at the top, making them harder to handle. And even the most powerful models are unlikely to handle the tall grass and weeds that the best gas-powered trimmers can tackle.

Price range: $25 to $75.

ELECTRIC BATTERY-POWERED TRIMMERS. Cordless trimmers combine the free range of gas trimmers with the convenience of corded electrics: less noise, easy starting and stopping, no fueling, and no exhaust emissions. But they're weak at cutting and run only about 15 to 30 minutes before the onboard battery needs recharging, which can take up to a day. They also tend to be pricey and heavy for their size (about 10 pounds). Models with the motor at the bottom of the shaft can be even harder to handle than the lighter corded versions.

Price range: $50 to $100.

Key features

All trimmers have a shaft that connects the engine or motor and controls to the trimmer head, where the plastic lines revolve. Curved-shafts are the most common and can be easier to handle when trimming up close. Straight-shafts tend to be better for reaching beneath bushes and other shrubs. Some models have a split shaft that comes apart so you can replace the trimmer head with a leaf blower, edging blade, or other yard tool, though we've found that some of these attachments aren't very effective.

Most gas-powered trimmers have two cutting lines, while many electrics use just one, which means they cut less with each revolution. Most gas and electric trimmers have a bump-feed line advance that feeds out more line when you bump the trimmer head on the ground; a blade on the safety shield cuts it to the right length.

Auto-feed systems add convenience by automatically feeding out new line as they sense a change in the centrifugal force exerted by a shortened line. But some auto-feed systems don't work very well and may compromise cutting performance. In either case, replacing the line usually involves removing and rethreading the empty spool. With some trimmers, you simply pull off the old spool and push on a new one.

Most gasoline models use two-stroke engines, which burn lubricating oil with the gasoline. Federal law requires manufacturers to slash exhaust emissions for new gas-powered trimmers by 70 percent by 2005, while California has required that emissions reduction since 2000. Some trimmers use inherently cleaner four-stroke engines, but these tend to weigh and cost more. Corded and battery models typically use a 1.8- to 5-amp motor.

To start most gas trimmers, you set a choke and push a primer bulb, then pull a starter rope. On most, a centrifugal clutch allows the engine to idle without spinning the line—safer and more convenient than models where the line continues to turn. On models without a clutch, the string is spinning while the engine is running. Electric-trimmer lines don't spin until you press the switch.

Some models make edging more convenient with a rotating head, shaft, or handle that makes the trimmer head easier to move to the vertical position. Heavier-duty models often offer a shoulder harness, which can ease handling and reduce fatigue. Other convenient features include easy-to-reach and easy-to-adjust switches, comfortable handles, and—on gas models—a translucent fuel tank.

Trimming safely

A trimmer's string can give you a painful sting even through clothing, draw blood on bare skin, and also fling dirt and debris. When you're trimming, wear gloves, long pants, sturdy shoes, safety glasses, and, with a gas trimmer, ear protection.

How to choose

PERFORMANCE DIFFERENCES. While almost any machine can trim a small, well-maintained lawn, some corded electric trimmers and all the battery-powered models in our most recent tests proved weak. As a rule with electric trimmers, the higher the amps, the better they cut. Slicing through tall grass and weeds generally requires a gasoline-powered trimmer, although our tests have shown no correlation between engine size and performance with these units.

RECOMMENDATIONS. Look for a trimmer that fits your physique, letting you work without stooping and maintain good balance so that your arms don't tire before the job is done. For competent performance on a range of trimming and edging tasks, you'll probably prefer a gas-powered model. Look for a cutting head with two strings for better performance. For smaller spaces and lighter-duty trimming, consider a corded electric trimmer. Look for one with the motor on top of the shaft for better balance and easier handling. Consider a cordless electric model only for the lightest of trimming chores.

Home 'Software'

Shoppers looking for things such as mattress sets, sheets and towels, or Oriental rugs and carpeting—home "software" as we call it—can face hard choices. Comparison shopping can be difficult in these categories. Price ranges for similar-looking items can be quite broad, model numbers can be obscure, often purposefully so, and product specifications spotty. The names of essentially identical mattress sets can vary from store to store.

Manufacturers often make little tweaks at the behest of retailers, which benefit by having a product under their own brand name. Buying sheets can be tricky because labeling isn't clear. Not all sheet manufacturers have caught up with changes in mattresses, so sheets labeled "deep-pocketed" don't necessarily fit a 12-inch-deep pillowtop mattress. Prices of Oriental rugs are lower than they were a decade ago, but it's still possible to pay more than you should for what you get. Shopping for wall-to-wall carpeting also poses pitfalls. Many stores provide little in the way of important information such as pile height or tufts per square inch. Buying even the humble towel requires unraveling the mysteries of pima, Supima, and other fibers.

Mattress sets

Once you've settled on the firmness and size you want, compare quality details and price from brand to brand and store to store.

If you think shopping for a car is an ordeal, try shopping for a mattress. Sure, you can lie down on a mattress, maybe even take it home for a 30-day "test drive." But try to peek at its innards and you'll be thrown out of the showroom. Worse still, while a Ford Taurus is a Ford Taurus nationwide, the names of essentially identical mattresses—called "comparables" by the industry—often differ from store to store. Independent bedding shops typically offer mattress sets from manufacturers' national lines. Major chains such as Macy's and Sears and telephone-order sources such as Dial-A-Mattress sell mattresses from the same manufacturers' lines but with names unique to the chain. Comparables are supposed to share basic components, construction, and firmness but may differ in color, fabric pattern, or quilting stitch. Consumers are the losers, since they can't comparison shop. This name game allows retailers to vary the price of similar mattresses by hundreds of dollars.

What's available

Sealy, Serta, and Simmons account for nearly three out of every four mattresses sold, but there are more than 35 other brands. The big makers offer no-frills models, but most people are more familiar with their flagship lines: Sealy Posturepedic, Serta Perfect Sleeper, and Simmons Beautyrest.

You can buy a mattress filled with water, foam, or air, but innerspring mattresses—named for their coiled steel springs sandwiched between layers of padding—remain the most widely purchased type. The padding, usually identical on top and bottom so you can flip the mattress, is generally made of several materials, including polyurethane foam, puffed-up polyester, or cotton batting. Mattresses used to be about 7 inches deep. Now they can range from 9 to 18 inches. If you buy a thicker mattress than what you have now, you may have to buy sheets with deeper pockets or corners.

Key features

Most stores have a cutaway or cross-section of at least some of the mattress sets on display. Here's what you should look for and ask about:

Ticking is a mattress' outermost layer and is usually polyester or a cotton-polyester blend. Low-end mattresses may have vinyl ticking, which can eventually stretch and sag. Fancier mattresses have damask ticking with the design woven into the fabric, not printed on it. Some also contain a bit of silk, which is more a marketing gimmick than any substantial benefit.

In most cases, **quilting** attaches a few layers of padding to the ticking. Stitch design varies and is largely an aesthetic consideration. Make sure stitches are uniform and unbroken; broken threads can allow the fabric to loosen and pucker. Top padding is generally polyurethane foam, with or without polyester batting. Batting provides a uniform, soft feel but tends to lose its loft faster than does a soft foam.

Middle padding lies below the quilted layer and often starts with foam. Convoluted foam, shaped like an egg carton, feels softer than a straight slab of the same type of foam, and it spreads your weight over a wider surface area, which should make you more comfortable. Soft, resilient foams feel almost moist to the touch. Foams that feel dry or crunchy won't spring back as readily. Other padding often consists of garnetted cotton (thick wads of rough batting that provide loft but compress quickly) and more foam of varied thickness and density. In some mattresses, firmness differs from area to area. One side may be firmer than the other, or a middle section may be firmer than the head or foot. A "test nap" is the only way to tell if a mattress is right for you.

Insulation padding lies directly on the springs and prevents you from feeling them. Commonly used bedding insulators include "coco pad," the fibrous matter from a coconut husk, and "shoddy pad," pieces of fabric that are matted and often glued together. Coco pad, especially in more than one layer, makes a mattress stiffer. Plastic webbing, nonwoven fabric, or a metal grid directly atop the springs can help keep them from chewing up the pad.

SHOPPING FOR A MATTRESS

Avoid the Pitfalls
Ads make it seem as if buying a mattress is as simple as picking up the phone or waltzing into a store. As you might suspect, it may not be that simple. Some tactics we have found:

THE BAIT AND SWITCH Low-ball ads tout name-brand mattress sets for less than $40. What they don't tell you is that these cheap mattresses are from the manufacturer's inferior "promotional" or "sub-premium" lines, some of which are so bad that few people would seriously consider buying them. Once you've bitten the hook, a salesperson is likely to steer you to a costlier, though sturdier, upgrade.

SLIPPERY PRICES Tags generally note a fictitious "list price," which you should not dream of paying, and a much lower discount price. Often the discount price is negotiable, too.

"BLOWOUT" SALES Ads make them seem rare, but they happen all the time. And a bargain isn't always all it's cracked up to be. Original prices are virtually mythical.

SAME NAME, DIFFERENT PRODUCT Product specifications and materials used can change at any time, though the model name remains the same. That means the floor sample in the showroom could be quite different from the mattress that arrives at your door.

CONFUSING JARGON You'll see mattresses classified as, say, premium, superpremium, ultrapremium, and luxury, and firmness levels described as pillow soft, plush, cushion firm, and superfirm or no firmness level at all. There can be dozens of variations within any line. Sealy, for instance, offers several quality and firmness levels. The descriptions of quality and firmness vary by brand—one company's firm may be harder than another's extra firm—and should be used as only a rough guide. The bottom line: You can't rely on product labels to tell you which mattress will give you the desired feel.

LATE DELIVERIES Many retailers promise you'll have your new mattress within 24 hours. But they don't always deliver on time. In our tests, many arrived 10 to 14 days late.

Extra support is added to certain areas—at the edge, say, so you have a solid place to sit when you tie your shoes. If you want extra support at the head, foot, sides, or center, ask whether the mattress beefs up those areas by means of more closely spaced coils, slabs of stiff foam inserted between the coils, thicker wire, or extra springs.

Coils are the springs that support you. While coil design doesn't affect a mattress' ability to withstand use and abuse, it does shape the bed's overall "feel." The wire in springs comes in a range of thicknesses, or gauges. As a rule, the lower the gauge number, the thicker and stiffer the wire and the firmer the mattress. The higher the gauge number, the thinner the wire and the softer the mattress.

Handles let you reposition the mattress on the box spring. They're not meant to support its full weight, which is why most warranties don't cover broken handles. Best are handles that go through the sides of the mattress and are anchored to the springs. Next best are

Anatomy of a sleep set

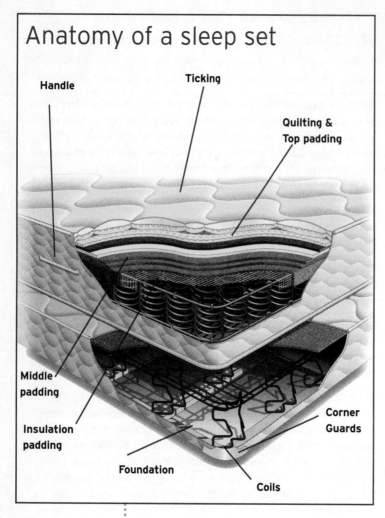

Handle

Ticking

Quilting & Top padding

Middle padding

Insulation padding

Foundation

Corner Guards

Coils

fabric handles sewn vertically to the tape edging of the mattress. Most common is the weakest design: handles inserted through the fabric and clipped to a plastic or metal strip.

The **foundation**, or box spring, can be a plain fiberboard-covered wooden frame, a wooden frame containing heavy-gauge springs, or even a metal frame with springs. A plain wooden frame, usually found with cheaper sleep sets, is adequate only if the wood is straight and free of cracks. Placing a mattress atop a plain wooden frame can make the mattress seem harder than it actually is. Corner guards help keep the foundation's fabric from chafing against the metal corners of the bed frame.

How to choose

PERFORMANCE DIFFERENCES. A firmer mattress won't resist permanent sagging better than a softer mattress. A thicker mattress sags more than a thinner mattress. And because all the permanent compression is within the padding layers, not the springs, more padding equals more potential for sagging.

RECOMMENDATIONS. The only way to judge mattress comfort is to try out a variety of brands and models in the store. (If you buy by phone, of course, you'll have to do your testing at home—after having made sure you can exchange an unsatisfactory mattress.) A good mattress will gently support your body at all points. Orthopedic experts generally recommend the firmest mattress that you find comfortable.

Never pay list price for a mattress. Sales are common, and deeper savings are often possible if you bargain. Spending more for a mattress gets you thicker padding, damask ticking, and perhaps a pillowtop—a cushion on both sides of the mattress that's filled with foam, wool, silk, or a down blend.

Mattress-by-phone businesses usually offer rock-bottom prices, especially if you persist in seeking low quotes, but you buy the bedding unseen and untried. Be sure you can exchange it. When you buy a mattress, buy a box spring, too; they perform as a unit. Putting a new mattress on an old box spring could void your warranty.

Oriental rugs

Intricate patterns, lustrous yarns, and artfully blended colors help explain the timeless allure of Oriental rugs. But some aren't from where the label says they're from—and some are overpriced.

Handmade rugs are less expensive than they were a decade ago, and there's a wider selection of patterns and colors. Machine-made rugs are improving in quality and come in increasingly varied designs. Synthetic yarns are also better able to mimic natural materials, while new looms permit 20 or more colors in a machine-made rug. Credit some of that windfall to computer-aided design and computerized weaving, which have led to faster production—and faster response to buyers' desires and to changes in fashion. The bad news: Many Oriental rugs are still overpriced for what they are. You can wind up with one that curls up, bleeds, or lies about its origins—or is less "antique" than it appears.

What's available

Technically, an Oriental rug is knotted by hand of wool, silk, cotton, or rayon, and has a raised pile, not a flat surface. Common parlance broadens that definition to include rugs made in an Oriental style. Such a rug can be made by hand or by machine; made of natural or synthetic fibers; and qualify as antique (made before 1915, as a rule), semiantique (made between 1915 and 1950), or contemporary. And it can be made in the traditional places—China, India, Iran (formerly Persia), Pakistan, Turkey—or elsewhere.

ORIENTAL RUGS: A PRIMER ON PATTERNS

Oriental rugs come in many different patterns. Four common ones—Heriz, Kirman, Sarouk, and Tabriz—are named for rug-making centers in Iran (formerly Persia). Heriz is usually a geometric pattern with a central medallion on a brick-colored field with a navy border. Kirman, Sarouk, and Tabriz are floral patterns. Kirmans can feature pastels or bright jewel tones. Sarouks often have a red background and sprays of flowers. An "American" Sarouk was woven in Persia in the 1920s or 1930s and was meant for the U.S. market; weavers used salmon-colored yarn that was hand-painted maroon in the United States. Tabriz can come in various designs.

Heriz

Kirman

Sarouk

Tabriz

Aubusson

Bokhara

Aubusson designs, originally found in flat-woven tapestry rugs from France, are typically made in China or India, where the thick wool pile is "carved," creating an embossed look.

Bokhara, named for a city in Uzbekistan where tribal rugs were sold, is generally a geometric design in which a smallish round mark called a "gul" or "elephant's foot" is repeated.

Historically, patterns and colors were specific to a city, village, or tribe. Today, designs are not restricted to their countries of origin. India, China, and Pakistan, the countries where the majority of handmade rugs are produced, turn out rugs in most of the traditional patterns and colors. As a result, you'll often see patterns preceded by the prefixes Indo-, Sino-, or Pak-. (The Federal Trade Commission requires labels to list the country of origin and the business name of the distributor.) Whatever its pattern, a rug is called "tribal" if it has been woven by members of a nomadic group. Such rugs tend to be small rather than room-sized.

Several other factors affect an Oriental rug's desirability beyond its price. While traditional Oriental rugs are made of wool, you'll also find them in silk, silk blends, and artificial fibers such as olefin. The typical price range for wool is between $12 and $75 per square foot compared with as little as $2 per square foot for olefin. All wools and weaves aren't created equal, however. Nor does the word "handmade" guarantee better quality.

You'll find new Oriental rugs of one kind or another at department stores, specialty shops, home centers, mass marketers, auction houses, mail-order companies, and Web sites. You'll also find semiantique and antique rugs sold by big-city rug dealers. Avoid shopping for rugs at "hotel auctions" for which you might receive a postcard announcing the sale. You can't return goods if you're not satisfied, and you may not get what you think you're getting.

Key considerations

Made by hand or machine? Handmade should mean hand-knotted; each strand of yarn has been tied to the rug's foundation by hand. Although the term conveys a certain cachet, the quality of those rugs depends on the skill of the maker. A good machine-made rug can be a better value than a poor-quality handmade one. Moreover, the overall quality of machine-made rugs is more consistent than that of handmade rugs. And if the wool and

---

Spotting a problem Oriental rug

Several common flaws and deceptions mean there's less to some Oriental rugs than meets the eye. Watch for:

CHEMICAL WASH
This common technique adds luster to wool and mutes colors so a new rug looks antique.
How to tell: Fold back the pile to expose the base of the fibers. The original colors are more garish.

SURROGATE SILK
Rayon pile on cotton backing is typical of the phony silk rugs sold at sales in hotels or at itinerant auctions. Its dyes generally won't be colorfast.
How to tell: Ask the dealer to burn a bit of yarn. Silk will smell like burning hair.

CURLING
One salesman told us the curled, Heriz-design rug we bought would flatten out after a few days on the floor. It didn't.
How to tell: Just look. This problem has a solution. Two-inch strips of vinyl can be sewn underneath the sides.

DRY ROT
Another common problem, particularly on some antique rugs.
How to tell: Bend sections of the rug with your hands. If you feel and hear something like breaking matchsticks, don't buy the rug.

construction are good, a machine-made rug should last as long as a handmade one—and those can last more than 100 years.

Still, machine-made rugs lack the subtleties of design or the unique character of hand-knotted rugs, and the best machine-made rug can't compare with the best handmade, which can take more than a year to make. Because labels need not identify whether the rug was made by hand or by machine, it pays to check for yourself. Here's how to recognize a handmade rug:

■ With the rug facing up, bend the pile back across the width of the rug—a process that is known as grinning. A handmade rug will have a small knot at each yarn's base, near the backing.

■ Look also at the fringe. In a handmade rug, it's usually an extension of the warp yarns—the foundation threads that run the length of the rug (as opposed to weft threads, running the width of the rug). In a machine-made rug, there are no knots, and the fringe is generally sewn on separately.

HOW GOOD IS THE WEAVE? An enthusiastic salesperson (and occasionally a tag) may boast that a rug has 200 knots per square inch, implying that knot count is an indicator of quality. It is—but only one of many. Rugs with an identical knot count can differ greatly in overall quality.

Other factors being equal, a higher count renders a more detailed design and will usually make for a longer-lasting rug. But the count will vary based on design (floral or curved designs generally require more knots than geometric designs) and the yarn's thickness (thin yarn allows for more knots). Expect a higher knot count to mean a higher price per square foot, too.

Clouding matters further, the method of counting varies with the type of rug. Chinese rugs have a line count—220, for example—representing the number of knots in a horizontal foot (across the rug's width). Contemporary Tabriz rugs are often graded by "raj," the number of knots in 2¾ horizontal inches, rounded to the nearest 10 (you'll see numbers such as 70

A PAINT JOB	TEA WASH	BLEEDING	HANDMADE VS. HAND-KNOTTED	APPLIED FRINGE
Paint on the back may hide areas where bleach used on the fringe wicked into the foundation. During cleaning, the paint will blacken the fringe. **How to tell:** Wipe a damp white cloth over the foundation and see if color comes off.	A wash of tea or dye can also make a new rug look antique. Tea washes aren't a problem unless they're done badly. **How to tell:** Look for splotches on the rug's back. Rub the pile with a wet white towel and see if the stain comes off.	Sometimes dye bleeds from the field onto the fringe, often during a chemical wash. **How to tell:** Peer at the area between a dark color and a lighter one, and at both ends of the fringe.	Some rugs are made with a tufting gun—operated by hand but a far cry from hand-knotting. **How to tell:** Check for hand-knotting. And be suspicious when cotton monk's cloth hides the latex backing that holds in the tufts.	Fringe on a handmade rug should be a continuation of the warp yarns; otherwise the rug may have been repaired. Although a separate fringe can be applied expertly, it can affect value. **How to tell:** Look for stitching or discontinuous warp yarns.

raj). Rugs from Pakistan often carry two numbers, such as 16/18. The first represents the number of knots in a horizontal inch; the second, the number of knots in a vertical inch.

Machine-made rugs have their own system for counting the density of yarns—points per square meter or tufts per square inch—but you'll see it less often. While actually counting the knots in a handmade rug may not be practical, you can tell a lot about a rug's weave by looking at its back. The weave should be fairly consistent, though the knots won't be perfectly uniform. And each color should be fairly consistent, though slight horizontal variations, called abrash, caused by yarns of different dye lots, are OK.

WHAT'S IT MADE OF? In general, **wool** is generally considered the best pile fiber for a rug: It wears extremely well, takes dyes well, doesn't mat, and is generally easy to clean. But wool quality is critical.

You can assess the quality of the wool in a new rug by running your hand back and forth a few times over the surface. If the rug sheds lots of fuzzy fibers on your hand or on the rug's surface, it is probably made of low-quality wool and will not hold up well. Very soft "sweater" or "garment" wool bends back and forth when vacuumed and is inappropriate in any rug, though you may see it in Chinese rugs with an Aubusson design. "Dead wool"—chemically separated from the hide of a dead sheep rather than shorn from a live one—feels dry and brittle or wiry, sheds easily, and won't hold up over time. It's found most often in very cheap rugs from India.

Some rugs have a "Wools of New Zealand" label, certifying that the rug is made of at least 80 percent New Zealand wool, which is of high quality. On a handmade rug, the certification also claims to mean that the rug was produced without child labor.

Olefin, also called polypropylene or a brand name such as Exellan, is a plastic fiber. It wears well but is hard to clean if stained with something oily. Labels generally warn against dry cleaning. Olefin can be a good choice in a basement or in any moist climate because it tolerates humidity and resists mold and mildew. Although the patterns and colors are the same as those used in wool Orientals, it's fairly easy to identify low-priced olefin. It has a somewhat artificial-looking shine, and colors tend to be flat or monochromatic. More-expensive olefin looks a lot like wool.

Silk rugs are fragile and hard to clean, and can be expensive. If the price of a silk rug seems too good to be true, the rug is probably rayon or mercerized cotton. If you're considering a silk rug, ask the seller to pull a small bit of yarn and burn it. When burned, silk smells like burned hair and leaves a small bead; rayon or cotton smells like burned paper. Cotton leaves ash, and rayon leaves no residue.

Also, beware of labels that say "art. silk." "Art." does not refer to the skills of a talented rug designer; it means artificial. Art. silk is rayon, and a poor fiber for rugs. "A. silk" and "faux soie" mean rayon, too. Many such rugs are made in China or India.

How to choose

PERFORMANCE DIFFERENCES. How well an Oriental rug holds up to cleaning depends on more than just its pile fiber. While the Federal Trade Commission requires that pile-fiber information be on the label, information about the backing fiber needn't be—and wasn't in the rugs we tested. That means "100 percent wool" refers only to the pile yarn, not the fringe or foundation, which is usually made of cotton or wool in handmade rugs and synthetic fiber or wool in machine-made rugs. That difference can become significant during cleaning, so it's important that the cleaner be a professional who can identify the fibers. Rugs with wool pile should generally be wet-cleaned; those with silk pile should generally be dry-cleaned. Rugs with rayon pile should always be dry-cleaned.

Colorfastness is another variable among Oriental rugs. Historically, Oriental rugs were colored with vegetable dyes, and some still are. Most new rugs are dyed with synthetic chemicals. Either way, rub a damp white cloth over dark portions of the pile. If color comes off on the cloth, the rug will bleed during cleaning.

White knots occur when warp yarns break during weaving and the weaver splices the pieces together. These knots eventually work their way to the surface of the pile and become more visible as the rug wears. A few white knots are inevitable, even in the hands of the best weavers, but avoid rugs liberally sprinkled with white knots. If you're tempted to cut them out, don't. You'll break the rug's backing and create a hole.

As for symmetry, no handmade rug will measure precisely, say, 4½ feet on each side, but the measurements should at least be close.

RECOMMENDATIONS. Your budget and your family life are the best guides to narrowing down your choices. For less expensive rugs, a good-quality machine-made wool rug combines good looks and practicality. We found well-made Couristan and Karastan rugs in attractive designs and colors and with a moth-resistant finish.

Consider a low-priced olefin rug ($7 to $9 per square foot) if you want something to cover the floor until you can afford something better. Another option is a dhurrie or kilim, which can provide a lot of decoration for a lot less money. Unlike traditional Oriental rugs, dhurries and kilims are flat-woven—they have no pile. Dhurries are made in India of cotton or wool. Kilims are made in Turkey, China, and Egypt, among other countries, and are usually made of wool. Although both are somewhat less durable than pile rugs, they should hold up for years, even in high-traffic areas. Wool will be somewhat more durable than cotton. One drawback: Kilims and dhurries don't mask stains as well as pile rugs, since there's nowhere for dirt to hide.

When buying pricier handmade rugs—or for that matter, any handmade rug—try to get a detailed receipt listing the country of origin, the fiber content of pile and foundation, the age, and (for new rugs only) the grade, as indicated by knot count. Sellers will often write "fine-quality Indo-Persian" or some such. That isn't good enough.

The Oriental Rug Retailers Association's code of ethics says rugs must be marked with a price, but many retailers ignore that guideline. Even when prices are shown, they're often a figment of the dealer's imagination. We found one Indo-Heriz with an original price of $1,259 marked down to $440. In fact, $440 is the price the rug should have been from the start. Be wary of discounts exceeding 20 percent; they're usually an indication that the original price has been inflated somewhere along the line.

Beware of auctions other than those by such well-known houses as San Francisco's Butterfield & Butterfield and Boston's Skinner Galleries. In any case, you'll need to be expert in judging rugs, and you can't return what you've bought. And wherever you buy, determine up front whether you can return the rug or take it home on approval. If you buy from a catalog or on the Web, you'll have to pay shipping charges if you return the rug.

Also remember that, true to the old stereotype, getting the best price on an Oriental rug usually involves some bargaining. You won't be able to do that via mail order, of course, and it may be hard in department stores, though you can always ask the salesperson to "do a little better." The best way to compare value is to calculate each rug's price per square foot. Finally, don't expect to reap a profit. Few Oriental rugs made after 1950 increase in value. The bottom line: Buy a rug you like at a price you like.

If you're considering an antique or silk rug, ask to take the rug home (some dealers require a deposit), get a due-back date in writing, and set up an appointment with a qualified independent appraiser. Most appraisers charge at least $100 per hour, so discuss your expectations beforehand. Avoid appraisers who charge a percentage of the rug's value as a fee and those who offer free appraisals.

MAINTAINING YOUR RUG. Good rugs deserve good care. In the past, rugs were hung over a sturdy pole and beaten. Today, you'll need a vacuum cleaner preferably with a beater bar. Vacuum the rug's surface at least twice a month. Because gritty dirt abrades the rug's backing, vacuum the back of the rug occasionally, too.

When it's time for a real cleaning, take the rug to a professional cleaner experienced with Oriental rugs. When the rug comes home, place it in a position 180 degrees from where it was before cleaning to equalize wear.

Sheets

Colors, patterns, materials, sizes—decisions abound. But at least finding sheets that fit extra-thick mattresses is easier than it used to be.

It's easy to become obsessed with style when you're selecting sheets. You can spend hours deciding whether to coordinate with the bedroom wallpaper, cozy up with a Laura Ashley vintage floral, or go minimalist with Calvin Klein. But even the most stylish bedding can lose its charm if the hems unravel after washing or you need to wrestle the fitted sheet over the mattress.

Sheets and pillowcases are either individually packaged and priced as "open stock," or sold as sets, with coordinating flat and fitted sheets plus two pillowcases (one for a twin). Accessories such as curtains, dust ruffles, and sham pillowcases may also be available.

The price of sheets can be affected by a stylish brand, but it also tracks with material type and thread count. Cotton-polyester sheets, still the most popular type, are generally less expensive, but a growing number of shoppers are choosing all-cotton. High-end sheets use premium cotton varieties including Egyptian, pima, and Supima. At the very expensive end of the price spectrum are a few linen or silk sheets.

What's available

Three manufacturers—Fieldcrest Cannon (owned by Pillowtex), Springs Industries, and WestPoint Stevens—account for about 70 percent of sales and make many different brands, including designer names.

Sizes include twin, full, queen, and king. While deep-pocket sheets are more widely available, especially through some catalog vendors, be sure to keep the receipt in case the claimed depth doesn't measure up.

Sheets made of cotton-polyester blends are renowned for easy care—less shrinkage, fading, and wrinkling. Some all-cotton sheets claim to be wrinkle-free, but we've found that they typically emerge from the dryer somewhat wrinkled, no better than a number of regular cottons and not as good as any of the blends. Regular cotton becomes combed cotton when it is carded (that is, combed) to removed short fibers and leave only the longest to be spun into yarn. In theory, the long fibers found in premium cottons should make a sturdier yarn that feels smooth and is less likely to pill. CONSUMER REPORTS tests, however, found that this doesn't necessarily hold true. Price range of a typical queen set: cotton/polyester, $30 to $150; all-cotton, $40 to $250 and up.

Key features

Thread count indicates the number of warp (lengthwise) and weft (crosswise) yarns, or threads, in a square inch of woven fabric. This is often regarded as the benchmark for quality in sheets. Sheets that have a thread count of 130 have thicker yarns. Sheets with a higher thread count have a tighter weave, finer yarns, a softer "hand," or feel, and a higher price. But we've found that above 180 or 200 threads per square inch, it's hard to detect any difference in softness.

Sheets made of woven fabric with plain weaves (muslin, percale, and variants) make up the majority of all sheet sales. Don't be surprised if you can't discern the differences in the various weaves—the detail is difficult to see without a magnifying glass.

Muslin, a plain weave (using a one-over, one-under pattern), has the lowest thread count—typically around 130—and the lowest price. It has a reputation for being coarse and scratchy and isn't widely sold. **Percale,** a fine, closely woven type of plain weave, is the most-prevalent fabric for sheets. The thread count usually ranges from 180 to 200. Percale sheets with a thread count of 220 to 250 are sometimes labeled **pinpoint.** A step up in price from regular percales, these use what's called a basket, or rib weave, in which two or more threads are grouped in a one-over, one-under weave pattern.

Widely perceived as luxury-class linens, **sateen** sheets have a slight sheen and a soft, smooth feel. This weave has one crosswise thread floated over four or more lengthwise threads. The thread count starts at about 230 and can climb to more than 300. (Sateens, which are typically all-cotton, are not related to the synthetic satin sheets of yesteryear, which were often slippery and uncomfortable.)

Flannel sheets, typically all-cotton, have a napped surface that produces a fuzzy appearance and a soft feel. **Knit** sheets are supposed to be as comfortable as a favorite T-shirt; indeed, they're very soft when new, less so after laundering (probably because of a finish that's removed in the wash).

How to choose

PERFORMANCE DIFFERENCES. In tests we found differences in softness, strength, and appearance generally related to fiber content and weave. Fit varied as well. Cotton-

<aside>
Basic mattress dimensions

Sizes can vary. For best results, use a measuring tape.

TWIN:
39x75 inches

EXTRA-LONG TWIN:
39x80 inches

FULL (DOUBLE):
54x75 inches

QUEEN:
60x80 inches

KING:
76x80 inches

WESTERN (CALIFORNIA) KING:
72x84 inches
</aside>

polyester blends generally had a pleasant feel, unlike the stiff blends of decades past. Sateens were very soft, but our tests showed they might not stand up as well as other types of sheets to everyday wear. Percale sheets, especially those made of cotton-polyester blends, are good in terms of strength.

The way corners are sewn—angled seam or straight seam—doesn't affect the fit or how easy it is to put a fitted sheet on a mattress. And neither type is stronger. When sheets failed our strength tests, the fabric tore before the seams broke.

Dark colors such as hunter green and navy blue sometimes faded considerably after 20 washings. But if you wash all the bedding together, the set should remain a consistent color.

RECOMMENDATIONS. Fit comes first. Measure your mattress and choose sheets sized appropriately. When shopping for yourself, you may wish to buy on sale—with frequent one-day events and scheduled "white sales," you won't have to wait long. Consider shopping outlets and off-price stores for discounts, but inspect items carefully for flaws in fabric or construction that could affect long-term durability, usability, or comfort.

Hold on to packaging and receipts until you've laundered the linens several times. It's a good idea to wash sheets before the first use to remove any finishes and get a better idea of the fit. If the sheets shrink, fade, or otherwise fail to live up to expectations, return them to the place of purchase. Be wary of "final sale" sheets (especially irregulars) that can't be returned.

LINEN LINGO

BEDSPREADS cover the whole bed, including the pillows and the box spring.

BLANKET COVERS go over wool blankets on the bed to keep them clean. They are thin and decorative, often with satin or lace trim.

COTTON is the most popular material for sheets. Many prefer the feel of 100 percent cotton, though cotton/poly blends are popular because they're cheaper and more wrinkle-resistant.

COVERLETS generally do not cover the pillows or the box spring. They often come with matching shams.

DROP refers to the length a bedspread or dust ruffle will extend as it "drops" toward the floor.

DUST RUFFLES, also known as bed skirts, are designed to dress up the box spring and hide any dust bunnies—or boxes, shoes, skis, etc.—that may be lurking under your bed.

DUVET and COMFORTER COVERS are one and the same. The cover is like a giant pillowcase or sham and covers just the top of the bed.

FLANGED refers to a decorative band of fabric, as on a pillowcase, that is flat instead of ruffled.

LINEN is a fabric woven from the fibers of the flax plant. It was once more widely used for sheets, napkins, and tablecloths, thus the terms "bed linen" and "table linen." Today, real linen's a luxury and the word is used generically. But linen sheets are still an option, if you can afford the price and don't mind a lot of ironing.

MATTRESS TOPPERS can include electric pads for warmth and sheepskin for coziness. The recommended minimum is a simple pad or cover to protect the mattress.

MERCERIZED cotton has a bit of a sheen to it.

SANFORIZED means preshrunk.

SHAMS are decorative pillowcases that are usually ruffled or flanged and tie or button closed, instead of being open at the end, like a pillowcase.

THERMAL LAYERING There's more than one way to make a bed, but technique does matter. A thermal blanket has little holes to trap air. If you use that over the sheet and use a regular blanket next, you will be warmer than if you do it the other way around. Similarly, electric blankets work best with another layer on top, with the top layer trapping the heat.

Towels

Even the best can change color, shrink, and distort significantly, so it's a good idea to check the retailer's return policy before buying.

All towels are not created equal. In addition to differences in size, color, softness, and absorbency, you may encounter unwelcome surprises. If a component of a towel's dye mixture isn't fixed properly, that component may disappear, altering the overall color of the towel. The metamorphosis can be so gradual that you don't realize it. Towels that shrink in length don't usually shrink much in width, and vice versa—it's all a function of how the towel is woven. Some towels shrink in the borders of each end, leaving them fat in the middle and flared at the ends.

What's available

Large retailers get their towels mainly from three manufacturers—Fieldcrest Cannon (owned by Pillowtex), Springs Industries, and WestPoint Stevens. Cotton bath towels typically cost between $5 and $25 and are sold at discounters such as Kmart, Target, and Wal-Mart, chains such as JCPenney and Sears, specialty stores such as Bed Bath & Beyond and Linens 'n Things, department stores, and mail-order catalogs. Sizes range widely from around 39x25 inches for the cheapest bath towels to a more generous 55x30 inches for pricier versions.

Key features

Aside from size, several other attributes explain the wide differences you will find in the price of towels, namely **thickness, fiber,** and **feel.**

As a rule, expect towels that are thick and densely woven to absorb more water than those that are thin and loosely woven. Thick towels may dry you better, but they also take longer in the dryer.

Regarding fiber, you'll see simply "cotton" as well as "premium" cottons: combed, Egyptian, pima, or Supima (a trademark for some pima cotton). With combed cotton, fibers are put through a process to eliminate short fibers and leave just the longer ones. Removing short fibers can help reduce shedding and pilling.

Egyptian cotton, grown along the Nile River, consists of long, strong fibers that are particularly lustrous. Pima cotton is the American version of Egyptian, grown in Arizona, California, New Mexico, and Texas. Towels made of premium cotton generally ranked higher in our tests than those made of ordinary cotton.

Softness sells, but don't buy a towel based solely on how it feels in the store. A finish is used to achieve that new-towel feel, and after a laundering or two the finish washes away. One way to keep towels soft through multiple washings is to use liquid fabric softeners or dryer sheets. There's a down side, though: Fabric softeners leave a waxy film on towels that reduces absorbency.

Check fading

When you purchase new towels, buy an extra washcloth in the same color and put it aside with the sales receipt. If you then have a serious problem with your towels fading after just a few times through the wash, you can return the faded towels to the store—and bring the unwashed washcloth with you as a point of comparison.

How to choose

PERFORMANCE DIFFERENCES. In our tests simulating about a year's worth of washing, many blue and green towels changed color. But only two of the bright red towels we tested bled in the wash—and just a little bit at that. Towel makers generally advise washing all dark colors separately, which is sensible. Practically all cotton towels shrink, even if you wash them in cold water and dry them on Low, as we did. Some of the worst shrinkers in our tests lost more than 9 percent in length—a loss of 4½ inches on a 50-inch towel. Another problem with some towels was pilling.

RECOMMENDATIONS. A towel that costs a few dollars is likely to be less absorbent, less soft, and smaller than a more expensive towel. But you don't have to spend top dollar for quality. When shopping, look for a thicker towel, which is usually more absorbent.

Discounters are a good source for inexpensive towels. Consider off-price stores or overstock outlets, too. Their towels may be irregular or come in limited colors, but prices can be half those charged by department and specialty stores. When buying colored towels in sets, compare them carefully under good lighting. Even towels of the same basic color will vary somewhat from one dye lot to another.

Wall-to-wall carpeting

Different types of fiber wear in different ways. Choose on the basis of where the carpet will go and how it will be used.

When you shop for carpeting you have to shop first for the fiber type, then the carpet brand. Highly advertised brands such as Anso from Honeywell, Stainmaster from DuPont, and Wear-Dated from Solutia are brands of nylon fiber, not brands of carpet. Because different retailers may sell the same carpet under different carpet brand names, comparison shopping is difficult. You'll probably have to take copious notes on carpets you like and look for samples with similar specifications in other stores. But basic information on things such as pile height and tufts per square inch is often lacking. You also need to consider installation.

What's available

Carpeting is sold at stores such as CarpetMax and Carpet One, which sell name brands as well as their own store brands; at home centers such as Home Depot and Lowe's; and at independent flooring stores, where you'll see carpet brands such as Aladdin and Philadelphia. Carpeting is also available by mail, from companies such as S&S Mills.

The price of a carpet depends largely on its fiber content, pile weight, and style. Wool is very expensive compared with synthetics. Nylon, the best-selling carpet fiber, typically costs more than polyester or olefin. Branded fiber tends to cost more than unbranded.

Wool, the standard against which synthetic carpets are measured, has outstanding resilience, comparable to that of nylon, so its crushing and matting resistance is very good. The best wool carpets are also known for their soft feel underfoot, though nylon can feel just as soft. But unlike nylon, wool may abrade. It also stains easily and tends to yellow in bright sunlight. Nylon is mildew resistant and offers good resilience and resistance to abrasion. Olefin, also known as polypropylene, generally resists staining, fading, abrasion, and moisture, making it a good choice for a basement or playroom. Polyester resists staining, but its resilience is only fair. Some polyester carpet is made from recycled plastic soda bottles.

Price range: $14 to more than $30 per square yard for nylon; $10 to $22 per square yard for olefin; $12 to $15 per square yard for polyester; and $30 to $60 per square yard for wool.

Key features

Generally, a heavier **pile weight**—the ounces of yarn per square yard—is considered better and is more expensive. A longer **pile height** is better if you want a luxurious look and feel. Pile whose height variations give it a textured look minimizes footprints or vacuum-cleaner tracks. A carpet with a high **tuft density** wears better. You can figure it by multiplying the number of tufts per inch, left to right, by tufts per inch, up and down. You can check tuft density by folding back a carpet sample. With a denser carpet, you won't see much backing peeking through. Like high tuft density, highly **twisted yarn** provides better resistance to wear. Labels may note that the yarn is heat set to help retain its shape.

Cut-pile styles, including saxony and plush, are made of yarn that's attached to the backing and cut at the top. The deeper and thicker the pile, the more luxurious the carpet may feel, but the more likely it is to retain dirt. Cut pile generally crushes under foot traffic more than other styles, so it's best reserved for low-traffic areas such as a formal living room or a master bedroom. Textured saxonies are better at hiding footprints.

In a **level loop,** yarn is looped over so both ends are attached to the backing. Short, densely spaced loops may not feel very soft, but they provide a smooth surface that wears well and is fairly easy to vacuum because there aren't crevices for dirt to sink into. High-density level loop is good for stairs, family rooms, and other high-traffic areas. Low-density level loop doesn't perform as well.

Berber is a variation of level loop, but with thicker yarn. Genuine Berber is handmade from wool. Less expensive Berber-style carpeting can be made of wool, nylon, olefin, or a nylon blend. The thicker yarn can snag, making this not the best choice for a foyer or hall.

Multilevel loop has long and short loops that give a textured appearance. The short loops create pockets that can make vacuuming difficult.

Retailers may include **padding** in the price of a carpet, but often it's a cheap grade. Low-density padding that you can easily compress between your fingers feels spongy underfoot and won't provide much support for the carpet. Better is medium-density padding made of prime urethane, a type of foam; rubber; rebond, made of leftover bits bonded with adhesive, hence its multicolored appearance; or pressed fiber, which is felt-like.

All new carpets emit volatile organic compounds (VOCs)—air pollutants associated with carpet manufacture—for a few days after installation. Though emissions are generally at a very low level, not everyone agrees what's safe. Current scientific evidence indicates that the level of VOCs emitted is probably not harmful to most. The Carpet and Rug Institute has made reduction of "4-PC," the most-odorous carpet VOC, a goal of its Indoor Air Quality Carpet Testing Program. Carpets, padding, and adhesives that pass may carry a "green label."

Look for the green label

The Carpet and Rug Institute can confirm that carpet and padding qualify for a "green label," which means the product meets industry standards regarding volatile organic compounds (VOCs). It also offers installation tips. Call 800-882-8846 or visit the organization's Web site at *www.carpet-rug.com.*

How to choose

PERFORMANCE DIFFERENCES. Branded nylons generally resist stains, while many un-branded nylons may not. In CONSUMER REPORTS tests, branded nylon, which is usually treated with stain and soil repellent before the backing is put on the carpet, generally performed better than unbranded. We analyzed the yarn in one unbranded model and saw why: More than twice as much stain repellent was on the top quarter-inch of the carpet as at the base of the yarn, indicating that repellent was sprayed only on the surface. Dense level loop and short cut-pile retained the least dirt after vacuuming. Multilevel loop and longer cut-pile models retained the most. With our worst performer, a multilevel-loop carpet, 70 percent of the dirt couldn't be vacuumed out. As for carpet wear, Home Depot's performance appearance rating (PAR) is a useful guide. It correlated closely with the CONSUMER REPORTS wear-test score. A carpet with a PAR of 4 to 5 is appropriate for moderate-to high-traffic areas.

RECOMMENDATIONS. Choose the most appropriate fiber, style, and construction for the room where the carpeting will go and then shop for color and price. For example, for a formal room, you might opt for the lustrous appearance and feel of cut-pile or wool. For a child's room or basement playroom, you'd be better off with olefin fiber for its stain and wear resistance—and a level-loop construction for easy vacuuming.

Most people arrange installation through the retailer, who sends employees or a subcontractor to do the job. Work out the details beforehand, and get them in writing. Decide, for example, who will be responsible for trimming doors, if that's necessary. Make sure installers double-glue seams—even seams under furniture. If you rearrange your furniture and expose a seam to foot traffic, fibers around an improperly glued seam can become fuzzy, and stitches may unravel.

When the installer arrives, ask to keep the identifying label from the plastic that the carpet comes wrapped in. That will probably be your only official record showing that you received what you ordered. Ask also for a scrap of the carpet, at least 12x24 inches, and file that along with the label, the sales receipt, and the warranty. This documentation can be important if you have a problem later. Have the installer inspect the carpet surface and backing for flaws before it's installed. Anything less than perfect warrants a call to the retailer.

You can minimize problems with VOCs by asking the installer to air out a new carpet for a day or so before installation. After it's installed, keep windows open and a fan going for two or three days. Make sure the installer seals seams with adhesives that have a CRI green label.

── A WARNING ABOUT WARRANTIES ──

Manufacturers and salespeople like to emphasize warranties. Some warranties promise to replace a carpet, others state they'll replace just the damaged area. But beware of the fine print: Coverage for "wear" or "staining" of a carpet, for example, may not mean what you probably think.

WARRANTIED "WEAR" refers to abrasion that leads to a loss of 10 percent of the fiber. While wool abrades, most modern synthetics don't, so for them the warranty is essentially meaningless. Stain warranties can also be misleading. To the consumer, a stain is a stain, whether it's from tea or an accident by a pet. But to manufacturers, the stains covered by warranties are generally caused by food dyes such as the ones in fruit drinks. (A good carpet cleaner can handle those.) Other stains—say, from mustard or acne cream (which can bleach dark fibers)—don't count. You may be offered an extended warranty that defines "stains" more broadly. Our advice: Save your money.

TO MAINTAIN A WARRANTY, you must prove that you cared for the carpeting as specified, so save receipts showing that it has been professionally cleaned.

Keeping It Shipshape

Equipment to keep your house clean, safe, and in working order continues to be refined. Manufacturers of cordless tools are now using nickel-metal hydride batteries, which are safer for the environment and claim to provide more power than a comparable nickel-cadmium battery.

Power and endurance are no longer an issue for a growing number of cordless drills. Some of the latest models are brawny enough for big jobs, yet light enough for around-the-house repairs. More sophisticated designs have made garage-door openers safer and far easier to program. Constantly changing "rolling codes" have also made these remote-controlled systems more secure from thieves. Wet/dry vacs are no longer relegated to the garage; smaller portable models are now marketed for kitchen duty. Upright vacuum cleaners, which historically have been more appropriate for carpeting, now also do well with bare floors. Canister vacs, which were always the way to go for bare floors, now likewise do a very good job with carpeting as well.

Fatal fires and litigation have underscored the need for two complementary types of smoke detection: ionization, the most common type, and photoelectric. A carbon-monoxide alarm is another indispensable safety device.

Circular saws

Circular saws are a mainstay for cutting the two-by-fours and plywood used in many home-improvement projects.

A circular saw is an essential tool for any but the most rudimentary workshop. Most have a power cord, but there are some cordless saws on the market.

What's available

Black & Decker, Craftsman (Sears), DeWalt, Makita, Milwaukee, Porter-Cable, and Skil brands account for most of the circular saws sold.

CORDED MODELS. These models run on an electric motor that can range from 10 to 15 amps. The higher the amps, the more power you can expect. Most models are oriented so the motor is perpendicular to the blade. Another type uses a "worm drive" design in which the motor is parallel to the blade; that gives a saw a lot of power, but at the expense of speed.

Price range: $40 to $140.

CORDLESS MODELS. These range from 14.4 to 24 volts. They usually have a smaller blade and a shorter run time than corded models.

Price range: $60 to $260.

Key features

Every saw has a big main handle and a stubby auxiliary **handle**; the former incorporates the saw's **on/off switch.** Some saws include an **interlock** you have to press before the on/off switch will work. This adds a level of safety, but can make the saw awkward to use.

Inexpensive saws have a stamped-steel **base** and thin housing; pricier models use thick, rugged material, such as plastic or cast aluminum, that stands up to hard use. A **blade** with two dozen large teeth cuts fast but can splinter the wood; a blade with 40 or more teeth gives a cleaner cut. The thinner the blade, the faster the cut and the less wasted wood. Typically, saws with a steel blade cut slower while models with a carbide-tipped blade cut fastest.

Bevel adjustment is used to change the angle of the cut from 0 to 45 degrees. The **depth adjustment** changes the blade's cutting depth. A circular saw works best when the teeth just clear the bottom of the wood. The **cutting guide**—the notch in the base plate that's aligned with the saw blade—helps you follow the cutting line you've drawn on the wood. A **blade-lock button** keeps the blade from turning when you change blades. The dust chute directs the sawdust away so you can see what you're doing.

How to choose

PERFORMANCE DIFFERENCES. Seconds count if you have a lot of wood to cut. Speed also affects safety; you're more likely to push a slow saw, dulling the blade quickly and over-heating the motor, or making the saw jam or kick back. CONSUMER REPORTS tests found that most corded saws have adequate torque for any typical home-workshop job. Battery-powered saws are much weaker. A weak saw could have trouble when used on thick hardwood or for other tough work.

Design points that can make a saw easy to use include a visible cutting guide, a blade that's simple to change and to adjust for depth and angle, good balance, a comfortable handle, and a handy on/off switch. How well the saw is constructed impacts its potential for a long, trouble-free life. It should have durable bearings, motor brushes that are accessible for servicing or replacement, a heavy-duty base, and rugged blade-depth and cutting-angle adjustments.

RECOMMENDATIONS. Judging from our tests, you can get a fine corded saw for as little as $60; for $120 to $160, you can get an excellent model. A cordless saw lacks the might for tough jobs but might do for occasional light work.

Whichever you buy, if it comes with a steel blade, replace it with a carbide-tipped one. Be sure to match the number of teeth with the material you want to cut; a blade for plywood, say, has more teeth than one for rough cutting.

All the saws are loud enough when cutting to warrant hearing protection. All kick up a lot of chips and dust, so safety glasses or goggles are a must. You should also wear a dust mask, especially when cutting pressure-treated lumber.

Cordless drills

Many of the latest models are powerful enough to handle construction and repair chores formerly reserved for corded models.

Better battery packs let today's cordless drills run longer and more power-fully per charge. The best can even outperform corded drills and handle deck construction and other big jobs before their batteries need to be recharged. Much of the credit goes to nickel-cadmium (NiCad) batteries, which can be charged hundreds of times. NiCads must be recycled, however, since the cadmium is toxic and can leach out of landfills to contaminate groundwater if disposed of improperly. Incineration can release the substance into the air and pose an even greater hazard. Some cordless drills have nickel-metal-hydride (NiMH) batteries, which don't contain cadmium and are safer for the environment.

What's available

Black & Decker and Craftsman (Sears) along with Ryobi and Skil are aimed primarily at do-it-yourselfers. Bosch, Craftsman Professional, DeWalt, Hitachi, Makita, Milwaukee, and Porter-Cable offer pricier drills with professional-style features.

Cordless drills come in several sizes, based on battery voltage. In general, the higher the voltage, the greater the drilling power. The most potent models pack 18 to 24 volts, while the 6- to 9.6-volt models are usually limited to light-duty use. In between are the 12- and 14.4-volt drills that often provide the best balance of high performance and affordability. There may still be some 24-volt models available online.

Sometimes, you'll also find a flashlight or a cordless saw bundled with a drill and sold as a kit. For the first time last year, sales of individual drills were flat, while the sale of drill kits grew.

Price range: $60 to $100 (6- to 9.6-volt); $40 to $140 (12-volt); $70 to $270 (14.4- and 18-volt); $300 to $370 (24-volt, available online).

Key features

Most cordless drills 12 volts and higher have two **speed ranges:** low for driving screws and high for drilling. Low speed provides much more torque, or turning power, than the high-speed setting, which is useful for drilling and boring holes. Most drills have a **variable speed trigger,** which can make starting a hole easier. An **adjustable clutch** is used to lower maximum torque, which can help you avoid driving a screw too far into soft wallboard or mangling the screw's head or threads once it's in. Most of today's models are also **reversible,** letting you easily remove a screw or back a drill bit out of a hole.

Most drills have a ⅜-inch **chuck** (the attachment that holds the drill bit), though some high-voltage, professional-grade models have a ½-inch chuck. In either case, most drills have replaced the little key needed to loosen and tighten the chuck with a **keyless chuck.**

Still other features make some drills easier to use. A **T-handle** in the center of the motor housing provides better balance than a **pistol grip** on the back, although a pistol grip lets you slide your hand up in line with the bit to better apply pressure. Models with two batteries let you use one while the other is charging. A **smart charger** charges the battery in an hour or less, rather than three hours or more for a conventional charger. Some smart chargers also extend battery life by adjusting the charge as needed. Many switch into a **maintenance** or **"trickle-charge"** mode after the battery is fully charged.

An **electric brake** stops a drill instantly when you release the trigger—a handy feature that helps you avoid damaging the workpiece and allows you to resume drilling or driving without waiting. Some models also include a **built-in bubble level;** others feature a **one-handed chuck** for easier bit changes.

How to choose

PERFORMANCE DIFFERENCES. In our tests, a 15.6-volt NiMH-powered drill ran longer than many 18-volt NiCad-powered models, yet weighed less. What's more, some 18-volt models can nearly equal a 24-volt drill's performance with less weight and a lower price tag. While higher voltage equals greater power, it also tends to mean added weight. That can make it tiring to hold a drill for any length of time, especially overhead.

RECOMMENDATIONS. A 24-volt cordless drill delivers power and endurance, but it can weigh up to 8 pounds and cost more than $300. If you're a contractor or serious do-it-yourselfer, you'll find plenty of power and endurance in a 14.4- or 18-volt model. The best selection is available in those sizes. They're also the best value. Drills with 12 volts or less are a dubious choice; although they are lightweight, many are suitable only for light-duty chores. What's more, recharging many of the least expensive models can take anywhere from 3 to 16 hours.

Look for a smart charger and two batteries, which often come with the better models. Whichever size drill you choose, make sure you're comfortable with its weight and ergonomics. And, if possible, try before buying.

Ratings: page 224

Garage-door openers

Garage-door openers are safer and more secure than ever. Some are also quieter and quicker. Because installation can be tricky, you may want to hire a professional.

Whether you're replacing a garage-door opener or buying one for the first time, technology is on your side. The latest ones require less force to automatically stop and reverse the door if it touches a person, a pet, or another obstructing object. Remote controls with constantly changing "rolling codes" thwart thieves. And unlike older models, which entailed lengthy code setting, the latest do most of that setup for you.

What's available

Most garage-door openers are made by one of two manufacturers. Chamberlain makes LiftMaster and Craftsman models, as well as its own brand. Overhead Door makes Genie and Genie Pro models as well as its own brand. Craftsman is by far the biggest-selling brand.

"Install-it-yourself" garage-door openers are sold at large retailers, such as Sears or Home Depot, while "professional" models are sold by installers and can have a higher price, though not always. Other differences can be found in the details. A professional model, for example, has a one-piece rail. Don't assume, however, that professional openers are necessarily sturdier or better.

Price range: $150 to $350, plus about $125 or so if you hire a professional installer.

Key features

Among components housed in the **power head** are the **motor,** the **drive pulley,** the **lights** that come on when the opener is operated, and, on most models, **travel-limit switches** that control when the door stops opening or closing. The motor of a garage-door

---

Disposing of NiCads

The makers of rechargeable batteries have established a nationwide program for recycling batteries. In response to a 1996 federal law, all rechargeables must now be easy to remove—if not always easy to replace—with simple household tools. That allows consumers to toss spent batteries in one of tens of thousands of battery-recycling bins at participating retailers such as RadioShack and Wal-Mart. To find a bin near you, call the Rechargeable Battery Recycling Corp. at 800-8-BAT-TERY (800-822-8837) or go to *www.rbrc.com.*

opener is one-half or one-third horsepower and either alternating current (AC) or the quieter direct current (DC). The **drive system** connects the motor to the trolley, which slides along a rail and raises and lowers the door. There are several types of drive system: **cogged-belt, chain-and-cable, screw,** and **straight-chain.**

The trolley can be disconnected so you can operate the door manually from inside the garage. With some screw-drive models, you must climb a ladder or use a broom handle to reconnect the trolley—an annoyance. An **electric eye** on most openers immediately stops and reverses the closing door if a light beam near the ground is broken—an important safety feature. An added **reverse feature** is designed to act as a backup if, say, you don't break the light beam and the door makes contact with you.

Most openers come with two remote controls and a **wall console** that includes a **door control, light switch,** and **vacation setting** to let you disable all or part of the system. A few models include an outdoor keypad.

How to choose

PERFORMANCE DIFFERENCES. All of the garage-door openers that we tested had ½-horsepower motors and lifted a 16-foot-wide test door with ease. Several models are especially quiet—a plus for light sleepers if there is a living space over the garage. Models with a cogged belt emitted 48 to 53 decibels (dBA), compared with 57 to 63 dBA for others tested. Most openers made a penetrating hum, though two screw-drive models made a less intrusive clatter. A DC motor helped several units operate quietly. In tests, most models took 12 to 13 seconds to open or close the door; the fastest opened the door in just 8 seconds, though it took as long to close the door as the others

RECOMMENDATIONS. Because solid performance and a high degree of safety are pretty much givens, you can choose a garage-door opener on the basis of cost and how quietly and quickly you want it to work. Choose a cogged-belt-drive model or one with a DC motor if quietness tops your wish list. Warranties can vary. The motor usually has a separate one. Ask the dealer to spell out terms before buying.

Because the job of installing a garage-door opener requires respectable mechanical skills and several hours, you may want to hire a professional. With most models, you usually have to assemble the rail pieces, hang the power head and rail from the ceiling, and attach the trolley to the door, along with wiring the electric eye, power head, and control console. Travel-limit switches can be hard

How garage-door openers work

On most garage-door openers, the motor in the powerhead (1) is connected by the drive system (2) to the trolley (3), which raises and lowers the door. Several new models use a cogged-belt drive system (4) which helps move the trolley and door more quietly. An electric eye stops and reverses the closing door if its light beam is broken. A backup does the same thing if the closing door touches a person, pet, or object.

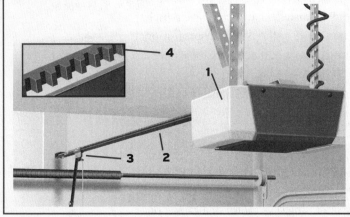

to adjust. A professional model's one-piece rail makes assembly easier, although its length—11 feet—may make it hard to bring home.

If you decide to install a garage-door opener yourself, set aside a day and get someone to help you. Before you begin, check the door's balance. When a properly balanced door is operated manually, it will stay in place wherever it is positioned and shouldn't take a lot of effort to open. If it isn't balanced, or if you want the springs checked for soundness, consider calling in a professional.

Smoke and CO alarms

Smoke alarms can cut by half your chances of dying in a house fire. Carbon monoxide detectors sniff out an invisible threat your senses can't.

A fire can start from a greasy pan on the stove or even from faulty wiring. Carbon monoxide (CO), another potentially deadly risk, may be generated by a malfunctioning furnace with a leaky heat exchanger, a blocked chimney, or a poorly vented water heater. Simply warming up a barbecue, car, mower, or snow thrower inside an attached garage creates CO, which can seep into living areas. To protect yourself and your family, you need two kinds of smoke detection—ionization and photoelectric—as well as CO detection.

Ionization smoke alarms use a harmless amount of radioactive material to sniff out fire. They tend to react quickly to fast-flaming fires, such as paper fires and those fed by flammable fluids. But they can be slow to detect the smoky, slow-starting bedding and upholstery fires that often kill sleepers. By contrast, the light beams and sensors of photoelectric alarms react much more quickly to smoke than they do to flames.

CO alarms are also essential. CO kills some 500 Americans and puts an estimated 10,000 in hospital emergency rooms each year. It displaces oxygen in the bloodstream, so it works slowly and is deadly above a certain level. The concentration of CO is measured in parts per million (ppm). While exposure to CO levels of 150 ppm for 1½ hours isn't likely to cause more than a headache for healthy adults, levels of 400 ppm for that duration can cause loss of consciousness and lead to brain damage or death. Pregnant women, children, the elderly, and those who are chronically ill are especially sensitive to CO and may experience problems at lower levels. A CO alarm can reveal the presence of this deadly gas before it becomes dangerous.

Many new homes have smoke alarms built in to comply with building codes. With interconnected built-in alarms, one alarm can trigger others. Additionally, many hardwired home-security systems incorporate smoke and CO sensors. If your home doesn't have a hardwired system, you'll have to install separate smoke and CO alarms.

What's available

First Alert accounts for more than half of the smoke-alarm market and, with Kidde-owned Nighthawk, sell the lion's share of CO alarms. Other major brands are Family Guard, Firex, and Lifesaver for smoke alarms, and American Sensors, Fyrnetics, and Senco for CO alarms.

Install-it-yourself smoke alarms run on batteries and typically go on ceilings or high on walls. Ionization alarms are still more common than photoelectric units, although a home needs both types of protection. Battery-powered dual-detection alarms combine ionization and photoelectric technologies, and provide the most complete coverage. Hardwired, interconnected smoke alarms are found in newer homes. You can also get models with built-in or separate strobe lights to alert the hearing impaired.

Price range: $10 and up for ionization smoke alarms, $20 and up for photoelectric and dual-detection smoke alarms.

CO detectors can be battery-powered, plug-in, or hardwired. Battery-powered CO alarms are usually mounted on a wall. Plug-in models go where there's an outlet. Some alarms combine an ionization smoke alarm and a CO alarm, although they lack the protection of a photoelectric smoke alarm.

Price range: $30 to $110.

Key features

Both smoke and CO alarms have a **horn** of at least 85 decibels, which sounds when an alarm detects smoke, flames, or carbon monoxide. Recent research suggests that young children may not be awakened by these alarms, so be sure to call or physically wake young children if one sounds. A **test button** lets you ensure that the alarm is working. CO alarms

Where to install smoke and CO alarms

Every home should have smoke and CO detection. A good approach is to place a smoke alarm or a pair of smoke alarms in each bedroom or in an area adjacent to the bedrooms, such as a hallway. A CO alarm should be placed so it can be heard throughout the home. If the bedrooms are upstairs or there is a basement, you'll need additional smoke detection and maybe additional CO detection as well.

Install smoke alarms on the ceiling at least four inches from the nearest wall—or high on the wall but at least four inches down from the ceiling—to keep them out of the "dead" space that smoke may miss. Since CO tends to mix with the room's air, a CO alarm, unlike a smoke alarm, needn't be on or near the ceiling. If the CO alarm has a digital readout, you'll want to put it where you can read it.

Avoid placing smoke alarms in corners and areas near windows, outside doors, or vents, where air currents can sweep smoke away from the alarm and delay or prevent its response. Cooking smoke, vehicle-exhaust gases, and bathroom humidity tend to trigger false alarms in kitchens and bathrooms.

Don't put a CO alarm in the garage—high CO concentrations will set it off. Avoid mounting near doors or windows because fresh air can cause misleadingly low CO readings.

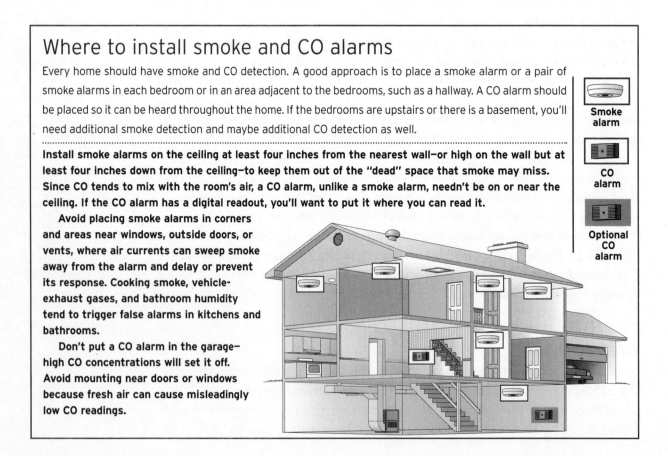

Smoke alarm

CO alarm

Optional CO alarm

and a few smoke alarms have a **hush button,** which silences the horn for several minutes. If there is still a threat, the alarm will sound again minutes later.

Most battery-powered alarms use a 9-volt cell that should be replaced annually; a **chirp warning** sounds when batteries are weak. You may also find alarms with a **long-life lithium battery.** Hardwired smoke alarms and plug-in CO alarms with **battery backup** can remain active during a power outage, while plug-in CO alarms with a **power cord** allow you to mount them on a wall or place them on a table.

CO alarms with a **digital display** tell you the concentration of CO. While alarms with this feature tend to cost more, we think the added premium is worth it. Most such alarms use a **liquid-crystal display** (LCD); models with **light-emitting diodes** (LEDs) may be easier to read in poor lighting, however.

How to choose

PERFORMANCE DIFFERENCES. Most smoke and CO alarms are UL- or CSA-listed, which means they comply with safety and other standards. In CONSUMER REPORTS tests, all of the ionization alarms reacted to smokeless, 3-foot-high flames within 30 seconds, while none of the photoelectric alarms responded to that kind of fire even after 3 minutes. But the photoelectric models reacted to our smoky fire within about 5 minutes, when visibility was still unimpeded; the ionization models took as long as 21 minutes to respond. By then, smoke had cut visibility significantly. The dual-detection alarms did well in both tests.

Most performance and safety standards require CO alarms to sound when levels reach 70 ppm and remain at that level for as little as one hour. In CONSUMER REPORTS tests of CO alarms, nearly all sounded within 15 minutes at a concentration of 400 ppm and within 50 minutes at 150 ppm. Most of the alarms silenced themselves within minutes of the air being cleared of CO. The most accurate digital displays came within 20 percent of actual levels. Other displays, however, were still accurate enough to be useful.

RECOMMENDATIONS. For basic protection, be sure there's a dual-sensor smoke alarm or both a photoelectric and ionization alarm on each floor of your home. Your home

---

AVOIDING FIRE AND CO DANGERS

The Consumer Product Safety Commission recommends inspections of your home's electrical wiring every 20 years. That's 20 years from the time the home was last inspected, not 20 years after you moved in. If you've added high-wattage appliances or renovated, you should consider an inspection sooner.

If you are experiencing flickering lights, hot outlets, or other warning signs of electrical fire, disconnect appliances on overworked circuits. Then hire a qualified, licensed electrician to inspect your home and make repairs. To find an electrician, start by asking your neighbors for recommendations. If your state requires licensing, check the electrician's license number with the appropriate state or county agency and contact the local Better Business Bureau about any previous complaints. When you hire the electrician, obtain an estimate in advance, and ask the electrician to list priorities and specify costs.

Remember that a safe home includes fire extinguishers and escape ladders. You should also plan escape routes and conduct fire drills.

To avoid problems with carbon monoxide, regularly inspect and maintain heating and other fossil-fuel-burning equipment and their venting systems. If an alarm sounds, throw open windows to ventilate the area and move everyone to fresh air immediately. Watch for symptoms of CO poisoning—including nausea, headache, dizziness, or drowsiness—and get immediate medical attention. Notify your fire department and utility provider. They'll bring the equipment needed to pinpoint the source of CO.

should also have at least one CO alarm.

When shopping for a smoke or CO alarm, try to make sure the unit was manufactured recently. Roughly one out of every six CO alarms we bought for our tests was at least two years old and did not meet current standards. All smoke and CO alarms should have a manufacture date stamped on the back, but you won't be able to see it without opening the package in the store. Ask a clerk for assistance.

Then test all smoke and CO alarms in your home at least monthly by pressing the test button. Replace batteries once a year—on an easy-to-remember date such as the Sunday in October when clocks return to Standard Time. Vacuum alarms regularly, since dust, insects, and cobwebs may clog vents and reduce an alarm's effectiveness or lead to false alarms. Replace smoke alarms every 10 years and CO alarms every five years, using the date stamp to help you keep track.

Vacuum cleaners

Fancy features and a hefty price don't necessarily mean improved cleaning ability. You'll find lots of competent models at a reasonable price.

Which type of vacuum cleaner to buy was once a no-brainer. Uprights were better for carpets, canisters for bare floors. Period. Now that distinction has been blurred, as more uprights can clean bare floors without scattering dust and more canisters do a very good job on carpeting.

You'll also see a growing number of features such as dirt sensors and bagless dirt bins as manufacturers attempt to boost convenience. Some of those features, however, may contribute more to price than function. Other, more essential features may not be found on the least-expensive models.

What's available

Hoover, the oldest and largest vacuum manufacturer, is a division of Maytag and offers roughly 50 models priced from $50 to $500. Many of the Hoover models are similar, with minor differences in features. And some Hoover machines are made exclusively for retail chain stores. Kenmore accounts for about 25 percent of all canister vacuums sold in the U.S.

Other players include Dirt Devil (made by Royal Appliance), which sells uprights and canisters as well as stick brooms and hand vacuums; Eureka, which offers low-priced models; and other brands such as Miele, Panasonic, Samsung, Sanyo, Sharp, and Simplicity, which are more likely to be sold at specialty stores. Upscale Aerus (formerly Electrolux) and Oreck vacs are sold in their own stores and by direct mail. Kirby and Rainbow models are still sold door-to-door.

UPRIGHTS. These tend to be less expensive and easier to store than canister models. A top-of-the-line upright may have a wider cleaning path, be self-propelled, and have a HEPA filter, dirt sensor, and full-bag indicator.

Price range: $50 to $1,300.

CANISTER VACUUMS. These tend to do well on drapes, under furniture—anywhere that is easier to reach with a hose. Most are quieter than uprights and more adept at cleaning on stairs and in hard-to-reach areas. You'll also find a growing number of models at the lower end of the price scale.

Price range: $150 to $1,500.

STICK VACS AND HAND VACS. Whether corded or cordless, these lack the power of a full-sized vacuum cleaner but can be handy for small, quick jobs.

Price range: $20 to $75.

Key features

Typical attachments include **crevice** and **upholstery tools.** Most vacuum cleaners also include an **extension wand** for reaching high places. Lately, many uprights have adopted a **bagless** configuration with a **see-through dirt bin** that replaces the usual bag. But we've found that emptying the bins can raise enough dust to concern even people without allergies.

The canister vacuums we've tested have a **power nozzle** that cleans carpets more thoroughly than a simple suction nozzle can. Also look for a **suction control** feature; found on most canisters and some uprights, it lets you reduce airflow for drapes and other delicate fabrics. When you're using an upright with attachments, having an **on-off switch for the brush** is a real plus; it protects you from injury, the power cord from damage, and furnishings from undue wear.

Generally, a vacuum cleaner **cord** is 20 to 30 feet long. While most uprights require you to manually wrap the cord for storage, canisters typically have a **retractable cord** that rewinds with a tug or push of a button.

Another worthwhile feature is manual **pile-height adjustment,** which can improve cleaning by letting you match the vacuum's height to the carpet pile more effectively than machines that adjust automatically. You'll also find more uprights with a **self-propelled feature** to make pushing easy, although that can also make them heavier and harder to carry up or down the stairs.

Some models have a **dirt sensor** that triggers a light indicator when the concentration of dirt particles in the machine's air stream reaches a certain level. But the sensor signals only that the vacuum is no longer picking up dirt—not whether there's dirt left in your rug. Result: You keep vacuuming longer, working harder and gaining little in cleanliness. A **full bag alert** indicates when the vac has a full bag (or bin on bagless models), which can reduce suction.

In the normal process of vacuuming, fine particles may pass through a vacuum's bag or filter and escape into the air through the exhaust. Many models are being marketed with the claim of **microfiltration** capabilities, which entails using a bag with smaller pores or a second, electrostatic filter in addition to the standard motor filter. Some vacuums have a **HEPA filter,** which may benefit someone with asthma. But many models without a HEPA filter performed just as well in Consumer Reports emissions tests as those with the special filters, because the amount of dust emitted depends as much on the design of the entire machine as on its filter.

Upright or canister?

You'll find both upright and canister vacuums that clean capably and are easy to use. While the best of both perform similarly overall, each has strengths and weaknesses. Base your decision on the kinds of cleaning you'll do, the features you need, and the amount you want to spend.

A vacuum's design can also affect how long it lasts. With some uprights, for example, dirt sucked into the machine passes through the blower fan before entering the bag–a potential problem, because most fans are plastic and vulnerable to damage from hard objects. Better systems filter dirt through the bag before it reaches the fan; while hard objects can lodge in the motorized brush, they're unlikely to break the fan.

Like bagless uprights and canisters, stick vacs and hand vacs typically have a messy dirt-collection bin. Some have a **revolving brush,** which may help remove surface debris from a carpet. Stick vacs can hang on a hook or, if they're cordless, on a wall-mounted charger base.

How to choose

PERFORMANCE DIFFERENCES. Better uprights and canisters clean carpet very well. Uprights can do an excellent job on bare floors, thanks in part to an on-off switch for the brush. We've found greater differences in overall performance among uprights than among canisters. Bagless vacs filter dust as well as bag-equipped models overall, but emptying their bins releases enough dust to make wearing a mask a consideration.

We have found stick vacs less impressive, with few excelling at all types of cleaning. Overall, hand vacs do a better job along wall edges than stick vacs because they come closer to the moldings and can angle into nooks and crannies.

High-end features such as dirt sensors don't necessarily improve performance. And ignore claims about amps and suction. Amps are a measure of running current, not cleaning power, and suction alone doesn't determine a vacuum's ability to lift dirt from carpeting. Some vacuums are extremely expensive—anywhere from $700 to $1,500 and more. CONSUMER REPORTS tests have shown that high-priced brands such as Aerus, Kirby, and Miele perform no better than many models that cost $150 to $300. Many of the least expensive uprights, however, sacrifice key features as well as performance.

RECOMMENDATIONS. Decide whether you prefer an upright or a canister. Then choose a model that performs well and has the right features for your kind of cleaning. If you have a variety of cleaning needs, you may want to consider getting more than one vacuum cleaner—an upright for carpets, a compact canister for when tool use is important, and a hand vac or stick vac for quick touch-ups around the kitchen and family room.

Ratings: page 275 Reliability: page 296

Wet/dry vacuums

Aimed at sawdust, wood chips, and spills, these machines are to regular vacs what pickup trucks are to sedans.

Wet/dry vacuums are meant for life's meaner tasks. Their place is typically in the workshop or garage, where their multigallon capacities and appetite for rough stuff make them right at home. Lately, manufacturers have been plugging their smallest portable models for kitchen duty: draining a clogged sink, sucking up soda spills, or picking up broken glass. Other capabilities can include use as a handheld blower for outdoor debris or as a pump. Wet/dry vacs of any size make poor housemates, however. Even the quietest are as loud as the noisiest household versions. And while their high-pitched whine is more annoying than dangerous, some are loud enough to make ear protection advisable. Still another concern is the fine dust these machines tend to spew into the air—a potential problem if you have allergies. But a high-efficiency cartridge filter significantly reduces those emissions and is available for many models.

What's available

Craftsman (Sears) and Shop-Vac account for three out of every four wet/dry vacs sold. Ridgid—sold mostly at Home Depot—and Genie are a distant third and fourth among leading brands. Ridgid and Craftsman models are made by the same manufacturer, Emerson Electric.

Wet/dry vacuums have claimed canister capacities ranging from 6 to 20 gallons for full-sized units and 1 to 2 gallons for compacts. Most units can fill about three-quarters of their canister with water before the float, an internal part designed to prevent overfilling and spilling, seals off the flow. Claimed peak motor power ranges from 1 hp for the smallest portables to more than 6 hp for the largest. The numbers denote peak horsepower, rather than actual output while in use, however. Larger models with more powerful motors tend to pick up debris or liquid faster, according to CONSUMER REPORTS tests. But some smaller units outperform larger ones. Use claims of canister capacity and peak motor power as a guide for comparing models within a brand or size group—not as an absolute.

Price range: compact, $30 to $70; full-size, $40 to $250.

Key features

A wet/dry vacuum's **hose** usually comes in one of two diameters: 1¼ inches or 2½ inches. Models with a wider hose tend to pick up liquids and larger dry debris more quickly. A **hose lock,** found in some models, secures the hose to the canister better than a simple press-on fit, which can release as you pull the hose.

Most models come with accessories. A **squeegee nozzle**—essentially a wide floor nozzle with a rubber insert—helps slurp up liquid spills more quickly and thoroughly. Other nozzles include a **utility nozzle** for solid objects and a **dirt** and a **crevice nozzle** for corners. Some nozzles include a **brush insert** for improved dry pickup. A **built-in caddie** allows the vacuum to hold all of these accessories conveniently, though some models provide other onboard storage.

Filters are another key feature. The two basic types include **cartridge** and **two-piece paper/foam.** Cartridge filters tend to be easier to service and can stay in during wet vacuuming; with a two-piece filter, you must remove the paper element for wet cleanup. A **high-efficiency cartridge filter** (about $20 to $30) reduces the fine dust spewed into the air. While it also reduces suction slightly, allergy sufferers should find the sacrifice worthwhile.

Other notable features include **large carrying handles** molded into the sides of the canister, which help you move the vacuum securely over ledges and up stairs. An **assist**

handle mounted at or near the top of the unit also makes jockeying these machine easier. Some models have **power cords** as short as 6 feet; look for one at least 15 feet long to avoid the safety risk of using an extension cord in standing water. A **drain spout** found in some models lets you simply open a drain, rather than lift and tilt the machine, while long **extension wands** reduce stooping.

How to choose

PERFORMANCE DIFFERENCES. A wet/dry vacuum's ability tends to track with its size. Compact models proved relatively wimpy in our tests, though they're fine for small areas and pint-sized spills. While all units we've seen pick up small wood shavings, chips, and sawdust, those with a wider hose suck up lighter dry and wet debris faster and often more thoroughly. Heavier dry waste tends to be a problem for all sizes, however.

RECOMMENDATIONS. Match the size of the vac with your needs. For example, models that hold 10 to 15 gallons can provide a good balance of size, power, and maneuverability. A large canister is handy for large spills. A large vac is harder to maneuver and store, however, while a small one must be emptied more often.

Maintenance includes cleaning the filter—typically about a five-minute job that involves removing it and brushing it clean (for paper elements) or washing it (for foam elements). An extra filter (about $15) you can quickly swap for a dirty one can come in handy, though changing filters is a messy task.

Hassle-Free Remodeling

Remodeling isn't redecorating. Redecorating means painting, buying new or recovering old furniture, hanging new draperies, and so on. Remodeling involves taking apart some portion of a home and building something different. It can be as straightforward as installing kitchen cabinets or modernizing a bathroom in the existing space. Or it can mean tearing out walls to make a larger space or adding a room or wing to a home. Redecorating is inconvenient. Remodeling is disruptive.

If you're married, a remodeling project should perhaps come with the equivalent of a manufacturer's warning label stating, "This project could be hazardous to your marriage." Just because you and your spouse have been living in your existing home, you may assume that both of you have similar tastes. Don't count on it. One of you may be dreaming of an all-white kitchen while the other sees bright colors on the walls and countertops. Despite the economy of late, in parts of the country, some of the best contractors are still heavily booked. There is a bright side if you're a homeowner eager to get a remodeling project started, though. A delay gives you time for the most cost-saving activities a homeowner can engage in: complete planning and thorough research of products, materials, and people.

Getting started

Most remodeling projects are evolutionary rather than revolutionary. They begin with dissatisfaction over your house the way it is. You could be feeling a twinge of envy that comes after seeing a friend's recent renovation, or a twinge in your back as you lug the laundry up from the basement for the third time in a day. The more you know what you need, and the surer you are about the styles and colors you like, the easier it will be to come up with a design. If you know you want something else but you're not sure what, clip pictures, plans, and suggestions out of magazines and newspapers. These will come in handy when you meet with an architect or a contractor. Instead of groping for words, you will be able to show pictures of what you want.

Assessing the status quo

Take a good look at what you already have. Analyze the room or rooms carefully, noting everything that's annoying, inconvenient, or just plain ugly. Ask questions such as these:

- Is the lighting functional and attractive?
- Do traffic patterns make sense?
- Do you need more storage space?
- Is there enough kitchen or bath counter space?
- Do the doors of kitchen appliances and cabinets open without bumping into anything?
- Can you get from refrigerator to range to sink with a minimum of walking back and forth? (Designers recommend a triangular arrangement.)
- Can more than one person prepare food (or get ready for work) at the same time?

This exercise in planning can go on for months, even years. (Of course, with some busy people, it can, by necessity, take place over a weekend.) Make lists of what you want and need, both for the immediate future and later years, when children leave the nest or aging parents move in.

If you start remodeling without a firm idea of what you intend to do, you're asking for higher costs, longer construction time, and an unhappy contractor.

Mapping out your dreams

To lend some reality to your plans, measure your house and draw the existing floor plan on quarter-inch graph paper. Obviously, if you're only remodeling one room or installing a bath, you don't have to measure the whole house, but at the very least you should be aware of what's beside, under, and over the area you're planning to work on. For instance, an added or relocated toilet will require a vent stack that has to go all the way up through the roof. Blending a 4-inch pipe into the decorative motif of the master bedroom can be a real challenge to a decorator.

Once you have all the dimensions, get a fresh piece of graph paper and translate your rough drawing to scale. Your goal is to draw a plan of the shell of the space you want to remodel. Use layers of tracing paper over the original drawing to make sketches of various layouts with a soft-lead pencil. Don't erase. Just flip over a new piece of tracing paper.

Anything you can do to visualize your project helps. You can also use kits (including paper cutouts shaped like furniture and walls) or software to experiment with layouts. Or use chalk or string to mark out a layout or the size of any components.

Drawing floor plans is the least expensive part of remodeling, so don't hold back. Play around with various changes. You can make one room out of two or three rooms, or two or three rooms out of one, or add baths and redesign kitchens with relative ease. It's best to leave the fireplace and chimney where they are and try to stay within the original walls. Once you start adding rooms and ells to the outside of the house, or dormers and a second story on top, you're getting into a whole new range of complications and costs. These floor plans are for information only.

Leave the creation of the working drawings to your designer, architect, or builder. Then he or she, not you, will be responsible for their accuracy. As you work, remember that this isn't a high-school project in which you must do all the work yourself or lose credit. If you run into a creativity block, ask for help.

Consulting an expert

RENT-AN-ARCHITECT. You can hire an architect on an hourly basis to review your plans and suggest creative approaches to solving problems. This type of service has become more common. If you're planning a major structural change, you might want to retain the architect for the creation of the working drawings and material specifications for your remodeling project. That is one way to ensure that your contractors will bid on the same project. You can also hire the architect to handle the bidding process, interview contractors, analyze bids, possibly do some negotiating, and help you select the winner.

If you don't have the time or inclination to oversee your own project, you can also hire an architect as a "clerk of the works" to oversee the job, sign off at each stage on the quality of the work and changes, and generally act for you on the job. Be aware that some contractors may not like this arrangement.

BUILDING-SUPPLY STORES OR LUMBERYARDS. If your budget is tight and you're worried that your plans might be bigger than your wallet, consult a local building-supply store or lumberyard. Many keep an estimator on staff who can tell you what your materials cost is likely to be, even based on your rough floor plans. The estimate will not include the cost of a general contractor or various subcontractors, but a good estimator should be able to give you a pretty good idea of where you stand. In return for this help, the estimator, of course, will expect the opportunity to bid on the building supplies you will need.

KITCHEN AND BATH SPECIALISTS. If a kitchen or bath remodeling is on your mind, you might explore your options with one or more of the many companies specializing in kitchen and bath projects. Remember that these suppliers are in business to sell materials, fixtures, and sometimes construction services and will be nudging you toward the high end of their lines. But you will ultimately make the final decisions.

SOLARIUM SPECIALISTS. If you want to add a single room to your house or even expand one, you might investigate the various solariums, or sunrooms, available on the

Putting it on paper

Sketches on graph paper can help you firm up your remodeling plans. Here's an approach you can follow.
1. Do a rough drawing of your existing floor plan. Measure and note all the distances.
2. Translate your drawing to scale.
3. Use tracing paper over the scale drawing to try out various ideas.

Keeping a log

Get a spiral-bound notebook and keep it with you when you go fixture shopping and during your conversations with your contractor. Use a page for each of the major items and appliances you need to buy. Note model numbers, prices, and locations as you find them. Keep a log of all meetings with your contractor, noting changes and additions along with the contractor's estimates. Remember to date items.

market. These lean-to-like structures are usually made of insulated glass on aluminum or wood frames. They can be used to solve a design problem by extending a living room, dining room, or kitchen a few feet, or they can be built on an existing porch or deck.

CARPENTERS AND OTHER CRAFTSPEOPLE. Don't overlook the possibility of a simple solution to your remodeling problems. Adding a bow window to the kitchen, taking out a wall between two small rooms, or tearing out the bathroom floor and replacing the sink with a new vanity may create the look or the space you need. Call in a carpenter to discuss the project. An experienced one will tell you how the job can be done and may come up with creative ideas or solutions.

DESIGN/REMODELING FIRMS. These fill the gap between a full-blown architect-generated design and one drawn on the back of an envelope by a carpenter. They provide conceptual drawings and estimates and also build what they design if you hire them to go the whole way.

The typical design/remodeling firm has a draftsman on staff. Many firms have made the move to computer-aided design (CAD) systems to create, with the push of a few keys, everything from deck designs and kitchens to a complete house.

Larger design/remodeling firms tend to treat the design and remodeling functions as separate operations. The construction side of the business is free to bid on projects originated by other designers or architects, and the design arm is free to sell its services separately. Many of the firms have subcontractors and craftspeople on staff and will be able to schedule them into your job. You're generally free to get estimates on the firm's designs from other contractors as well.

Selecting materials and products

You will get more accurate bids from your contractors and will be better able to compare bids if you stipulate the appliances, cabinets, fixtures, and materials you want in your new space. Otherwise, one bid may be based on low-end products and another on high-end. Make a list of the items you want with model numbers and prices.

If you have trouble making decisions, you're in for a difficult time. There are hundreds of decisions to be made and you need to make them in a timely manner to prevent work from coming to a halt. The floor can't be laid if you're still debating the merits of tile over linoleum in the bathroom. All kitchen work will stop if you take too long to select the style and composition of your cabinets. So do as much of the decision-making as possible as soon as possible.

In Chapter 7, "Fresh Starts," you can compare various options regarding components, such as countertops, faucets, and interior lighting. Chapter 1, "Kitchen & Laundry," discusses the major kitchen appliances available. Those and other sections of this book will help you make informed choices, but you must make the decisions that balance your budget with your dreams. It may help to see and touch the products. Consider visiting distributors' showrooms, lumberyards, building-supply warehouses, plumbing-supply stores, carpet-supply houses, appliance vendors, and wallpaper and decorating stores. A caveat: You will be strongly tempted by beautiful and costly choices. If you simply must have, say, an $800 faucet set for your kitchen, try to balance it with a low-priced but adequate dishwasher.

Choosing a contractor

Don't count on newspaper advertisements or the phone book. The best contractors don't have to advertise. They get work through satisfied customers' referrals. Consult friends and neighbors who have had work done. Another source is the National Association of Home Builders (*www.nahb.com*). After a little pointing and clicking, you can bring up contact information for local builders' associations in your region. These in turn, usually have member directories to help you find a contractor. Kitchen-and-bath shops or other suppliers may try to steer you to contractors they use regularly, but don't feel you must use one of them.

Call the Better Business Bureau or a local consumer-affairs agency for complaint histories of the contractors you're considering. One or two gripes shouldn't necessarily induce you to look elsewhere. But be wary of a contractor with more problems than that. You'll also want to check with the appropriate agency to see if the contractor is properly licensed and insured. Some states or counties as well as many large cities or townships license contractors; other jurisdictions require them to be registered. As a rule, licensing entails passing a test to measure competency, while registering involves only payment of a fee. If a problem arises, a government agency may be able to pursue a licensed or registered contractor on your behalf.

Licensing won't guarantee success, but it indicates a degree of professionalism and suggests that the contractor is committed to his or her job. The same holds true for membership in or certification by an industry group such as the National Association of the Remodeling Industry (NARI), the National Kitchen & Bath Association, or the NAHB Remodeling Council—usually a sign of someone who is in business for the long run and not the quick buck. NARI will even try to resolve disputes between member

---

SPOTTING A QUESTIONABLE CONTRACTOR

A warning signal should sound in your head if you encounter any of the following:

A contractor who makes unsolicited phone calls or visits. Be especially wary of people who offer a bargain price, claiming that they're doing a job in the neighborhood and have leftover materials.

A contractor whose address can't be verified, who uses only a post office box, or who has only an answering service and no separate listing in the telephone book.

A contractor who isn't affiliated with any recognized trade association.

License or insurance information you can't verify.

A contractor who can't (or won't) provide references for similar jobs in your area.

The promise of a hefty discount—but no mention of the total cost of the job.

The promise of a deep discount if the contractor uses your home as a "demo."

High-pressure sales tactics or threats to rescind a special price if you don't sign on the spot.

A contractor who tries to scare you into signing a contract by claiming that your house puts you at peril (i.e., "Your electrical wiring could start a fire if it isn't replaced.")

contractors and homeowners, if requested.

When checking references, ask whether the contractor is insured and, if applicable, licensed to do the work. If, for example, someone gets hurt or your neighbor's property is damaged by an unlicensed or uninsured contractor, you could wind up paying. It's wise to know what your homeowners' insurance covers before work starts.

No matter how you find potential contractors, be sure to ask for a list of previous customers; then call them or, better yet, visit their homes to look at the work. Ask some penetrating questions such as these:

■ Would you hire this contractor again?
■ Were you satisfied with the quality of the work?
■ How did the contractor handle cleanup each day?
■ Was the contractor easy to talk to?
■ How did the contractor handle differences and work changes?
■ Was the job completed on time and at the bid? If not, why not?

You might also ask the contractor for a list of his or her building-material suppliers. Call them to see if the contractor has an account or pays for items upon delivery. Most suppliers are willing to extend credit to financially reliable contractors.

Do you need a general contractor?

Typically, if your job requires more than three subcontractors, a general contractor may be a good idea. A general contractor can free you from such burdens as maintaining a work schedule, obtaining necessary permits, and resolving disputes with suppliers. He or she will have more leverage than you do with subcontractors, since you're only a one-time job. In a tight labor market, that could be important. A general contractor may get discounts at lumberyards and supply houses. Whether or not these savings are passed on to you or retained as part of the contractor's fee is something that should be covered in the contract.

Evaluating bids

Industry groups recommend that you get a written estimate from at least three contractors. An estimate should detail the work to be done, the materials needed, the labor required, and the length of time the job will take. Obtaining multiple estimates is a good idea. An estimate can evolve into a bid—a more detailed figure based on plans with actual dimensions. Seeking more than one bid will increase your odds of paying less. Once agreed to and signed by you and the contractor, a bid becomes a contract.

The cheapest bid isn't always the best. Homeowners who accept a rock-bottom bid may wind up less satisfied overall than those willing to pay more. One bidder may be using smaller-diameter copper tubing or cheaper tile. He or she may also be bidding on exactly what you say you want, without making it clear that your pre-World War II house may also need new wiring and water lines, which will cost extra.

Make sure all bidders are bidding on the same specifications and job description. Take the time to choose materials and fixtures yourself, since you may not always like or agree with the contractor's selections. The term "comparing apples to oranges" may well have been invented during the bidding process.

Know your plans. It can be costly to change job specifications after the work has begun. Revising your plans can add substantially to cost overruns, with changes resulting in lengthy delays. A less-than-straightforward low bidder is counting on these changes to make the job profitable.

Negotiating a fair contract

A contract spells out all the terms of the work, helping you and the contractor minimize misunderstandings and wasted effort caused by poor instructions. It should include the contractor's name and address, license number, a timetable for starting and finishing the job, a payment schedule, names of subcontractors, and the scope of work to be done.

Other basic items include a specification of materials and equipment needed, demolition and clean-up provisions, approximate start and finish dates, terms of the agreement, and room for signatures and the date. Watch out for binding arbitration provisions that limit your right to sue in the event of a dispute.

An excellent addendum to a contract is the contractor's statement of what isn't included. This will include the assumptions the contractor has made about your job, such as that the existing wiring and plumbing lines are adequate, that the homeowner will pay for all trash removal, that the subflooring is sound, that the existing baseboards and window trim will be usable, and so on.

MODEL CONTRACTS

For help in writing a contract, consider tapping into the expertise of industry associations:

■ **The American Homeowners Foundation offers a comprehensive model contract ($8 or two for $9) that can save you time and headaches when coming to terms with a contractor. To order, call 800-489-7776 or visit** *www.americanhomeowners.org.*

■ **The American Institute of Architects can supply excellent fill-in-the-blanks contract forms for virtually any type of building project. Prices vary. To order, call 800-365-2724 or visit** *www.aia.org.*

Do your homework and specify the materials and brand names of all the products, appliances, and fixtures to be used. The contract should also give the contractor the burden of obtaining all building permits. Most municipalities have a building code; the person who obtains the permit is usually liable if the work doesn't come up to code.

It's common to pay for a project in stages over the course of the work, especially as key materials and supplies are delivered. Try to limit the down payment to 10 percent or less. Contractors who ask for a substantial amount up front may use your money to hire help to finish their previous job, leaving you to fume at delays. In some states, it's illegal to require large deposits. Some projects, however, require deposits on components that have to be made to order—kitchen cabinets, for instance. In such a case, a higher down payment may be required and justified.

Your contractor should agree to resolve problems that arise during the course of work rather than afterward. They might readily fix sloppy plastering or a leaky roof as soon as it's pointed out but be less willing to fix it later on. That's a good reason to hold back part of the final payment until after a job is completed. You can negotiate such terms and include them in the contract. Withholding the last 5 to 10 percent of the money for 30 days isn't an unreasonable stipulation.

Never make the final payment until you have obtained signed mechanic's-lien waivers or releases from all subcontractors and suppliers. These are basically receipts acknowledging payment for goods and services; they free you from third-party claims on your property in the event that you pay the contractor but he or she doesn't pay subcontractors or suppliers.

Doing it yourself

If you have a fairly uncomplicated remodeling project in mind and think you can handle it yourself, you will need three things:

Time

Unless you're experienced, chances are you'll take longer to do a job than a professional carpenter or plumber would. And, unless you're retired, you probably have something else to do eight hours a day or more during the week. This could dim some of your enthusiasm for a lengthy stint of after-work and weekend labor. If your project is in the basement, attic, or some closet out of the main traffic area, the extra time may not matter. But if you have put the kitchen or a bathroom out of commission, you could quickly find yourself working in a pretty anxious family environment.

Talent

Remember, you'll be doing something for perhaps the first time that a contractor has done many times. You'll take longer and probably make more mistakes than the professional. Most people underestimate the scope of a building task and overestimate their skills; try to be realistic in your appraisals of both.

Tools

Figure in the cost of new tools and mileage for trips to the hardware store in your project estimates. Do you have access to a truck to deliver oversized items or will you need to rent one. Most projects require specialized tools. Hanging a door, for example, needs a router, special bits, and setup jigs for both the hinges and lock sets.

If you have some doubts about your ability to handle a remodeling task by yourself but still want to be involved and save some money, consider hiring a contractor who will let you work with him or her as an unpaid assistant. That way you can take over some of the simple yet time-consuming tasks such as sanding, puttying, painting, cleaning up each day, or just holding up one end of a plank. Be sure to work out this arrangement with your contractors before they bid on the job. Some will welcome your help; others may not.

There are hundreds of good books dedicated to the do-it-yourselfer, offering step-by-step descriptions, drawings, and photos covering virtually any home project you may have. Check your local bookstore or library. There are also Web sites that can offer you help. Search the NAHB Web site *(www.nahb.com)* for the project you have in mind for step-by-step help.

Obtaining financing

Because you may be living with the financial consequences of a costly project for years to come, start by answering two questions: What will the improvement you want to make add to the resale value of your home? And what's the best way to pay for the job?

Projects that add value

If you're planning to stay in your home for a while, the most important reason for remodeling is your own comfort and convenience. The project you choose may also add to the value of your home. You won't recoup your entire investment; some projects yield better returns than others. *Remodeling* magazine performs an annual survey to determine the cost vs. value ratio of remodeling projects. For their 2003 report, go to *www.remodel ing.hw.net.* If you do decide to remodel, use the newer homes in your neighborhood as a benchmark.

Most upgrades are appealing to potential purchasers. Adding a second bathroom to a one-bathroom house, for example, is a big plus. But adding a swimming pool or hot tub may make your house less desirable to safety-conscious potential buyers who have small children. Other cost-effective upgrades include remodeling an aging kitchen and converting a master bedroom into a suite by linking it to a dressing area and private bath.

Keep good records and hold on to contractors' receipts. Money spent on home improvements adds to the "cost basis" of your home and reduces the capital-gains tax that may be due when you sell. You'll need complete records of your outlays to do your income-tax return the year you sell. Don't wait until you get organized. Get a box, or select a drawer and throw all the receipts, contracts, change orders, bills, and memos into it. You can sort it out later.

Paying cash

Because even a relatively modest home improvement such as replacing siding or adding a deck can cost well over $5,000, paying for remodeling projects out of current income or readily available savings can place a huge strain on a household's budget. With sufficient planning and saving, you may be able to finance modest home improvements—siding, kitchen cabinets, windows—without resorting to borrowing.

Another way to self-finance a project is by tapping your other investment accounts—selling some mutual-fund holdings, for example. But think this option through carefully. You should determine that the combination of additional comfort and home-value appreciation will be worth more to you than the return you could expect by leaving your money where it is.

One option you should consider only as a last resort is using a credit card to pay for a significant home improvement. Unless you're prepared to pay off the full amount when you receive your monthly statement, you'll begin to incur stiff interest charges, sometimes at an annual rate of 18 percent or higher.

Smart ways to borrow

Using loans that can be paid off in installments may be the only way to make remodeling affordable. Borrowing can have distinctive advantages—if you shop for loan terms and choose a reputable lender. Avoid unsecured personal loans; at today's average interest rate of about 12 percent, they can be almost as costly as using a credit card.

The best source of collateral you have for a remodeling loan is the equity you've already accumulated in your home. Your lender might also offer you a larger loan based on the increased value of your home after the remodeling. Interest rates on loans based on home equity are usually the lowest a homeowner can find anywhere. On top of that, interest you pay on a home-equity loan is apt to be tax-deductible, further reducing your cost of borrowing.

There are several ways to borrow against your home equity. Here's a look at the pros and cons of each:

HOME-EQUITY LOANS. Also known as second mortgages, these provide a lump sum of money at a fixed rate of interest. They're available through credit unions, banks, home-finance companies, and even some big brokerage houses that cater to retail customers. Borrowing limits usually range from 70 to 80 percent of the value of your house, minus any amount outstanding on your first mortgage. Some banks are now offering far more—up to 125 percent of home value in some instances—but CONSUMER REPORTS strongly advises against such a loan. The reason: You owe more than your house is worth.

Home-equity loans are most often repaid over 10 to 20 years, although terms range from 5 to 30 years. In late 2003, the average interest rate on home-equity loans nationwide was around 6 percent, but rates can vary widely, so shop carefully. Financing companies, such as Household Finance, typically market their loans to borrowers with spotty credit histories and charge interest rates up to 5 percentage points higher than commercial banks.

A home-equity loan can be a good way to pay for a relatively costly renovation, such as a new bathroom, a home-office addition, or some other large project that you can expect to complete within a period of several weeks. These are jobs for which you want to lock in a favorable fixed-interest rate so you can budget your payments, knowing that rising rates won't cause them to rise.

HOME-EQUITY LINES OF CREDIT. These differ from closed-end home-equity loans in that they generally allow a homeowner to draw upon his or her available equity when needed. Most credit lines allow the borrower simply to write a check; the interest charges vary with the rates prevailing when the credit is tapped. As a homeowner pays off past borrowings, the credit line is replenished. Some financial institutions charge a nominal annual fee to keep the credit line open, though most do not.

Home-equity lines of credit are the most flexible way to borrow money for home improvements. You may want to consider a credit line if you plan to do a series of remodeling projects, working with several different contractors over an extended period of time. For example, you may plan to re-side your home this spring, build a deck next summer, and replace windows the following fall. With an open credit line, you needn't apply for a separate loan for each of these projects, and you can take advantage of favorable interest-rate trends. In late 2003, the average interest rate on home-equity lines of credit nationwide was about 3¾ percent.

CASH-OUT REFINANCING. With the average rate on a conventional 30-year fixed-rate mortgage at around 6 percent (in late 2003), you may want to consider cash-out refinancing. This allows you to replace your current mortgage with a larger new one. For example, if you currently owe $80,000 on the mortgage you took out when you originally bought your home, you may be able to refinance that loan and expand the amount you borrow to, say, $100,000. That $20,000 difference is cash you can use to pay for a major home renovation.

A cash-out refinancing may be especially worth considering if interest rates are at least a percentage point below the rate of your original mortgage. If that's the case, you may discover you can have access to funds you need for remodeling while keeping your monthly mortgage payment only a little above—or even no more than—what it had been before you refinanced. Don't forget that you may face substantial closing costs based on the full amount you borrow, but these costs have been coming down.

A FIRST MORTGAGE. This can help if you're buying a home that's in immediate need of refurbishing. You'll be able to amortize the remodeling costs over the full 30-year life of your new home loan. The advantage, of course, is that you can begin renovations that will make your home more livable soon after you move in. The lender may increase the appraised value of your home considering the proposed renovations.

But there are some downsides. If borrowing more results in your down payment's falling below 20 percent of the total amount of the loan, you may be required by your lender to pay private mortgage insurance (PMI). The premiums for PMI, which protects your lender against the risk that you will default on your loan, can add significantly to your monthly mortgage payment for years.

SPECIAL BANK LOANS. These can help when rehabilitating a home. Some programs are limited to borrowers who live in disadvantaged neighborhoods or whose annual income does not exceed the median of their communities; others are available to anyone. Ask your bank or other financial institution whether it offers home-improvement mortgage loans, rehabilitation mortgage loans, home-improvement loans, or second mortgages from the government-sponsored agencies Fannie Mae or Freddie Mac. Or call Fannie Mae at 800-732-6643 for a referral to lenders near you.

ENERGY-EFFICIENCY LOANS. Some utility companies work with local lenders to make it less costly for homeowners to undertake energy-efficient renovations, such as installing new windows or insulating an attic. Families with incomes of up to $30,000 per year can qualify for interest-free loans ranging from $500 to $4,000. Those with higher incomes are eligible for loans with an annual interest rate of just 5 percent. Some companies promote their rebate and loan offerings through bill inserts or billboards. Fannie Mae, the government-sponsored agency that buys home loans from lenders to resell on the secondary market, buys and resells energy loans.

A caveat: Some utilities are abandoning these programs to cut costs and to be more competitive as the industry becomes deregulated. To find out whether there are any special programs in your area, call your local utility and ask if it sponsors home-energy audits, rebate programs, and low-cost loans.

Correcting mistakes

If you have ever rearranged furniture, you'll have some idea of how slim the chances are that your remodeling will come off without any hitches or changes. Things look different in real life than on paper. If some aspect of the remodeling bothers you and you don't change it, it will go on bothering you. There are several kinds of mistakes:

■ Things that are done correctly but look wrong.

■ Things that are done wrong but look OK. The flooring is laid east to west rather than north to south. You catch it but not before it has all been laid. Talk it over with your contractor. Is it really worth holding his or her feet to the fire to change it or could you adjust?

——— LIVING WITH WORK IN PROGRESS ———

You may think of it as your home, but to your contractors, it's their workplace. They'll arrive each morning on their schedule—usually between 7 and 8 a.m. If those hours don't fit your family's usual schedule, change it.

On the first day, show the crew which bathroom they can use, put out some towels, give them room in your fridge to store their lunches and sodas, give them permission to use your water, and set out some glasses. Let your contractor use your phone to line up the next day's subcontractors or check on deliveries.

Set aside room in the garage for the crew's tools. If workers keep their tools at your place, they save time packing and unpacking; what's more, they have to show up each day. Also consider letting the crew use the garage as a workshop and place to store cabinetry or other materials as they're delivered.

Children and construction projects don't mix. Your children will not agree with this, but it is dangerous and your workers should not have to act as babysitters or unplug their saws and drills after every use. Arrange for summer camp or recruit your family or neighbors for day-care help.

As work progresses, particularly if it involves some of the basic operations in your life such as the kitchen or bathrooms, your life is going to become difficult. You will be living with dust and noise. If your contractor is kind, he or she will leave you the use of your kitchen sink, refrigerator, and stove for as long as possible or move your appliances into another room. When the water in the kitchen is turned off, you may have to wash dishes in the bathtub.

If you are adding a room to an outside wall, the contractor shouldn't break through the wall into your home until the very last step. This will isolate all the dust and noise for most of the project.

There may come a time when it would be best to move out for a few days to a motel or a relative's or friend's home. It's not advisable to go on an extended vacation because you really should check in each day to preview and review the work being done.

■ Things that are done wrong and look wrong. There are only two electrical outlets over the kitchen counter, and the plans call for six. You are entitled to have your contractor correct the mistake at his expense. It will ease the atmosphere, however, if you have caught such a mistake before the wallboard is up. Visit the job regularly, and set up meetings with your contractor to go over what has just been done and what is coming up next.

When there is a problem, talk it over with the contractor. He or she may have some ideas for correcting the problem. If not, it is time for a change order. If you caught the problem early, it's possible that a lot of work will not have to be torn out. That is why you should check how the job is progressing every day.

A change order should be regarded as a new contract. Your contractor should furnish you with an estimate of the costs involved in time and materials, and you should sign off on those revisions and calculate the additional expenses into your budget. It is for this reason that you should budget 20 percent for unanticipated problems.

Wrapping up the project

Don't be discouraged if the work seems to slow to a crawl as the project nears its end. You and the family are sick and tired of the daily mess, the noise, and having to share your house with a bunch of people with power tools and dirty boots. The hammering will be slower, the sounds of the power saw shorter and farther apart. You are at the finish-carpentry phase of the project.

Finish carpenters are the elite of the business. No more than one or two will be on your project. Their job is to install the kitchen cabinets, baseboards, moldings, and window surrounds. They may spend all day in your new master bedroom closet hanging rails and building shelving. They are probably working as fast as they should.

After the skilled carpenters come the painters. Their work, too, seems to go slower than you will think it should. It might be two or three days before they even open a can of paint. This, too, is how it should be done. All those nail holes and corner gaps have to be puttied and sanded.

Finally it's time for the final tour of the spaces with your contractor and the creation of the infamous "punch list"—problems that need to be addressed before final payment is tendered. The tour can become like a victory lap after a race won. You get a chance to offer congratulations for the work done. Or you may have been harboring long-suppressed gripes about doors that stick, corners that gap, and missing window locks and light fixtures. But save it. Your contractor also has a list, and he or she can see these things as well as you can. Fixtures may be on back-order, or the people who can correct some of the problems are already on the next job but will be back to finish your home.

Remember that the contractor wants you to be happy with the work because you may be the source of a future job, either directly or via a referral, and you should still have 5 to 10 percent of his or her last payment in the bank. If all is in order or soon will be, release the check. If there is an $80 light fixture still to come, withhold that amount and pay the rest. Be sure to ask for the owner's manuals and warranties for all the newly installed

It's all in the timing

Don't let your contractor tear out the old kitchen cabinets or bathroom fixtures until the replacements you ordered from the factory are sitting in your garage. Deliveries can be weeks or even months late. And make sure everything is correct in terms of style and is free of damage.

appliances. Note that most warranties start from the moment of installation, not from the date of purchase.

Making the final payment doesn't mean you are without recourse if things crop up later. Your contract probably calls for at least a year's guarantee on workmanship and materials. You should recognize that projects made of wood will move as they gain and lose moisture, that foundations will shift, that cracks will appear. This is all normal, as your contractor knows. If you have a door that sticks, he may put off calling on you until all the doors have had a chance to move and he can send someone in to adjust them all at once.

You are now free to move about in your new space. Enjoy it. You have earned some quiet time.

Fresh Starts

The skyrocketing costs of buying a new home have led more and more people to get creative with the one they're living in now. Sometimes a little refreshing is all it takes to make an old home feel new again. A coat of paint can give your home's interior or exterior a fresh look. Wallpaper can develop the personality of a room and hide minor flaws. A wood floor can bring an elegant, classic look to a living room. A kitchen can be transformed with new cabinetry, countertops, and flooring. Roofing and siding products are essential to a home's integrity. Improvements such as these make a home nicer to live in and can add to its value.

In response to the growing trend to refeather the nest, retailers of all shapes and sizes have what a homeowner needs for projects large or small. Warehouse-sized home centers such as Home Depot and Lowe's put an extensive selection of home-improvement products in one place, often at very low prices. Local hardware stores, specialty shops, and lumberyards sometimes deliver superior service. While relatively few people actually buy home-improvement products through Web sites, many take advantage of the unparalleled access to product information that the Internet delivers.

Cabinetry

If you're remodeling a kitchen or bathroom, you'll almost surely devote planning and money to cabinets. Be sure they're well made, since they're subject to heavy use.

Essentially, a kitchen cabinet is nothing more than a box with a door or drawer in the front. But many details distinguish those boxes: the materials they're made of, whether they're stock, semicustom-made, or custom-made, and how they're put together. The type of wood used affects the cabinet's price. Some store displays may boast that the cabinets are "all wood." That can mean they're made of plywood or particleboard. But few stock or even custom-made cabinets are made entirely of solid-wood boards.

What's available

Before you delve into the details, you should understand the basic varieties of cabinet.

STOCK. The most affordable type, these come in standard styles off-the-shelf from kitchen-remodeling stores and home centers. Most are built to a manufacturer's standard selection of styles in standard dimensions. Stock cabinets range in width from about 9 to 48 inches in 3-inch increments. Since kitchens don't come in standard dimensions, installers use filler strips—boards matching the cabinet finish—to take up the odd few inches between cabinet and wall. Stock cabinets and filler pieces usually can be delivered in a week or so.

SEMICUSTOM. These come in more sizes, materials, finishes, trim choices, and with more storage accessories than stock cabinets. This range of choices allows them to be truly customized for each kitchen application. They're sold at home centers, cabinet dealerships, and in kitchen showrooms. They're available in the manufacturer's stock styles and finishes and standard widths—though you can have base cabinets built taller than the standard 36-inch height or shallower than the standard 24-inch depth for a custom look. You can also add or subtract height or width. Delivery time is longer and the price is generally 20 percent to 30 percent higher than for standard stock cabinets.

Which is right for your kitchen?

Cabinet types

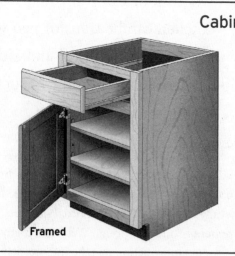

Framed

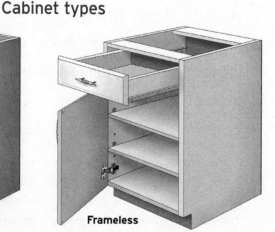

Frameless

CUSTOM. These are made to order, and, as such, are the most costly option. You or your kitchen designer can specify the style, materials, shapes, and sizes. You can hire a carpenter to build custom cabinets. Expect to pay dearly (anywhere from 30 to 100 percent more than for semicustom) and to wait six weeks or longer for construction on site.

Key features

SURFACES. The modern answer to painted paneled doors, **Thermofoil** consists of polyvinyl-chloride sheets heated and molded to a sculpted fiberboard substrate. Thermofoil-faced doors and drawers are easy to spot—they have a seamless finish. Salespeople like to point out that Thermofoil cabinets have few areas to trap dust and dirt. Indeed, the material is very easy to clean and resists scratches and staining, although it does occasionally yellow with age

Laminates come in an endless variety of colors and textures, including wood grain (although you probably won't mistake laminate for the real stuff). They're usually used on flat, contemporary-looking doors and drawer fronts. Laminated surfaces can be damaged by heat and dryness—from a range, for example. Sometimes referred to as low-pressure laminate, **melamine** is often used in the interior of mid- to high-priced cabinets. The material chips fairly easily and can bubble and lift from the underlying particleboard when exposed to high humidity. But it is not as fragile as low-end materials such as vinyl or paper.

You can get the look of solid wood without the cost by choosing cabinets of **wood veneer,** a thin sheet of wood laminated to plywood or a composite such as particleboard. You can tell the difference between solid wood and veneer by comparing the grain on the outside and inside of the door. If the grain doesn't match, the panel is veneered. **Solid wood** may not necessarily be superior to a laminate veneer or Thermofoil and may actually be more prone to warping or cracking.

FRAMING. Framed cabinets have horizontal rails and vertical stiles that frame the door and drawers. **Decorative hinges** attach the door to the frame. Traditional styles with

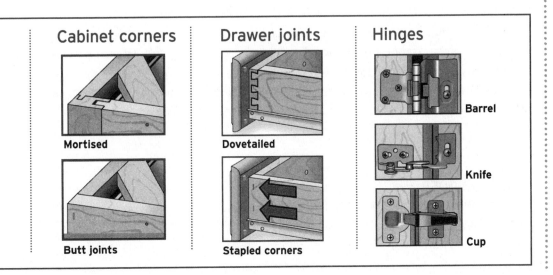

Cabinet corners — Mortised, Butt joints

Drawer joints — Dovetailed, Stapled corners

Hinges — Barrel, Knife, Cup

paneled doors and a wood finish usually distinguish framed cabinets. The **face frame** provides extra support, which helps keep the cabinet square during installation.

With **frameless cabinets,** the doors are attached directly to the cabinet sides with hinges that are hidden from view when the door is closed. Plain, contemporary styles are usually frameless. These cabinets provide slightly more interior room and easier access, but they're tricky and time-consuming to install. **Cross rails** add rigidity and stability, particularly important when installing frameless cabinets.

JOINING DETAILS. Look for **mortised corners** in better-quality framed cabinets, **doweled corners** in frameless models. By comparison, inexpensive cabinets often have simple **butt joints** in which the back and sides are glued and then nailed or screwed together. Corners are sometimes reinforced with braces.

HINGES. Stainless-steel hinges and **screws** help cabinets hold up over the long haul. In CONSUMER REPORTS high-humidity tests, plain-steel hinges began to rust. Good hinges should automatically close a cabinet door when it's left slightly ajar. Some types of hinges are **adjustable,** so doors can be realigned if they sag or shift over time. **Cup hinges** are designed to be totally concealed when the door of a cabinet is closed. Ask when you buy if they are adjustable (most are). Cup hinges generally limit the door opening to about 115°. **Knife hinges,** like cup hinges, can be concealed when the door is closed, but most aren't adjustable. Knife hinges allow the door to open almost 180°. **Barrel hinges** are an inexpensive hinge generally used on framed cabinets. A narrow cylinder is visible when the door is closed. Most aren't adjustable. Barrel hinges allow doors to open about 160°. Cabinets need a solid anchor to the wall (called a **hanger rail).** Base cabinets have a rail at the top; wall cabinets have one at top and one at bottom.

SHELVES. These should extend the full depth of the cabinet for maximum storage. **Nonadjustable shelves,** though sturdy, offer no flexibility. **Adjustable shelves** can be positioned to suit oversized stock pots or flat frying pans. Choose **metal** or **wood supports** for adjustable shelves when there's an option. Beware of plastic clips, which can be flimsy and can bend under weight.

DRAWERS. CONSUMER REPORTS tests have shown that the most durable drawers have a box made of solid wood and a separate front attached to the box. **Dovetailed** or **doweled joints** hold better than stapled ones. Press down on the drawer bottom to see if it's sturdy. Those made of thin hardboard sagged under weight in our tests. In most cabinets, **drawer rollers** move on tracks mounted on the sides of the cabinet. Look for **full-extension slides** that allow access to the entire drawer.

END PANELS. Choose base cabinets with **plywood** end panels if you can. When exposed to high humidity (for example, next to a dishwasher), plywood held up better than particle board in CONSUMER REPORTS tests.

How to choose

PERFORMANCE DIFFERENCES. To a certain extent, you get what you pay for with kitchen cabinets. Less expensive ones might have stapled drawers, which don't hold up particularly well; a thin hardboard drawer bottom, which can separate from the rest of the drawer under a heavy load; and a vinyl or paper interior surface. You won't find a significant difference in quality between medium- and high-priced cabinets. With both, you can expect drawers and doors that can withstand severe impact. But you may also get an inferior finish.

For bathrooms, CONSUMER REPORTS testing found wood veneer or laminate cabinets to be more durable than ones faced with wood-grain paper or foil. Solid wood wouldn't be our first choice; humidity may warp the doors.

RECOMMENDATIONS. The choice of installation contractor is as important a decision as the choice of materials. Make sure the contractor will provide a warranty separate from the one provided with the cabinets. When your cabinets are delivered, examine them to make sure they are the same style and finish as those you saw in the store and that they have not been damaged. To check installation, look at the cabinet doors to be sure none are out of alignment; be sure doors and drawers move smoothly.

Countertops
A countertop has to withstand considerable punishment over a long period of time. And it needs to look good.

What's available

BUTCHER BLOCK. Butcher-block countertops are made of hardwoods; maple is the most common, though red oak and teak also are used. A slab of butcher block is useful for chopping and slicing, but it can become marred with everyday use. Butcher block is relatively easy to install and repair. The wood will almost certainly become scratched, nicked, burned, or stained as it's used; fortunately, it can be sanded and resealed. Butcher block should either be treated regularly with mineral oil or beeswax, or it should be sealed with a varnish suitable for food-preparation surfaces. Wood is vulnerable to fluctuations in humidity, so butcher block is a poor choice for over a dishwasher or near a sink, where it can get wet frequently.

CERAMIC TILE. Ceramic tile comes in an almost limitless selection of colors, patterns, and styles. A professional or an adept do-it-yourselfer can install it easily. You can use tile to customize a countertop—on a backsplash or island top. Tile set into the counter near the range can serve as a built-in trivet. Glazed tiles are highly resistant to stains, scratches, and burns. And repairs are relatively easy and inexpensive. Grout can be tinted to match or contrast with the tiles, but the joints can trap crumbs and soak up unsightly stains. Cleaning it can be difficult unless the grout is sealed. Tile can be scratched by hard, sharp objects and can chip or crack if hit hard enough.

ENGINEERED STONE. This artificial material is a variation of solid surfacing that is made primarily of small stone chips combined with resins and pigments. Engineered stone can look much like granite but has a more uniform appearance. It's resistant to stains, heat, and abrasion and never needs sealing. However, engineered stone doesn't withstand impact—especially a blow to the edge—as well as real granite.

GENUINE STONE. The most popular stones for kitchen countertops, granite and marble come in a spectrum of colors. They also stand up to almost any type of physical abuse, resisting scratches, nicks, and scorching from hot pans. Granite is the tougher material. Marble is slightly softer and more prone to staining and etching from the acids in foods and cleaners. The stone's cold surface also makes it ideal for keeping pastry dough cool and firm while it's being rolled or kneaded. Both granite and marble should be sealed with a protective, penetrating sealer that's applied periodically.

Because these are natural materials, the grain you see in a display may not be the same as in the stone delivered to your kitchen. But most suppliers will allow you to inspect and choose the stone slabs. Genuine stone is expensive, partly because it's heavy and difficult to install. Stone tiles are less expensive—and lighter weight—than thick slabs. Special equipment may be needed to move the slabs, which have to be arranged to match color and grain. Without sealing, polished granite can stain easily, and the stains may be difficult to remove. Limestone, slate, soapstone, and sandstone are also used as countertops, though they are softer than either granite or marble.

LAMINATE. Laminates such as Formica and Wilsonart are lightweight and relatively easy to install, although edge treatments add to installation cost and complexity. Laminate is the most popular countertop material, probably because it comes in hundreds of colors and patterns and the price is right. Typically it consists of a colored top layer over a dark core; when laminate covers the top and edge of a countertop, part of that core shows as a dark line. Some manufacturers offer laminates colored all the way through. These cost a bit more, but they show no dark line and any surface scratches will be less visible.

Prefabricated seamless countertop-and-backsplash—known as postformed counter—is also available. Laminate is not as durable as other materials. Caustic substances, such as drain cleaner, can ruin the finish, and direct flame will scorch the surface. Solid colors and shiny finishes readily show scratches and nicks. Damaged areas can't be repaired. Water can seep through seams or between the countertop and backsplash, weakening the material underneath or causing the laminate to lift.

SOLID SURFACE. Solid-surface materials, which imitate marble and other types of stone, are sold under various brands: Avonite, DuPont Corian, Formica Surell, Nevamar Fountainhead, and Wilsonart Gibraltar. Solid-surface countertops are reasonably durable

An array of choices

Let your budget and your own sense of style be your guide, since all of these materials are both practical and pleasing.

Tile

Engineered stone

Granite

Solid surface

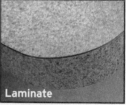
Laminate

Butcher block

but expensive; they're best installed by a contractor who has been certified by the manufacturer. Made of polyester or acrylic resins combined with mineral fillers, they come in various thicknesses and can be joined almost invisibly into one apparently seamless expanse. These materials can be sculpted to integrate the sink and backsplash and routed to accept contrasting inlays.

Scratches and nicks don't show readily on solid surfaces and can be buffed out with an abrasive pad; some gouges can be filled. Repair of a solid-color surface tends to be less discernible than repair of a surface that mimics a granite pattern. Prolonged heat may cause a solid-surface material to discolor.

How to choose

The overall kitchen design that you've chosen and your budget will determine which material is most appropriate. Butcher block, laminate, and ceramic tile tend to be the least expensive, with some ceramic tiles costing as little as $4 a square foot, installed. Solid-surface materials range from $40 to $75 per square foot, and engineered stone starts at about $50 a square foot. Genuine stone can run as little as $50 per square foot up to as much as $300 a square foot.

PERFORMANCE DIFFERENCES. Our tests over the years have shown more differences between types of countertop than between brands of a type. Overall, engineered stone and granite are the toughest, closely followed by ceramic tile. Butcher block is the most vulnerable, mostly because the wood can be so easily scratched and gouged.

RECOMMENDATIONS. Comparison shopping and research at home centers or kitchen-design outlets can go a long way toward helping you make the right choice. Listed above are the leading materials, but just about anything that's hard and flat—from plate glass to sheets of zinc—can make a countertop. Concrete and stainless steel are two other options. The more exotic your choice, the more important it is to find a capable installer. You don't want to pay for sloppy work on material that's costing you hundreds of dollars for every square foot.

Faucets

Fixtures for kitchens and bathrooms range widely in price. Some of the newest models have improvements aimed at making them last longer.

According to manufacturers, most homeowners put style first, durability second, and function last in their search for a new kitchen or bathroom faucet. The style issue isn't surprising, considering kitchens and bathrooms are some of the most remodeled spaces in a home. But there's more to think about when choosing a faucet.

What's available

The most familiar names in kitchen and bath faucets include American Standard, Delta, Eljer, Kohler, Moen, Peerless, Price Pfister, and Sterling. Kitchen and bath faucets fall into two basic styles: Single-handle faucets that regulate flow and temperature with one lever or knob and two-handle faucets that let you control hot and cold water independently. With the latter, the handles are 4 or 8 inches apart and require sinks with suitably spaced plumbing holes.

Price range for faucets: $50 to $2,400 or more.

Key features

Deep inside the faucet is the key working component—the valve that shuts off the flow of water. There are many designs.

A traditional **washer-and-seat** faucet—a compression-valve design—relies on rubber or neoprene washers attached at the bottom of each handle stem to stop the flow of water as the handle is screwed down against a metal valve seat. While simple and easy to service, this system requires a lot of maintenance. The washers eventually become brittle, compressed, or worn; the small screws that attach them corrode; and the valve seats wear down under repeated friction and pressure. Annoying leaks and drips are the result. Most U.S. manufacturers have replaced this system with valve and flow-control options that are more durable. In some cases, though, the newer designs require more involved repairs than the older ones do.

Ball valves are what you'll find on some single-handle faucets. Introduced in the early 1950s, this design includes a metal ball housed in a brass or plastic sleeve. Turning the faucet handle in any direction moves the ball, which regulates both water temperature and flow. Ball valves are available on both kitchen and bathroom faucets.

Ceramic or **stainless-steel disks** use perforated disk-shaped regulators to control water flow. The disks rotate in pairs or against a fixed plate, often within a cartridge assembly. Repairs typically can involve replacing the entire cartridge.

Another cartridge design encompasses a single bored cylinder valve with **O-rings** that seal it within the faucet body. While the O-rings can be replaced individually, typically the whole cartridge

---

A MATTER OF TASTE

Whichever faucet you choose, look for a lifetime warranty for its internal valve as well as its finish. Then consider which faucet style you prefer and what you're willing to pay.

BASIC: $60 to about $180. This category includes single- and dual-handle chrome and epoxy-finish models with either a standard or a gooseneck-style spout. Choose chrome if you're especially concerned about scratches, epoxy if you want a range of color options.

MIDRANGE: $170 to $350. Choices for this category include everything for "basic" plus models with a pull-out spout and a chrome or epoxy finish, and models with a standard spout in PVD. Decide whether you prefer the array of finish choices offered by PVD, or the look and utility of a gooseneck or pull-out spout.

HIGH-END: $250 to $750 or more. Options here include all of the foregoing plus more expensive PVD finishes. For sinks with two or three bowls, make sure the faucet can reach all of the bowls. If you're buying a sink and faucet together, you can ease faucet installation by checking that the sink holes match the connections for the faucet. If they don't, you'll have to cover unused holes in the sink with a base plate (often included with the faucet) or, if possible, drill more holes as needed.

is replaced. Manufacturers are so confident about the durability of these new valves that most faucets now come with a lifetime warranty against leaks and drips. The warranty covers only the faucet, however, and not the labor to repair or replace it.

Spouts can be fixed or can swivel side to side. They can be standard, pull-out, or gooseneck-shaped. With the **pull-out** type, the single spout doubles as a sprayer that can be pulled out to rinse dishes and pots and pans. Gooseneck spouts are useful for washing large objects or filling buckets. Some kitchen faucets have **integrated water filters,** which you must change regularly. You can also buy filters that attach to the outlet of the faucet.

Traditional **finishes** include chrome and epoxy-coated metal. The finish you'll see on many new faucets is known as **physical vapor deposition,** or PVD. Sold by various manufacturers under the trade names Brilliance, LifeShine, Vibrant, Pforever Pfinish, and others, these brass-, silver-, copper-, nickel- and titanium-hued finishes are said to be bonded to the faucet body. CONSUMER REPORTS has tested the durability of these and the more traditional finishes, and found them all to be very durable. Most faucet manufacturers offer a lifetime warranty against corrosion, tarnishing, and discoloration on all finishes. The warranty covers only parts, not labor.

How to choose

PERFORMANCE DIFFERENCES. You don't have to buy a manufacturer's priciest line to get a good faucet. Most faucets share many of the same basic parts. Even a relatively inexpensive faucet often has many of the functional qualities of a pricier model.

The simpler the mechanism, the fewer parts that can break or wear out. A single-lever model has only one flow regulator, while faucets with separate handles have two. Pull-out spouts with hoses protected by a flexible metal sleeve will be less easily damaged than those with unprotected hoses. And any long gooseneck faucet is more vulnerable to accidental bumps simply because there's more surface area in harm's way. Remember, too, that faucets with ornate spouts and other intricate styling details tend to have surface contours and crevices that invite soap-scum and mineral-scale deposits.

RECOMMENDATIONS. Match the faucet to the hole configuration in your sink. Choose based on style and utility. Don't forget to check the warranty. You can get a lifetime warranty on even low-priced faucets. Several manufacturers have also made do-it-yourself installation easier with top-mount fittings and tools-free connectors.

Floor varnish

Refinishing a wood floor requires a combination of art and craft. Which varnish you choose rests largely on the look and durability you want, plus your time constraints.

You know it's time to refinish a wood floor when its finish is worn through or the surface is badly nicked. Deep gouges, split or warped boards, and other damage, however, are signs that a wood floor needs more than a face-lift—it needs to be repaired or replaced.

Whether you refinish the floor yourself or hire a pro, expect days of disruption, dust,

Scratch resistance

Tests of faucet durability showed that even nylon scouring pads could leave scratches on chrome, epoxy-coated metal, or PVD-finished faucets if scrubbing was vigorous enough. Consider choosing a faucet with a brushed or satin finish in chrome or PVD to help hide scratches.

and, with solvent-based varnish, fumes. You also face significant cost and convenience differences between water-based and solvent-based varnish—key reasons why choosing the right one for your needs is critical no matter who applies it.

What's available

Three major brands of floor varnish are Flecto Varathane, Minwax, and Pro Finisher (available only at Home Depot). Water-based varnishes dry faster and allow easier cleanup, making the application process a bit less onerous. Solvent-based varnishes tend to go farther and cost less per square foot. The catch: Their longer drying time means more days to finish the job—and possibly more money you'll pay a pro if you hire the job out. Solvent-based varnishes leave an amber finish. Water-based products dry pale and practically clear; if you prefer the amber hue, you'll have to stain the wood first.

Price range per gallon: water-based, $30 to $45; solvent-based, $10 to $40.

Key features

Sheen levels range from satin to high gloss. Varnishes with a satin finish showed the least appearance change in a CONSUMER REPORTS abrasion test—a plus for busy rooms. We found that low-gloss finishes went on smoothest with the fewest imperfections. They were also less likely to raise the wood grain—a condition in which the wood fibers "stand up" and create a rough surface.

Varnishes typically contain polyurethane—a resin designed to resist surface wear and provide a tough, no-wax finish that's easy to clean using a damp mop.

Solvent-based—also known as oil-based—products use a solvent such as mineral spirits to deliver the resins that eventually form the finish. Water-based products hold their resins within an emulsion. Solvent-based varnishes tend to contain more solids than water-based products, which is why manufacturers estimate greater coverage and recommend fewer coats for solvent-based types. Solvent-based products require mineral spirits for cleanup, generate more volatile organic compounds (VOCs), and are combustible.

Water-based varnishes tend to have lower levels of VOCs. Along with their distinctive odor, VOCs pose the possibility of headaches and nausea for those particularly sensitive to chemical odors. If you're applying varnish yourself, consider wearing a respirator with an organic filter cartridge (about $20 to $40). With water-based varnishes, brushes and varnish spills can be cleaned with water.

How to choose

PERFORMANCE DIFFERENCES. Solvent-based varnishes have long enjoyed a reputation for greater resistance to wear and scratches—a reason why most varnish manufacturers recommend them for high-traffic areas. In CONSUMER REPORTS' real-life foot-traffic tests, this proved to be true. Dirt also became less imbedded in flooring finished with solvent-based varnishes than in those finished with water-based varnishes.

Bright, sunny rooms are one place where water-based varnishes have an edge. All of those we tested withstood intense exposure to lab ultraviolet (UV) light without changing color. By comparison, all of the solvent-based products we tested darkened. In spill tests, none of the varnished floors were damaged by vodka, beer, wine, cola, or water. But most were damaged by detergent, and a few were damaged by coffee, vinegar, or ammonia.

RECOMMENDATIONS. Start by deciding whether you'll hire a contractor or do the job yourself. Consider hiring a pro if the floor is especially uneven or needs repair. Then choose which type of varnish to use. Water-based varnish provides faster drying time, easier cleanup, and excellent ultraviolet resistance. Solvent-based varnish leaves an amber finish, and drying time between coats is longer and cleanup messier. It also tends to darken under ultraviolet light, but stands up better to high-traffic areas.

All varnishes require multiple coats, particularly in high-traffic areas. You'll wait only an hour or two for each coat of water-based varnish to dry, compared with anywhere from five hours to overnight for most solvent-based products. Water-based varnishes require more coats for heavy traffic—typically four, compared with three for most solvent-based products. You or a flooring contractor could get all of those coats down in one long day using a water-based varnish. You'll still have to wait anywhere from 12 hours to a day or two for any varnish to cure before it can handle heavy traffic, however.

Flooring: Vinyl tiles and sheets

Also called resilient flooring, vinyl may not be as elegant as wood or ceramic tile, but its durability and easy cleanup make it a smart choice for kitchens and other high-traffic areas.

A lack of variety will never be a problem if you're considering vinyl flooring, which comes in a vast array of patterns and colors. Prices are relatively low, and installation is easy; roughly half of those who buy sheet vinyl and some 90 percent of those who buy vinyl tiles lay down the flooring themselves.

What's available

The market leader in vinyl flooring is Armstrong. Other major brands include Congoleum and Mannington. Home centers such as Home Depot and Lowe's are discount sources of flooring, but you'll probably get more personal attention at a specialty store. Stores that sell flooring can also arrange installation. Vinyl flooring comes two ways, in sheets and as tiles. Sheet vinyl generally costs $10 to $35 per square yard. Tiles typically measure per square foot and cost 50 cents to $2 each.

Key features

Peel-and self-stick tiles are clearly the easiest vinyl flooring to install and repair. But **sheet vinyl** offers a seamless look. You'll find two types of sheet vinyl: **Perimeter-bonded** floors, which are glued down only around the edge of the room and along any seams, and **fully-adhered** flooring, which is laid in a coat of mastic that's spread over the entire subfloor. The two types are similar in cost and performance. Perimeter-bonded floors do a better job of hiding small surface imperfections in the subfloor since they're not stuck down; fully adhered vinyl lays flatter and is less likely to bubble up. The latter is installed almost exclusively by professional installers.

Vinyl flooring typically has a **protective coating,** or "wear layer," made of urethane or vinyl. Urethane proved more resistant than vinyl in CONSUMER REPORTS scuff and abrasion tests. The type of wear layer didn't seem to make a difference when CONSUMER REPORTS tested for puncturing. Sheets, however, performed better than tiles in the puncture test. Most sheets resisted puncture; most tiles didn't because they lacked the sheet vinyl's cushioned layer.

Textured surfaces hide dents best. We loaded various weights onto indentation tools of different diameters (made especially for our tests) to simulate the effect of high-heeled shoes and furniture legs pressing into flooring. Most of the products bounced back from the depressions left by furniture, but few recovered completely from the heel test, which was more severe.

With the **rotogravure,** or roto, printing method, colors and patterns are printed on the surface of the base layer. In the more intricate **inlaid printing method,** the design is embedded in the vinyl. Models with inlaid printing tend to cost more, but they don't always prove to be the most durable.

How to choose

PERFORMANCE DIFFERENCES. With vinyl flooring, you usually get more by spending more. In CONSUMER REPORTS tests, the most expensive products weren't necessarily the best, but most performed very well. The cheapest products were consistently among the worst. Expect to spend at least $1.50 per square foot of floor space to get a sheet or tile that will hold up well.

In our tests, several sheet-vinyl products were excellent overall, and most performed at least very well. Several of the vinyl tiles were very good, but as a group they fell somewhat short of the sheets. No matter how good the vinyl floor, it will not match ceramic tile's ease of cleaning and ability to maintain its appearance. The drawbacks of ceramic tile, however, are its propensity to crack if heavy objects are dropped on it and the high cost of installation.

Vinyl tends to be less slippery than other flooring types. When wet, only one vinyl tile in CONSUMER REPORTS tests proved to be as slippery as the wood, glazed-ceramic, and laminate flooring we tested.

RECOMMENDATIONS. If you plan to install the floor yourself, you're better off with vinyl tiles, as opposed to sheets. The no-wax variety is the easiest to maintain. Be sure to buy tiles in sealed boxes with the same lot number to avoid lot-to-lot color variations. Buy extras so you can redo mistakes and replace tiles that become damaged.

Flooring: Wood and wood alternatives

Natural wood flooring has staying power and an attractive warmth, but easier-to-install copycats may sometimes be a better choice.

Solid wood remains many people's ideal for floors. Indeed, hardwood flooring can increase a home's resale value and speed its sale, according to the National Association of Realtors. Oak is the most popular and readily available choice. Others include maple, cherry, and hickory. Pine, a softwood, costs less. Solid wood flooring comes prefinished or unfinished.

Alternatives to solid wood include plastic laminate and engineered wood. Both are easier and cheaper to install. Laminate mimics wood (or tile or marble) by using a photograph of the real thing beneath its clear surface layer. Engineered-wood flooring incorporates a thin veneer of real wood over structural plywood. It costs about the same as solid wood. You'll also see bamboo flooring and parquet wood tiles.

What's available

You'll find wood and wood-look flooring at flooring suppliers and lumberyards as well as at mass merchandisers and home centers such as Home Depot, Lowe's, and Wal-Mart. Flooring suppliers tend to have the widest selection, particularly for exotic woods, while mass merchandisers and home centers usually offer the lowest prices.

The many brands of wood flooring include Anderson, Bruce, Harris-Tarkett, Hartco, and Permagrain. Brands of plastic-laminate flooring include Armstrong, Congoleum, Formica, Mannington, Pergo, Tarkett, and Wilsonart.

Price range, per square foot: prefinished solid wood, $4 to $7.25; engineered wood, $5 to $9; plastic-laminate, $3 to $4.50. Add about $3 per square foot if you have the flooring installed professionally.

Key features

WITH PREFINISHED SOLID WOOD. Narrow boards are called strips; wide ones, planks. Most are ¾-inch thick or less. A finish layer protects the flooring from spills, stains, and wear. Thicker flooring is usually nailed to a plywood subfloor; thinner flooring is stapled or glued. Thinner flooring can also cover above-ground concrete using a vapor barrier. For nailing into wood, you'll need a manual or pneumatic nailer (about $20 per day to rent). You can usually refinish solid wood several times before it is sanded down to its tongue joints.

WITH ENGINEERED WOOD. A wear layer protects the wood veneer—usually ⅛-inch thick or less—on top of construction-grade plywood. Instead of the painstaking nailing needed to put down a solid-wood floor, engineered wood is usually stapled down (the most secure method) or glued to the subfloor, though sometimes it can be floated the way

A QUICK GUIDE TO REFINISHING FLOORS

Varnishing a floor is rigorous work. These tips can help you survive the three to four days you may need to cover a moderate-sized area.

WHEN TO WORK. Do the job in warm weather, since you'll need to open doors and windows for maximum ventilation. Don't rush. Try to work when humidity is low and rain isn't in the forecast, since high humidity extends drying time.

WHAT YOU'LL NEED. Buy a broomstick applicator, lamb's-wool pads, and brushes (natural bristle for solvent-based varnish, synthetic for water-based) for applying varnish to the floor's perimeter. You'll also need tack cloths; plenty of sandpaper in three grit levels, from coarse to fine; a sharp scraper for getting into corners; goggles; a dust mask; painters gloves; and mineral spirits for solvent-based cleanup (use plain water for water-based varnish). Also count on renting a drum sander, an edge sander, a wet/dry vac, and a buffer—about $110 per day for all four.

TOTAL COST. Expect to pay about $180 to $200 for varnish and supplies for a moderate-sized, 200-square-foot area. Figure on paying from $300 to $600 to have a flooring contractor do the work.

Steps to follow if you decide to do it yourself:

1. SETTING UP Move the furniture out and then sweep the floor. Seal off the area you're working in with drop cloths or old bed sheets to keep dust contained.

2. SANDING To remove old varnish and smooth the surface of the wood, pass the drum sander evenly over the old finishing, moving in smooth, straight lines parallel to the planks. Work in several passes, starting with coarse-grit sandpaper and progressing to fine-grit until the old finish is removed and the surface is smooth and even. Follow each pass of the drum sander with the edge sander along baseboards and other tight spots, using the same progression of sandpaper. Tips: Be sure the mechanism that holds each machine's sandpaper and dust collector is secure before leaving the rental shop. Keep all sanding machines moving while in use to prevent them from gouging the surface. Maintain even pressure and a steady pace. When starting or stopping, tilt the sanding portion upward. Also be sure to sweep up after each sanding pass to prevent damage from grit.

3. DUSTING After sanding, sweep up every trace of sawdust and grit, then follow up with a wet/dry vac so debris isn't trapped in the varnish. You can also use a household vacuum. Wipe up the last bits of dust with tack cloths. Tips: Before you dust, remove the bed sheets that sealed off the area to keep them from adding dust to the floor. Be sure to dust walls, door frames, and other spots throughout the area before applying varnish.

4. VARNISHING Open all windows and doors to maximize ventilation. Begin by brushing varnish around the floor perimeter and other hard-to-reach areas. Then pour a thin line of varnish at the point farthest from the door, running parallel to the wood planks, and spread it in a continuous line with the lamb's wool. Tips: Overlap each pass, angling the pad away from the area you just covered to push excess varnish onto the new area to get smoother results. Using a watering can may make it easier to pour varnish onto the floor.

5. BETWEEN COATS Prepare the fully dried surface for subsequent coats using a buffer or oscillating sander and fine-grit screen. Tips: Make sure the surface is dry by

SANDING

VACUUMING

BUFFING

VARNISHING

using your thumbnail to check that the film is hard. Then vacuum and dust the surface again with tack cloths before applying the next coat.

6. WRAP-UP When floors are dry, move furniture back in. Let varnish cure from 12 hours to a day or two before walking on it a lot.

plastic-laminate flooring is. You may be able to refinish engineered wood—by lightly sanding and varnishing it—at least once, depending on the thickness of its veneer. (Most manufacturers recommend that a professional do this.)

WITH PLASTIC LAMINATE. Here, too, a wear layer protects against spills, stains, and wear and covers the pattern layer—essentially a photograph of wood, tile, marble, slate, or some other material. A fiberboard core supports the top layers. Plastic-laminate planks are interlocked with or without glue and held in place by their own weight in what is called a floating floor. A foam layer goes between the laminate and the subfloor. A vapor barrier is recommended between the subfloor and the foam layer if moisture is a concern. An alternative approach is gluing the flooring to the subfloor. Once the wear layer becomes worn or damaged, it can't be sanded and refinished. You may be able to do minor touch-ups with kits sold by flooring manufacturers. If not, you'll have to replace the offending section or— if problems are widespread—the entire floor.

How to choose

PERFORMANCE DIFFERENCES. Most of the solid-wood products resisted spills very well in Consumer Reports tests, and they should be able to stand up to close encounters with party drinks and other common household liquids. In a long-term foot-traffic test, the laminates held up better than most solid wood flooring and all of the engineered wood flooring. Among the laminates, some brands were better than others in resisting denting, but all were much more dent-resistant than other types of flooring.

Plastic laminates proved impervious to stains from mustard, wine, and acidic liquids, although most of the solid-wood and engineered-wood flooring were close behind. All of the plastic-laminate products we tested came through hours of ultraviolet exposure in our lab with their original colors intact. Ultraviolet light from the sun and or from halogen lamps can change the color of real wood.

RECOMMENDATIONS. First determine whether you'll install the flooring yourself or hire a contractor. Your decision may affect which type of flooring you decide upon. Plastic-laminate flooring offers relatively easy installation and a tough surface for busy rooms. It mimics wood and other materials but is better at resisting abrasion, scratches, and dents than prefinished solid-wood flooring and engineered-wood flooring. One noticeable drawback of plastic laminate is its faux-wood pattern, which can look unnaturally consistent over a large area. With real wood, each strip or plank has its own unique grain.

Prefinished solid wood is less damage-resistant and harder to install (you may want to hire a pro), but it offers authenticity and warmth. It can also be refinished several times; damaged or worn plastic-laminate flooring must be replaced.

Engineered-wood flooring offers a true wood surface without the painstaking nailing needed to put down a solid-wood floor. Unlike most solid-wood flooring, an engineered-wood floor can go in a basement or other damp area because of the added dimensional stability of its layered construction.

But you won't save money by choosing an engineered floor; it costs about as much as solid wood and generally can't be refinished as often. Always purchase an extra box of flooring for future repairs.

Types of wood flooring

Plastic laminate

Engineered wood

Solid wood

Interior lighting

Lighting adds to the ambience of a room in two ways: the look of the fixtures and the light they throw off. Styles range from unobtrusive to dramatic.

Lighting choices have progressed far beyond soft-white, three-way bulbs in table lamps. Several different types of bulbs now deliver all the light you've grown accustomed to, and some can do it far more economically. You'll also find thousands of fixtures that can bathe a room in light, illuminate a small area, or focus light in a pinpoint beam. And prices range from a few dollars to a few thousand dollars.

What's available

Lighting stores, home centers, and even some well-stocked hardware stores carry a wide variety of lighting. There are three main categories.

AMBIENT. All rooms require ambient lighting for overall illumination. A collection of light sources is the traditional solution. How much ambient light you need depends largely on the activities in the room and the color of the walls. For example, a workshop needs bright, uniform lighting; a bedroom or foyer can be evenly but less brightly lit. Dark colors absorb light, so you need a lot more wattage with hunter green walls than with pale peach. Recessed ceiling fixtures are the usual choices for ambient light, although track lighting and wall-mounted sources are also good choices.

TASK. Rooms such as kitchens, family rooms, bedrooms, and bathrooms need task lighting to augment the ambient lighting. Kitchens may require a light fixture directly over the counter or the cooktop. Lights mounted under the front edge of cupboards provide shadow-free light for working.

In other rooms, a desk lamp helps with tasks such as paying bills, while a reading lamp lets you curl up with a good book. In the bathroom, good lighting around mirrors eliminates shadows so you can see what you're doing when shaving or applying makeup. Track lights and hanging ceiling fixtures are both excellent choices for task lighting.

ACCENT. This light plays up decorative elements—a painting, sculpture, or plant. It's a nice addition in a foyer, a formal living room, or a dining room. Accent lighting can show off china in a glass-front cabinet, or it can be installed above cabinets to soften their hard edges. Uplights, wall-washers, sconces, and track lighting can all provide effective accent lighting in a home.

Key features

Traditional **incandescent bulbs** are still the most commonly used in most homes—60 watt, three-way, soft white, and so on. They're inexpensive and typically last about 1,000 hours.

Halogen bulbs, unlike ordinary incandescent bulbs, are filled with a halogen gas. They're a bit pricier than regular incandescents, but they tend to last about 2,000 hours.

Introduced more than a decade ago, **compact fluorescents** are gaining popularity. These bulbs can last about 5,000 hours or more and now cost less than $10. They're three to four times more energy efficient than incandescent bulbs, with some providing about the same light as a 100-watt incandescent while using only about 25 to 30 watts. You could put one in a fixture designed for, say, a 60-watt incandescent bulb to safely increase light output.

How to choose

PERFORMANCE DIFFERENCES. You get what you pay for. Halogen bulbs produce intense, very white light that can bring out the colors in a room. Compact fluorescent bulbs are the priciest type, but they last longer than halogen or incandescent bulbs. The light of a compact fluorescent bulb is difficult to distinguish from that of an incandescent bulb. But the former needs some time to warm up to full brightness. And it may need to be used for 100 hours or so before its brightness level stabilizes. Some bulbs get a little brighter after that; some slightly dimmer.

A compact fluorescent bulb may interfere with the remote control of your TV set, VCR, or hi-fi system. It may also cause static in an AM radio or cordless phone.

RECOMMENDATIONS. When shopping for fixtures, don't limit your choices to what is on display. Most lighting stores have catalogs from the manufacturers and will order the fixtures you want. A special order lets you select the finish you want—brass, chrome, and so on.

Some utilities offer rebates for compact fluorescent bulbs. You can shorten the lives of compact fluorescent bulbs if you use them improperly, however. Many are not meant to be used with dimmer switches or outdoors.

Paint, exterior
The best paint can improve your home's appearance and protect it from the weather for up to 10 years.

While a fresh coat of paint on the siding and trim will give your house curb appeal, exterior paint isn't just for show. It provides an important layer of protection against moisture, mildew, and the drying effects of the sun.

What's available

Major brands include Ace, Behr (sold at Home Depot), Benjamin Moore, Dutch Boy, Glidden, Sears, Sherwin-Williams, True Value, and Valspar (sold at Lowe's). You'll also see many brands of paint sold regionally.

Exterior paints come in a variety of sheens. The dullest is flat, followed by low-luster (often called eggshell or satin), semigloss, and gloss. The flatter finishes are best for siding, with the lowest-sheen variety the best choice if you need to mask imperfections. Glossy paint is most often used for trim because it highlights the details of the woodwork and the paint is easy to clean.

Price range: $15 to $30 a gallon.

Key features

The choice of color affects a paint's longevity. Some pigments are inherently more vulnerable to the damaging effects of sunlight. Blues are the most likely to change color by fading or turning a greenish yellow. Yellowish-tan paints are also subject to color change.

How to choose

PERFORMANCE DIFFERENCES. Our tests of exterior paints are very severe, exposing painted panels on outdoor racks angled to catch the maximum amount of sun. One year of testing is approximately equal to three years of real-life exposure.

CONSUMER REPORTS tests have found that the grade of paint matters. "Good" or "economy" grades don't weather as well as top-of-the-line products. Using a cheaper grade of paint means you'll spend more time and money in the long run because you'll need to repaint more often. "Contractor" grades of paint that we've tested also tended to be mediocre.

Generally, most paints will look good for at least three years, and some should look good for about six. Most also do a good job of resisting the buildup of mildew and preventing the wood from cracking.

RECOMMENDATIONS. Only a few brands consistently perform well no matter what the color. They include M.A. Bruder and California, both sold mainly in the East, and the Glidden Spred Dura national brands.

Paint, interior

Plenty of high-quality, durable wall paints are available to brighten your rooms. And you won't need to endure as many fumes as in years past.

A fresh coat of paint is an easy, inexpensive way to freshen a room. Today's paints are significantly better than their predecessors of even a few years ago in several important respects: They spatter less, keep stains at bay, and have ample tolerance for scrubbing. They also resist the buildup of mildew (important if you're painting a kitchen, a bath, or a basement room that tends to be damp). Some are labeled low-VOC.

What's available

Major brands include Ace, Behr (sold at Home Depot), Benjamin Moore, Dutch Boy, Glidden, Sears, Sherwin-Williams, True Value, and Valspar (sold at Lowe's). You'll also see designer names such as Martha Stewart, Bob Vila, and Ralph Lauren, as well as many brands of paint sold regionally.

You'll find several types of paints for interior use. Wall paints can be used in just about any room. Glossier trim enamels are used for windowsills, woodwork, and the like. Kitchen and bath paints are usually fairly glossy and formulated to hold up to water and scrubbing and to release stains.

Price range: $15 to $30 per gallon.

Key features

Paint typically comes in a variety of sheens—**flat, low luster,** and **semigloss.** The degree of glossiness can be different from one manufacturer to another. Flat paint, with the dullest finish, is the best at hiding surface imperfections, but it also tends to pick up stains and may be marred by scrubbing. It's well suited for formal living rooms, dining rooms, and other spaces that don't see heavy use.

A low-luster finish (often called eggshell or satin) has a slight sheen and is good for family rooms, kids' rooms, hallways, and the like. Semigloss, shinier still, usually works best on kitchen and bathroom walls and on trim because it's generally easier to clean. Low-luster and semigloss paints look best on smooth, well-prepared surfaces, since the paint's shine can accentuate imperfections on the wall.

Most brands come in several tint bases—the uncolored paint that forms the foundation for the specific color you choose. The tint base largely determines the paint's toughness, resistance to dirt and stains, and ability to withstand scrubbing. The colorant determines how much the paint will fade. Whites and browns tend not to fade; reds and blues fade somewhat; bright greens and yellows tend to fade a lot.

Cures for the color blues

The right paint color can make the difference between a pleasing, inviting space and a room that no one ever really enjoys. If you can't change the room lighting, you'll have to change the paint, once you understand some basics about natural and artificial light.

■ Fluorescent light enhances blues and greens but makes warm reds, oranges, and yellows appear dull. The yellow glow of incandescent light enhances warm colors.

■ Sunlight changes throughout the day and throughout the year. A color that looks fine on a sunny day may be awful when the clouds roll in.

■ Northern light seems cool; southern light appears warm.

■ Wall texture and paint gloss also affect color. A glossy finish reflects more light, so colors look brighter. Flat paints and textured walls absorb light, so colors appear darker.

■ When you're planning colors, collect the largest color swatches you can find and tape them to the wall. That way, you can study them at different times of day and under different lighting conditions. It's often smart to buy a quart of a color and paint a test square on the wall.

How to choose

PERFORMANCE DIFFERENCES. CONSUMER REPORTS tests have shown that few paints hide the old color in one coat, so plan on applying two coats. Regular semigloss paints designed for kitchens and baths are formulated to be easy to clean; our tests show that some brands are especially stain resistant and handle scrubbing extremely well. Some semigloss paints can remain sticky even after they've dried, however, meaning flowerpots or other windowsill knick-knacks can get stuck to the surface.

Drying time is the biggest difference we've discovered between regular paints and those labeled low-VOC. Low-VOC paints dry very fast. You have to work quickly to avoid marks from overlapping roller strokes as well as brush marks around trim. Brushes and rollers may be harder to clean after applying a low-VOC paint.

RECOMMENDATIONS. Most paint manufacturers offer three levels of quality—essentially, good, better, and best.

Decades of CONSUMER REPORTS tests have clearly shown that it makes sense to buy top-of-the-line paints. Many of the leading brands produce paints that have delivered very good or excellent performance in our tests. The Behr and Valspar paints sold at Home Depot and Lowe's, respectively, make good all-around choices.

Roofing shingles

Many homeowners are opting for laminated shingles that mimic wood or slate, even though they cost and weigh more than the popular three-tab variety.

When replacing a roof, most people opt for three-tab or laminated fiberglass shingles (both are a type of asphalt shingle named after the substance that holds them together). In less than 10 years, extreme temperatures and sunlight can crack, curl, and split shingles, rain and sleet can wear them down, and wind can tear them apart. But they can last much longer—25 years or more—if you choose the right kind, and the right installation.

What's available

Major brands of asphalt shingles include CertainTeed, GAF, Tamko, and Owens Corning.

Asphalt shingles are essentially large rectangles made of fiberglass mats coated with asphalt. They are coated on the bottom surface with sand, talc, or other mineral fillers to make them stiff and to counter the asphalt's stickiness. The top surfaces are typically coated with granules colored with a hard ceramic glaze. These granules also protect the asphalt from the sun's ultraviolet rays and add weight to the shingle so it can better resist wind.

Since asphalt shingles first appeared more than 80 years ago, they've mostly been the same familiar three-tab format—a piece of shingle made of three 12-inch-wide tabs notched by slots. Shingles with a fiberglass mat, instead of the traditional organic mat, came out in the early 1970s and now account for the majority of asphalt shingles sold.

Laminated shingles (also called "architectural" or "dimensional") are a more expensive type of asphalt shingle. They commonly consist of two or more shingle layers laminated together to create a three-dimensional effect that mimics wood or slate in each laminated shingle. They tend to weigh more than three-tab fiberglass shingles.

The usual shingle size is 12x36 inches, though "metric" shingles (13x39 inches) are also available. Some brands use nonstandard sizes for their laminated shingles. Most manufacturers also offer shingles that have zinc or copper particles mixed in with the surface granules. These metal oxides help prevent the formation of algae, which can be a problem in some regions. Homeowners who have seen black streaking on their roof should consider algae-resistant shingles for their next replacement.

Shingles are sold in "bundles" that typically contain one-third "square" of three-tab shingles (a square is enough to cover 100 square feet) and one-fourth square of laminated shingles.

Price range: $30 to $60 per square (190 to 240 pounds per square) for three-tab; $40 to $140 per square (260 to 450 pounds per square) for laminated.

How to choose

PERFORMANCE DIFFERENCES. While laminated shingles did better than three-tab shingles overall in CONSUMER REPORTS tests, the best three-tab shingles rival the best laminates

---

— UP ON THE ROOF —

The roofing you choose affects longevity and affordability. The table below shows how economical fiberglass shingles are compared with other choices. We've based the comparison on the labor charges and the 3,100 square feet of material needed to roof a 2,300-square-foot house, including the garage and porch. (For fiberglass, the range uses the price of a CR Best Buy three-tab shingle at one extreme, the average price of laminated fiberglass at the other.)

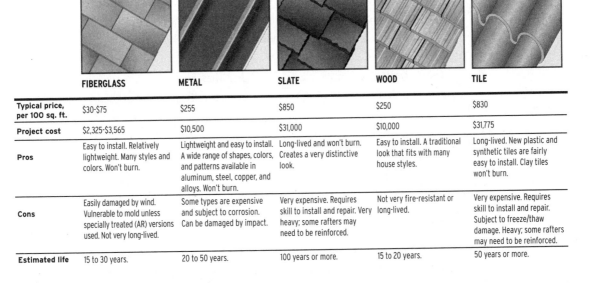

	FIBERGLASS	METAL	SLATE	WOOD	TILE
Typical price, per 100 sq. ft.	$30-$75	$255	$850	$250	$830
Project cost	$2,325-$3,565	$10,500	$31,000	$10,000	$31,775
Pros	Easy to install. Relatively lightweight. Many styles and colors. Won't burn.	Lightweight and easy to install. A wide range of shapes, colors, and patterns available in aluminum, steel, copper, and alloys. Won't burn.	Long-lived and won't burn. Creates a very distinctive look.	Easy to install. A traditional look that fits with many house styles.	Long-lived. New plastic and synthetic tiles are fairly easy to install. Clay tiles won't burn.
Cons	Easily damaged by wind. Vulnerable to mold unless specially treated (AR) versions used. Not very long-lived.	Some types are expensive and subject to corrosion. Can be damaged by impact.	Very expensive. Requires skill to install and repair. Very heavy; some rafters may need to be reinforced.	Not very fire-resistant or long-lived.	Very expensive. Requires skill to install and repair. Subject to freeze/thaw damage. Heavy; some rafters may need to be reinforced.
Estimated life	15 to 30 years.	20 to 50 years.	100 years or more.	15 to 20 years.	50 years or more.

Except as noted, cost-data research by RSMeans, a product line of Reed Construction Data, a leading provider of construction-information products. Data for house size and required materials provided by the National Association of Home Builders, an industry trade group.

in performance and cost as little as $30 per square. They can be a satisfactory choice if you're looking to curb costs.

Three-tab shingles generally have a 20- to 30-year prorated warranty. Some manufacturers also provide full-replacement value for 10 years. Prorated warranties for laminated shingles often run even longer—sometimes for the life of the house.

RECOMMENDATIONS. Fiberglass shingles are a long-term investment, both from a quality and aesthetic standpoint. When deciding to put on a new roof, consider how long you'll stay in your house. If it's only a few years—and the existing roof isn't that bad—you may want to let the next owner take on this expense. And even if you'll be staying there for a while, consider how the shingles you choose will affect your home's resale value down the road. That may mean balancing your personal taste with the need for your home to fit in with others in the neighborhood.

New shingles can be placed over a single existing layer that doesn't show signs of damage. (Look for damage from within the attic, or check topside for soft spots or undulations.) Don't add a third layer; the rafters may not support the weight and it may be illegal in some locales. Shingles should be nailed (four nails per shingle in most areas, six where it's windy), not stapled.

Even the best fiberglass shingles won't last if the plywood or solid-board sheathing beneath them is in poor shape. When installing new shingles, replace any rotted, warped, or split sheathing. Also replace or reinforce any rafters that are badly cracked or bowed. Proper attic ventilation is also a key to long-lived roof shingles, since excess heat buildup can hasten their deterioration. Have the installer eliminate any air-flow obstructions around the soffit, ridge, and gable-end vents.

Replace all roof underlayment and flashing when a complete tear-off of old roofing is done. Buy an extra bundle of shingles so you'll have matching shingles handy for spot repairs.

Before you sign the dotted line, see that the contract spells out all details. Ask the roofing contractor for the shingle manufacturer's warranty—especially the full-reimbursement period, which is more meaningful than the total warranty. And keep a wrapper from one of the bundles of shingles so you can identify exactly what was installed should you need to use the warranty.

Many brands are now "certifying" installers who can offer a labor warranty at an additional cost. Be sure to obtain proof of this certification from the installer.

Siding

New siding ranks high on the payback scale. You may recoup more than 70 percent of your investment should you decide to sell your home.

Sooner or later, most houses need new siding, either because the old siding has deteriorated or because you want something that's easier to maintain. While you can choose nearly anything that sheds water and blocks drafts, vinyl siding is by far the most popular option, accounting for about half of all siding sold. In fact, it has virtually eliminated aluminum as an option.

What's available

Siding materials are sold at lumberyards and, increasingly, home centers. Here are the most common choices:

VINYL. Leading brands include Alcoa, Alside, CertainTeed (which also makes Wolverine and Ashland-Davis products), Crane, Georgia-Pacific, Heartland, LP Vinyl Siding, Napco, Reynolds, and Royal Building Products.

Universal quality standards that require consistent thickness and industry-standard levels of resistance to fading and wind have helped raise the bar for this popular material. Vinyl is easy to work with and requires little maintenance. It generally holds color well and comes in many colors, textures, and profiles. It can't match wood, however, for showing fine trim details. And vinyl siding may crack in extreme cold if struck by a hard object.

Price per square foot uninstalled: about $0.45 to $1.90.

WOOD SHINGLES/CLAPBOARD. Both of these materials offer the appeal of real wood (usually cedar or pine) and traditional styling, and can be stained, painted, or left natural. They are also available already primed or painted, which can be a real convenience. Both shingles and clapboard are durable and tend to resist impacts, even in cold weather. One downside is the amount of maintenance these choices require if painted or stained, plus they can be damaged by water and insects.

Price per square foot uninstalled: about $0.70 to $3.45.

FIBER CEMENT. Providing the look of wood but requiring less maintenance, fiber-cement siding is starting to supplant the natural stuff. This cement-based product with reinforcing fibers shouldn't need to be repainted as frequently as wood and resists impacts and insects. But it's relatively brittle, and can be damaged if water gets absorbed and then freezes.

Price per square foot uninstalled: about $0.85 to $2.55.

MASONRY. This classic siding option includes brick, stucco, and stone. Pluses include low maintenance and resistance to impacts and insects. On the downside, it's pricey, requires periodic refinishing if painted, and may, like fiber cement, be damaged by freezing water. Brick veneers require periodic repointing (removing and replacing old, crumbling mortar), while cracks in stucco will also need to be repaired.

Price per square foot uninstalled: about $2.45 to $10 or more.

SIMULATED STUCCO. An alternative to cement-based stucco, this polymer-based product resists insects and creates a waterproof barrier when properly applied. Simulated stucco can trap moisture, however—a problem that has resulted in litigation by some home-

CLOSE-UP

MORE DEPTH
Deeper-profile siding (left) looks more like wood and appears straighter than shallow-profile siding.

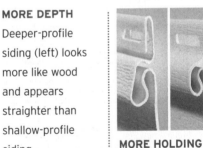

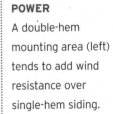

MORE HOLDING POWER
A double-hem mounting area (left) tends to add wind resistance over single-hem siding.

GOOD FORM
Added bends gave the few dutchlap styles we tested (right) more rigidity than clapboard styles of the same model.

owners. What's more, it may fade or require refinishing, can be damaged by impacts, and is expensive to install.

Price per square foot uninstalled: about $1.80 to $2.40.

Key features

Vinyl siding offers a variety of colors and trim accessories, along with surface textures that include wood-grain, smooth, and simulated brush strokes. Shapes or profiles include a single 8-inch "lap" board per strip, along with double and triple laps, dutchlap, and even simulated shingles and shakes. Double-hem mounting areas tend to provide more attachment strength than single-hem systems.

Wood shingles and clapboard come in a variety of widths and thicknesses, and in rough or smooth surface textures.

Fiber-cement siding includes different profiles and surface textures, while masonry includes a variety of brick, stone, and stucco styles.

How to choose

PERFORMANCE DIFFERENCES. While vinyl-siding manufacturers often tout thickness as an attribute, CONSUMER REPORTS tests have shown that color retention and rigidity are more important in helping some vinyl siding look better than others.

Wood shingles and clapboard provide a traditional look many like, but require considerable upkeep.

SIDING CHOICES

Weigh the look you like against price and upkeep. The table below compares vinyl with four other common choices, based on the 3,200 square feet of siding needed to cover the average new 2,300-square-foot house. To choose the right siding for your needs, balance its appearance against its cost and maintenance requirements. Expect to add at least $3,000 for painting or staining. You'll also pay extra for removing old siding and other related work.

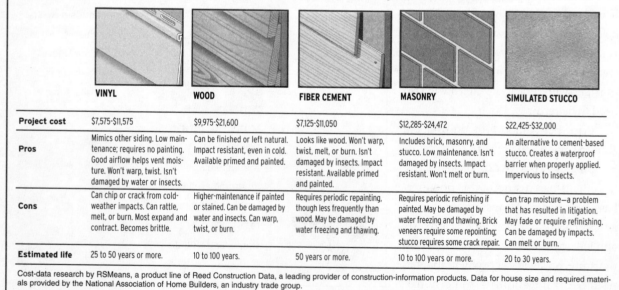

	VINYL	WOOD	FIBER CEMENT	MASONRY	SIMULATED STUCCO
Project cost	$7,575-$11,575	$9,975-$21,600	$7,125-$11,050	$12,285-$24,472	$22,425-$32,000
Pros	Mimics other siding. Low maintenance; requires no painting. Good airflow helps vent moisture. Won't warp, twist. Isn't damaged by water or insects.	Can be finished or left natural. Impact resistant, even in cold. Available primed and painted.	Looks like wood. Won't warp, twist, melt, or burn. Isn't damaged by insects. Impact resistant. Available primed and painted.	Includes brick, masonry, and stucco. Low maintenance. Isn't damaged by insects. Impact resistant. Won't melt or burn.	An alternative to cement-based stucco. Creates a waterproof barrier when properly applied. Impervious to insects.
Cons	Can chip or crack from cold-weather impacts. Can rattle, melt, or burn. Most expand and contract. Becomes brittle.	Higher-maintenance if painted or stained. Can be damaged by water and insects. Can warp, twist, or burn.	Requires periodic repainting, though less frequently than wood. May be damaged by water freezing and thawing.	Requires periodic refinishing if painted. May be damaged by water freezing and thawing. Brick veneers require some repointing; stucco requires some crack repair.	Can trap moisture—a problem that has resulted in litigation. May fade or require refinishing. Can be damaged by impacts. Can melt or burn.
Estimated life	25 to 50 years or more.	10 to 100 years.	50 years or more.	10 to 100 years or more.	20 to 30 years.

Cost-data research by RSMeans, a product line of Reed Construction Data, a leading provider of construction-information products. Data for house size and required materials provided by the National Association of Home Builders, an industry trade group.

Fiber-cement siding is a lower-cost, easier-maintenance option, while masonry and simulated stucco provide classic good looks and little upkeep—but are costly to install.

Professional installation adds at least as much to the project cost as the materials, though rates vary enough to warrant getting several estimates.

RECOMMENDATIONS. Consider vinyl first if, like many people, you want a moderately priced, low-maintenance siding. And choose the color from actual siding samples, since colors in catalogs may not be accurate.

Be sure the contractor who installs the siding is properly licensed, if applicable, and is insured for workers' compensation and liability. And have the contractor fix uneven or rotting sections of wall before putting up the new siding. If existing siding is made with asbestos and you want it removed, consult an asbestos-abatement contractor.

Sinks

Unless unique shapes or exotic materials are must-haves, you can find high quality in low-priced enamel, stainless-steel, and acrylic models.

Whether you're looking to add a bit of character to your kitchen or simply replace a chipped porcelain sink, you'll find a plethora of styles, colors, and finishes to suit your needs.

What's available

Choices include enamel finishes, stainless steel, and polyester or acrylic resins. In most home centers and plumbing-supply stores, you'll find brands such as American Standard, Eljer, Elkay, Kohler, and Moen.

Price does not relate to quality or durability, so this is one place in a kitchen makeover where you can save a few bucks. The more expensive sinks are usually made of enamel over cast iron, heavy-gauge stainless steel (the lower the gauge number, the thicker the steel), or solid-surface resins made to mimic granite, marble, and other natural materials.

Less expensive models are typically enamel on steel, thin-gauge stainless, or an acrylic-resin film that looks like enamel over a molded fiberglass substrate.

Key features

Bowl depth typically ranges from about 6 to 10 inches. More depth means more room to wash and rinse big things like mixing bowls. A deep bowl also means more protection from splashing. **Drains** can be centered or positioned to the rear of the bowl. The latter provides more clearance and more flexible storage in the cabinet below.

Stainless-steel models with **sound-deadening pads** on the underside muffle the sounds of dish clatter best. Enamel on iron surfaces are noisiest. All types deaden the sound of running water to some extent.

Sinks designed with a rim around the top simply drop into a hole cut into the counter-top surface. Those without a rim install under the counter, which requires different mounting methods and more skill.

How to choose

Kitchen décor is an obvious influence. A stainless-steel sink is a good choice if you want to emulate the pro style. For a more traditional look, consider enameled or acrylic-resin sinks; they come in a wide range of colors. Solid-surface can be made to merge seamlessly with countertops and backsplashes.

PERFORMANCE DIFFERENCES. All surfaces resist staining well, even when stubborn stains, such as a tea bag or mustard, sit for hours. Stainless steel requires a bit more scrubbing than other types, but it will come clean. Drain cleaner can be difficult to remove from enamel finishes.

Enamel-coated and stainless-steel surfaces resist scratches well and won't be burned by a hot pot. CONSUMER REPORTS engineers found that a $400 enamel-over-cast-iron sink can chip just as easily as a $100 enamel-on-steel one. And an expensive stainless-steel model can dent as readily as less-expensive models.

The color of a solid-surface sink runs throughout the material, so you can also buff out superficial scratches or burns. Dropping a very heavy object on some solid-surface sinks can cause them to shatter. If that happens, you'll have to replace the sink.

Acrylic-resin sinks don't chip and are least likely to dent or break under impact. Scratches show up, and they can't be buffed away. Hot pots can cause permanent damage to the surface.

RECOMMENDATIONS. You can probably find the look you want and the function you need for $100 to $200. Choices in this price range include enamel over steel, thin-gauge stainless steel, and acrylic.

High-priced models—such as heavy-gauge steel, enamel over iron, and solid-surface sinks—range from about $200 to $450. Beyond aesthetics, functionally there is no point in paying a premium for thick-gauge stainless or enamel over cast iron.

Toilets

Low-flush toilets use 1.6 gallons of water per flush and are the only toilets on the market today. Still, performance varies among models and brands.

Some of the first low-flush toilets on the market earned a reputation for being problematic because they required two or more flushes to do their job—and often clogged in the process.

Many of the newer models that were tested work quite well on a single flush. But there are large differences in performance—even within a given brand.

What's available

Most major manufacturers offer an extensive array of models in different designs and colors and in a range of prices.

Gravity-flush toilets are the most common design. They work like old-fashioned toilets, using water pouring from the tank to clear the bowl and push waste down the drain. The performance of some gravity-flush toilets no doubt contributed to the conventional wisdom that low-flush toilets generally clogged or needed two flushes. While some that we tested recently worked well, others didn't do a very good job of clearing solid waste. This type of toilet is fairly easy to install and inexpensive to maintain.

Pressure-assist toilets use a pressure tank to force water into the bowl. They work very well as long as household water pressure is at least 25 pounds per square inch. Pressure-assisted toilets tend to be pricey and noisy. Their raucous whoosh can be disconcerting.

Vacuum-assist models work well and quietly, but there aren't many on the market. This type of toilet uses a vacuum chamber inside the tank to help pull water and waste down the drain. Vacuum-assist toilets use the same kind of early-closing flush and fill valves that gravity-flush toilets do, so they're simple to maintain.

Gravity-flush models tend to be the least expensive. Vacuum-assist models cost more. Pressure-assist toilets are at the high end of the price range, generally $300 or more. Within types, more money does not buy better performance, just more upscale design.

Price range: $100 to $600 (colors cost more).

Key features

Bathroom remodeling is the most common reason to buy a new toilet. Depending upon the configuration of the new bathroom, you may want a round-front or elongated **bowl.** A round-front style is generally a better choice for a small bathroom than an elongated one. Two-piece designs, with a tank that bolts onto the bowl, are less expensive than one-piece designs. Toilets are available in several different "rough-in" dimensions—the clearance to the back wall needed to connect to the water line. The most common rough-in is 12 inches.

How to choose

PERFORMANCE DIFFERENCES. A gravity flush toilet is a good choice for bathrooms near bedrooms where quiet is important. Pressure-assist models might be best reserved for powder rooms some distance from the bedrooms, and in households with strong enough water pressure. Vacuum assist should work well in any bathroom in the house.

RECOMMENDATIONS. If you're shopping for a new toilet, decide if you want a gravity flush, vacuum assist, or pressure assist model. A pressure-assist toilet should be the choice when clogging is a concern. You can make any older toilet more water-efficient by placing a water-filled bottle in the tank or installing a special flapper valve. Those measures are likely to worsen flushing performance, however.

Ratings: Page 267

How the main toilet types work

GRAVITY

The tried-and-true mechanism, which depends on water dropping from the tank into the bowl and trap to move waste down the drain.

PRESSURE ASSISTED

The china covers a tank of pressurized water. It expands with a loud whoosh when you flush, adding force to help push waste away. Most work mechanically. Noise is the biggest drawback of a pressure-assist toilet.

VACUUM ASSISTED

A vacuum chamber inside the tank works like a siphon to pull air out of the trap below the bowl so that it can quickly fill with water to clear waste.

Wallpaper

You'll find a broad array of colors, patterns, and textures. Vinyl-coated paper, which is relatively durable and easy to clean, is the popular choice of material.

Wallpaper, or wall covering, offers myriad decorating solutions. It can do things that paint can't. It can make a high-rise living room feel like a country cottage or give a small foyer the look of an art-deco stage set. Wallpaper can also hide some minor flaws in imperfect walls and add architectural interest to boring, boxy rooms.

What's available

Wallpaper is sold in home centers, paint-and-wallpaper stores, and decorator showrooms. You can also buy it on the Internet. A single manufacturer—Imperial Home Décor Group—makes about half the wallpaper brands. Another big chunk of the market, including the Village and Waverly brands, belongs to F. Schumacher. Other wallpaper makers include Blonder, Brewster Wallcovering, Eisenhart Wallcoverings, and York Wall Coverings.

The price you see in a book, on a display, or on an Internet site isn't the price you pay. The stated price is for a single roll. But wallpaper doesn't come in single rolls. It comes in double and triple rolls that look like single rolls. You probably won't have to pay double or triple the stated price, though. Retailers commonly discount wallpaper by 30, 40, or 50 percent or more. Expect to cover about 60 to 70 square feet per double roll.

Widths vary. So-called American rolls range from 18 to 36 inches wide; more often than not they are 27 inches wide. Euro, or metric, rolls are generally 20 to 21 inches wide.

Wall covering comes in three basic types at a broad range of prices:

PLAIN PAPER. This type of wall covering—often a reproduction of an antique pattern—is expensive, largely because it's usually made in limited quantities, printed in small mills, or even handcrafted. Plain paper has no protective coating, so it can't tolerate scrubbing.

VINYL. Most wallpaper is paper or fabric coated with vinyl. It may be called paper-backed vinyl, vinyl-coated paper, expanded or textured vinyl, or even (incorrectly) solid vinyl. Vinyl by any of its names is the most widely sold wall covering because it's the easiest to hang and relatively simple to maintain. Many vinyl wallpapers are prepasted—the adhesive is activated when you wet the paper.

FABRIC AND GRASS CLOTH. If you have the money (and decorator connections, and a very tidy family), you can cover your walls in pure silk. But you're more likely to find grass cloth—heavily textured wall covering made of jute, linen, or grasses, woven and bonded to backing. Grass cloth is fairly expensive and difficult to install.

Key features

Many patterns have a **repeat,** which is the vertical distance between repetitions of an image on the roll. The repeat can be less than an inch to more than two feet. A large repeat may mean lots of wasted paper. Failing to properly match the pattern means amateurish results. When considering left-to-right alignment, a **random match** will be the most cost-effective. It matches no matter how adjoining strips of paper are aligned.

A **straight match** is easy to cut and align because the pattern follows a straight horizontal line. You do have to allow for the pattern repeat, though. A **drop match** means that the pattern on the left edge of the paper isn't the same as the pattern parallel to it on the right. So when you hang a new sheet, you have to position it, or "drop" it, to align the design.

Pretrimmed means there's no extra blank white paper on the edges of the roll. That's handy because it's a chore to trim that excess perfectly straight. **Strippable** products leave a minimum of adhesive behind, so it's easy to clean off the wall if you decide to switch to paint. With **peelable** wall coverings, a thin layer of the backing is left on the wall to serve as a liner for new wallpaper.

How to choose

PERFORMANCE DIFFERENCES. Wall coverings hold up to wear and tear in various ways. Resistance to staining depends on the construction. Plain-paper wall coverings are vulnerable. You have a better chance of removing stains from vinyls, but they aren't impervious. Resistance to fading depends largely on the color of the wallpaper, not the brand or type. CONSUMER REPORTS has found that wall coverings with a lot of bright-yellow pigment (including some greens, oranges, and beiges) fade the most.

Most of the vinyls we've tested held up impressively to scrubbing with a soft nylon brush. Plain paper, which can't tolerate scrubbing, may be labeled "spongeable" or "wipable." But watch out when using cleaning products. In CONSUMER REPORTS tests, a nonabrasive bleaching cleanser left faded areas on several brands. An ammonia-based spray cleaner left spots on several darker patterns.

RECOMMENDATIONS. The easiest type to hang is vinyl—it holds up well and is often easy to handle. The easiest patterns to hang are large florals, toiles, and random patterns. A pattern with a random match, a straight match, or a short drop match will give you the fewest headaches. Beware of stripes; if walls aren't perfectly straight where they meet in corners or at the ceiling, stripes will emphasize the problem. Grass cloth is easy to stain while hanging. The reflective surface of foils calls attention to every flaw. Dark colors may show the white backing if seams are less than perfect.

Ask for sizable samples to take home, even if you have to pay a small fee for them. Hang the swatches on a wall to see how the wallpaper will look in the room at different times of the day and at night.

Some retailers substitute their own model numbers for the manufacturers' numbers to frustrate comparison shopping. You can often overcome this, however, if you have the name of the sample book and the page number of the pattern.

If you plan to hire someone to hang wallpaper for you, get at least three estimates. The amount that contractors charge varies by region.

Some Web sites (such as *usawallpaper.com* and *doit yourself.com*) offer free calculation pages to help you estimate the number of rolls you'll need for a job. Because colors can vary from one production run to another, it's best to buy all the wallpaper you'll need at the same time, and to make sure all the rolls have the same run number. Buy an extra roll or two, in case you make a mistake, or for future repairs.

Well-matched

A pattern with a drop match (top) takes careful alignment. A pattern with a straight match (bottom) aligns horizontally.

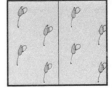

Windows

Upgrading to energy-efficient windows will likely improve your comfort and your home's aesthetics, but it will take years to recoup the initial outlay from energy savings.

You'll probably want to install new windows when you're remodeling, when the old ones have deteriorated, or when you want windows that are easier to wash and maintain.

Modern windows incorporate a frame made of all-vinyl or wood, the latter often covered in vinyl or aluminum, with two panes of glass.

To cut energy use, those panes are separated with air or another gas and sometimes specially coated. Improved comfort in the summer and winter is the major benefit, and slightly reduced heating or cooling costs will be an added bonus.

What's available

Window styles include double hung, sliding, hopper, awning, casement, and bay. The major brands are American Craftsman, Andersen, CertainTeed, Crestline, Marvin, Pella, Simonton (which also makes Sears models), and Weather Shield.

Some brands are sold at home centers such as Home Depot, Lowe's, and Menards. But most brands, including Sears, are typically purchased by contractors through distributors. Some windows come in custom sizes; others in stock sizes only. The materials that make a window frame can affect energy efficiency, maintenance, and price.

Price range: $150 to more than $400 for 3x5-foot, double-hung, double glazed windows.

VINYL. These frames are easy to maintain, but they aren't usually available in many colors. And they are sometimes difficult to match with existing woodwork. Vinyl windows are often sold as a low-cost choice. Many were lower-performing models in our tests.

ALUMINUM. As vinyl frames have become more popular, aluminum frames have become less

---

┌─ HOW TO DECODE LABELS ─┐

Standardized labels are supposed to make it easier to shop for windows, but use is not universal.

THE NFRC LABEL. Alaska, California, Florida, Massachusetts, Minnesota, Oregon, Washington, and Wisconsin require windows to be certified by the National Fenestration Rating Council. In other states, many certified products bear the NFRC label even though it's not required. On the label are figures for U-factor, solar-heat-gain coefficient, and visible-light transmittance, each ranging from zero to 1. U-factor is a measure of thermal performance that describes a window's ability to conduct heat. The inverse of the U-factor—the R-factor—describes insulating ability. The higher the R-factor (or the lower the U-factor), the better a window will keep your home cool in summer and warm in winter.

SOLAR-HEAT-GAIN COEFFICIENT refers to the amount of sunlight that radiates through the windows from outdoors. A high number means the window allows the sunlight's heat to get indoors—a desirable trait in a northern Minnesota winter but thoroughly unwelcome in a Houston summer.

VISIBLE-LIGHT TRANSMITTANCE refers to the amount of visible light entering a room. A window with a high number will allow in more light.

THE ENERGY STAR LABEL. So far, only a few manufacturers participate in the federally sponsored Energy Star label program. The label digests the data from the NFRC label and identifies a window as suitable for a specific region. You need only look at the map on the Energy Star label to see whether the window is appropriate for your area. However, not all windows have the Energy Star label. Many unlabeled windows may actually be more energy efficient.

so. The biggest drawback is that they allow heat to escape. That can make the area around the window chilly. In places with cold winters, a simple aluminum frame can become cold enough to condense moisture or frost on the inside, but where winters are mild, aluminum can be a good choice for its durability. If you are set on buying aluminum-framed windows, choose ones that have "thermally broken" frames, with insulating material between interior and exterior components.

WOOD. For elegance, wood is difficult to beat, although it usually costs more than vinyl and requires painting or staining and other maintenance. To minimize maintenance where it's usually needed most—the exterior side—many manufacturers cover, or clad, the wood in vinyl or aluminum. Wood composite frames—some made from a mixture of wood fibers and plastic resins—are supposed to combine the durability of wood with the low upkeep of plastics.

Anatomy of an energy-efficient window

The frame of a low-maintenance energy-efficient window is typically made of vinyl or of wood clad in vinyl or aluminum. Glazing usually consists of two panes of glass sealed around the edges and often treated with a low-E coating. In CONSUMER REPORTS tests, most windows appeared to be well-made but differed in their ability to withstand temperature extremes, wind, and rain.

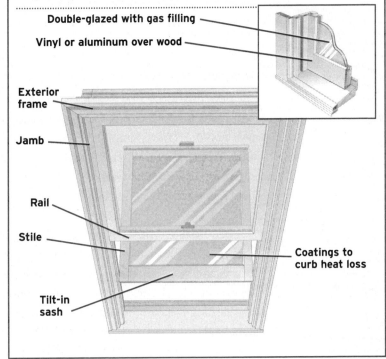

Double-glazed with gas filling
Vinyl or aluminum over wood
Exterior frame
Jamb
Rail
Stile
Tilt-in sash
Coatings to curb heat loss

Key features

Three types of glazing are commonly available: single, double, and triple. A single pane of glass, or single-glazed, allows the highest transfer of energy and offers little insulation against frigid winters and searing summers. **Double-glazed** windows have two panes of glass. A few manufacturers offer **triple glazing.**

The gas between the glass has a bearing on the quality of insulation. Plain old air works fine and is standard for some brand lines. **Argon gas,** which provides better thermal performance, is standard in other brand lines; sometimes it is a step-up option. A few top-of-the-line windows incorporate **krypton gas,** which provides incrementally better insulation.

Double- and triple-glazed windows are sealed assemblies so they retain any special gas between the panes and also keep out moisture, which can condense between the panes. Should the seal fail, moisture, water droplets, and fogging between the glass panes can occur.

Clear glass lets a relatively large amount of radiant energy (heat in from the sun during the summer, heat out from your home during the winter) to pass through. **Low-E coatings** (the "E" stands for emissivity, or the ability of a surface to emit heat) enhance the insulation quality of a window by making it reflect heat.

These coatings reduce some of the visible light that passes through the glass and may give a tinted appearance. The view out at night may be impeded somewhat. The coatings can be fine-tuned for different climates—a southern or a northern window, for example.

Most new double-hung windows have **tilting sashes,** a very handy feature that lets you pivot them inward for easier cleaning. With most, you simply flip a lever or two to tilt the sash inward. But with some, you must pull the sash out of the track.

Mullions are decorative vertical elements that separate panes of glass. To help keep out water, some windows have a thin **lip**—a strip of wood or vinyl about an inch high—that rises from the sill. You'll need to work around it when installing a room air conditioner.

How to choose

PERFORMANCE DIFFERENCES. CONSUMER REPORTS has found most windows do a very good or excellent job at sealing out a fairly strong wind when the outside thermometer registers 70° F. Only a handful do well at sealing out a high wind when the outside temperature drops to zero. When it's that cold, weather stripping and other components can stiffen or shrink. Our tests have shown that aluminum frames are durable. But we have found windows with frames made of vinyl- or aluminum-clad wood can perform well, too.

RECOMMENDATIONS. If you're replacing windows, choose those that are designed for your region's climate. Cooling costs predominate in southern regions, so look for double glazing and a low-E coating. Give first consideration to windows with a low solar-heat-gain coefficient. The Department of Energy recommends that the number be 0.4 or lower.

Heating bills are of concern in northern regions. Give priority to well-insulated, double-glazed windows that are draft-free. A low-E coating isn't essential in places where summers aren't particularly hot. In central regions, both heating and cooling are concerns. As in southern regions, look for double glazing and a low-E coating. You'll also want high insulating performance and a solar-heat-gain coefficient of 0.55 or lower.

Heating, Cooling, & Filtering

The quality of the indoor air we breathe and the tap water we drink remains a concern for many. To address these concerns, there is an array of filtering products on the market, many of which do the job quite well. Before buying, however, consumers should make sure they truly need these products. If you're buying equipment for heating or cooling your home, you need to compare the premium you'll pay for the most energy-efficient model with the savings it will bring.

Air cleaners

Whole-house and single-room air cleaners have limitations, but both types can provide relief from some indoor pollutants when other measures don't work.

Indoor air is more polluted than the air on the other side of the window, according to estimates by the U.S. Environmental Protection Agency. Further, the American

Certification

The Association of Home Appliance Manufacturers certification label for portable air cleaners gives the clean-air delivery rate (CADR)–measured at the high fan setting in cubic feet per minute–for dust, tobacco smoke, and pollen. The higher the CADR, the faster a machine will clean the air. CONSUMER REPORTS conducts tests at the low and high settings.

Lung Association cites indoor pollution as a health hazard for millions of Americans with asthma or allergies. Indoor pollutants may include visible particles of dust, pollen, and smoke, as well as invisible combustion by-products such as carbon monoxide and nitrous oxide, along with other gaseous invaders such as fumes from carpet adhesives and upholstery.

Two commonsense solutions are ensuring proper ventilation and controlling the pollutant at the source. If dust is a problem, you might want to replace wall-to-wall carpeting with bare floors or area rugs, which won't trap allergens. Frequent vacuuming may help, though some vacuum cleaners stir up dust. You can lessen the effects of pet dander by designating pet-free rooms, particularly bedrooms. A properly vented range hood can rid kitchen air of smoke and odors, while an exhaust fan in a bathroom can help squelch mold, mildew, and odors.

Air cleaners may be the next step when those measures aren't enough. But only people with respiratory problems are likely to benefit from using such devices. Even then, experts say, air cleaners may not be consistently effective. Don't rely on an air cleaner to protect you from carbon monoxide, odors, viruses, or dust mites.

If your house has forced-air heating and cooling, choose an appropriate whole-house furnace filter or professionally installed cleaner for your system. If your house doesn't have forced-air heating and cooling, your only option is a room air cleaner.

What's available

WHOLE-HOUSE AIR CLEANERS. Major brands include Aprilaire, Honeywell, Lennox, Trane, and Trion. Whole-house cleaners range from inexpensive fiberglass furnace filters to electronic precipitators, which must be installed professionally in a home's duct system.

Furnace filters range from plain matted-fiberglass (about $1), meant to trap large particles of dust and lint, to electrostatically charged pleated filters ($15 to $25) designed to attract pollen, lint, pet dander, and dust.

Electronic-precipitator air cleaners impart an electrical charge to particles flowing through them, then collect the particles on oppositely charged metal plates or filters. These more elaborate systems must be fitted into ductwork and wired into the house's current. Most have a collector-plate assembly that must be removed and washed every one to two months.

Price: about $400, plus $200 or more for installation.

ROOM AIR CLEANERS. Sharper Image has surpassed other brands as the market leader. Other notable brands include Bionaire, Friedrich, Holmes, Honeywell, Hunter, and Whirlpool. Most room air cleaners weigh between 10 and 20 pounds. They can be round or boxy, and can stand on the floor or on a table.

Room air cleaners can work quite well, even on dust and cigarette-smoke particles, which are much smaller and harder to trap than pollen and mold spores. They aren't good at trapping gases, however.

Two technologies predominate. The most common is a filter system in which a high-efficiency particulate air (HEPA) filter mechanically strains the air of fine particles. The other dominant technology uses an electronic precipitator that works like those in some whole-house systems, with a fan to move air through them.

The Association of Home Appliance Manufacturers (AHAM), a trade group, tests and rates room air cleaners using a measurement known as clean air delivery rate (CADR), which is determined by how well a filter traps particles and how much air the unit moves. Separate CADRs are listed for dust, tobacco smoke, and pollen. (While most manufacturers participate in this voluntary program, some models do not have an AHAM-certified performance rating.) We've typically found the AHAM-certified CADRs to be accurate. If whole-house air cleaners and filters are labeled, they carry a minimum efficiency reporting value (MERV). The higher the MERV, the better for trapping small particles.

Price range: $110 to $600. Annual filter cost: $30 to $220.

Key features

Whole-house air cleaners generally are available in a range of standard sizes. Some manufacturers say their filters are treated with a special antimicrobial agent, presumably to prevent bacterial growth on the filter. We've not evaluated those claims.

Room air cleaners typically use a **fan** to pull air into the unit for filtration. Some models with an electronic precipitator or a HEPA filter incorporate **ionizing circuitry** that uses powered needles or wires to charge particles, which are more easily trapped by the filter. But this ionization may also make the particles stick to walls or furnishings, possibly soiling them. The process of ionizing particles also creates ozone, which can be a respiratory irritant. An **indicator** in most models lets you know when to change the filter.

HEPA filters are supposed to be replaced annually and can cost more than $100—sometimes as much as the room air cleaner itself. **Prefilters,** which are designed to remove odors and/or larger particles, are generally changed quarterly, while washable prefilters should be cleaned monthly. An electronic precipitator's **collector-plate assembly** must be removed and washed every month or so; it slides out like a drawer, and you can put it in a dishwasher or rinse it in a sink.

Most room air cleaners have a **handle,** while some heavier models have **wheels. Fan speeds** usually include low, medium, and high. A few cleaners use a **dust sensor** and an **air-quality monitor** designed to raise or lower the fan speed automatically, depending on conditions. Our tests of one model with this feature found that it did not respond well to very small particles in the air.

How to choose

PERFORMANCE DIFFERENCES. CONSUMER REPORTS tests of furnace filters and whole-house air cleaners found that the better ones were effective with dust but not smoke. The filters may also restrict air flow through the system, adversely affecting the performance of your furnace or air conditioner. Electronic-precipitator filters were most effective against dust and smoke, and they restrict airflow much less.

Room air cleaners provided varying levels of performance in our tests, with no one type—HEPA filter or electronic precipitator—clearly outdoing the others. When set at high, the best did a very good job of clearing a room of dust and smoke; other models were only good or fair. Most of the room air cleaners were easy to use. Electronic-precipitator models cost less to run than HEPA units because they don't require you to replace an expensive filter. The Sharper Image Ionic Breeze, Honeywell Environizer, and Hoover Silent Air were far less effective than any other air cleaner tested.

RECOMMENDATIONS. Choose an air cleaner based on the size of your air-quality problem. Among whole-house models, one of the better pleated electrostatic filters may be all you need; consider an electronic precipitator if someone in your home smokes or has a chronic respiratory problem, such as asthma. Also be sure that a whole-house filter fits snugly in its mount, since leaks can make it less effective. (You can seal gaps with weather stripping.)

If you decide to get a room air cleaner, choose one that's appropriately sized for the room. We suggest looking for a model with a CADR of at least two-thirds of the room's area, assuming an 8-foot ceiling. For example, a 12x15-foot room—180 square feet—needs a model with a CADR of at least 120 for the contaminant you want to remove (dust, smoke, or pollen, for example).

The CADR printed on the packaging assumes you'll run the air cleaner at high speed. If you think you'll use medium or low speed to reduce noise, compensate by getting a model with a CADR that is a bit higher than suggested for the room size. Also note that a room with a high ceiling requires a model with a correspondingly higher CADR. Follow instructions when placing a room air cleaner to ensure it will work effectively. Some models can sit against a wall; others need to go in the middle of the room.

Ratings: page 204, 206

Air conditioners

Falling prices make individual room air conditioners an inexpensive alternative to central-air systems for cooling one or two rooms.

Once a high-priced convenience, relatively precise electronic controls with digital temperature readouts have replaced vague "warmer" and "cooler" settings on a growing number of lower-priced air conditioners. Added efficiency is also trickling down the price scale. Many models have a higher Energy Efficiency Rating (EER) than the federal government requires: The minimum EER for air conditioners below 8,000 British thermal units per hour (Btu/hr.) is 9.7; it's 9.8 for those with 8,000 to 13,999 Btu/hr.

What's available

Fedders, GE, Kenmore (Sears), and Whirlpool are the leading brands of room air conditioners. You'll find cooling capacities that range from 5,000 Btu/hr. to more than 30,000 Btu/hr. The majority of room air conditioners in stores are small and midsized units from 5,000 to 9,000 Btu/hr. Large models (9,800 to 12,500 Btu/hr.) can also be found.

Price range: about $100 to more than $600 (small to midsized, depending mostly on cooling capacity); $270 to $475 (large).

Key features

An air conditioner's exterior-facing portion contains a **compressor, fan,** and **condenser,** while the part that faces a home's interior contains a fan and an **evaporator.** Most room models are designed to fit double-hung windows, though some are built for casement and slider windows and others for in-wall installation.

Most models have adjustable vertical and horizontal louvers to direct airflow. Many offer a **fresh-air intake** or **exhaust setting** for ventilation, although this feature moves a relatively small amount of air. An energy-saver setting on some units stops the fan when the compressor cycles off. **Electronic controls** and **digital temperature readouts** are becoming common. A **timer** lets you program the unit to switch on (say, half an hour before you get home) or off at a given time. More and more models also include a **remote control.** Some models install with a **slide-out chassis**—an outer cabinet that anchors in the window, into which you slide the unit.

How to choose

PERFORMANCE DIFFERENCES. Most room air conditioners we've tested do a fine job of cooling. But we've found wide variations in quietness. We've also found significant differences in how well models direct airflow to the left or right. That's important if the mounting window is off to one side, rather than centered in the wall, so you can direct cool air toward the room's center.

RECOMMENDATIONS. Start by determining the right size air conditioner for the room: One that's too large may not dehumidify properly, while one that's too small may not adequately cool the space. Then check the unit's EER on the yellow EnergyGuide tag to see how efficient it is compared with other models.

ESTIMATING YOUR COOLING NEEDS

Use the chart to determine roughly how much cooling you'll need for a space with an 8-foot ceiling.

1. At the bottom of the chart, find the square footage of the room that you want to cool.

2. From there, move up the chart until you reach the shaded band that represents the type of space above your room: the thickest band represents an occupied area; the medium-width band, an insulated attic; the thinnest band, a noninsulated attic.

3. Within the band, move down for a room facing mostly north or east; up for a room facing mostly south or west.

4. Read across the left to find the Btu/hr. figure.

5. From that figure, subtract up to 15 percent for a northern climate, or add up to 10 percent for a southern climate. Subtract 30 percent if you'll use the unit only at night. If more than two people regularly occupy the area, add 600 Btu/hr. for each additional person. And add 4,000 Btu/hr. if the area includes the kitchen.

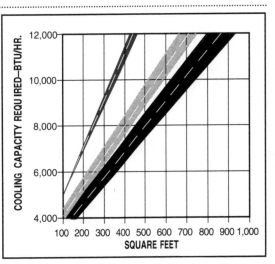

A typical room air conditioner can weigh anywhere from 40 to 100 pounds, making installation a two-person job. Once the air conditioner is in, maintain it by cleaning its air filter every few weeks; some units have an indicator that tells you when it's time to clean or change the filter.

Central-air systems

You'll find a central-air system in nearly every house built in the South and Southwest. Proper installation and maintenance mean more than the brand.

Room air conditioners are an economical alternative for cooling a room or two in regions with relatively short summers. But for many parts of the country, you'll need a central air-conditioning system that can cool the entire house. Unlike a room air conditioner, which is a self-contained unit, the most common central air-conditioning system comprises cooling equipment connected to ducts that distribute air throughout the home. A new minimum-efficiency standard is scheduled for 2006.

What's available

Major brands of central-air systems are American Standard, Bryant, Carrier, Coleman Evcon, Comfortmaker, Goodman, Heil, Janitrol, Lennox, Rheem, Ruud, Trane, and York. More important than brand, however, is how well the contractor sizes, fabricates, and installs the system, which efficiency level you choose, and how well you maintain the system once it's installed.

The most common central-air system is a split system, where refrigerant circulates between an indoor coil and a matching outdoor condenser with compressor. Refrigerant cools the air, dehumidifying it in the process, and a blower circulates it via ducts throughout the house. A heat-pump system functions like the central-air system but provides both heating and cooling. An air-source heat pump is most appropriate for areas with mild winters. When used as an air conditioner, a heat pump discharges heat from the house either into the air outside or deep into the ground. In cold months, a heat pump extracts heat from the ground or the outside air to warm the house.

Price range: $3,000 for the equipment if you're replacing an old system; $6,000 or more if you need ductwork installed because you're starting from scratch or upgrading a forced-air heating system. Ground-source heat pumps cost even more.

Key features

The system's efficiency is expressed as the **Seasonal Energy Efficiency Rating (SEER),** which describes how much cooling the unit delivers based on a partial load over the entire season. A SEER of 10 denotes a low-efficiency unit, a SEER of 11 to 12 medium-efficiency, and one of 13 or above high-efficiency. Size and cooling capacity are synonymous. Size is measured in **British thermal units per hour (Btu/hr.)** or in **"tons,"** with one ton of cooling equaling 12,000 Btu/hr.

Central-air systems also differ in their key components. While all use a compressor to pump refrigerant to the evaporator and condenser, some have scroll-type compressors that tend to be quieter and more efficient than reciprocating types because they have fewer moving parts. According to contractors we surveyed, reciprocating compressors are more repair-prone. Most manufacturers offer both types.

Pairing new equipment with old can cause problems. If you replace only one component, you have what is called a **field-matched system,** which may require more repairs than a totally new one. With **damper-zoned cooling,** a large or multistory house is often divided into several heating and cooling zones to improve temperature control. This type of system is complex and may have a relatively high repair rate. However, when designed correctly, it does improve the temperature uniformity in the home. An alternative is the installation of multiple independent heating and/or cooling systems. While more expensive, this can provide better temperature control in a large home where each floor of the home has its own system.

How to choose

PERFORMANCE DIFFERENCES. According to the contractors Consumer Reports surveyed, units with a SEER of 11 to 12 hold up best. Contractors told us that high-efficiency systems tend to be more complex, however, with more that can go wrong. Low-cost, low-efficiency builders' models also require more repairs, perhaps due to design shortcuts, the contractors said.

RECOMMENDATIONS. Improper installation can make even the best system work poorly. Systems with ductwork that's too small can result in poor cooling or excessive noise in one or more rooms. Also troublesome are ducts that leak or lack insulation. A contractor can seal seams and joints and insulate sections of ductwork that run in spaces that aren't cooled or heated, such as attics or crawl spaces.

Along with your climate and the size of the space you need to cool, consider your existing heating and cooling equipment. If you have a central cooling system or a forced-air heating system, you already have the ductwork; all you may need a contractor to do is replace or add the basic hardware components of the central-air system. That's a significant savings, since installing

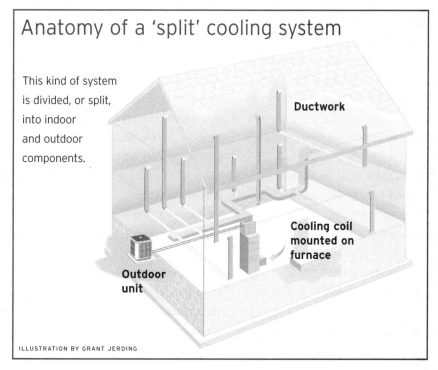

Anatomy of a 'split' cooling system

This kind of system is divided, or split, into indoor and outdoor components.

Ductwork

Cooling coil mounted on furnace

Outdoor unit

ILLUSTRATION BY GRANT JERDING

ducts in a typical new home or retrofitting them to an existing one can add thousands of dollars to the bill. Adding ducts to a very old house may require significant construction costs. Ducts that already serve a heating system may have to be upgraded to accommodate the higher airflow that a central-cooling system requires. Because heating ducts may not have the best air-supply locations in each room, they can compromise cooling-system performance.

If you have an ailing split cooling system more than a decade old, consider total replacement of inside and outside units, rather than a major repair. (This is also a good time to consider the addition of a whole-house air cleaner. See page 187.) While only one of these system's major components typically fails, replacing the whole system at once usually is more cost-effective. What's more, unmatched major components can compromise efficiency and lead to additional repairs.

You can also take several steps to ensure a quality installation. For starters, be wary of contractors who base estimates merely on house size or vague rules of thumb. A contractor who bids on your job should calculate required cooling capacity by using a recognized method such as the Air Conditioning Contractors of America's Residential Load Calculation Manual, also called Manual J.

COST-CONSCIOUS COOLING

Time-honored steps keep cooling costs down and extend the life of a central-air system.

Keep up maintenance

■ Clean or replace the air conditioner's filter frequently–monthly during heaviest use.

■ Get annual, detailed equipment inspections.

■ Keep fallen leaves, grass clippings, dryer lint, and other dirt and debris away from the system's outdoor condenser. And keep the condenser coils clean, following manufacturer's instructions.

■ Cut back grass and foliage to permit easy airflow around the house and the condenser.

■ See that leaks in ducts are sealed and that the ducts in uncooled spaces are insulated.

■ Don't block vents or grills inside the house.

■ Caulk and install weather stripping.

Work with the weather

■ Raise the thermostat setting as much as you can without overly sacrificing comfort. For every degree you raise the setting, you can expect to cut your cooling bills by 3% or more.

■ Keep sunlight out, especially in the afternoon in rooms facing west.

■ Keep exterior doors and windows closed when running the air conditioner during the day. At night, turn it off and open the windows to draw in cooler air.

■ Plant trees and shrubs to keep the house and the air conditioner's outdoor component in the shade, yet still allow air to circulate. Deciduous trees in particular provide effective and attractive climate control by letting sunlight through in the winter but blocking it in the summer.

Keep heat down

■ Ceiling fans can keep air moving in the rooms you occupy and allow you to comfortably cut back air-conditioner use. To conserve electricity, avoid running a fan in an unoccupied room.

■ Use the oven sparingly in summer; avoid baking in midday. Run the dishwasher, washing machine, or dryer in the evening, when electricity rates may be lower and heat from those appliances won't increase the demands on central air conditioning.

■ Lamps, TVs, and other appliances produce some heat, so turn them off when not in use. Position them away from the air conditioner's thermostat. Use compact fluorescent lights if possible; they generate less heat and use less electricity than incandescents.

An additional reference for assessing ductwork needs is Manual D. The result will be a detailed, room-by-room analysis of your cooling needs. Ask for a printout of all calculations and assumptions, including ductwork design. Finally, try to negotiate an overall price that includes a service plan with regular inspections, discounts on repairs, and a labor warranty.

Heating systems

Size, efficiency, and the contractor's competence are more important than brand names. A new unit could cut your heating bills, but don't count on a fast return on your investment.

Efficient heating will do more than just save on fuel bills. Properly installed, a new furnace can distribute heat more evenly and continuously than an old one, making your home a cozier place. Because new furnaces burn less fuel than their predecessors, they produce less carbon dioxide—and have less impact on the environment.

Despite the improved efficiency and comfort of most new furnaces, it is generally more cost-effective to repair a furnace than to replace it. An exception is when a key component such as the heat exchanger or control module fails. Then you're probably better off replacing the furnace, especially if the unit is more than about 15 years old. The average furnace typically lasts about 18 years.

What's available

Most new central-heating systems across the country use a gas furnace. Heat pumps, predominantly electric appliances, are the preferred way to heat in the South and Southwest, where winters are mild and electricity is relatively cheap. Oil furnaces are mostly used in older homes in the Northeast and Midwest.

GAS FURNACES. The major brands of gas furnaces are Amana, American Standard, Armstrong, Bryant, Carrier, Comfortmaker, Goodman, Heil, Janitrol, Lennox, Rheem, Ruud, Tempstar, and Trane. All offer units in a range of rated capacities and efficiencies. A gas furnace heats air and uses a blower to circulate it through ductwork. How efficiently a furnace converts gas into heat is reflected in its annual fuel-utilization efficiency (AFUE) rating, which is measured as a percentage. The higher that percentage, the more heat the furnace can wring from each therm (100,000 Btu) of gas—and the lower the environmental impact of its emissions. Gas furnaces generally have become more efficient. A unit made in the early 1970s typically has an AFUE of about 65 percent. Today the lowest efficiency allowed by federal law for new gas furnaces is 78 percent; the most efficient models have an AFUE as high as 97 percent.

HEAT PUMPS. The major brands of heat pumps are Bryant, Carrier, Heil, Janitrol, Lennox, Rheem, Ruud, Trane, and York. These units wring heat from outdoor air and pump it into your home using a blower. When it gets hot outside, they run in reverse and act as an air conditioner, drawing heat from indoor air and pumping it outdoors. When the temperature drops, heat pumps can't produce as much heat and must be supplemented,

Hiring a contractor

In the end, it's the contractor who will make the biggest difference in how well the installation of a furnace, heat pump, or central-air system goes. Seek referrals and get price quotes from at least three contractors. Some utilities install and maintain furnaces. Contractors who bid on your installation should show you proof of bonding and insurance, plus any required contractor's licenses. Check with your local Better Business Bureau and consumer-affairs office for complaint records. It's a plus if technicians are certified by North American Technician Excellence (NATE), a trade organization, and have several years' experience.

often with built-in electric elements that kick in automatically and provide expensive, less-efficient heating. Size (or capacity) is measured in British thermal units per hour (Btu/hr.). Efficiency is reflected in the unit's heating seasonal performance factor, or HSPF. The ratings for new heat pumps range from 6.8, the minimum allowed, to about 10. Models that use the ground outside as a place to extract or dissipate heat are more efficient but more expensive to install. Higher-efficiency models cost more.

OIL FURNACES AND BOILERS. These oil-fired counterparts to gas furnaces draw oil from a tank located in the basement, garage, or underground. Only homeowners who already own an oil unit and who live in a region where oil is widely distributed are likely to consider this option. It's better to install the tank in the basement; in-ground tanks may eventually leak, posing an environmental hazard and requiring an expensive cleanup. Some oil dealers sell insurance against tank leakage; CONSUMER REPORTS recommends it if you have an older underground tank.

IN-FLOOR RADIANT HEATING SYSTEMS. These systems turn a home's floors into radiators. Heated water from a boiler is routed through special plastic tubing installed on the subfloor and covered with concrete, gypsum-based concrete, or built-up finished flooring. Alternately, an electric heating grid can be used in lieu of the water piping. While radiant heating systems are relatively slow to warm up and cool down, they provide even heat with no drafts or noise. And they're an effective way to warm large areas—especially those with high ceilings. These systems also offer flexible energy options that include an oil- or gas-fired boiler, a solar water heater, or, in some regions, the home's potable hot-water system. Electric heating grids are less efficient than a heat pump—and electricity is more than three times as expensive as other heating fuels, based on national heating prices.

Key features

With gas furnaces, **variable-speed blowers** can deliver air more slowly (and often more quietly) when less heat is needed. Heat can then be delivered more continuously, with fewer swings in temperature and airflow. **Variable heat output,** available on some furnaces with variable blower speed, can further increase efficiency and comfort by automatically varying the amount of heat the furnace delivers, usually between two levels. The furnace can then deliver heat more continuously than a fixed heat output allows.

A refinement on that idea is **infinitely variable air speed and heat output.** Also referred to by the heating industry as "full modulation," a system so equipped is said to maintain a clean burn and proper fuel-air ratios across a spectrum of operating conditions. Rheem, for one, offers a fully modulating gas furnace.

Another option is **zone heating,** which employs a number of thermostats, a central controller, and a series of dampers that control airflow to deliver more or less heating or cooling to meet the different "loads" in various parts of the home. The larger the home, as a rule, the more useful zone heating is. That's especially true if sections of the home vary a lot in their heating or cooling needs. But contractors have told CONSUMER REPORTS that furnaces connected to zoned ductwork require more repair than furnaces connected to single-zone systems. An alternative is to install multiple independent heating/cooling systems. For instance, separate systems can be installed on the first and second floors of a large home.

In older gas furnaces, a continuously burning **pilot light** ignites the burners. But that design has largely been supplanted by more efficient alternatives such as **intermittent, direct-spark,** or **hot-surface ignition.**

To draw more heat from the air they burn, furnaces with an AFUE of 90 percent or higher have a **second heat exchanger**—the component that draws heat from the burned gas. Because the exhaust is cooler when it leaves that second exchanger, it may yield acidic condensation. To prevent acid from causing corrosion, the second exchanger is made of stainless steel, lined with plastic or otherwise protected. **Air filters** trap dust and reduce airborne particles. When installing a new heating system, it is a good time to think about upgrading your system's air cleaner, and replacing or installing a new cooling system.

WHEN IT'S TIME TO REPLACE YOUR HOT-WATER HEATER

A water heater isn't something you buy on impulse or upgrade as new features become available. Odds are, you don't think about it at all until it breaks or dies completely. That's when virtually all replacement purchases are made. Water heaters are fairly long-lived—most are warranted for a decade or more. When they do give out, it usually happens suddenly as water leaks out through corrosion in the tank.

Most water heaters are gas or electric. Electric water heaters are more efficient when it comes to storing water. But because electricity is relatively expensive, gas heaters are cheaper to operate. Oil-fired water heaters are also available in locales such as the Northeast and Midwest, but they are comparatively expensive and represent a small fraction of the total number installed in homes. Solar- and heat-pump-operated water heaters make up a small part of the market. These use gas or electricity as a backup heat source.

American, A.O. Smith, Bradford, Rheem, State, and White are among the major manufacturers of hot-water heaters. In major retail stores, you'll find brands such as GE, Hotpoint, and Kenmore (Sears). There is some variety in the different models, though the brands compete mainly on warranty and price. Plumbers who buy direct from whole-sale suppliers may offer to install water heaters branded by one of the manufacturers. These are generally utilitarian, no-frills units, but they too offer a range of storage capacity and warranty options. If the unit breaks or needs service, your only recourse is the plumber, who may refer you to the supplier or the manufacturer for satisfaction. That may not be a problem if you deal with the same plumber for all your home's needs. Service warranties for appliances are also available through third-party repair providers such as Sears Home Central.

When you need to replace your hot-water heater, start by determining whether your old unit is big enough for your needs now and in the future. A typical, 40-gallon unit ranges from $175 to $350, depending on warranty and efficiency. That size may be fine for most families, but if yours may grow—or you're planning to install a hot tub or whirlpool bath—consider stepping up to a 50-gallon or an even larger model. While you'll pay more initially, a larger water heater costs about the same per year to operate as a smaller unit. Conversely, empty nesters probably don't need extra capacity. Opting for a smaller unit will only save a little on installation costs—and it may mean you'll run out of hot water.

In areas where the water is corrosive or has a high mineral content, choosing a model with a longer warranty may make sense (most warranties are divided between service, parts, and tank). And whichever heater you buy, ask if the service warranty covers labor.

How to choose

PERFORMANCE DIFFERENCES. Size can make a difference. A furnace that's too small won't keep the house comfortable during extreme cold. Partly to avoid that possibility, contractors may sell furnaces that are too large for the home they're installed in. Unfortunately, a unit that's too large will cost more and may not work properly. Also, upgrading to a larger or high-efficiency furnace may require the installation of larger ducts. Without the larger ducts, the increased air flow needs of the furnace can create a noisy system.

The more efficient a furnace, generally, the lower your energy bill for heating. But you also have to figure in other costs. For instance, the electricity to run its blowers and other components is not considered in the AFUE rating, but the cost can be significant. Higher-efficiency models may have special installation requirements, such as new, revised, or special vents (needed for a furnace with an AFUE of 90 percent or more or if other appliances such as a gas-fired water heater share a vent or chimney with the furnace). All this can easily add several hundred dollars to the installed cost of a new furnace.

Some contractors we surveyed said the most efficient gas furnaces (those with, say, an AFUE of 90 percent or more) tend to need more repair than other models. These high-efficiency furnaces tend to have more components that can break down and are more likely to use new designs that are not yet tried-and-true. (More than half of the contractors we surveyed also cited new furnace designs as more repair-prone.)

RECOMMENDATIONS. Choosing a competent contractor is more important than considering brand. But based upon subscriber responses to our annual questionnaire, American Standard and Trane were more reliable than the average gas furnace. To be sure of correct capacity, choose a contractor who will take the time to calculate heating needs by using an industry-standard calculation such as the Air Conditioning Contractors of America's Manual J. Such a calculation accounts for climate as well as your home's size, design, and construction.

Generally the more efficient the gas furnace, the more expensive it will be. A gas furnace with an AFUE of 90 percent can cost $1,000 more than a similarly sized unit with an AFUE of 80 percent. That additional cost can generally be recouped over the lifetime of the furnace. Just how quickly the expenditure is recovered depends not only on the unit's AFUE but also on its electrical consumption, how well your home retains heat, and your region's climate. In regions where winters are especially harsh, the payback time may be only a decade or so.

When comparing models, make sure the contractor's estimate for each choice considers the cost of any changes to venting. And insist that the contractor estimate annual operating costs by basing them on the unit's AFUE and electrical consumption, information on your home, and the region where you live. Salespeople have the information needed to make these calculations easily and accurately. Weigh the differences in operating costs against the prices for various units, along with their features.

If a model that fits your needs and priorities has an AFUE in the mid-90 percent range or above, ask the contractor about any reliability problems that might exist. Some manufacturers' basic (usually low-efficiency) models may have less generous warranties than their premium models. Consider a service contract that includes an annual inspection of your furnace.

Thermostats

Electronic setback thermostats offer far more flexibility and energy-saving potential than the electromechanical models they are replacing.

You can cut your energy costs by as much as 20 percent by lowering your home's thermostat 5° F at night and 10° F during the day when no one is home—or raising it comparably when cooling. Setback thermostats can take much of the hassle out of doing that by handling the adjusting for you. While you'll still find a few electro-mechanical models with a 24-hour timer, they can't match the control and flexibility of today's electronic models. Many models let you program different temperatures for different days.

What's available

The major brands are Honeywell, Hunter, Lux, and White Rodgers. Some programmable electromechanical and electronic thermostats allow only two daily temperature periods. Others models let you set one schedule for weekdays, another for weekends, usually with four temperature periods each day. Seven-day electronic models let you pick different programs for different days, with four possible temperature periods per day.

Price range: $30 to $150.

Key features

All electronic thermostats have a **liquid crystal display** that shows time of day and room temperature. Some also display the temperature you've programmed, whether the heating or cooling system is supposed to be on, and which programmed period is in effect. Some models can be briefly **illuminated,** handy in a dark room. Another feature on some displays is an **indicator** that tells you when the filter of a forced-air system should be replaced, based on operating time.

Most models come with a **factory-set program** you can adjust to your needs. This feature also makes programming easier, since you're refining an existing program, rather than creating one from scratch. Some models are **detachable** from the wall mount, allowing you to punch in your preferences from your sofa or another location. Many models include **abbreviated instructions** on their outer case. All models have **temperature-adjustment buttons** that allow you to temporarily override the

---

— GETTING WITH THE PROGRAM —

Programming most electronic setback thermostats is simple, thanks largely to preinstalled setback programs and abbreviated instructions inside the cover. Here are the steps for most:

1. To start programming or review a program, push the Prog, View Prog, or Set Schedule button. Pushing the button repeatedly takes you along each program period—identified on the display by name (wake, day, evening, and sleep) or number (1 through 4).

2. Set temperature for the period displayed by pushing the Up or Down arrows.

3. Set the start time by pushing the Set Clock or Set Time button and then either an Ahead or Back button or an Up or Down arrow.

4. End programming by pushing Run Program or Return. Most thermostats automatically return to the "run" mode if you forget this step. Most seven-day models have a Copy button to duplicate settings between days—easier than creating a new program for each day.

programmed temperature until the next programmed period, when the temporary setting is automatically cancelled.

A **hold button** allows you to override the programmed temperature until you cancel it. A variation allows you to set the temperature override for up to a month or more—handy when you go on business trips or vacations.

Most thermostats prevent frequent on/off cycling of the cooling system. A few models provide **secondary automatic backup switches** for turning the heat off if the house is in danger of overheating—or turning it on if temperatures drop far enough for the pipes to freeze, for example. While most units are **battery-powered** and use one, two, or three AA alkaline batteries, some White Rodgers models draw power from the heating or cooling system and continue working even if their batteries die. A **low-battery indicator** for battery models should generally provide ample warning.

How to choose

PERFORMANCE DIFFERENCES. Most of the thermostats that we've tested have been quite good at responding to changes in room temperature. Factory-installed setback programs, logical dials and buttons, and helpful prompts on the display make programming intuitive with most units. Indeed, you should be able to program most electronic thermostats without checking the manual.

RECOMMENDATIONS. A unit that allows one schedule for weekdays and another for weekends is probably fine for most people. Consider a seven-day model if your daily schedule tends to vary—say, if children are at home earlier on some days than others. If you're replacing a thermostat that has a mercury switch, be careful not to break the tube that holds the mercury, a toxic substance. Contact your local recycling or hazardous-materials center for advice on proper disposal of the thermostat. Or you can go online to the Thermostat Recycling Corporation's Web page for more information at *www.nema .org/index_nema.cfm/664.*

Also, be sure to change the thermostat's batteries once a year, even if they're still good, to prevent your heating or cooling system from shutting down in case the batteries die. You can always pop the old ones into another device to use whatever battery life remains.

Water filters

Many are good at removing pollutants such as lead and chlorination by-products. They can also remove off-tastes and odors.

Most drinking water in the U.S. is safe. But if you have any qualms about the quality of your tap water—or simply don't like its taste—you may want to consider getting a water filter. While boiling your tap water can protect against some organisms, it won't remove stable compounds that can affect water's taste; nor will it remove lead.

Facts about your water supply can help you decide. A federal law requires larger water utilities to send an annual "Consumer Confidence Report" to their customers before July 1 each year that explains what's in the water when it leaves the treatment plant.

Some states have required such reports for years. If you don't find such a report in your mail, you may find the information at a public library, in a local newspaper, or on a utility company or local municipality Web site. People with a well must have testing done on their own—the EPA recommends having well water tested annually. The local health department can identify the pollutants specific to your region. See "If you drink well water," at right for more information.

What's available

Major water-filter brands are Brita, Culligan, GE, Kenmore (Sears), Omni, and Pur. There are several different types, some cost less to maintain than others.

CARAFES. Generally made of plastic, these are simple to use and typically come in a half-gallon size or larger. Many can fit in the door of a fridge. Filter changes are usually required after processing 40 gallons—the equivalent of two to three months of typical use.

Price range: half-gallon size, $20. Annual cartridge cost: $50 to $110.

FAUCET-MOUNTED FILTERS. Models that attach to your faucet are compact and easy to install. The filter should generally be changed at least every two to three months.

Price range: $20 to $45. Annual filter cost: $50 to $120.

UNDERSINK SYSTEMS. These attach to the cold-water line beneath a sink. The housing can be attached to a wall or cabinet back. Typically, filtered water is drawn through a separate faucet. Some systems include that faucet. Their cartridges last long, generally six months. Some have multiple cartridges. Professional installation is recommended.

Price range: $55 to $180. Annual cartridge cost: about $45 to $170.

REVERSE-OSMOSIS SYSTEMS. These undersink models use a special membrane to remove contaminants. Larger and more expensive than other undersink systems, they can take up most of the space beneath a sink. Removing dissolved minerals is their strength. Their cartridges last long, generally six months. But these units require maintenance, including periodic sanitizing with bleach. Aside from distillers, these are the only units certified to filter out arsenic. Professional installation is recommended.

Price range: about $235. Annual cartridge cost: about $45 to $80.

WHOLE-HOUSE (POINT-OF ENTRY) SYSTEMS. These hook up to your home's water main, so you can use filtered water for bathing, laundry, and dishes. If your tap water contains sediment, a whole-house system can protect your appliances and eliminate periodic cleaning of clogged faucet aerators. Professional installation is recommended.

Price range: $35 to $55. Annual cartridge cost: about $15 to $50.

Key features

Some carafe, faucet-mounted, and undersink filters have a **flashing light, color indicator,** or other device signaling the need for a new filter cartridge. Slower-than-usual water flow may also tell you that it's time to replace the cartridge, since flow tends to slow or stop as impurities collect in the filter. Faucet-mounted, undersink, and reverse-osmosis filters allow you to choose unfiltered water for cleaning or washing.

If you drink well water

The EPA's Safe Drinking Water Hotline, 800-426-4791, provides useful information. The agency can also help you find a lab to evaluate water for a variety of contaminants. Check *www.epa.gov /safewater/faq /sco.html* for a lab certified by your state to test potable water. Some state health departments offer free or inexpensive kits for residential wells. Severe contamination will likely require more protection than the filters we tested.

How to choose

All tested filters made removal claims. Those claims are certified by one of the following: CSA International (CSA), National Sanitation Foundation International (NSF), Underwriters Laboratories (UL), or the Water Quality Association (WQA). To ensure that the filter you buy will remove a contaminant, its label should specify that the filter is lab-certified for that substance. Some manufacturers offer replacement cartridges, each designed to remove different contaminants. You can use those interchangeably, if they're the same size and brand as the cartridge included with the filtering system. Check these Web sites to see if a model you're considering handles the contaminants you want removed from your water: *www.CSA-international.org; www.nsf.org; www.UL.com;* and *www.wqa.org.* Search the certified-product listings for "drinking water treatment units."

PERFORMANCE DIFFERENCES. In CONSUMER REPORTS tests, all models except for the whole-house filters are fine for removing both lead and chloroform, which is sufficient for most people's needs. Most models were good, very good, or excellent at removing off-tastes.

Most undersink models delivered water more quickly and were less prone to clog than faucet-mounted models and carafes. Slowest were the reverse-osmosis systems; they delivered water at about 50 minutes per half-gallon—too slow for most households. They also wasted about 5 gallons for each gallon purified.

While whole-house filters can provide filtered water to every tap in the house, we found there are probably better choices when significant taste or contamination issues exist.

RECOMMENDATIONS. Remember that water filters are designed to purify water that's already safe to drink—not to make contaminated water safe. Filters cannot purify microbiologically contaminated water. Boiling remains the only short-term answer. Long term, the water utility must clean its existing water source or find a better one. Consider your daily water use to help determine the filtering equipment you need. A carafe filter might be fine if you need to filter only a relatively small amount of water at a time. Also determine how often you'll have to change filters, which affects annual costs; follow the manufacturer's recommended replacement schedule, since bacteria can thrive inside a filter. Also consider the type and degree of contamination; severe contamination will likely require more protection than the filters discussed here.

Beyond this, compare notes with neighbors and notify the water utility and local health officials if you suspect contamination. The latter can help locate the problem and eliminate it at its source.

Ratings: page 284

Reference

Ratings Pages 204-285

HOW TO USE THE RATINGS To find out important information on making your choice, read the buying-advice article on the product you're interested in. The Overall Ratings table gives you the big picture on how well the product performed in CONSUMER REPORTS tests. "Recommendations and notes" gives model-by-model details. Use the handy key numbers to move quickly from table to details.

Availability for most products is verified especially for this book. Some tested models may no longer be available. Models similar to the tested models, when they exist, are listed in the Ratings chart or in the "Recommendations and notes." Such models differ in features, not essential performance, according to manufacturers.

Finding reliable brands Page 287
Brand locator Page 297
Index Page 303

Air cleaners, room

If you have a forced-air heating/cooling system, choose a whole-house air cleaner. Otherwise, look for a room-sized cleaner that's designed to cover an area slightly larger than the one you need to treat. That way, you may be able to run it on low and still get adequate cleaning. The top three can quickly clear smoke and dust from a room; the worst is little better than nothing at all. With most room air cleaners, the cost of electricity and replacement filters can be substantial. The high-scoring Friedrich C-90A, $500, performs impressively at Low speed and has a filter that can be washed.

In performance order

Ratings key: Excellent ◉ · Very good ◓ · Good ○ · Fair ◒ · Poor ●

Key number	Brand & model (Similar models, in small type, comparable to tested model.)	Price	Type	Annual cost — Energy	Annual cost — Filter	Overall score	Dust — High	Dust — Low	Smoke — High	Smoke — Low	Noise — High	Noise — Low	Ease of use	Area (sq. ft.)
1	**Friedrich** C-90A	$500	EP	$56	$72		◉	○	◓	○	◒	◒	○	480
2	**Kenmore** 83202 83200, Whirlpool AP51030HO	350	F	84	220		◓	○	◓	○	◓	○	○	500
3	**Whirlpool** AP45030HO	270	F	64	130		◓	○	◓	○	◓	○	○	500
4	**Bionaire** BAP-1300 Holmes HAP675RC	225	F	63	132		◓	◒	◓	◓	◒	○	○	490
5	**Honeywell** Enviracare 50250	180	F	115	156		◓	◒	◓	◒	◓	○	○	390
6	**Vornado** AQS35	200	F	124	43		◓	◒	◓	◒	●	○	◒	400
7	**Hunter** 30400	180	F	146	90		○	◒	◓	◒	◓	○	○	400
8	**Hunter** HEPAtech 30375	150	F	106	128		○	◒	◓	◒	●	◒	○	440
9	**Hunter** 30170	160	F	57	88		◒	●	◒	◒	○	○	○	290
10	**Holmes** HAP650 GE (Wal-Mart) 106653	160	F	45	95		○	●	◒	◒	◒	◉	○	340
11	**Austin** Health Mate 400	400	F	93	30		◒	●	◒	●	◒	◒	◒	200
12	**Holmes** HAP625 GE (Wal-Mart) 106643	120	F	25	60		◒	●	◒	●	○	◒	○	210
13	**Honeywell** Enviracare 18150	160	F	43	100		◒	●	◒	●	◒	◒	○	230
14	**Honeywell** Enviracare 17000 17005	110	F	54	125		◒	●	◒	●	◒	◒	◒	200
15	**Hoover** SilentAir 4000	300	EP	7	36		●	●	●	●	◉	◉	◒	9
16	**Sharper Image** Ionic Breeze Quadra (SI637)	350	EP	4	-		●	●	●	●	◉	◉	○	14
17	**Honeywell** ⬛ Environizer 90200	200	EP	6	-		●	●	●	●	◉	◉	◒	2

⬛ Discontinued, but may still be available.

See report, page 187. Based on tests published in Consumer Reports in October 2003, with updated prices and availability.

Ratings

Guide to the Ratings

Overall score is based on air-cleaning ability, noise, and ease of use. In the **type** column, **EP** denotes an electrostatic precipitator; **F** a HEPA filter. **Dust** and **smoke** scores reflect the ability to clear air of those particles at **high** and **low** speeds in a short-term, sealed-chamber test. Dust scores also indicate prowess with pet dander and larger particles, such as pollen; smoke scores also indicate prowess with other small particulates, as from cooking. For (15), (16), and (17), we used only the high setting in calculating overall score. **Noise** is based on instrument measurements and judgments at the highest and lowest speeds. **Ease of use** covers the control layout, changing the filter or cleaning collector plates, and moving the machine. **Area** is given to the nearest 10 square feet, based on AHAM guidelines. For (11), (15), (16), and (17), which do not have AHAM certification, we calculated approximate area. **Price** is approximate retail. **Annual cost** is our estimate based on operating the cleaner continuously. **Energy cost** is based on an electricity rate of about 8 cents per kilowatt-hour. **Filter cost** is based on the manufacturer's suggested retail price and recommended replacement schedule.

—— WILL AN AIR CLEANER ADDRESS YOUR NEEDS? ——

You should be able to rely on an air cleaner to deal with: Dust, smoke particles, pollen, and pet dander. Don't rely on an air cleaner to protect you from: Carbon monoxide, odors, viruses, and dust mites (they rarely become airborne).

Basic actions that may be more effective and less costly than using an air cleaner:

ELIMINATE CAUSES

■ Ban indoor smoking.

■ Remove sources of pollution, such as pressed-wood (particleboard) products. Avoid getting pets if you're allergic.

■ Get dust mites out in the laundry with the hottest water you can. Avoid furnishings that accumulate dust.

■ Vacuum with a low-emissions machine.

VENTILATE ROOMS

■ Open the windows whenever weather and outdoor air quality permit.

■ Use outdoor-venting exhaust fans in kitchen and baths to reduce moisture that can breed bacteria, insects, and dust mites.

■ Properly vent heating equipment and appliances. Keep the equipment, chimneys, and vents in good repair.

CONTROL HARMFUL GASES

■ Test for radon with a kit from a home center. If levels are too high, have a contractor fix the problem.

■ Use chemicals outdoors. Try to keep solvents and pesticides outdoors. If you use them indoors, open windows and vent with a fan.

■ Use a carbon-monoxide alarm.

Ratings

Air cleaners, whole house

If you have a forced-air heating/cooling system, you can make a noticeable improvement in air quality by simply installing a filter. The 3M Filtrete Ultra 1250, $15, tops the Ratings for filters that you install yourself. Although the most expensive of its type, with an annual upkeep of $60, it's a standout for dust removal. If someone in your home smokes or has a chronic breathing problem, consider adding an electronic precipitator to your system. The four electronic models tested were 30 times more effective than conventional fiberglass furnace filters. But they cost between $600 and $700 plus installation. Three professionally installed whole-house cleaners combine excellent overall performance with a moderate price and operating cost: the Aprilaire 5000, the Trane Perfect Fit TFE210A9FR2, and the Honeywell F50, all $600. The Trane imposes the smallest restriction on airflow.

In performance order

Excellent ● Very good ◕ Good ○ Fair ◑ Poor ●

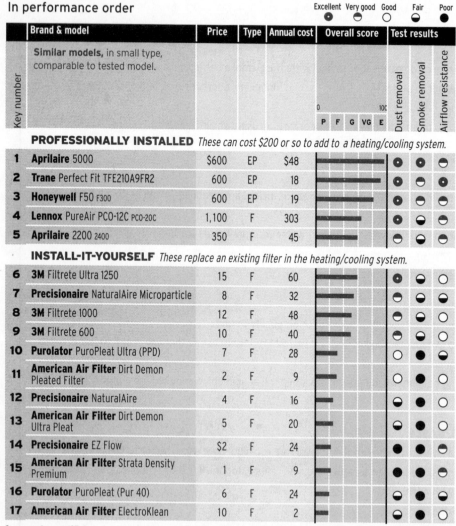

Key number	Brand & model *Similar models, in small type, comparable to tested model.*	Price	Type	Annual cost	Overall score	Dust removal	Smoke removal	Airflow resistance
	PROFESSIONALLY INSTALLED *These can cost $200 or so to add to a heating/cooling system.*							
1	**Aprilaire** 5000	$600	EP	$48		●	●	◑
2	**Trane** Perfect Fit TFE210A9FR2	600	EP	18		●	◑	●
3	**Honeywell** F50 F300	600	EP	19		●	◑	◑
4	**Lennox** PureAir PCO-12C PCO-20C	1,100	F	303		●	◑	◑
5	**Aprilaire** 2200 2400	350	F	45		◑	◑	◑
	INSTALL-IT-YOURSELF *These replace an existing filter in the heating/cooling system.*							
6	**3M** Filtrete Ultra 1250	15	F	60		●	◑	○
7	**Precisionaire** NaturalAire Microparticle	8	F	32		◑	◑	◑
8	**3M** Filtrete 1000	12	F	48		◑	◑	○
9	**3M** Filtrete 600	10	F	40		◑	◑	○
10	**Purolator** PuroPleat Ultra (PPD)	7	F	28		○	●	◑
11	**American Air Filter** Dirt Demon Pleated Filter	2	F	9		○	●	○
12	**Precisionaire** NaturalAire	4	F	16		◑	●	○
13	**American Air Filter** Dirt Demon Ultra Pleat	5	F	20		◑	●	○
14	**Precisionaire** EZ Flow	$2	F	24		●	●	◑
15	**American Air Filter** Strata Density Premium	1	F	9		●	◑	○
16	**Purolator** PuroPleat (Pur 40)	6	F	24		◑	◑	◕
17	**American Air Filter** ElectroKlean	10	F	2		◑	●	○

See report, page 187. Based on tests published in Consumer Reports in October 2003, with updated prices and availability.

Ratings

Guide to the Ratings

Overall score is based mainly on the ability to remove dust and smoke particles from a test chamber equipped with duct-work to simulate one room within a house with forced-air heating and cooling. In the **type** column, **EP** denotes an electro-static precipitator; **F** a furnace filter, which can include an electrostatic filter, fiberglass, pleated paper, or extended media. Under **test results, dust removal** and **smoke removal** scores reflect the ability to clear the air of those parti-cles in our short-term test. Dust scores also indicate how well the machine is likely to work on pet dander and larger parti-cles, such as pollen; smoke scores indicate prowess with other small particulates, as from cooking. **Airflow resistance** reflects how freely the model allows air to pass through it; a low score can signal a filter that may adversely affect the overall performance of the heating/cooling system. **Price** is approximate retail, not including installation. **Annual cost** is based on an electricity rate of about 8 cents per kilowatt-hour, the manufacturer's suggested retail price for filters, and the manufacturer's recommended replacement schedule. For (5), the annual cost includes operating the ultraviolet lights (not tested) built into the unit.

Ratings

Blenders

You don't need to spend a bundle to get a decent blender. Most of the models we tested, even inexpensive ones, were competent at various tasks. Many have specific strengths, so choose one that suits your needs. If you make mostly fruit smoothies or icy drinks such as piña coladas, look for a model that did well in those tests. Regardless of wattage, most models had the oomph to crush ice. While all of the tested models have some shortcomings, most were judged good for convenience and were reasonably easy to use. Both the Sharp EJ-12GD, $40, and the Black & Decker ProBlend BL600, $45, were adept at all tasks and low-priced.

In performance order

Excellent ● Very good ◕ Good ○ Fair ◖ Poor ●

Key number	Brand & model (Similar models, in small type, comparable to the tested model.)	Price	Overall score (0–100)	Convenience	Icy drinks	Smoothies	Purée	Glass jar	Plastic jar	Stainless-steel jar	Removable blade	Controls	Dishwasher-safe jar
1	**Bosch** MMB 9110 UC	$300		○	◕	◕	◖		●		●	D	●
2	**Juiceman** Smoothie JMS6	125		○	◕	◕	○		●			T	
3	**Oster** In2itive 6710 6700	100		○	◕	◕	◖		●		●	T	●
4	**KitchenAid** KSB3[WH]	90		○	◕	○	◖	●			●	T	●
5	**Sharp** EJ-12GD[W]	40		○	○	◕	◖	●			●	T	●
6	**Black & Decker** ProBlend BL600	45		○	○	◕	◖	●			●	P	●
7	**Oster** 6643	40		◖	○	◖	◖	●			●	P	●
8	**Hamilton Beach** Blend Master Ultra 5225[O]	35		○	◖	◖	◖	●			●	P	●
9	**KitchenAid** KSB5[SSOB]	135		○	◕	○	●			●	●	T	●
10	**T-Fal** Magiclean 67940	45		○	◖	◕	◖		●		●	D	●
11	**Proctor-Silex** 50171R12 57171	25		○	◖	○	◖		●		●	P	
12	**Oster** 6646	45		◖	○	◖	◖	●			●	P	●
13	**Oster** 6641	27		○	◖	◕	◖		●		●	P	
14	**Hamilton Beach** Turbo Twister 5615[O] 🄳 Smoothies & More 52153	35		○	◖	○	◖		●		●	P	

🄳 Discontinued, but similar model is available. Price is for similar model.

See report, page 33. Based on tests published in Consumer Reports in July 2003, with updated prices and availability.

Ratings

Guide to the Ratings

Overall score is based primarily on performance and convenience. We judged how well each model made icy drinks, fruit **smoothies**, vegetable **purée**, and more. For **convenience,** we judged ease of cleaning and replacing blade; clarity of controls and jar markings; pouring ease; and jar balance. **Price** is the approximate retail. Under **brand & model,** bracketed letters or numbers are the color code. A dot indicates that a model has the feature listed. Under controls, **P=push buttons, D=dial, and T=touchpad.**

CONTROLS VARY IN USABILITY AND CLEANABILITY

TOUCHPAD

Pros: Flat, smooth controls are easiest to clean. Some models have programmed settings to eliminate guesswork about time and speed.

Cons: Must often press twice—on and desired speed—to activate. On models lacking speed settings, must press up or down arrow repeatedly to reach desired speed. On programmables, small displays are hard to read.

PUSH BUTTONS

Pros: Easy to change from one speed to another with a single touch.
Cons: Hardest type of control to clean.

DIAL

Pros: Easier to clean than push buttons.
Cons: To move from low to high speed (or vice versa), must rotate dial through complete range.

SWITCH

Pros: Easier to clean than push buttons.
Cons: Limits available speeds to one or two, sometimes with a pulse option.

Ratings

Camcorders

Digital camcorders offer the widest range of tape formats, the best selection of models, and the best overall performance. A digital camcorder that uses MiniDV or D8 format is the best all-around choice, especially for people who don't want to spend a lot. The **CR Best Buy** Sony DCR-TRV350 and the Canon ZR60, both $500, are two very good, inexpensive choices. Digitals that record directly onto a DVD are best-suited for those who can afford to spend more and who want their home videos on a durable, easily stored medium. For a bargain-priced DVD camcorder, try the Panasonic VDR-M30PP, $800, the least-expensive DVD recorder we tested. Analog camcorders' main advantage is a low price. Picture quality is about what you'd expect from a rental video. The Sony CCD-TRV318, $300, is one of the easiest to use and has the best low-light performance of the analogs we tested.

In performance order

Legend: Excellent ● | Very good ◕ | Good ○ | Fair ◔ | Poor ●

Key number	Brand & model	Price	Format	Overall score (P–F–G–VG–E)	Picture quality	Ease of use	Image stabilizer	Audio quality	Weight (lb.)	Battery life (min.)
	DIGITAL MODELS									
1	**Canon** Elura50	$800	MiniDV		◕	○	●	○	1.0	60
2	**Panasonic** VDR-M30PP	800	DVD-RAM, -R		◕	○	●	◕	1.2	NS
3	**Panasonic** PV-DV73	700	MiniDV		◕	◕	◕	◔	1.4	NS
4	**Panasonic** PV-GS50	700	MiniDV		◕	◕	◕	○	1.0	NS
5	**Sony** DCR-TRV350 A CR Best Buy	500	D8		◕	○	●	◕	2.2	80
6	**Hitachi** DZ-MV350A	850	DVD-RAM, -R		◕	○	●	○	1.2	45-50
7	**Sony** DCR-PC105	1,000	MiniDV		◕	○	◕	◔	1.2	80-90
8	**Sony** DCR-TRV80	1,500	MiniDV		◕	○	●	◕	1.8	95
9	**Canon** ZR60	500	MiniDV		◕	◕	◕	◕	1.4	75
10	**Canon** ZR70MC	700	MiniDV		◕	◕	◕	○	1.4	140
11	**Hitachi** DZ-MV380A	1,000	DVD-RAM, -R		◕	○	●	○	1.4	45-50
12	**Sony** DCR-TRV22	700	MiniDV		◕	◕	◕	◔	1.4	90
13	**JVC** GR-DX75	600	MiniDV		◕	◔	○	◔	1.2	65
14	**Sony** DCR-TRV33	800	MiniDV		◕	○	◕	◔	1.4	90
15	**Panasonic** PV-GS70	900	MiniDV		○	◕	◕	◔	1.2	NS
16	**Sony** DCR-TRV38	900	MiniDV		○	○	●	◕	1.6	70
17	**JVC** GR-DV500	600	MiniDV		○	◕	○	◕	1.6	70
18	**Canon** Optura 20	900	MiniDV		○	◕	◕	◔	1.6	60
19	**JVC** GR-D70	480	MiniDV		○	○	◕	●	1.4	70
20	**Sharp** VL-Z7U	600	MiniDV		○	◔	◕	◔	1.2	100
21	**Samsung** SCD27	500	MiniDV		◔	○	◕	◔	1.4	90

Ratings

Key number	Brand & model	Price	Format	Overall score (P F G VG E)	Picture quality	Ease of use	Image stabilizer	Audio quality	Weight (lb.)	Battery life (min.)
ANALOG MODELS										
22	**Sony** CCD-TRV318	$300	Hi8		◒	◓	●	◒	2.0	120
23	**JVC** GR-SXM250	250	SVHS/ET-C		◒	◓	◑	●	2.4	75
24	**Canon** ES8600	280	Hi8		◒	○	◑	◒	2.0	90
25	**Samsung** SCL810	230	Hi8		◒	◓	–	◒	2.0	90

See report, page 60. Based on tests published in Consumer Reports in November 2003, with updated prices and availability.

Guide to the Ratings

Overall score is based mainly on picture quality; ease of use, image stabilizing, and audio quality carried less weight. **Picture quality** is based on the judgments of trained panelists who viewed static images shot in good light at standard speed (SP) for tape and "fine" mode for DVDs. **Picture quality** in low light was nearly always fair or poor. **Ease of use** takes into account ergonomics, weight, how accurately the viewfinder frames scenes, and contrast in the LCD viewer. **Image stabilizer** indicates how well that circuitry worked. **Audio quality** represents accuracy using the built-in microphone, plus freedom from noise and flutter. **Weight** includes battery and tape or disk. **Battery life** is as stated by the manufacturer, using the LCD viewer. Turning off the viewer typically extends battery life by 10 to 40 minutes. "NS" indicates that the manufacturer did not provide the specification for battery life. Price is approximate retail. **Recommendations & notes** lists noteworthy features and some minor shortcomings.

Recommendations and notes

MOST CAMCORDERS HAVE: Tape counter. Backlight-compensation switch. Manual aperture control. High-speed manual shutter. Manual white balance. Simple switch for manual focus. Audio dub. Tape-position memory. Audio fade. Transitional effects. S-video signal out. Video fade. Full auto switch. Quick review. Optical zoom: 10x. LCD size: 2.5 inches. **MOST DIGITAL CAMCORDERS HAVE:** A/V input. Microphone jack. Still image digital capture.

DIGITAL MODELS

1 CANON Elura 50 **Very good.** Image stabilizer worked very well. Autofocus worked very well. Relatively compact. Audio practically free of flutter at slow speed. LCD size: 2 in. Lacks backlight compensation switch and manual aperture control. Canon has been among the more repair-prone brands of digital camcorders. Similar: Elura40MC.

2 PANASONIC VDR-M30PP **Very good.** Image stabilizer worked very well. Audio was somewhat free of background noise. Audio practically free of flutter at slow speed. Poor picture quality in low light (if used in "Auto" mode or with manual settings). How to load the tape or battery isn't obvious. Battery must be removed before connecting DC power. Uses proprietary A/V cable. Has video fade but lacks audio dub.

3 PANASONIC PV-DV73 **Very good.** Easy to use, overall. Audio practically free of flutter at slow speed. LCD size: 3.5 in. Poor picture quality in low light (if simply used in "Auto" mode). Battery must be removed before connecting DC power. Lacks A/V input.

4 PANASONIC PV-GS50 **Very good.** Easy to use, overall. Relatively compact. Audio practically free of flutter at slow speed. Uses proprietary mini jack to S-video connector. Autofocus failed to work in some situations. Poor picture quality in low light (if simply used in "Auto" mode). Battery must be removed before connecting DC power.

5 SONY DCR-TRV350 **A CR Best Buy Very good.** Good low-light picture quality. Image stabilizer worked very well. Has a built-in video light. Optical zoom: 20x. Discontinued, but similar DCR-TRV250[ ] is available.

Ratings

Recommendations and notes

6 HITACHI DZ-MV350A **Very good.** Relatively lighweight. LCD viewer is easy to see in bright light. Image stabilizer worked very well. You have to remove the battery before connecting a power cord. Uses proprietary A/V cable.

7 SONY DCR-PC105 **Very good.** Image stabilizer worked very well. Relatively compact. Audio practically free of flutter at slow speed. Uses proprietary A/V cable. Can't load tape if mounted on tripod. Lacks a high-speed manual shutter.

8 SONY DCR-TRV80 **Very good.** Image stabilizer worked very well. LCD size: 3.5 in. Poor performance in low light. Similar: DCR-TRV 70.

9 CANON ZR60 **Very good.** Easy to use. Good picture quality in low light if manual settings are used. Optical zoom: 18x. Autofocus failed to work in some situations. Lacks slow-speed manual shutter, built-in titles, custom titles, and still image digital capture. Canon has been among the more repair-prone brands of digital camcorders. Similar: ZR65MC.

10 CANON ZR70MC **Very good.** Easy to use and good in low light if manual settings are used. Optical zoom: 22x. But the autofocus didn't work in some situations. Lacks a slow-speed manual shutter. Canon has been among the more repair-prone brands of digital camcorders.

11 HITACHI DZ-MV380A **Very good.** Image stabilizer worked very well. Audio practically free of flutter at slow speed, but autofocus failed to work in some situations. How to load the tape or battery isn't obvious. Battery must be removed before connecting DC power. Uses proprietary A/V cable. Lacks manual aperture control, audio dub, tape position memory, and transitional effects.

12 SONY DCR-TRV22 **Good.** LCD viewer is easy to see in bright light. Similar: DCR-TRV19.

13 JVC GR-DX75U **Good.** Excellent audio accuracy. Relatively compact. Audio practically free of flutter at slow speed. Optical zoom: 16x. Somewhat hard to use, overall. Autofocus failed to work in many situations. Poor picture quality in low light. Uses proprietary A/V cable. Can't load tape if mounted on tripod. Lacks quick review, tape position memory, transitional effects, and microphone jack. JVC has been among the more repair-prone brands of digital camcorders. Similar: GR-DX95.

14 SONY DCR-TRV33 **Good overall.** Poor performance in low light. Lacks simple switch for manual focus.

15 PANASONIC PV-GS70 **Good.** Audio practically free of flutter at slow speed. Battery must be removed before connecting DC power.

16 SONY DCR-TRV38 **Good overall.** LCD viewer (3.5 in.) is easy to see in bright light. Image stabilizer worked very well. Poor performance in low light. Similar: DCR-TRV39.

17 JVC GR-DV500 **Good.** Easy to use, overall. Audio practically free of flutter at slow speed, but autofocus failed to work in many situations. Poor picture quality in low light (if simply used in "Auto" mode). Can't load tape if mounted on tripod. Can't change battery if mounted on tripod. Has video fade. Lacks quick review, tape position memory, and transitional effects. JVC has been among the more repair-prone brands of digital camcorders. Similar: GR-DV800.

18 CANON Optura 20 **Good overall.** Good performance in low light, but only if manual settings are used. Optical zoom: 16x. LCD size: 3.5 in. Lacks slow-speed manual shutter. Similar model: Optura 10.

19 JVC GR-D70 **Good.** Audio practically free of flutter at slow speed, but autofocus failed to work in many situations. Optical zoom: 16x. Poor picture quality in low light (if simply used in "Auto" mode). Audio had very noticeable background noise. Can't load tape if mounted on tripod. Lacks quick review, tape position memory, transitional effects, and microphone jack. JVC has been among the more repair-prone brands of digital camcorders. Similar: GR-D30.

20 SHARP VL-Z7U **Good.** Excellent audio accuracy, but somewhat hard to use overall. Audio practically free of flutter at slow speed. Poor picture quality in low light (if simply used in "Auto" mode). Uses proprietary A/V cable. Lacks high-speed manual shutter, quick review, tape position memory, transitional effects, and microphone jack. Similar: VL-Z3U, VL-Z5U.

21 SAMSUNG SC-D27 **Good.** Excellent audio accuracy. Autofocus worked very well. Audio practically free of flutter at slow speed. LCD size: 3.5 in. Only fair picture quality at standard speed. Poor picture quality in low light (if simply used in "Auto" mode). Can't load tape if mounted on tripod. Lacks manual white balance, simple switch for manual focus, transitional effects, and A/V input. Similar: SCD23.

Ratings

Recommendations and notes

ANALOG MODELS

22 SONY CCD-TRV318 **Good.** Easy to use. Good low-light picture quality. Image stabilizer worked very well. Optical zoom: 20x. Fair picture quality at standard speed, poor picture quality at low speed. Can't load tape if mounted on tripod. Lacks slow-speed manual shutter, manual white balance, quick review, audio dub, date search, tape position memory, A/V input, microphone jack, and still image digital capture. Similar model: CCD-TRV118.

23 JVC GR-SXM250 **Good.** Easy to use, overall. Autofocus worked very well. Optical zoom: 16x. Only fair picture quality at standard speed. Image stabilizer only slightly effective. Audio had very noticeable background noise. Relatively bulky. At slow speed, audio quality was hampered by flutter. Audio had very noticeable background noise. Lacks manual aperture control, audio dub, transitional effects, A/V input, microphone jack, and still image digital capture.

24 CANON ES8600 **Good.** Good picture quality in low light if manual settings are used. Optical zoom: 22x. Only fair picture quality at standard speed. Can't load tape if mounted on tripod. Lacks manual aperture control, slow-speed manual shutter, manual white balance, audio dub, custom titles, date search, tape position memory, A/V input, microphone jack, and still image digital capture.

25 SAMSUNG SCL810 **Fair.** Easy to use, overall. Excellent audio accuracy. Autofocus worked very well. Optical zoom: 22x. Only fair picture quality at standard speed. Lacks image stabilizer, manual aperture control, high-speed manual shutter, manual white balance, quick review, audio dub, tape position memory, transitional effects, A/V input, microphone jack, and still image digital capture.

Ratings

Circular saws

If you're a serious do-it-yourselfer, look for a top-rated circular saw, which can cost $140 to $160. But you can get a fine saw for less. Among lower-priced saws, consider the Black & Decker CS1000, $40. Battery-powered saws such as the DeWalt DW939K, $260, lack the power for tough jobs but might do for occasional light work. The worm-drive DeWalt DW378GK, $155, outperformed the others in its class, but was noticeably slower than the best of the regular saws, and is primarily for contractors.

In performance order

Ratings key: Excellent ● · Very good ◗ · Good ○ · Fair ◖ · Poor ●

Key number	Brand & Model	Price	Overall Score (0–100, P F G VG E)	Cutting Speed	Power	Ease of Use	Construction	Weight (lb.)	Amps [1]
REGULAR SAWS									
1	**Milwaukee** 6390-21	$140		●	●	●	●	11	15
2	**DeWalt** DW369CSK	140		●	●	◗	●	11	15
3	**DeWalt** DW364K	160		●	●	◗	●	12½	15
4	**Makita** 5740NB **A CR Best Buy**	90		●	○	●	◖	8½	10.5
5	**Makita** 5007NBK	130		●	●	○	●	11	13
6	**Craftsman** (Sears) Professional 27108	100		◗	●	●	◗	11	15
7	**Bosch** 1658K	110		◗	○	◗	○	11	13
8	**Black & Decker** CS1000	40		○	◗	○	○	11	11
9	**Black & Decker** CS1010K	50		○	◖	○	○	11	12
BATTERY-POWERED SAWS									
10	**DeWalt** DW939K	260		◗	●	○	○	8½	18
11	**Craftsman** (Sears) Professional 27119	200		○	●	◗	○	10	18
12	**Makita** BSS730SHK	480		○	●	○	◖	9½	24
13	**Bosch** 1659K	300		○	●	○	○	9	18
WORM-DRIVE SAWS									
14	**DeWalt** DW378GK [2]	155		◗	●	◗	●	13	15
15	**Skil** HD77	160		◖	●	○	◖	16	13
16	**Craftsman** (Sears) Professional 2761	140		◖	●	○	◖	16	13

[1] For battery-powered saws, figure is in volts. [2] Hybrid design.

See report, page 128. Based on tests published in Consumer Reports in August 2002, with updated prices and availability.

Ratings

Guide to the Ratings

Overall score is based mainly on cutting speed, power, and ease of use. **Cutting speed** is how fast each saw crosscut and ripped a series of 2x12 pine and a 24-inch sheet of ¾-inch-thick hardboard; the best were up to four times as fast as the slowest. **Power,** measured with a dynamometer, indicates how well a saw can handle thick or hard wood. **Ease of use** shows how easy it was to use the cutting guide, adjust depth and bevel, and change blades, as well as our judgment of the saw's balance and handle comfort. **Construction** includes our assessment of bearings, access to motor brushes, and ruggedness of the base, housing, and adjustments. **Weight** is to the nearest half-pound with blade and, for cordless models, battery. **Price** is approximate retail.

Recommendations and notes

ALL MODELS HAVE: Blade guard that retracts when you push the saw forward. Cutting depth adjustable to at least 3½ inches. Cutting angle adjustable to 45 degrees. Most have: Carbide 7¼-inch blade. Blade lock to make blade changes easier. One-year warranty.

REGULAR SAWS

1 MILWAUKEE 6390-21 **Excellent.** Adjustable handle. Heavy-duty base.

2 DEWALT DW369CSK **Excellent.** Blade brake. Heavy-duty base. Earlier version of saw was subject of safety recall.

3 DEWALT DW364K **Excellent.** Blade brake. Heavy-duty base.

4 MAKITA 5740NB **A CR Best Buy Excellent.** Heavy-duty base. Safety interlock button. Attached wrench for blade change. Newest version has different front handle. An earlier version of saw was the subject of safety recall.

5 MAKITA 5007NBK **Excellent.** Heavy-duty base. Sharp bevel-angle guide can contact fingers on front handle.

6 CRAFTSMAN (Sears) Professional 27108 **Very good.** Heavy-duty base. Extra-long cord. Padded switch.

7 BOSCH 1658K **Very good.** Blade-wrench storage.

8 BLACK & DECKER CS1000 **Good.** Not supplied with carbide blade or blade lock. Short cord. Base less substantial. Blade-wrench storage. 2-yr. warranty.

9 BLACK & DECKER CS1010K **Good.** Not supplied with carbide blade. Short cord. No blade lock. Base less substantial. Blade-wrench storage. 2-yr. warranty.

BATTERY-POWERED SAWS

10 DEWALT DW939K **Good.** Safety interlock button. Blade-wrench storage.

11 CRAFTSMAN (Sears) Professional 27119 **Good.** Safety interlock button. Blade-wrench storage.

12 MAKITA BSS730SHK **Good.** Blade brake. Heavy-duty base. Safety interlock button, but it's awkward to use. Blade-wrench storage. Bevel adjustment has fasteners front and rear.

13 BOSCH 1659K **Good.** Blade brake. Safety interlock button, but it's awkward to use. Blade-wrench storage.

WORM-DRIVE SAWS

14 DEWALT DW378GK **Excellent.** Heavy-duty base. Not double-insulated. Hybrid design.

15 SKIL HD77 **Good.** Extra-long cord. Not supplied with carbide blade. Poor dust ejection. Not double-insulated.

16 CRAFTSMAN (Sears) Professional 2761 **Good.** Not supplied with carbide blade. Not double-insulated. Poor dust ejection.

Ratings

Coffeemakers

Most automatic drip coffeemakers are capable of brewing good coffee, so focus on convenience features such as clear cup markings and easy-to-read displays and controls. The top-rated Cuisinart Brew Central DCC-1200, $100, has a host of handy features. For less money, consider any of the four **CR Best Buys:** the Black & Decker Smart Brew Plus DCM2500, $35, Black & Decker Smart Brew DCM2000, $25, Braun Aromaster KF 400, $20, and Mr. Coffee AR12, $20. Among thermal-carafe models, the Mr. Coffee Thermal Gourmet is a very good choice at a reasonable price.

In performance order

Excellent Very good Good Fair Poor

Key number	Brand & model	Price	Overall score	Auto on/off
			0 — 100	
			P F G VG E	
REGULAR MODELS				
1	**Cuisinart** Brew Central DCC-1200	$100		•
2	**Black & Decker** Smart Brew Plus DCM2500 **A CR Best Buy**	35		•
3	**Krups** ProAroma 12 Plus Time 453-71	100		•
4	**Black & Decker** Smart Brew DCM2000 **A CR Best Buy**	25		
5	**Braun** Aromaster KF 400 **A CR Best Buy**	20		
6	**Mr. Coffee** AR12 **A CR Best Buy**	20		
7	**Hamilton Beach** Flavor Plus 43421	40		•
8	**Proctor-Silex** Easy Morning 41331	20		
9	**Black & Decker** Spacemaker ODC325	75		
10	**Mr. Coffee** PL12	20		
11	**Mr. Coffee** PLX20	30		•
12	**Proctor-Silex** Simply Coffee 46871	20		
13	**Proctor-Silex** Simply Coffee 46801	20		
THERMAL-CARAFE MODELS				
14	**Capresso** MT500 440	160		•
15	**Krups** AromaControl Therm Time 199-73	100		•
16	**Mr. Coffee** Thermal Gourmet TC80	43		
17	**Black & Decker** Thermal Select TCM300	35		

See report, page 16. Based on tests published in Consumer Reports in December 2002, with updated prices and availability.

Ratings

Guide to the Ratings

Overall score is based on convenience. Tests included ease of filling, loading grounds, pouring, cleaning, and using controls. **Auto on/off** models are programmable, have a clock, and shut off after two hours. Thermal models shut off immediately. **Price** is approximate retail.

Recommendations and notes

Models listed as similar should offer performance comparable to the tested model, although features may differ.

EXCEPT AS NOTED, ALL: Have drip-stop, "on" light, one-year warranty, clear cup markings in reservoir and/or on front-facing fill tube, or have removable reservoir with markings. Load without removing basket. Glass carafes have markings; most have flip-top lid.

REGULAR MODELS

1 CUISINART Brew Central DCC-1200 **Excellent, with many features and unusual design, but expensive.** 12 cups. Adjustable hotplate. Small-batch control. Water filter. Cleaning cycle. Remove lid to fill carafe. Three-year warranty.

2 BLACK & DECKER Smart Brew Plus DCM2500 **A CR Best Buy Very good, with good price and features.** 12 cups. Long cord; storage. But markings on side. Tested model sold only at Kmart. Similar: DCM 2575, DCM 2550.

3 KRUPS ProAroma 12 Plus Time 453-71 **Very good and feature-rich, but expensive.** 12 cups. Adjustable hotplate. Brew-strength/ small-batch controls. Water filter. Long cord; storage. Remove lid to fill carafe. Harder to program. Similar: 453-42.

4 BLACK & DECKER Smart Brew DCM2000 **A CR Best Buy Inexpensive and very good, if very basic.** 12 cups. But markings on side. Tested model sold only at Kmart and Target. Similar: DCM2050, DCM2075.

5 BRAUN Aromaster KF 400 **A CR Best Buy Inexpensive and very good, if very basic.** 10 cups.

6 MR. COFFEE AR12 **A CR Best Buy Inexpensive and very good, if very basic.** 12 cups. Similar: AR13, ARX20, ARX23.

7 HAMILTON BEACH Flavor Plus 43421 **Very good.** 10 cups. Brew-strength control. Long cord; storage. Two-year warranty. Similar: 43424, 43425, 43321

8 PROCTOR SILEX Easy Morning 41331 **Very good, but inconveniences.** 12 cups. Brew-strength control. But carafe harder to control when full. Two-year warranty. Similar: 41334.

9 BLACK & DECKER Spacemaker ODC325 **Very good if a bit expensive; mounts under cabinet.** 12 cups. Basket, reservoir pull out. Long cord; storage. But less brew than other 12-cup models. Sold only at Kmart, Target, Wal-Mart. Similar: ODC325N.

10 MR. COFFEE PL12 **A basic, low-cost model.** 12 cups. Basket harder to close (overflowed when not closed securely) and harder to replace on hinges. Similar: PL13.

11 MR. COFFEE PLX20 **Very good and reasonably priced, but inconveniences.** 12 cups. Basket harder to close (overflowed when not closed securely) and harder to replace. Display hard to read. Auto setting not obvious. Similar: PLX23.

12 PROCTOR-SILEX Simply Coffee 46871 **Basic model.** 12 cups. Brew-strength control. But basket won't sit upright on counter. Carafe harder to control when full. Six-month warranty. Similar: 46831.

13 PROCTOR-SILEX Simply Coffee 46801 **Inexpensive, but lacks conveniences.** 12 cups. Basket won't sit upright on counter. Carafe harder to control when full. Must remove basket to load. No drip-stop or "On" light. Uncoated hotplate. Markings on carafe only. Six-month warranty.

THERMAL-CARAFE MODELS

14 CAPRESSO MT500 440 **Very good, but expensive; sleek silver-metal-and-black design and many features.** 10 cups. Small-batch setting. Water filter. Carafe easier to handle than other thermals. Long cord; storage. Fill tube with markings on side.

15 KRUPS AromaControl Therm Time 199-73 **Very good, but expensive; with contemporary rounded design.** 10 cups. Long cord; storage. Similar: 199-46, 197-46, 197-73, 229-45, 229-46, 229-70.

16 MR. COFFEE Thermal Gourmet TC80 **Very good, and reasonably priced for a thermal-carafe model.** 8 cups. Long cord; storage. Similar: TC81.

17 BLACK & DECKER Thermal Select TCM300 **Reasonably priced for a thermal-carafe model, but inconveniences.** 8 cups. "On" light not easily visible. Basket hard to open/close. Sold only at Target.

Ratings

Cooktops

Electric smoothtops offer quick heating and easy-to-clean glass surfaces. While most electric cooktops heated quickly on their high settings and provided very low heat when turned down, most gas models didn't perform as well as the electrics on their low settings. Among electrics, the Kenmore 4270, $450, offers slightly faster heating than the Frigidaire Gallery GLEC30S8C, $500, but lacks bridge elements. Gas cooktops provide easily adjustable flame controls and choices ranging from basic to pro style. Among gas models, the Jenn-Air JGC8536AD, $850, offers excellent quick heating and two high-heat burners, while the Maytag MGC6536BD, $700, excelled at low-heat simmering. Consider the Magic Chef CGC2536AD, $350, if you're willing to trade style and features for a low price. A look at the prices for both categories reveals little correlation between price and performance.

In performance order

Ratings legend: Excellent ● · Very good ◕ · Good ○ · Fair ◑ · Poor ●

Key number	Product (Similar models, in small type, comparable to tested model except that they're 36 inches wide, have an extra element or warning zone, and cost about $100 more.)	Price	Overall score (0–100, P F G VG E)	Heating, high	Heating, low	No. of elements, low	Elements, medium	Elements, high	Bridge element	Touch controls
	ELECTRIC COOKTOPS									
1	**Frigidaire** Gallery GLEC30S8C[S] **A CR Best Buy** GLEC36S8C[ ]	$500		◑	●	1	2	1	●	
2	**GE** Profile JP930TC[WW] JP960TC[ ]	740		◑	●	1	2	1	●	
3	**GE** Profile JP939BH[BB]	1,200		◑	●	1	1	2		●
4	**Kenmore** (Sears) 4270[2] **A CR Best Buy** 427I[ ]	450		●	●	1	2	1		
5	**Kenmore** (Sears) Elite 4402[2]	600		◑	●	1	2	1	●	
6	**Jenn-Air** JEC8430AD[W]	560		◑	●	1	2	1		
7	**Thermador** CEP304Z[B]	1,300		◑	●	2		2		●
8	**Whirlpool** Gold GJC3034L[P] GJC3634L[ ]	650		◑	●	1	2	1		
9	**Bosch** NES73[2] NES93[2]	1,000		◑	●	1	2	1		●
10	**Amana** AKT3040[WW] AKT3650[ ]	550		◑	◑	1	2	1		

Ratings

Key number	Product	Price	Overall score (P F G VG E, 0–100)	Heating, high	Heating, low	No. of burners, low	Burners, medium	Burners, high	Stainless-steel	Glass	Enamel	Continuous grates
	GAS COOKTOPS											
11	**GE** Monogram ZGU375NSD[SS] ZGU375LSD [1]	$1,300	▬▬▬▬▬	◑	●		4	1	●			●
12	**Jenn-Air** JGC8536AD[S] **A CR Best Buy**	850	▬▬▬▬	●	◑	2	1	2	●			●
13	**Maytag** MGC6536BD[W] MGC6430BD[ ] **A CR Best Buy**	700	▬▬▬▬	○	●	1	3	1			●	●
14	**Thermador** SGSX365Z[S]	1,500	▬▬▬	◑	◑		2	3	●			●
15	**GE** Profile JGP962TEC[WW]	1,100	▬▬▬	◑	○	2	2	1	●			●
16	**Magic Chef** CGC2536AD[W]	350	▬▬▬	○	◑		4	1			●	
17	**Amana** AKS3640[SS]	600	▬▬▬	○	◑		4	1				●
18	**Kenmore** (Sears) Elite 3303[2]	750	▬▬▬	◑	○	1	2	1		●		●
19	**Kenmore** (Sears) Elite 3321[3]	900	▬▬▬	◑	○	2	2	1				●
20	**Frigidaire** Gallery GLGC36S8C[B] GLGC30S8C[ ]	600	▬▬	○	◑	2	2	1		●		●
21	**Bosch** NGT93[5]	900	▬▬	◑	◐	1	3	1				●

[1] 36-inch propane-only model.

See report, page 37. Based on tests published in Consumer Reports in September 2003, with updated prices and availability.

Guide to the Ratings

Overall score includes high- and low-heating performance. **Heating, high** denotes how quickly the highest-powered element or burner heated 6⅓ quarts of room-temperature water to a near-boil. **Heating, low** shows how well the least-powerful element or burner melted and held chocolate without scorching it and whether the most powerful, set to low, held tomato sauce below a boil. **Price** is approximate retail. Under **Product,** brackets show a tested model's color code. Similar-model cooktops have the same highest and lowest elements or burners; other details may differ.

All 30-inch electric cooktops have: Four elements with rated powers ranging from 1,200 to between 2,200 and 2,500 watts. Expandable elements. Glass cooktop. Hot-surface indicator lights. A one-year full warranty. **Most have:** Control knobs. Limited five-year warranties on glass and elements. A 40-amp circuit requirement.

All 36-inch gas cooktops have: Control knobs. Sealed burners with lift-off base and cap for cleaning. A 120-volt connection requirement. A one-year full warranty. **Most have:** Five burners with rated power for low heat between 5,000 and 6,500 Btu/hr. and for high heat between 12,000 and 15,000 Btu/hr. A propane conversion kit.

Ratings

Cookware

You don't have to pay top dollar to get even heating, comfortable handles, easy cleaning, and durability. Among nonstick sets, the two **CR Best Buys,** Simply Calphalon Nonstick, $200 for 8 pieces, and Cook's Essentials, $125 for 10 pieces, are good choices for those on a budget. If you want an uncoated set, consider the Wolfgang Puck Bistro Collection. It has 20 pieces (including a 6-piece tool set and a nonstick frypan) and costs $150.

In performance order

Legend: Excellent ◉ Very good ◖ Good ○ Fair ◐ Poor ●

Key number	Brand & Model (material)	Price	Overall score	Pieces	Even heat	Durable coating	Cleanup
NONSTICK SETS							
1	**Calphalon** Simply Calphalon **A CR Best Buy** (anodized aluminum)	$200		8	◉	◖	◉
2	**Emerilware** by All-Clad (anodized aluminum)	350		10	◉	◖	◉
3	**Cook's Essentials A CR Best Buy** (stainless steel)	110		10	◖	◖	◉
4	**Scanpan** Titanium New Tek Classic (aluminum)	330		8	◖	◖	◉
5	**Cuisinart** Stick Free (stainless steel)	200		7	◖	◖	◉
6	**Meyer** Anolon Titanium (anodized aluminum)	400		10	◖	◖	◉
7	**Meyer** Circulon Steel (stainless steel)	150		8	○	◖	◖
8	**T-Fal** Encore Hard Enamel (enamel on aluminum)	80		8	◖	◖	◉
9	**Nordic Ware** Rangeware Pro (aluminum)	100		8	●	◖	◉
UNCOATED SETS							
10	**Wolfgang Puck** Bistro Collection (stainless steel)	150		20	◉	◖	○
11	**Tools of the Trade** Belgique Gourmet (stainless steel, copper)	250		12	◉	–	○
12	**Magnalite** Classic (aluminum)	115		8	◖	–	◐
13	**Wearever** Easy Pour and Strain (stainless steel)	80		8	◖	◖	○
14	**Emerilware** by All-Clad (stainless steel)	150		7	◖	–	○
15	**Calphalon** Simply Calphalon (stainless steel)	150		8	◖	○	○
16	**Cuisinart** Multiclad (stainless steel)	200		7	○	–	○

See report, page 18. Based on tests published in Consumer Reports in December 2002, with updated prices and availability.

Guide to the Ratings

Overall score is based on performance and convenience. Each set includes at least these pieces: one 9.5- to 11-inch frypan with no lid, a stockpot/Dutch oven (usually 5- to 6.5-qt.) with lid, and a 2- to 3-quart saucepan with lid. To test for **even heat,** we cooked frypan-sized pancakes at 400° F on a gas cooktop and gauged how evenly they browned. To test for **durable coating** on nonstick sets, we had a mechanical arm rub a steel-wool pad over the frypan's surface. **Cleanup** scores are based on the ease of removing a baked-on sauce of flour, milk, and butter from saucepans. Recommendations and notes include judgments on handle sturdiness, which indicate how well the frypans fared when we tried to bend the handle with up to 75 lb. of force and to loosen it by moving the pan up and down with 1.5 times its own weight inside. **Price** is approximate retail for the set.

Ratings

Recommendations and notes

All cookware sets: Can be used on gas, electric coil, and electric smoothtop ranges. **Except as noted all:** Are dishwasher-safe and oven-safe to at least 425° F. Have a limited lifetime warranty. Have riveted handles, which are strong but can be hard to clean. Have handles that did not come loose in our tests and that stayed cool enough to hold without a potholder even while boiling water. Offer additional open stock.

NONSTICK SETS

1 CALPHALON Simply Calphalon **A CR Best Buy** (anodized aluminum) **Almost as good as set above, but a fraction of the price and lighter weight.** Not dishwasher-safe. Handles uncomfortable. 10-year warranty. Extras: 1-qt. saucepan & lid, 8-in. frypan.

2 EMERILWARE (anodized aluminum) **Well equipped, simmers very well.** But not dishwasher-safe. Heavy. Extras: 3-qt. sauté pan & lid, 3.5-qt. casserole & lid, 8-in. frypan. Made by All-Clad.

3 COOK'S ESSENTIALS A CR Best Buy (stainless steel) **Very good, especially simmering.** But oven-safe only to 350°. Glass lids. Lifetime warranty. Extras: 1-qt. saucepan & lid, 12-in. sauté pan & lid, 8-in. frypan. No open stock. Available only from QVC.

4 SCANPAN Titanium New Tek Classic (aluminum) **Impressive overall.** But unriveted handles less comfortable and less well balanced than most. Heavy. Glass lids. Lifetime warranty. Extras: 1- qt. saucepan & lid, 8-in. frypan.

5 CUISINART Stick Free (stainless steel) **Very good value.** But saucepan handles got hot. Lifetime warranty. Extras: 2-qt. steamer insert, 8-in. frypan.

6 MEYER Anolon Titanium (anodized aluminum) **Very good.** But saucepan handles got hot. Heavy. Lifetime warranty. 8-qt stockpot. Extras: 3-qt. saucepan & lid, 5-qt. sauté pan & lid, 8-in. frypan.

7 MEYER Circulon Steel (stainless steel) **Commendable cooking.** But oven-safe only to 350°. Shallow ridges slightly impede cleaning. Lifetime warranty. 8-qt. stockpot. Extras: 1.5-qt. saucepan & lid, 8-in. frypan.

8 T-FAL Encore Hard Enamel (enamel on aluminum) **There are better sets.** Lightweight, with comfortable, no-rivet handles. But oven-safe only to 350°. Lifetime warranty. Extras: 1-qt. saucepan & lid, 7.5-in. frypan, 3-piece tool set, recipe book.

9 NORDIC WARE Rangeware Pro (aluminum) **Choose another.** Stockpot couldn't hold simmer, stockpot handles got hot. Extras: 1.5-qt. saucepan & lid, 8-in. frypan. Limited open stock.

UNCOATED SETS

10 WOLFGANG PUCK Bistro Collection (stainless steel) **Well equipped, cooks well.** 8-in. frypan is nonstick. Glass lids. Lifetime warranty. 8-qt. stockpot. Extras: 3- and 4-qt. saucepans & lids, 10-in. casserole & lid, steamer insert, 11-in. frypan & lid, 6-piece tool set. Sold through Home Shopping Network. Open stock sold through www.wpcookware.com.

11 TOOLS OF THE TRADE Belgique Gourmet (stainless steel, copper) **Very good performance.** Comfortable handles. Lifetime warranty. 8-qt. stockpot. Extras: 1- and 3.5-qt. saucepans & lids, 12.5-inch frypan & lid, steamer insert. Sold only at Macy's and other Federated Department Stores. Nonstick frypan available in open stock.

12 MAGNALITE Classic (aluminum) **Very good overall.** But oven-safe only to 350°. Stockpot handles got hot. Uncomfortable, no-rivet handles. Some spouts. Heavy. 50-yr. warranty. Extras: 1-qt. saucepan & lid, meat rack. Limited open stock.

13 WEAREVER Easy Pour and Strain (stainless steel) **Good value for basic set.** But oven-safe only to 350°, frypan handle not well balanced. Some spouts. Glass lids. Frypan is nonstick. Heavy. Lifetime warranty. Extras: 1-qt. saucepan & lid, lid for frypan.

14 EMERILWARE (stainless steel) **Very good.** Handles uncomfortable. Glass lids. Can use in broiler. Heavy. Lifetime warranty. Extras: 3-qt. casserole & lid. Made by All-Clad.

15 CALPHALON Simply Calphalon (stainless steel) **Cooks evenly, but handles uncomfortable.** Can use in broiler. Glass lids. Heavy. 10-yr. warranty. Extras: 1-qt. saucepan & lid, 8-in. frypan.

16 CUISINART Multiclad (stainless steel) **A princely sum for pauper performance.** Saucepan handles got hot. Can use in broiler. Lifetime warranty. Extras: 1.5-qt. saucepan & lid.

Dishwashers

You can get very good or even excellent washing for $350 or a little less, but expect to pay more for the quietest operation and most flexible loading. Stainless-steel tubs, front panels, and designs with hidden controls add to the cost. The two Bosch models that top the Ratings are strong performers, and the Bosch SHU43C0, $580, is a good value. However, Bosch has been among the more repair-prone brands. Two **CR Best Buys** offering excellent washing with minimal noise are the Maytag MDB5600AW, $400, and the Kenmore (Sears) 1634, $330. Both have been reliable brands.

In performance order

Ratings scale: Excellent ● | Very good ◖ | Good ○ | Fair ◑ | Poor ●

Key number	Brand & model	Price	Overall score	Washing	Energy use	Noise	Loading	Ease of use	Cycle time (min.)	Sensor	Stainless-steel tub
1	**Bosch** SHU66C0[2] SHI66A0[ ] SHV66A0[ ] SHY66C0[ ]	$850		Excellent	Fair	Excellent	Very good	Very good	105	●	●
2	**Bosch** SHU43C0[2] SHU53A0[ ]	580		Excellent	Fair	Excellent	Very good	Good	105	●	●
3	**Kenmore** (Sears) 1637[2] 1636[ ] 1736[ ] 1737[ ]	520		Excellent	Very good	Good	Very good	Excellent	135	●	
4	**Kenmore** (Sears) Elite 1648[2] 1649[ ] 1748[ ]	870		Excellent	Very good	Excellent	Very good	Excellent	145	●	●
5	**KitchenAid** KUDI01IL[BL] KUDI01FL[ ] KUDI01DL[ ]	550		Excellent	Very good	Very good	Good	Very good	130	●	●
6	**Miele** G894SC G694SC	1,300		Excellent	Very good	Very good	Very good	Very good	135		●
7	**Kenmore** (Sears) 1638[2] 1646[ ] 1647[ ] 1738[ ] 1746[ ] 1747[ ]	570		Excellent	Very good	Very good	Very good	Very good	145	●	
8	**KitchenAid** KUDP01DL[WH] KUDP01FL[ ] KUDP01IL[ ]	800		Excellent	Good	Very good	Very good	Very good	130	●	
9	**KitchenAid** Superba KUDS01FL[WH] KUDS01DL[ ] KUDS01IL[ ]	950		Excellent	Good	Very good	Excellent	Very good	130	●	
10	**Maytag** MDB8600AW[W] MDB9600AW[ ]	600		Excellent	Good	Very good	Very good	Very good	110	●	
11	**Frigidaire** Professional PLDB998C[C] PLDB999C[ ] PLDS999C[ ]	500		Excellent	Good	Good	Good	Excellent	115	●	
12	**Maytag** MDB7600AW[W] MDBF750AW[ ] MDBH970AW[ ] MDBTT79AW[ ]	500		Excellent	Good	Very good	Excellent	Very good	120	●	
13	**Whirlpool** Gold GU1500XTL[Q]	570		Excellent	Good	Very good	Very good	Very good	135	●	
14	**Maytag** MDB9150AW[W]	750		Excellent	Good	Good	Very good	Excellent	130	●	●
15	**GE** Profile PDW8200J[WW] PDW8280J[ ] PDW8400J[ ] PDW8480J[ ]	650		Excellent	Good	Very good	Very good	Very good	120	●	●
16	**Maytag** MDB5600AW[W] MDB6600AW[ ] MDBF550AW[ ] MDBH950AW[ ] MDBTT59AW[ ] **A CR Best Buy**	400		Excellent	Good	Very good	Very good	Excellent	135	●	
17	**Whirlpool** DU943PWK[Q] DU950PWK[ ] DU951PWK[ ] DUL200PK[ ]	350		Excellent	Good	Good	Good	Very good	105	●	
18	**Whirlpool** Gold GU1200XTL[Q] DUL300XTL[ ]	500		Excellent	Good	Very good	Good	Excellent	130	●	
19	**Fisher & Paykel** DD603[W]	1,200		Excellent	Very good	Very good	Very good	Very good	115		
20	**GE** GSD6900J[BB] GSD6860J[ ]	500		Excellent	Good	Good	Excellent	Excellent	120	●	
21	**GE** Profile PDW8600J[BB] PDW8680J[ ]	850		Excellent	Good	Very good	Excellent	Excellent	120	●	●

Similar models, in small type, comparable to tested model. Price shown is for white or black finish, except for Frigidaire (11), which has a stainless-steel finish.

Overall score scale: 0 — 100, P F G VG E

Key number	Brand & model	Price	Overall score (0–100, P F G VG E)	Washing	Energy use	Noise	Loading	Ease of use	Cycle time (min.)	Sensor	Stainless-steel tub
22	**Kenmore** (Sears) 1634[2] 1734[ ] **A CR Best Buy**	$330	▬▬▬	◉	⊖	⊖	○	⊖	145		
23	**GE** GSD6600G[WW] GSD6200J[ ] GSD6260J[ ] GSD6660G[ ]	460	▬▬▬	◉	○	○	⊖	●	120	●	
24	**Kenmore** (Sears) 1552[2] 1652[ ]	350	▬▬▬	◉	⊖	◐	⊖	⊖	105		
25	**Maytag** MDB6650AW[W]	615	▬▬▬	⊖	⊖	○	○	●	85		●
26	**Maytag** Performa PDB4600AW[W]	330	▬▬▬	◉	⊖	◐	○	●	90		
27	**Admiral** DWB1000A	270	▬▬▬	⊖	⊖	○	○	⊖	95		
28	**Kenmore** (Sears) 1522[2] 1532[ ] 1622[ ]	280	▬▬▬	⊖	⊖	◐	○	⊖	95		
29	**Whirlpool** DU900PWK[Q] DU909PWK[ ] DUL100PK[ ]	300	▬▬▬	⊖	⊖	○	◐	○	100		
30	**Asko** D3250 D3350 D3450	1,100	▬▬▬	◐	●	⊖	○	○	90		●
31	**Whirlpool** DU920PWK[B] ▣ DU911PWK[ ] DU910PWK[ ]	330	▬▬▬	○	⊖	○	⊖	○	95		
32	**Haier** ESD200	400	▬▬▬	◐	●	○	○	○	100		●
33	**Frigidaire** FDB710L[C] FDB510L[ ] FDB750R[ ]	235	▬▬▬	◐	⊖	○	○	⊖	85		

▣ Discontinued, but similar models are available. Price is for similar models.

See report, page 20. Based on tests published in Consumer Reports in February 2003.

Guide to the Ratings

Overall score is based mainly on washing, but also factors in noise, energy and water use, loading, and more. Overall and energy-use scores may differ from those in earlier reports because we have raised our standard of excellence to reflect new, more-efficient models. **Washing** judges results with a full load of very dirty dishes, glasses, and flatware. **Energy use** is for the normal cycle. **Noise** was judged by listeners, aided by sound-level measurements. **Loading** reflects ability to hold extra place settings and oversized items. **Ease of use** considers controls and other factors. Under **brand & model**, a bracketed letter or number is the color code. **Cycle time** (rounded to nearest 5 minutes) is for a normal cycle, including heated dry, if available. A **sensor** adjusts water usage and cycle time to the amount of soil on dishes. A **stainless-steel finish** adds $60 to $130 to prices shown. **Price** is approximate retail. **Most have** a self-cleaning filter, which requires no maintenance but may add to the noise level.

Ratings

Drills, cordless

Decide whether you need raw power for decks and other big jobs, easy handling for around-the-house tasks, or—like most buyers—some combination of the two. For mundane tasks and the occasional deck, consider the **CR Best Buy** 18-volt Ryobi HP1802MK2, $100. It's nearly as capable overall as the top-rated drills, yet it weighs less and costs about half as much. Increasingly, drills with less than 14.4 volts are not worth buying. Even the highest-scoring 12-volt model we tested rated no better than a "Good" and offered less for its price. Odds are, you'll also find models in the 9.6-volt category disappointing for all but the lightest-duty tasks. Consider them only if you value minimal weight and cost over performance.

In performance order

Ratings key: Excellent ● | Very good ◕ | Good ○ | Fair ◒ | Poor ●

Key number	Brand & Model	Price	Weight (lb.)	Overall Score	Overall power	Run time	Charge time	Handling
18-VOLT DRILLS								
1	**DeWalt** DW987K-2	$270	6.0		●	◕	●	○
2	**Craftsman** (Sears) Professional 27124	200	6.5		◕	◕	●	○
3	**DeWalt** DW929K-2	200	4.6		◕	○	●	◕
4	**Ryobi** HP1802MK2 **A CR Best Buy**	100	5.1		◕	○	●	◕
5	**Black & Decker** FSD182K-2	110	5.2		◕	○	○	○
6	**Grizzly** G8596	70	4.2		○	◕	●	◕
14.4-VOLT DRILLS								
7	**DeWalt** DW928K-2	180	4.3		◕	◕	●	◕
8	**Makita** 6228DWAE	160	3.8		○	◕	◕	●
9	**Ryobi** HP1442MK2	85	4.2		○	◕	●	◕
10	**Black & Decker** FSD142K-2	90	4.4		○	◕	○	○
11	**Grizzly** G8595	55	3.4		◕	○	○	◕
12-VOLT DRILLS								
12	**DeWalt** DW927K-2	140	4.0		◕	◕	●	◕
13	**Makita** 6227DWE	130	3.4		○	◕	●	◕
14	**Black & Decker** FSD122K	70	3.5		◕	◕	○	○
15	**Ryobi** HP1202MK2	70	3.4		◕	●	◕	◕
9.6 VOLT AND BELOW								
16	**DeWalt** DW926K-2	$100	3.4		◕	●	●	●
17	**Black & Decker** CD9600K	60	2.9		◕	●	●	◕

See report, page 129. Based on tests published in Consumer Reports in January 2003, with updated prices and availability.

Ratings

Guide to the Ratings

Weight is to the nearest tenth of a pound for the drill and battery pack. **Overall score** is based on overall power, run time, charge time, and handling. **Overall power** denotes drilling speed and torque, or twisting force. **Run time** reflects work per battery charge, measured on a dynamometer. **Charge time** is how much time it takes to fully recharge a discharged battery. **Handling** includes weight, balance, and effort needed to position the head. **Price** is approximate retail. **Recommendations & notes** list noteworthy features and some minor shortcomings.

Recommendations and notes

ALL TESTED CORDLESS DRILLS HAVE: A keyless chuck. A reversible drive. **MOST HAVE:** A smart charger with 1-hour charge time. Two speed ranges: slow (0 to about 400 rpm) for driving screws, and fast (about 0 to 1,100-1,650 rpm) for drilling holes; single-speed models have a range of 0 to 600-800 rpm, which tends to compromise their driving and drilling performance. A variable clutch with at least 16 settings for limiting the tool's maximum torque. A ⅜-inch chuck (½-inch for 18- and 24-volt models, except as noted). A trigger lockout for safety. Bit storage. Two NiCad battery packs. A carrying case. A one-year warranty.

18-VOLT DRILLS

1. **DEWALT** DW987K-2 **Powerful and well-equipped, but heavy.** Three speed ranges.

2. **CRAFTSMAN** (Sears) Professional 27124 **Capable and well-equipped, but heavy.**

3. **DEWALT** DW929K-2 **Capable and light.** ⅜-inch chuck.

4. **RYOBI** HP1802MK2 **A CR Best Buy Lots of performance for the money.** Magnetic screw holder. 2-year warranty.

5. **BLACK & DECKER** FSD182K-2 **Capable, but charging takes 3 to 6 hours.** ⅜-inch chuck. Quick-connect bit change. 2-year warranty.

6. **GRIZZLY** G8596 **Light, though otherwise unimpressive.** ⅜-inch chuck. Extra bits. Only one battery. Charging takes 3 to 5 hours.

14.4-VOLT DRILLS

7. **DEWALT** DW928K-2 **Capable overall.**

8. **MAKITA** 6228DWAE **Light and well-balanced.** No bit storage.

9. **RYOBI** HP1442MK2 **OK.** Magnetic screw holder. 2-year warranty.

10. **BLACK & DECKER** FSD142K-2 **OK, but charging takes 3 to 6 hours.** Quick-connect bit change. Level light. ½-inch chuck. 2-year warranty.

11. **GRIZZLY** G8595 **There are better choices.** Only one battery. Charging takes 3 to 5 hours.

12-VOLT DRILLS

12. **DEWALT** DW927K-2 **Power offset by relatively short run time.**

13. **MAKITA** 6227DWE **Light and well-balanced, but otherwise unimpressive.** No bit storage.

14. **BLACK & DECKER** FSD122K **There are better choices.** Charging takes 3 to 5 hours.

15. **RYOBI** HP1202MK2 **There are better choices.** Charging takes 3 to 5 hours.

9.6 VOLT AND BELOW

16. **DEWALT** DW926K-2 **Best of an unimpressive group.** Well-balanced and well-equipped.

17. **BLACK & DECKER** CD9600K **There are better choices.** Only one battery. Charging takes 16 hours.

Ratings

Dryers

All the full-sized dryers we tested were very good or excellent performers with ample capacity. For spacious capacity and superb drying, consider the quiet GE Profile DPSB620EC, $600. For fine performance at a low price, look to the **CR Best Buy** Kenmore 6280, $410, or Frigidaire Gallery GLER642A, $350. A pricier dryer may offer fancier styling, touchpad controls, a porcelain top, a stainless-steel drum, and extras such as programmability and numerous cycles—none essential in our view. A compact washing machine and dryer is an option when space is tight, but most are pricey. A stackable full-sized washer and dryer offer more capacity and usually cost less.

In performance order

Rating symbols: Excellent ● · Very good ◕ · Good ○ · Fair ◑ · Poor ⬤

Key number	Brand & model	Price	Overall score (P F G VG E)	Drying performance	Capacity	Noise	Drying rack	Stainless-steel drum	Custom programs	Optional extended tumble
FULL-SIZED DRYERS										
1	**GE** Profile DPSB620EC[WW]	$600		●	●	●	•	•	•	•
2	**Kenmore** (Sears) 6280[2] **A CR Best Buy**	410		●	●	◕				
3	**Kenmore** (Sears) 6490[2]	440		●	●	○	•			
4	**Whirlpool** Gold GEQ9800L[W]	450		◕	●	●				•
5	**Kenmore** (Sears) Elite HE3 8483[2]	900		◕	●	●	•			•
6	**LG** DL-E5932W	900		◕	●	●	•	•	•	•
7	**Maytag** Neptune MDE7500AY[W]	800		●	●	○			•	•
8	**Kenmore** (Sears) Elite 6408[2]	770		◕	●	●	•			•
9	**Kenmore** (Sears) Elite HE3 8282[2]	900		◕	●	●	•			•
10	**Whirlpool** Duet GEW9200L[W]	880		◕	●	●	•			•
11	**Whirlpool** Gold GEW9868K[Q]	680		◕	●	◕				•
12	**Whirlpool** LEQ8000J[Q]	420		◕	●	◕				•
13	**Whirlpool** Gold GEW9878J[Q]	560		●	●	◕				•
14	**Kenmore** (Sears) Elite 6206[2]	770		◕	●	●	•		•	•
15	**Frigidaire** Gallery GLER642A[S] **A CR Best Buy**	350		◕	◕	◕	•			•
16	**KitchenAid** KEYS850J[W]	500		◕	●	●	•			•
17	**Maytag** Atlantis MDE8400AY[W]	600		◕	●	●	•			•
18	**GE** DPXH46EA[WW]	450		◕	◕	○	•			•
19	**Maytag** Atlantis MDE8600AY[W]	570		◕	◕	◕	•			•
20	**Maytag** Performa PYE4500AY[W]	400		◕	●	○				•
21	**GE** DWSR405EB[WW]	400		○	●	◕	•			•
22	**Maytag** Performa MDE3500AY[W]	480		◕	●	◕				•
23	**Hotpoint** NWSR483EB[WW]	300		○	●	◕				•
24	**Maytag** SDE5701AY[W]	450		○	●	◕				•
25	**Roper** RES7648K[Q]	350		○	●	○				

Ratings

Key number	Brand & model	Price	Overall score			Test results			Features			
			0 — 100	P F G VG E		Drying performance	Capacity	Noise	Drying rack	Stainless-steel drum	Custom programs	Optional extended tumble
COMPACT DRYERS												
26	**Miele** Novotronic T1576	$1,200				◓	◑	○		●		
27	**GE** DSKS433EB[WW]	400				○	◑	○				

See report, page 23. Based on tests published in Consumer Reports in August 2003, with updated prices and availability.

Guide to the Ratings

Overall score is based primarily on drying performance, capacity, and noise. Also factored in: Convenience (not shown), which considers controls, accessibility, and overall ease of use. All tested models were very good for convenience except the two tested compact dryers Miele Novotronic T1576 and GE DSKS433EB[WW], which scored lower. **Drying performance** combines tests on various-sized loads of different fabric mixed, including cotton, permanent press, and delicates. **Capacity** ranges from about 4 cubic feet for compacts to 7.5 cubic feet for the largest models; all could handle our 12-pound load. **Noise** reflects judgments by panelists. **Price** is approximate retail. Under **brand & model,** bracketed letters or numbers are color codes.

Recommendations and notes

Models judged excellent for drying were noticeably better than lower-rated units at leaving a load damp for ironing and drying delicates at low heat.

FULL-SIZED DRYERS

1 GE Profile DPSB620EC[WW] **Excellent overall.** Impressive on large loads. Delicates temperature lower than most, an advantage. Large door opening. Touchscreen controls. Damp dry signal to remove clothes for ironing. Gas equivalent: DPSB620GC[ ].

2 KENMORE (Sears) 6280[2] **A CR Best Buy Very good.** Superb drying for a good price. But warmer than most on delicates. Impressive on large loads. Fewer features than most. Similar: 6282[ ], 6481[ ]. Gas equivalent: 7280[ ], 7282[ ], 7481[ ].

3 KENMORE (Sears) 6490[2] **Very good overall.** Impressive on large loads. Large door opening. Similar: 6492[ ], 6493[ ]. Gas equivalent: 7490[ ] 7492[ ], 7493[ ].

4 WHIRLPOOL Gold GEQ9800L[W] **Very good, but warmer than most on delicates.** Impressive on large loads. Gas equivalent: GGQ9800L[ ].

5 KENMORE (Sears) Elite HE3 8483[2] **Very good overall.** Delicates temperature lower than most, an advantage. Damp dry signal to remove clothes for ironing. Touchscreen controls. Gas equivalent: 9483[ ].

6 LG DL-E5932W **Very good overall.** Delicates temperatures lower than most, an advantage. Damp dry signal to remove clothes for ironing.

7 MAYTAG Neptune MDE7500AY[W] **Very good.** Touch screen. Impressive on large loads. Damp dry signal to remove clothes for ironing. Similar: MDE5500AY[ ]. Gas equivalent: MDG5500AW[ ], MDG7500AW[ ].

8 KENMORE (Sears) Elite 6408[2] **Very good overall.** Delicates temperature lower than most, an advantage. Damp dry signal to remove clothes for ironing. Touchscreen controls. Gas equivalent: 7408[ ].

Ratings

Recommendations and notes

9 KENMORE (Sears) Elite HE3 8282[2] **A very good dryer, though pricey.** Touchpad controls. Very quiet. Pedestal available to raise dryer door to a comfortable height. Gas equivalent: 9282[ ].

10 WHIRLPOOL Duet GEW9200L[W] **Very good.** Much like the Kenmore (Sears) Elite HE3 8282[2]. Exceptionally quiet. Large door opening. Gas equivalent: GGW9200L[ ].

11 WHIRLPOOL Gold GEW9868K[Q] **Very good.** Very quiet. Impressive on large loads. Touchpad controls. Gas equivalent: GGW9868K[ ].

12 WHIRLPOOL LEQ8000J[Q] **Very good performance for the price.** But fewer features than most. Impressive on large loads. Similar: LEQ9858L[ ]. Gas equivalents: LGQ8000J[ ], LGQ9858L[ ].

13 WHIRLPOOL Gold GEW9878J[Q] **Impressive on large loads and delicates.** Discontinued, but similar GEW9878L[ ] is available. Gas equivalent: GGW9878L[ ].

14 KENMORE (Sears) Elite 6206[2] **Very good.** Delicate temperatures lower than most, an advantage. Large door opening. Touchpad controls. Gas equivalent: 7206[ ].

15 FRIGIDAIRE Gallery GLER642A[S] A **CR Best Buy** A very **good, no-frills machine.** Impressive on large loads. Gas equivalent: GLGR642A[ ].

16 KITCHENAID KEYS850J[W] **Very good.** Delicate temperatures lower than most, an advantage. Discontinued, but similar KEYS850L[ ] is available. Gas equivalent: KGYS850L[ ].

17 MAYTAG Atlantis MDE8400AY[W] **Very good overall.** Delicates temperature lower than most, an advantage. Large door opening. Moisture monitor. Gas equivalent: MDG8400AY[ ].

18 GE DPXH46EA[WW] **Very good.** Impressive on large loads and delicates. Gas equivalent: GE DPXH46GA[ ].

19 MAYTAG Atlantis MDE8600AY[W] **Very good.** Moisture monitor. Similar: MDE7600AY[ ]. Gas equivalents: MDG7600AW[ ], MDG8600AW[ ].

20 MAYTAG Performa PYE4500AY[W] **Very good, no-frills machine.** Drum opening smaller than most. Gas equivalent: PYG4500AY[ ].

21 GE DWSR405EB[WW] **Very good.** Not as good at drying as other sensor models. Large door opening. Gas equivalent: GE DWSR405GB[ ].

22 MAYTAG Performa MDE3500AY[W] **A very good, no-frills machine.** Moisture monitor. Gas equivalent: MDG3500AW[ ].

23 HOTPOINT NWSR483EB[WW] **A very good, spartan machine.** But no moisture sensor. Large door opening. Gas equivalent: NWSR483GB[ ].

24 MAYTAG SDE5701AY[W] **Very good, but warmer than most on delicates.** Moisture monitor. Large door opening. Gas equivalent: SDG5701.

25 ROPER RES7648K[Q] **VERY GOOD, BUT WARMER THAN MOST ON DELICATES.** No moisture sensor. Fewer features than most. Gas equivalent: RGS7648K[ ].

COMPACT DRYERS

26 MIELE Novotronic T1576 **Very good overall.** Delicates temperature lower than most, an advantage. Door opening smaller than most.

27 GE DSKS433EB[WW] **Good overall.** Controls on front of dryer.

Ratings

DVD players

Excellent picture quality is a hallmark of DVD players. Almost any of the dozen or so progressive-scan, single-disc players priced at $100 or less, as well as the three standard players, will deliver excellent picture and sound quality in typical use. For playing home-recorded or special music discs, check that the player can handle them. If you want to connect the player to your receiver via the digital-audio connection, make sure the output matches the input on the receiver.

In performance order

Ratings key: Excellent ● Very good ◐ Good ○ Fair ◑ Poor ●

Key number	Brand & model	Price	Overall score (P F G VG E)	Picture quality	Ease of use	Coaxial digital-audio output	Optical digital-audio output	JPEG image files	Video CDs	WMA audio files
	PROGRESSIVE-SCAN, SINGLE-DISC PLAYERS									
1	**JVC** XV-N44SL	$100	▬▬▬▬	●	◐	●	●	●	●	
2	**JVC** XV-N55SL	120	▬▬▬▬	●	●	●	●	●	●	
3	**Panasonic** DVD-S55	130	▬▬▬▬	●	◐		●	●	●	
4	**Pioneer** DV-260	80	▬▬▬▬	●	●	●	●	●	●	
5	**Pioneer** DV-363	100	▬▬▬▬	●	●	●	●	●	●	
6	**Mitsubishi** DD-6040	120	▬▬▬▬	●	●	●	●	●	●	
7	**Toshiba** SD-3900	100	▬▬▬▬	●	◐	●	●	●	●	
8	**Aspire** Digital AD-1100	130	▬▬▬▬	●	◐	●	●			
9	**Sharp** DV-SL20	180	▬▬▬▬	●	◐	●				
10	**Sony** DVP-NS725P	150	▬▬▬▬	●	●	●	●		●	
11	**Hitachi** DV-P735U	110	▬▬▬▬	●	◐	●				
12	**Onkyo** DV-SP301	145	▬▬▬▬	●	●	●	●	●	●	●
13	**Philips** DVD727	100	▬▬▬▬	●	◐			●		◐
14	**Samsung** DVD-HD931	300	▬▬▬▬	●	◐	●	●	●		
15	**RCA** DRC230N	90	▬▬▬▬	●	◐	●	●	●	●	
16	**V, Inc.** Bravo D1	200	▬▬▬▬	●	◐			●		
17	**Zenith** DVB312	80	▬▬▬▬	●	◐	●		●		●
18	**Philips** DVD726	90	▬▬▬▬	●	◐			●		
19	**Samsung** DVD-P230	80	▬▬▬▬	●	◐			●		
20	**RCA** DRC212N	80	▬▬▬▬	●	◐	●	●	●	●	●

Ratings

Key number	Brand & model	Price	Overall score	Test results		Features				
			0 100 P F G VG E	Picture quality	Ease of use	Coaxial digital-audio output	Optical digital-audio output	JPEG image files	Video CDs	WMA audio files
PROGRESSIVE-SCAN, MULTIDISC PLAYERS										
21	**Onkyo** DV-CP701 (6 discs)	290	▬▬▬▬▬	●	●	●	●	●	●	●
22	**Panasonic** DVD-F85 (5 discs)	150	▬▬▬▬▬	●	●	●	●	●	●	●
23	**Sony** DVP-NC665P (5 discs)	180	▬▬▬▬	●	◐	●	●	●	●	
24	**Samsung** DVD-C631P (5 discs)	120	▬▬▬▬	●	◐	●	●	●		●
25	**Philips** DVD 795SA (5 discs)	280	▬▬▬▬	●	◐	●	●	●	●	●
STANDARD SINGLE-DISC PLAYERS										
26	**Sony** DVP-NS325	100	▬▬▬▬	●	◐	●		●	●	●
27	**Toshiba** SD-2900	80	▬▬▬▬	●	◐	●		●	●	●
28	**Apex** AD-1225	60	▬▬▬	●	○	●		●	●	●

See report, page 70. Based on tests published in Consumer Reports in December 2003.

Guide to the Ratings

Overall score is mainly based on picture quality; ease of use is also factored in. **Picture quality** indicates the sharpness and detail of video images. For progressive-scan models, the score reflects performance with both conventional TVs and HDTVs. **Ease of use** is our assessment of remote control, console front panel, setup menu, key playback functions, and features. **Price** is approximate retail. Under Features, **JPEG image files** and **video CDs** indicate ability to read digital photos and video files on CDs. **WMA audio files** indicates ability to play music files stored on CD in this format.

Recommendations and notes

All tested models: Play DVDs and CDs, CD-R and CD-RW discs, and MP3 audio files on CDs. Played DVD-R discs, DVD+R discs, and DVD+RW discs in our tests. Have composite-video, S-video, and component-video outputs.

PROGRESSIVE-SCAN, SINGLE-DISC PLAYERS

1 JVC XV-N44SL **Excellent.** Better than most at playing damaged DVDs. Similar: XV-N40BK.

2 JVC XV-N55SL **Excellent.** Similar: XV-N50BK.

3 PANASONIC DVD-S55 **Excellent.** Has DVD-Audio playback and Dolby Digital and DTS decoders. Has center-channel dialog enhancement. If using receiver to decode digital multichannel sound, unit will connect only via optical digital-audio input.

4 PIONEER DV-260 **Excellent.**

5 PIONEER DV-363 **Excellent.**

6 MITSUBISHI DD-6040 **Excellent.** But some progressive-scan playback less clear than that of other units with this capability. Better than most at playing damaged DVDs. Lacks virtual surround sound, a potential issue if you use only two speakers. 6-mo. warranty on labor.

7 TOSHIBA SD-3900 **Excellent.** Better than most at playing damaged DVDs and CDs. Has center-channel dialog enhancement. Plays back some older audio CDs with excessive treble.

8 ASPIRE Digital AD-1100 **Excellent.** Includes Dolby Digital decoder (needed only if your receiver lacks it). Has no multilingual setup menu. Plays back some older audio CDs with excessive treble. 12-mo. warranty on labor.

Ratings (sidebar)

Recommendations and notes

9 SHARP DV-SL20 **Excellent, though somewhat pricey.** Better than most at playing damaged DVDs. If using receiver to decode digital multichannel sound, unit will connect only via coaxial digital-audio input.

10 SONY DVP-NS725P **Excellent.** But when playing back most movies on DVD, progressive-scan video is not as smooth as that of most other units tested.

11 HITACHI DV-P735U **Excellent.** If using receiver to decode digital multichannel sound, unit will connect only via coaxial digital-audio input. Lacks ability to output DTS digital audio to receiver.

12 ONKYO DV-SP301 **Excellent.** Lacks virtual surround sound, a potential issue if you use only two speakers. 12-mo. warranty on labor.

13 PHILIPS DVD727 **Excellent.** Better than most at playing damaged CDs. Lacks virtual surround sound, a potential issue if you use only two speakers.

14 SAMSUNG DVD-HD931 **Excellent.** Has Digital Visual Interface (DVI) output for high-resolution video connections to HDTVs with this input, although the DVI 1080i output was incompatible with some test HDTVs. 12-mo. warranty on labor.

15 RCA DRC230N **Excellent and well-priced for a progressive-scan model.** Better than most at playing damaged DVDs. Plays back some older audio CDs with excessive treble.

16 V, INC. Bravo D1 **Excellent.** Has firmware-upgradable Digital Visual Interface (DVI) output for high-resolution video connections to HDTVs with this input. But lacks audio dynamic range control, virtual surround sound (a potential issue if you use only two speakers), and multilingual setup menu. Plays back some older audio CDs with excessive treble.

17 ZENITH DVB312 **Excellent and well-priced for a progressive-scan model.** Better than most at playing damaged DVDs. If using receiver to decode digital multichannel sound, unit will connect only via coaxial digital-audio input. Plays back some older audio CDs with excessive treble.

18 PHILIPS DVD726 **Excellent and well-priced for a progressive-scan model.** Better than most a playing damaged CDs. If using receiver to decode digital multichannel sound, unit will connect only via coaxial digital-audio input. Lacks virtual surround sound, a potential issue if you use only two speakers.

19 SAMSUNG DVD-P230 **Excellent and well-priced for a progressive-scan model.** But progressive-scan playback of most movies on DVD is no smoother than that of standard players. If using receiver to decode digital multichannel sound, unit will connect only via coaxial digital-audio input. Plays back some older audio CDs with excessive treble. 12-mo. warranty on labor.

20 RCA DRC212N **Very good and well-priced for a progressive-scan model.** But not as easy to use as others. Has center-channel dialogue enhancement. Lacks console display.

PROGRESSIVE-SCAN, MULTIDISC PLAYERS

21 ONKYO DV-CP701 **Excellent, though pricey.** Better than most at playing damaged CDs. Lacks virtual surround sound, a potential issue if you use only two speakers. 12-mo. warranty on labor.

22 PANASONIC DVD-F85 **Excellent and well-priced.** Includes DVD-Audio playback. Has Dolby Digital and DTS decoders. Has center-channel dialog enhancement. If using receiver to decode digital multichannel sound, unit will connect only via optical digital-audio output.

23 SONY DVP-NC665P **Excellent.** But when playing back most movies on DVD, progressive-scan video is not as smooth as that of most other units tested. 12-mo. warranty on labor.

24 SAMSUNG DVD-C631P **Excellent and well-priced.** But progressive-scan playback of most movies on DVD is no smoother than that of standard players. Plays back some older audio CDs with excessive treble. 12-mo. warranty on labor.

25 PHILIPS DVD 795SA **Excellent.** High price gets you SACD playback, along with Dolby Digital and DTS decoders. Has center-channel dialog enhancement.

SINGLE-DISC PLAYERS

26 SONY DVP-NS325 **Excellent.** Better than most at playing damaged CDs. If using receiver to decode digital multichannel sound, unit will connect only via coaxial digital-audio input.

27 TOSHIBA SD-2900 **Excellent.** Has center-channel dialog enhancement. If using receiver to decode digital multichannel sound, unit will connect only via coaxial digital-audio input.

28 APEX AD-1225 **Very good overall, though not as easy to use as others.** Lacks console display, audio dynamic range control, and virtual surround sound (a potential issue if you use only two speakers). Plays back some older audio CDs with excessive treble, and failed to play CD-audio portion of hybrid SACD discs.

DVD recorders

DVD recorders differ little in basic performance. All offer superb images and sound when playing a prerecorded DVD or a recording of a high-quality source made in 1- or 2-hour mode. You can pack 4 to 6 hours of content onto a blank DVD, but you'll get more detail and less graininess with settings that offer 1- or 2-hour recordings. If you'll play recordings on the recorder itself and want the most recording flexibility, these models are good choices: Panasonic DMR-E60, $550, Samsung DVD-R4000, $500, and Panasonic DMR-E50, $500. They can use DVD-RAM discs, which let you begin watching recordings before they're completed. If you want recordings that can be played on most DVD players, two good choices are the Magnavox MDV630R, $450, and the Philips DVDR 75, $600.

In performance order

Ratings key: Excellent ● / Very good ◕ / Good ○ / Fair ◔ / Poor ●

Key number	Brand & model	Price	Overall score (P F G VG E, 0–100)	Disc types	Playback picture quality	Recording picture quality: 1 or 2 hr.	Recording picture quality: 6 hr.	Ease of use	Coaxial digital-audio output	Optical digital-audio output
1	**Panasonic** DMR-E60	$550		DVD-R, DVD-RAM	●	●	○	●		●
2	**Samsung** DVD-R4000	500		DVD-R, DVD-RAM	●	●	○	●		●
3	**Panasonic** DMR-E50	500		DVD-R, DVD-RAM	●	●	○	●		●
4	**Sharp** DV-RW2	500		DVD-R, DVD-RW	●	●	◕	◔		●
5	**Magnavox** MDV630R	450		DVD+R, DVD+RW	●	●	○	◔	●	
6	**Philips** DVDR 75	600		DVD+R, DVD+RW	●	●	○	◔	●	
7	**Sony** RDR-GX7	800		DVD-R, DVD-RW, DVD+RW	●	●	○	◔	●	●

See report, page 70. Based on tests published in Consumer Reports in December 2003.

Ratings

Guide to the Ratings

Overall score is based mainly on picture quality; ease of use is also factored in. **Disc types** indicates the types of discs on which each player can record. **Playback picture quality** indicates sharpness and detail with prerecorded discs. All were tested with conventional TVs; all but the Maganvox (5) were also tested with HDTVs. **Recording picture quality** for **1 or 2 hr.** and **6 hr.** is for discs recorded in those modes. In 4-hr. mode (not displayed), all were good. **Ease of use** assesses the remote control, console front panel, setup menu, basic functions, and features. **Price is approximate retail.**

Recommendations and notes

All tested models have: Composite-video, S-video, and stereo audio inputs for recording. One-touch recording. Ability to record near-CD-quality stereo audio using Dolby Digital compression. Composite-video, S-video, and component-video outputs. Parental controls. Resume-play function. Ability to play DVD-video and CD-audio discs. Ability to play CD-R, CD-RW, DVD-R, DVD+R, and DVD-RW (video mode) discs. Dolby Digital and DTS multichannel digital-audio outputs. Two-channel (stereo) analog-audio output. Front-panel A/V inputs.

1 PANASONIC DMR-E60 **Excellent overall.** Plays DVD-Audio discs in stereo mode only. Has 16-event/1-month timer for time-shift recordings. Displays JPEG picture files from CompactFlash and PC cards (other media supported with adapter, not supplied).

2 SAMSUNG DVD-R4000 **Excellent overall.** Has 16-event/1-month timer for time-shift recordings.

3 PANASONIC DMR-E50 **Very good overall.** But poor performance when playing back damaged DVD-Video discs in our tests. Has 16-event/1-month timer for time-shift recordings.

4 SHARP DV-RW2 **Very good overall.** Excellent performance when playing back damaged DVD-Video discs and audio CDs in our tests. Has 8-event/12-month timer for time-shift recordings. Lacks 6-hour recording mode for DVD-R recordings.

5 MAGNAVOX MDV630R **Very good overall.** Excellent performance when playing back damaged DVD-Video discs in our tests. Has 2.5-hour (instead of 2-hour) recording mode. Has 6-event/12-month timer for time-shift recordings.

6 PHILIPS DVDR 75 **Very good overall.** Has 2.5- and 3-hr. recording modes. Has 6-event/12-mo. timer for time-shift recordings.

7 SONY RDR-GX7 **Very good overall.** Has 1.5- and 3-hour recording modes. Has 30-event/1-month timer for time-shift recordings.

DVD/VCR combos

DVD-VCR combinations are space-efficient; they allow you to combine a DVD and VCR in a space little bigger than a stand-alone unit of either type. They eliminate hooking up an extra device. However, you won't be able to record most DVD movies on videotape because of copy restrictions on DVDs. In our tests, DVD-VCR combination units were almost indistinguishable in overall performance in DVD playback and videotaping. Choose by price and features. Based on our previous tests of VCRs, we think it's safe to shop for a stand-alone recorder based on price and features.

In performance order

Excellent ● Very good ◐ Good ○ Fair ◖ Poor ●

Key number	Brand & model	Price	Overall score (P F G VG E)	Picture quality: DVD	Picture quality: VHS (SP/EP)	Ease of use: DVD	Ease of use: VCR	Coaxial digital-audio output	Optical digital-audio output	JPEG image files	Universal remote
1	**Panasonic** PV-D4743	$160		●	○	◐	◐		•	•	•
2	**Hitachi** DV-PF73U	180		●	○	◐	◐	•			•
3	**Samsung** DVD-V3500	170		●	○	◐	◐	•	•	•	•
4	**Sony** SLV-D300P	200		●	○	○	◐	•	•		•

See report, page 90. Based on tests published in Consumer Reports in December 2003.

Guide to the Ratings

Overall score is based mainly on DVD and VCR picture quality; ease of use is also factored in. **DVD picture quality** indicates sharpness and detail with prerecorded discs. **VCR** scores are based on recordings made in standard and extended-play modes. **Ease of use** assesses the remote control, console front panel, setup menus, basic functions, and features. Under Features, **JPEG image files** indicates ability to read digital photos on CD. **Price** is approximate retail.

   All tested models have: Progressive-scan DVD video output. Composite-video and RF VCR and DVD output. S-video and component-video DVD output. Parental controls. Dolby Digital multichannel audio output for DVD. Two-channel analog audio output. One-touch recording. Ability to play DVD-video and CD-audio discs, CD-R, CD-RW, MP3-format, DVD+R, DVD-R, and DVD-RW (video mode) discs. Single-disc DVD player. Front-panel A/V inputs.

Ratings

Food processors & choppers

Any of the food processors we tested can handle basic chopping and slicing. Most are adept at shredding, and several purée well. However, the processors costing less than $55 don't have enough power to knead bread dough without laboring. The inexpensive models were also noisy. The Cuisinart DLC-5, $85, a **CR Best Buy**, doesn't come with many extras, but this midsized processor performs the basics very well (including kneading) and is well-priced.

Though smaller and less versatile than processors, choppers can be handy for little tasks, such as mincing garlic or herbs. For basic tasks, the Cuisinart DLC-1, $30, and the Cuisinart Mini Prep Plus DLC-2A, $45, both chop very well.

In performance order

Ratings legend: Excellent ◉ · Very good ◕ · Good ○ · Fair ◐ · Poor ●

Key number	Brand & model (Similar models, in small type, comparable to tested model.)	Price	Overall score (P F G VG E, 0–100)	Weight (lb.)	Claimed/measured capacity (cups)	Slicing	Shredding	Puréeing	Noise
	FOOD PROCESSORS								
1	**KitchenAid** Professional KFP670[WH] KFP650[ ], KFP600[ ]	$240		14	11/10	◉	◉	◐	◐
2	**Cuisinart** DLC-5 **A CR Best Buy**	85		11	7/8	◉	◉	◐	◐
3	**Cuisinart** Pro Custom II DLC-8S	200		13	11/10	◉	◉	◐	◐
4	**Cuisinart** Power Prep Plus DLC2014	300		15	14/12	◉	◉	◐	○
5	**KitchenAid** Ultra Power 7 KFP450[WW]	130		10	7/7	◉	◐	◐	◉
6	**KitchenAid** Little Ultra Power KFP350[WH] KFP300[ ]	100		10	5/6	◉	◐	◐	◐
7	**Cuisinart** Prep 11 Plus DLC-2011	300		13	11/9	◉	◉	○	◉
8	**Kenmore** 69703 KFP-70	140		11	7/7	◉	◉	○	◉
9	**Cuisinart** Little Pro Plus	70		7	3/4	◐	◐	◐	◉
10	**DeLonghi** Cucina DFP880	300		15	12/11	◐	◐	◐	◉
11	**Black & Decker** Quick 'N Easy Plus FP1400 FP1300	40		6	8/9	◐	◐	◐	●
12	**Hamilton Beach** 70550 🅳 70550R	30		6	8/8	◐	◐	●	◐
13	**GE** 106622F (Wal-Mart)	40		6	9/9	◐	◐	●	◐
14	**Black & Decker** Power Pro II FP1500	55		7	10/9	◐	◐	○	◐

🅳 Discontinued, but similar model is available. Price is for similar model.

Ratings

Key number	Brand & model	Price	Overall score	Claimed capacity (cups)	Test results		
	Similar models, in small type, comparable to tested model.		0 100 P F G VG E		Chopping	Puréeing	Noise
	CHOPPERS						
15	**Ultimate Chopper** CH-1	$60		¾	◖	○	◖
16	**Cuisinart** DLC-1	30		2½	◖	◖	◒
17	**Cuisinart** Mini Prep Plus DLC-2A	45		3	◖	○	◒
18	**Black & Decker** EHC600 Ergo	25		2	◖	◒	○
19	**Black & Decker** SC400	20		2	○	○	◒
20	**Hamilton Beach** 72600 72610	25		3	○	◒	○
21	**GE** Deluxe 106848 (Wal-Mart)	20		3	○	◒	○

See report, page 33. Based on tests published in Consumer Reports in December 2003.

Guide to the Ratings

Overall score is based on performance and noise, and also reflects convenience factors. **For processors:** We judged each model's proficiency at **slicing** vegetables, **shredding** potatoes and cheese, and **puréeing** peas and carrots. (All processors chopped effectively.) For **choppers:** We judged proficiency at **chopping** onions, beef, and almonds and at **puréeing. Noise** was judged based on the unit's highest speed. **Weight** of processors is rounded to the nearest pound and includes the base, bowl, lid, and chopping blade. Capacity of processors is as claimed by the manufacturer, then as measured by us (dry). **Capacity** of choppers is as claimed by the manufacturer. **Price** is approximate retail. Under **brand & model,** bracketed letters are color codes.

Most processors and choppers have: A one-year warranty. **All processors have:** A clear plastic bowl with locking lid. S-shaped chopping blade. At least one slicing/shredding disk. Plastic food pusher. Most are dishwasher safe. **All choppers have:** A clear plastic bowl and lid. Chopping blade. All are dishwasher safe.

Ratings

Generators, portable

Models judged very good in our power-delivery tests came closest to meeting their wattage claims and maintained the voltage needed to keep devices from overheating. Best for most emergency needs are the **CR Best Buy** Generac Wheelhouse 5500 1646 and the Troy-Bilt 5550 01919, both $650. If low noise is most important, check out the Honda EU3000is, $1,800, and the Yamaha EF3000iSE, $1,900.

In performance order

Ratings legend: Excellent ◉ Very good ◕ Good ○ Fair ◔ Poor ●

Key number	Brand & model	Weight (lbs.)	Price	Overall score (P F G VG E, 0–100)	Watts (claimed)	Run time (hr.)	Power delivery	Ease of use	Noise	Wheels	Oil guard	Fuel gauge
	SMALL (3,000 TO 4,000 WATTS) *Best for bare essentials, recreation, or powering tools.*											
1	**Honda** EU3000is	132	$1,800		2800	7	◕	○	◉		•	•
2	**Yamaha** EF3000iSE	153	1,900		2800	7	◕	◕	◉	•	•	•
3	**Generac** 4000EXL 1645	142	750		4000	7.5	◔	◉	○	•	•	
4	**Craftsman** 32330	90	450		3000	2	○	◔	○			
5	**Coleman** Powermate Premium PM0543000.17	105	400		3000	2	◔	○	◔			
	MIDSIZED (4,500 TO 7,000 WATTS) *Fine for most emergency needs.*											
6	**Generac** Wheelhouse 5500 1646 [2] **A CR Best Buy**	157	650		5500	6.5	◕	◕	○	•	•	•
7	**North Star** 8000 TFG 165938F [1]	260	2,000		6600	6	◕	◕	◔		•	•
8	**Craftsman** 32560	157	750		5600	6.5	◕	◕	◕	•	•	•
9	**Troy-Bilt** 5550 01919 [3] **A CR Best Buy**	156	650		5550	6.5	◕	◕	◕	•	•	•
10	**Coleman** Powermate Premium Plus PM0545005	133	500		5000	6	○	◔	○		•	
11	**Honda** EG 5000XK1	148	1,350		4500	2.5	○	○	◔		•	

[1] *Sold only at Northern Tool.* [2] *Sold only at Home Depot.* [3] *Sold only at Lowes.*

Based on tests published in Consumer Reports in November 2003.

Guide to the Ratings

Overall score is based on power delivery, noise, run time, and ease of use. **Watts (claimed)** are the maximum for continuous operation, as stated by the manufacturer. **Run time** denotes hours per tankful of fuel rounded to the nearest half-hour, based on full load capacity. **Power delivery** reflects how much wattage models delivered, how well they maintained the minimum voltage needed to safely run motorized appliances, and their power quality. **Ease of use** denotes ease of starting and moving, as well as panel access, features, and other controls. **Noise** reflects sound levels measured at 50 feet with generators operating 3 feet from a building. **Weight** is to the nearest pound without fuel. **Price** is approximate retail.

Ratings

Home theater in a box

A home theater in a box is the easiest and usually the cheapest path to surround sound, with prices starting below $300. All these systems include a receiver and six speakers, plus wiring and instructions that make setup a relative snap. Be sure there are enough connections for your needs because some models skimp on inputs and outputs. If you're looking for a model with a DVD player, the Sony HT-1800DP, $450, holds only one disc, but its separate components offer flexibility, and its receiver has ample connections. If you don't need a DVD player, the Onkyo HT-S760B, $500, is very good. It costs more than other models without DVD players, but has more inputs and offers 6.1 support.

In performance order

Ratings key: Excellent ● | Very good ◕ | Good ○ | Fair ◔ | Poor ●

Key number	Brand & model	Price	Overall score (P F G VG E)	Sound quality	Ease of use	Features	No. of discs	Digital-audio in (optical/coaxial)	Composite-video in/out	S-video in/out	Component-video in/out	Powered subwoofer	Onscreen display	Front-panel input
MODELS WITH DVD PLAYER														
1	**Sony** HT-1800DP	$450		◕	◕	◔	1	1/1	3/1	0/1	0/1	●		
2	**Sony** HT-C800DP	400		◕	○	○	5	0/0	1/0	0/0	0/1		●	
3	**Panasonic** SC-HT900	500		●	○	◔	5	1/0	0/0	0/1	0/1	●	●	
4	**Panasonic** SC-MT1	400		●	○	◔	1	0/0	0/0	0/1	0/1			
MODELS WITHOUT DVD PLAYER														
5	**Sony** HT-DDW750	300		◕	◕	◕	–	1/1	3/1	0/0	0/0	●		
6	**Onkyo** HT-S760B	500		◕	◕	◕	–	2/1	4/1	4/2	2/1	●		●
7	**Kenwood** HTB-306	350		◕	◕	◔	–	1/2	3/1	2/1	0/0			
8	**RCA** RT-2600	280		○	○	○	–	2/1	4/1	2/1	0/0			●
9	**Kenwood** HTB-206	300		◕	○	◔	–	1/2	3/1	0/0	0/0			

See report, page 73. Based on tests published in Consumer Reports in November 2003, with updated prices and availability.

Guide to the Ratings

Overall score is based mostly on sound quality. **Sound quality** represents the accuracy of the amplifier, front speakers, subwoofer, and center-channel speaker. **Ease of use** reflects the design of the front panel and the remote control, legibility of controls, and ease of setup. **Features** reflects the presence or absence of useful features. The inputs and outputs shown are on the receiver, if that is separate from the DVD player. On models with DVD players, the S-video and component-video outputs can be used only with a TV. **Price** is approximate retail.

Recommendations and notes

ALL TESTED MODELS HAVE: A receiver and six speakers: front left and right, center, rear-surround left and right, and sub-woofer. Decoders for Dolby Digital, DTS, Dolby Pro Logic surround audio, and other digital-signal processing (DSP) modes. An FM tuner that scored very good in our tests. An AM tuner (not tested for this report) that should be good or fair, based on previous testing. Headphone jack. Mute button. Wiring and setup instructions. No phono input. **MOST TESTED MODELS:** Have bass and treble adjustment, receiver-display dimmer, at least 30 radio-station presets, sleep timer, and 1-yr. warranty. Lack on-screen display (OSD) feature, front-panel A/V inputs, loudness control, or bass-boost switch. Most with DVD player cannot play DVD-Audio and SACD discs.

MODELS WITH DVD PLAYER

1. SONY HT-1800DP **Very good.** Includes stand-alone single-disc DVD player. Has optical and coaxial digital-audio inputs and 2-yr. warranty. Lacks 5.1 inputs for external digital-audio decoders. Front and rear-surround speakers 6x3.75x5 in. (HWD), 1.8 lb. each; center speaker 3.75x9.25x5 in., 2.2 lb.; subwoofer 12.75x10.75x16 in., 21.6 lb.

2. SONY HT-C800DP **Very good.** Includes integrated five-disc DVD player. Has on-screen display, and bass-boost switch. 2-yr. warranty. Lacks 5.1 inputs for external digital- audio decoders. No S-video connection, sleep timer or treble adjustment. Front and rear-surround speakers 6x3.75x5 in. (HWD), 1.8 lb. each; center speaker 3.75x9.25x5 in., 2.2 lb.; subwoofer 12.75x10.75x14.25 in., 14.7 lb.

3. PANASONIC SC-HT900 **Very good.** Can play DVD-audio discs. Includes integrated five-disc DVD player. Has on-screen display. Optical digital-audio input only. Lacks 5.1 inputs for external digital-audio decoders. No treble adjustment. Front and rear-surround speakers 42x10x10 in. (HWD) standing (21.75x3.25x4 in. wall- mounted), 9 lb. each; center speaker 5.5x10x5.75 in. standing (3.75x9.75x4 in. wall-mounted), 3.4 lb.; subwoofer 17.75x6.25x17.75 in., 26.3 lb.

4. PANASONIC SC-MT1 **Very good.** Includes integrated single-disc DVD player. Can play DVD-audio discs. But lacks digital-audio input from other devices, such as digital-cable box or satellite receiver. Lacks 5.1 inputs for external digital-audio decoders. No treble adjustment. Front and rear-surround speakers 9x4.25x4.25 in. (HWD), 2 lb. each; center speaker 5.5x10x5.75 in., 3.4 lb.; subwoofer 17.75x6.25x17.75 in., 25.6 lb. 15 radio station presets.

MODELS WITHOUT DVD PLAYER

5. SONY HT-DDW750 **Very good.** Has optical and coaxial digital-audio inputs and 2-yr. warranty. Lacks component- and S-video input/output, requiring you to connect DVD player, digital-cable box, or satellite receiver directly to TV for best picture quality. Lacks 5.1 inputs for external digital-audio decoders. Front and rear-surround speakers 6x3.75x5 in. (HWD), 1.8 lb. each; center speaker 3.75x9.25x5 in., 2.1 lb.; subwoofer 12.75x10.75x16, 21.1 lb.

6. ONKYO HT-S760B **Very good.** Has optical and coaxial digital-audio inputs, front-panel A/V inputs, and 2-yr. warranty. Has 5.1 inputs for external digital-audio decoders. Front speakers 16.5x7.5x9.5 in. (HWD), 11.8 lb. each; rear-surround speakers 10.5x7x5 in., 3.9 lb. each; center speaker 6.25x15.25x8 in., 7.8 lb.; subwoofer 20.25x11x15.75 in., 29.5 lb. Similar model: HT-S767C has 6-disc DVD player.

7. KENWOOD HTB-306 **Very good, but relatively few features for the price.** Has optical and coaxial digital-audio inputs, bass-boost switch, and loudness control. Has 5.1 inputs for external digital-audio decoders. Lacks component-video input/output, requiring you to connect HD-capable devices directly to similarly capable TV for very best picture quality. No sleep timer. Front and rear-surround speakers 7x4x5 in. (HWD), 2.1 and 1.7 lb. each respectively; center speaker 4x8x5 in., 2.2 lb.; subwoofer 13x12x17.75 in., 16.9 lb.

8. RCA RT-2600 **Very good.** Has optical and coaxial digital-audio inputs and front-panel A/V inputs. Has 5.1 inputs for external digital-audio decoders. Lacks component-video input/output, requiring you to connect HD-capable devices directly to similarly capable TV for very best picture quality. No receiver-display dimmer or sleep timer. Front and rear-surround speakers 7x4.75x4.5 in. (HWD), 2.9 and 2.2 lb. each respectively; center speaker 4.75x7x4.5 in., 2.9 lb.; subwoofer 14x8x13.5 in., 10.6 lb.

9. KENWOOD HTB-206 **Good.** Has optical and coaxial digital-audio inputs, bass-boost switch, and loudness control. Has 5.1 inputs for external digital-audio decoders. Lacks component-video input/output, requiring you to connect HD-capable devices. No sleep timer. Front speakers 7x4x5.75 in., 1.9 lb.; rear-surround speakers 7.25x4x5.75 in. (HWD), 1.5 lb. each; center speaker 4x8x5.75 in., 2 lb.; subwoofer 14.75x8x14.75 in., 13.7 lb.

Ratings

Kitchen knives

If you frequently cook gourmet meals, you might appreciate the superior precision, control, and comfort afforded by the expensive knives that top the Ratings. You can get fine quality for far less, however. The two **CR Best Buys,** Farberware Pro Forged, $90 for nine pieces, and Chicago Cutlery Metropolitan, $60 for eight pieces, are very good choices. And, at $130 for seven pieces, the Oxo MV55-PRO offers excellent performance and value. If you prefer no-maintenance knives, the Cutco ($80 for two pieces) was very good overall. Much more economical is the Farberware Classic set ($20 for 12 pieces).

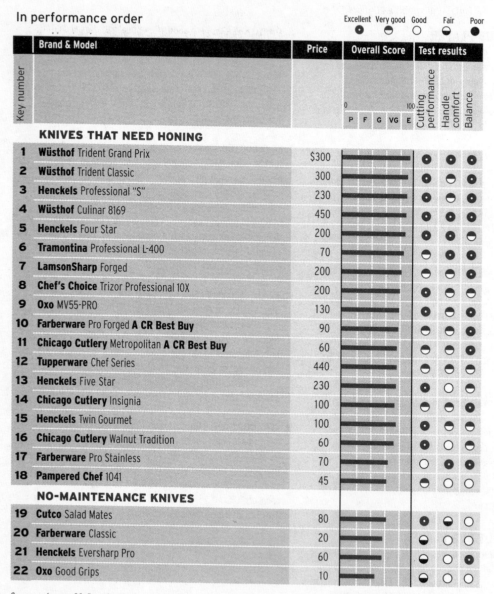

In performance order

Ratings key: Excellent · Very good · Good · Fair · Poor

Overall Score scale: 0 — 100 (P F G VG E)

Key number	Brand & Model	Price	Overall Score	Cutting performance	Handle comfort	Balance
	KNIVES THAT NEED HONING					
1	**Wüsthof** Trident Grand Prix	$300		Excellent	Excellent	Excellent
2	**Wüsthof** Trident Classic	300		Excellent	Very good	Excellent
3	**Henckels** Professional "S"	230		Excellent	Very good	Excellent
4	**Wüsthof** Culinar 8169	450		Excellent	Excellent	Excellent
5	**Henckels** Four Star	200		Excellent	Excellent	Excellent
6	**Tramontina** Professional L-400	70		Very good	Excellent	Excellent
7	**LamsonSharp** Forged	200		Very good	Very good	Very good
8	**Chef's Choice** Trizor Professional 10X	200		Excellent	Very good	Very good
9	**Oxo** MV55-PRO	130		Excellent	Very good	Very good
10	**Farberware** Pro Forged **A CR Best Buy**	90		Very good	Very good	Excellent
11	**Chicago Cutlery** Metropolitan **A CR Best Buy**	60		Very good	Very good	Excellent
12	**Tupperware** Chef Series	440		Very good	Very good	Very good
13	**Henckels** Five Star	230		Excellent	Good	Very good
14	**Chicago Cutlery** Insignia	100		Very good	Very good	Very good
15	**Henckels** Twin Gourmet	100		Excellent	Very good	Very good
16	**Chicago Cutlery** Walnut Tradition	60		Excellent	Good	Very good
17	**Farberware** Pro Stainless	70		Good	Excellent	Excellent
18	**Pampered Chef** 1041	45		Very good	Good	Good
	NO-MAINTENANCE KNIVES					
19	**Cutco** Salad Mates	80		Excellent	Very good	Good
20	**Farberware** Classic	20		Fair	Excellent	Good
21	**Henckels** Eversharp Pro	60		Fair	Good	Poor
22	**Oxo** Good Grips	10		Very good	Good	Good

See report, page 30. Based on tests published in Consumer Reports in December 2002, with updated prices and availability.

Ratings

Guide to the Ratings

Brand and model is line we tested; we judged only chef's, slicing, utility, and paring knives in a line. **Overall score** is based mainly on cutting performance and handle comfort and balance but factors in corrosion resistance and, for no-maintenance knives, blade-edge durability. **Cutting performance** reflects how well each type cut through foods. **Handle comfort** and **balance** are based on the chef's knife. **Price** is approximate retail for the smallest available set that includes all or most of the four tested knives and typically a block and steel. If sets do not include all four knives, we note missing ones and their approximate price. Recommendations and notes indicate number of pieces in the set, blade type, and handle material if not hard plastic or composite.

Recommendations and notes

MOST KNIVES TESTED IN THESE SIZES: chef's, 8 inches; slicing, 8 to 10 inches; utility, 4 to 6 inches; paring, 3 to 4 inches.

KNIVES THAT NEED HONING

1 WÜSTHOF Trident Grand Prix **Forged.** 8-piece set. Better for wet grip than most. Heavier than most.

2 WÜSTHOF Trident Classic **Forged.** 8-piece set.

3 HENCKELS Professional "S" **Forged.** 7-piece set.

4 WÜSTHOF Culinar 8169 **Forged.** 6-piece set (not included: utility, $65). Stainless-steel handles. Heavier than most.

5 HENCKELS Four Star **Forged.** 7-piece set (not included: slicer, $82).

6 TRAMONTINA Professional L-400 **Forged.** 3-piece set (not included: slicer, $35). Heavier than most.

7 LAMSONSHARP Forged **Forged.** 6-piece set. Wood handles; more prone to damage but offer better wet grip than most. Blade more likely to corrode than most. Maker will sharpen for free (you pay shipping).

8 CHEF'S CHOICE Trizor Professional 10X **Forged.** 3-piece set (not included: slicer, $125). Better for wet grip than most. Heavier than most.

9 OXO MV55-PRO **Stamped.** 7-piece set. Rubber-coated steel handles are bulky but offer better wet grip than most. Blade more likely to corrode than most.

10 FARBERWARE Pro Forged **A CR Best Buy Forged.** 9-piece set. Handles are bulky. Utility knife too small and flexible.

11 CHICAGO CUTLERY Metropolitan **A CR Best Buy Stamped.** 8-piece set. Handles are bulky. Lighter than most.

12 TUPPERWARE Chef Series **Forged.** 8-piece set (not included: slicer, $65). Heavier than most. Utility knife too small and flexible. Sold mainly through in-home parties.

13 HENCKELS Five Star Forged. **7-piece set.** Handles are bulky. Blade more likely to corrode than most.

14 CHICAGO Cutlery Insignia **Forged.** 10-piece set. Heavier than most.

15 HENCKELS Twin Gourmet Stamped. **7-piece set.** Gap between handle and blade. Blade more likely to corrode than most.

16 CHICAGO Cutlery Walnut Tradition **Stamped.** 6-piece set. Wood handles are bulky and more prone to damage but offer better wet grip than most. Gap between handle and blade. Lighter than most.

17 FARBERWARE Pro Stainless **Forged.** 8-piece set. Stainless-steel handles. Utility knife is serrated.

18 PAMPERED Chef 1041 **Stamped.** 2-piece carving set (not included: chef's knife, $26; utility, $19; paring, $15). Lighter than most. No sharpening steel; some knives come in a storage/sharpening case. Sold through sales representatives only.

NO-MAINTENANCE KNIVES

19 CUTCO Salad Mates **Stamped.** 2-piece set (not included: chef's knife, $94; slicer, $69). Blade more likely to corrode than most. Chef's and paring knives are fine-edged; slicing and utility knives are serrated. Maker will sharpen for free (you pay shipping). Sold through sales representatives only.

20 FARBERWARE Classic **Stamped.** 12-piece set. Better for wet grip than most. Gaps between handle and blade. All tested knives are serrated. Lighter than most.

21 HENCKELS Eversharp Pro **Stamped.** 7-piece set. Gap between handle and blade. All tested knives are serrated. Lighter than most.

22 OXO Good Grips **Stamped.** 2-piece set (not included: chef's knife, $12; slicer, $9). Handles are bulky and have fins that can trap food. Lighter than most. Chef's and paring knives are fine-edged, slicing and utility knives are serrated.

Ratings

Microwave ovens

Competent performance overall makes most of these microwave ovens a safe bet. Among countertop models, the GE JE 1860, $165, combines performance, space, and features. Consider the slightly smaller GE JE 1460, $130, **a CR Best Buy,** for its value, the Panasonic Genius NN-T993, $180, for larger meals, and the Kenmore 6325, $100, another **CR Best Buy,** if counter space is tight. If you want an over-the-range microwave, consider the competent and spacious LG Glide & Cook, $450, and Kenmore Elite 6468, $450. If you don't mind giving up shortcut keys, the **CR Best Buy** Panasonic Genius NN-S262, $350, is a very good choice. If performance and controls outweigh capacity, look to the Whirlpool Gold GH8155XM, $450.

In performance order

Ratings legend: Excellent ● | Very good ◕ | Good ○ | Fair ◑ | Poor ⬤

Key number	Brand & model (Similar models, in small type, comparable to tested model.)	Price	Watts	Capacity (cu. ft.) claim	Capacity (cu. ft.) test [1]	Overall score	Evenness	Auto defrost	Ease of use
MIDSIZED COUNTERTOP These offer a lower price and smaller footprint, 21x17 in. (WxD) for many.									
1	**Kenmore** (Sears) 6325[2] **A CR Best Buy**	$100	1200	1.2	0.9		○	●	◑
2	**Panasonic** Genius NN-S563[B]F NN-S553[ ]F [2]	110	1350	1.2	0.8		◑	◑	○
3	**Emerson** Professional Series MW8108[P]	90	1100	1.0	0.8		◑	◑	◑
LARGE COUNTERTOP These are bigger inside as well as outside, 24x19 in. (WxD) for many.									
4	**GE** JE1860[W]H	165	1100	1.8	1.2		◑	◑	●
5	**GE** JE1460[B]F **A CR Best Buy**	130	1150	1.4	1.0		◑	◑	◑
6	**GE** Profile JE2160[B]F	160	1200	2.1	1.5		◑	◑	◑
7	**Kenmore** (Sears) 6234[9]	110	1200	1.6	1.2		◑	●	◑
8	**Kenmore** (Sears) Elite UltraWave 6236[9]	150	1200	1.4	1.2		○	◑	●
9	**Panasonic** Genius NN-T993[S]F NN-S953[ ]F [2], NN-S963[ ]F	180	1350	2.2	1.6		◑	◑	◑
10	**Goldstar** MA2120[W]	120	1200	2.1	1.5		◑	●	◑
11	**Whirlpool** MT4145SK[Q]	130	1100	1.4	1.0		◑	○	◑
12	**Sharp** Carousel R-121[O] R-120[ ] [2] [3]	250	1100	1.5	1.0		◑	○	◑
13	**Whirlpool** MT4140SK[B]	140	1100	1.4	1.0		○	○	◑
OVER-THE-RANGE (OTR) These are stylish and free up counter space, but they require installation.									
14	**Whirlpool** Gold GH8155XM[B] MH8150XM[ ] [2]	450	1000	1.5	0.7		◑	●	●
15	**GE** Profile Spacemaker 2.0 JVM2070[B]H JVM2050[ ]H	525	1100	2.0	1.1		◑	◑	◑
16	**LG** Glide & Cook LMVM1945S[B]	450	1100	1.9	1.8		○	◑	◑
17	**Kenmore** (Sears) Elite 6468[2]	450	1200	2.0	1.8		○	●	◑
18	**Panasonic** Genius NN-S262[B]F NN-S252[ ]F [2] **A CR Best Buy**	350	1200	1.9	1.0		○	◑	◑
19	**LG** Scroll 'n Cook LMV915NV	500	1000	1.9	1.0		○	○	◑
20	**GE** Spacemaker JVM1850[B]F JVM1870[ ]F	375	1000	1.8	0.9		◑	◑	◑

Key number	Brand & model	Price	Watts	Capacity (cu. ft.) claim	test [1]	Overall score (0–100, P F G VG E)	Evenness	Auto defrost	Ease of use
OVER-THE-RANGE (OTR) *These are stylish and free up counter space, but they require installation.*									
21	**Kenmore** (Sears) 6264[9] 6262[ ] [2]	350	1000	1.6	0.8		○	○	◉
22	**Sharp** Carousel R-175[0]	350	1100	1.6	0.8		◐	◐	◉
23	**Amana** ACO1860A[B] ACO1840A[ ]	400	1000	1.8	0.9		○	○	◐
24	**GE** Spacemaker JVM1650[B]B JVM1640[ ]H [2]	345	1000	1.6	0.8		○	◐	◐
25	**Maytag** MMV5186AA[S]	430	1000	1.8	0.9		○	◐	◐
26	**Sharp** Carousel R-151[0] R-150[ ] [2]	250	1000	1.5	1.0		◐	◐	○
OTR SPEED-COOK *Fine for regular heating, but browning can be a challenge.*									
27	**Kenmore** (Sears) Elite 6379[9]	750	1100	1.7	0.8		◐	◉	◐
28	**Whirlpool** Gold GH9177XL[B]	700	1100	1.7	0.8		◐	◉	◐

[1] Test measurements are with turntable on. [2] Similar model has no sensor. [3] Designed for under-cabinet mounting.

See report, page 31. Based on tests published in Consumer Reports in January 2004.

Guide to the Ratings

Overall score is based mostly on cooking evenness, defrosting ability, and ease of use. **Watts** and **capacity (claim)** are as listed on the product or packaging. **Capacity (test)** reflects our measure of usable space based on the turntable or sliding tray. **Evenness** is how uniformly the model heated a dish of cold mashed potatoes. **Auto defrost** denotes how completely and evenly the program defrosted 1 pound of frozen ground beef. **Ease of use** is how easily ovens can be set without guidance. **Price** is approximate retail. Under brand & model, the color code is bracketed. Similar models, in small type, have the same wattage and capacity as those tested and should perform comparably, though features may vary.

Ratings

Mixers

Most stand and hand mixers will whip, mix, and mash acceptably. The KitchenAid Classic K45SS, $215, a **CR Best Buy,** is a stand mixer that excels at everything from meringue to double batches of bread dough. The less-expensive Sunbeam Mixmaster 2366, $80, is a decent performer across the board. Hand mixers good for most tasks are the Cuisinart CountUp HTM-9LT, $70, the KitchenAid Professional 9 KHM9P, $80, and the KitchenAid Ultra Power Plus 7KHM7T, $70. All easily handle cookie dough and have touchpad controls and digital speed display.

In performance order

Ratings legend: Excellent ● | Very good ◒ | Good ○ | Fair ◔ | Poor ●

Key number	Brand & model (Similar models, in small type, comparable to tested model.)	Price	Overall score (P F G VG E)	Bowl	Capacity (qt.)	Weight (lb.)	Whipping time	Mashing	Mixing	Kneading	Convenience	Noise
STAND MIXERS												
1	**KitchenAid** Classic K45SS[WH] K45SSD[ ] **A CR Best Buy**	$215		SS	4½	24	Excellent	Very good	Excellent	Excellent	Very good	Good
2	**KitchenAid** Ultra Power KSM90PS[WW]	230		SS	4½	24	Excellent	Very good	Excellent	Excellent	Very good	Good
3	**KitchenAid** Artisan KSM150PS[WW]	250		SS	5	23	Excellent	Good	Excellent	Excellent	Very good	Good
4	**DeLonghi** DSM700	300		SS	5	16	Excellent	Good	Very good	Very good	Good	Very good
5	**Sunbeam** Mixmaster 2366 2367, 2369	80		G	4	10	Good	Good	Good	Good	Good	Good
6	**GE** 106772 (Wal-Mart)	30		G	4	8	Good	Good	Good	Very good	Good	Good
7	**Hamilton Beach** Power Deluxe 64695	35		G	4	8	Good	Very good	Good	Good	Good	Fair

Key number	Brand & model	Price	Overall score (P F G VG E)	Whipping time	Mashing	Mixing	Convenience	Noise	Whisk	Interchangeable beaters	Wire beaters	Slow-start
HAND MIXERS												
8	**Cuisinart** CountUp HTM-9LT D HTM-9LB	$70		Excellent	Excellent	Excellent	Very good	Poor	•		•	•
9	**KitchenAid** Professional 9 KHM9P[WH]	80		Excellent	Very good	Excellent	Very good	Very good	•		•	•
10	**KitchenAid** Ultra Power 5 KHM5DH[WH] KHM3[ ], KHM5TB[ ]	55		Very good	Very good	Excellent	Very good	Very good	•		•	
11	**Braun** Multi Mix 4-in-1 M880	50		Very good	Good	Excellent	Very good	Very good		•		
12	**KitchenAid** Ultra Power Plus 7 KHM7T[WH]	70		Very good	Good	Excellent	Very good	Very good			•	•
13	**Black & Decker** Power Pro MX77 D MX77W5	10		Good	Very good	Very good	Good	Very good	•			

Key number	Brand & model	Price	Overall score (0–100) P F G VG E	Whipping time	Mashing	Mixing	Convenience	Noise	Whisk	Interchangeable beaters	Wire beaters	Slow-start
	HAND MIXERS											
14	**Oster** 2496	$27		◕	◖	○	○	○	•	•		
15	**Black & Decker** Power Pro MX45	20		○	◖	○	○	●		•		
16	**GE** 106651 (Wal-Mart)	20		◖	○	○	○	○	•	•	•	
17	**Hamilton Beach** MixMate Ultra 62680 62681	20		○	◖	◖	○	◖		•		
18	**Proctor-Silex** 5 62515	10		◖	○	◖	◖	○		•		

D *Discontinued, but similar model is available. Price is for similar model.*

See report, page 33. Based on tests published in Consumer Reports in December 2003.

Guide to the Ratings

Overall score is based on performance and noise, plus convenience factors. All mixers made excellent whipped cream and meringue; **whipping time** reflects how fast they did so. Hand mixers took from about 1 to 3 minutes; stand mixers, from about 1 to 7½ minutes. We also judged proficiency at **mashing** potatoes, **mixing** cookie dough, and, for stand mixers, **kneading** bread. **Convenience** considers factors such as ease of using controls and inserting and removing beaters. **Noise** was judged at the unit's highest speed. **For stand mixers:** Under **bowl,** "SS" means stainless steel, "G" means glass. **Capacity** is as claimed by the manufacturer. **Weight,** to the nearest pound, includes mixer, bowl, beaters, and cord. **Price** is approximate retail. Under **brand & model,** bracketed letters are color codes. **Most stand and hand mixers have:** A one-year warranty. **All stand and hand mixers have:** Three or more speeds. **All stand mixers have:** Dough hooks. **All hand mixers have:** Speed control on handle. Beater-eject mechanism.

Power blowers

Among the handheld blowers most people buy, electrics rule. Besides outperforming the best gas-powered models, electric handhelds cost and weigh less while freeing you from fueling, pull-starting, and periodic tune-ups. Among the best electrics are two **CR Best Buys,** the Toro Super Blower Vac 51591, $70, and the Weed Eater 2595 Barracuda, $50. But if you can't drag an extension cord around, consider a gasoline-powered model. The **CR Best Buy** Weed Eater BV 1650, $100, is a good value if loosening debris isn't a priority. A lighter model worth considering is the John Deere BH25, $190. For large properties, the Echo Pro Lite PB260L, $300, is less noisy.

In performance order

Ratings scale: Excellent · Very good · Good · Fair · Poor

Key number	Brand & model	Price	Weight (lb.)	Overall score	Sweeping	Loosening debris	Vacuuming	Handling	Noise at 50 ft.	Noise at ear
	Similar models, in small type, comparable to tested model.			0 — 100 (P F G VG E)						
ELECTRIC HANDHELD BLOWERS										
1	**Toro** Super Blower Vac 51591 **A CR Best Buy**	$70	7		Fair	Excellent	Excellent	Excellent	Good	Good
2	**Toro** Ultra Blower Vac 51598	100	7.5		Fair	Excellent	Excellent	Excellent	Good	Good
3	**Weed Eater** 2595 Barracuda **A CR Best Buy**	50	7		Excellent	Very good	Very good	Good	Good	Good
4	**Toro** Rake and Vac 51573	65	6.5		Good	Very good	Excellent	Very good	Good	Good
5	**Black & Decker** Leaf Hog BV2500	70	7		Fair	Very good	Excellent	Very good	Very good	Good
6	**Weed Eater** 2540 Groundskeeper	40	7		Good	Good	Good	Good	Good	Good
7	**Black & Decker** FT1000	40	6		Fair	Good	N/A	Very good	Very good	Good
8	**Craftsman** 79940	70	7		Fair	Good	Good	Good	Good	Good
9	**Weed Eater** 2510 Groundsweeper	30	5		Fair	Good	N/A	Good	Fair	Good
10	**Craftsman** 79943	60	7		Fair	Good	Good	Very good	Good	Good
GASOLINE HANDHELD BLOWERS										
11	**Echo** PB-230LN PP-231LN [2]	200	11		Good	Very good	N/A	Good	Good	Fair
12	**John Deere** BH25	190	8.5		Good	Excellent	N/A	Very good	Good	Good
13	**Weed Eater** BV 1650 **A CR Best Buy**	100	11.5		Fair	Good	Good	Good	Good	Fair
14	**Craftsman** 79712 79412 [2]	100	11		Good	Good	N/A	Good	Good	Fair
15	**Craftsman** 79734 79434 [2]	130	11		Good	Good	Good	Good	Fair	Poor
16	**Echo** ES-210 ES-211 [2]	200	9.5		Good	Good	Fair	Good	Good	Good
17	**Weed Eater** FL 1500 Featherlite	80	7.5		Fair	Good	N/A	Good	Fair	Good

Ratings

Key number	Brand & model	Price	Weight (lb.)	Overall score						Test results					
				P	F	G	VG	E		Sweeping	Loosening debris	Vacuuming	Handling	Noise at 50 ft.	Noise at ear

GASOLINE BACKPACK BLOWERS

Key number	Brand & model	Price	Weight (lb.)	Overall score	Sweeping	Loosening debris	Vacuuming	Handling	Noise at 50 ft.	Noise at ear
18	**Makita** RBL500	$400	24.5		◉	◓	N/A	◉	○	●
19	**Solo** 470 D 471-KAT [2]	420	24		◉	◉	N/A	○	○	◓
20	**Stihl** BR340L	300	20.5		◓	◓	N/A	◉	○	◓
21	**Echo** Pro Lite PB260L	300	16		◓	◓	N/A	◉	◓	◓

[1] Price includes optional bag ($35). [2] Similar models comply with California emissions rules and typically are sold in California only. **D** Discontinued, but similar model is available. Price is for similar model.

See report, page 106. Based on tests published in Consumer Reports in September 2003, with updated prices and availability.

Guide to the Ratings

Overall score is based on sweeping and loosening performance, handling, noise, and where applicable, vacuuming. **Weight** is to the nearest half-pound in blower mode. **Sweeping** is how quickly blowers moved large leaf piles. **Loosening** is how quickly models removed embedded leaf particles from the lawn. **Vacuuming** is how quickly blowers picked up leaves and how well they mulched them. **Handling** includes ease of maneuvering while blowing and ease of controls and mode changes. **Noise** includes our measurements **at 50 feet** and at ear level. Models rated excellent or very good at 50 feet should meet typical limits of 65 decibels (dBA). For **noise at ear,** models rated fair and poor emitted 91 to 99 dBA and, we think, should be used with hearing protection. **Price** is approximate retail.

Ratings

Power sanders

You'll find many competent sanders, especially among the versatile random-orbit and finishing types. Two very good choices for most uses are the Craftsman 27957, $80, and the Ryobi RS241, $30, a **CR Best Buy.** Consider the Craftsman for its fine overall performance and the Ryobi for its easier handling and low price. If getting into corners is critical, try the Black & Decker FS500, $30, also a **CR Best Buy.** For sanding large or uneven areas, look for a belt sander. The top-scoring Porter Cable 352VS, $180, is best for large, horizontal surfaces, while the lighter Makita 9911, $130, offers easier vertical sanding. We recommend that you wear hearing protection with any model that scored less than a good in our noise tests.

In performance order

Ratings legend: Excellent ● · Very good ◖ · Good ○ · Fair ◐ · Poor ●

Key number	Brand & model (Similar models, in small type, comparable to tested model.)	Price	Weight (lb.)	Overall score (0–100: P F G VG E)	Speed by type	Controls	Dust capture	Handling by type	Noise	Dust bag	Vac connection	Easy paper change
RANDOM-ORBIT *Most versatile; 5-inch-diameter models can handle some rough- and most finish-sanding.*												
1	**Craftsman** (Sears) 27957	$80	3.6		Excellent	Excellent	Very good	Good	Good	●	●	●
2	**DeWalt** DW423K	90	3.5		Very good	Excellent	Excellent	Good	Good	●	●	●
3	**Makita** BO5012K	100	3.1		Very good	Excellent	Excellent	Very good	Good	●	●	●
4	**Ryobi** RS241 **A CR Best Buy**	30	3.0		Very good	Good	Good	Excellent	Good	●	●	●
5	**Porter Cable** Quicksand 333 / 333VS	60	3.6		Good	Good	Good	Very good	Good			
6	**Craftsman** (Sears) 11623	40	2.9		Good	Good	Fair	Very good	Very good			
FINISHING *Good for corners; ⅓-sheet models are best for larger areas.*												
7	**Makita** BO3700 (⅓-sheet)	85	3.7		Good	Fair	Very good	Excellent	Excellent	●		●
8	**DeWalt** DW411K	55	3.0		Very good	Excellent	Good	Very good	Fair			
9	**Porter Cable** 340K	50	2.7		Very good	Very good	Good	Fair	Fair			
10	**Black & Decker** FS350 (⅓-sheet)	40	2.9		Very good	Excellent	NA [1]	Excellent	Fair		●	
11	**Craftsman** (Sears) 11632 (⅓-sheet)	60	3.7		Excellent	Very good	Good	Good	Good	●		
12	**Black & Decker** FS500 **A CR Best Buy**	30	2.7		Very good	Good	Good	Good	Good			
13	**Makita** BO4552K	50	2.5		Very good	Fair	Very good	Good	Fair	●		
14	**Skil** 7230	20	3.0		Very good	Good	NA	Excellent	Fair			●
15	**Craftsman** (Sears) 11627	30	2.6		Fair	Good	NA	Good	Fair			

Ratings

Key number	Brand & model	Price	Weight (lb.)	Overall score (0–100, P F G VG E)	Performance					Features		
					Speed by type	Controls	Dust capture	Handling by type	Noise	Dust bag	Vac connection	Easy paper change
DETAIL *Strictly for finish-sanding tight corners; you'll need a random-orbit or finishing sander for most other work.*												
16	**Ryobi** CFS1500K Cat	$30	1.8	▬	○	◐	NA	●	◐			•
17	**Craftsman** (Sears) 11680 Mouse	40	1.4	▬	○	○	NA	◐	◐			•
BELT *Best for quickly sanding large or uneven surfaces; not meant for finishing or extended overhead sanding.*												
18	**Porter Cable** 352VS	180	11.3	▬▬▬	●	●	○	◐	●	•		•
19	**Makita** 9911	130	6.6	▬	○	●	●	●	◐	•		
20	**Skil** 7313	50	5.3	▬	○	○	◐	○	◐	•		
21	**Ryobi** BE318	50	6.8	▬▬	○	◐	◑	●	●	•	•	
22	**Black & Decker** BR400	60	7.2	▬	○	○	◐	◐	●	•		

1 *NA means no collection bag.*

Based on tests published in Consumer Reports in January 2004.

Guide to the Ratings

Overall score is based on sanding speed, controls, dust capture, handling, and noise. **Speed by type** denotes the amount of hardwood and softwood removed in 5 minutes—important for rough-sanding with a belt sander, less so for other types used mostly for finish-sanding. We used coarse, 80-grit paper for belt sanders, finer 100-grit paper for random-orbit and finishing types, and still-finer 120-grit paper for detail sanders based on their different emphases. Belt sanders that excelled in speed removed four times as much wood in 5 minutes as similarly rated finishing sanders. **Controls** includes handle and switch design, and other usability judgments. **Dust capture** is the percentage of sanded wood captured by the bag. **Handling by type** denotes maneuverability and freedom from vibration. We emphasized easy, one-handed operation for most sanders and two-handed use for belt sanders. **Noise** is based on tests with a sound meter. **Weight** reflects our measurement to the nearest tenth of a pound. **Price** is approximate retail.

Ratings

Ranges

You can buy a competent coil-type electric range for as little as $400. Spend more and you'll get added stylishness and conveniences like a trendy glass smoothtop instead of coils, higher-power elements, a convection feature for the oven, and stainless-steel trim. The Frigidaire FEF366A[S], $555, **a CR Best Buy,** offers very good performance and outstanding value. The highly-rated GE JBP80WF[WW], $750, and GE JBP82WF[WW], $850, are both excellent performers. If smoothtop styling isn't a must, consider an electric-coil model, which offers the ultimate in quick cooktop heating.

You can count on impressive performance from a gas range for as little as $550. Spend a bit more and you typically get stainless-steel trim, higher-heat burners, and—increasingly—a convection option for oven cooking, though the time saved with this feature tends to be minimal. Pricier models (about $1,500 to $2,000) also include dual-fuel ranges, which pair a gas cooktop with an electric oven, though dual-fuel stoves delivered no clear benefits in our tests.

In performance order

Ratings key: Excellent ● | Very good ◕ | Good ○ | Fair ◔ | Poor ●

Key number	Brand And Model	Price	Overall Score	Cooktop High	Cooktop Low	Oven Baking	Oven Broiling	Oven Capacity
ELECTRIC SMOOTHTOP RANGES								
1	**GE** JBP80WF[WW]	$750		◕	●	◕	◕	●
2	**GE** JBP82WF[WW]	850		◕	●	◕	◕	●
3	**Kenmore** (Sears) Elite 9901[2]	1,200		●	●	◕	◕	◕
4	**Maytag** Accellis MER6750AA[W]	1,000		◕	●	◕	●	○
5	**Maytag** Gemini MER6769BA[W]	1,000		◕	●	◕	◕	◕
6	**Maytag** Gemini MER6872BA[W]	1,550		◕	●	◕	◕	◕
7	**Kenmore** (Sears) 9582[2]	1,050		●	●	◕	○	◕
8	**Maytag** PER5710BA[W]	600		◕	◕	●	◕	◕
9	**Frigidaire** FEF366A[S] **A CR Best Buy**	555		◕	◕	◕	◕	◕
10	**KitchenAid** KERC500H[WH]	750		●	●	◕	◕	◕
11	**GE** Profile JS968SF[SS]	1,750		●	●	◕	◕	◕
12	**Jenn-Air** JES8850AA[W]	1,600		◕	◕	○	○	○
13	**Whirlpool** Polara GR556LRK[P]	1,800		◕	●	○	○	○
GAS RANGES								
14	**GE** Profile JGBP85WEB[WW]	950		○	●	◕	●	◕
15	**Maytag** Gemini MGR6772BD[W]	1,350		◕	◕	◕	◕	◕
16	**Magic Chef** CGR3742CD[W]	625		○	●	●	●	◕
17	**Maytag** MGR5880BD[W]	1,100		○	●	●	○	◕

Key number	Brand And Model	Price	Overall Score (0–100) P F G VG E	Cooktop High	Cooktop Low	Oven Baking	Oven Broiling	Oven Capacity
18	**Maytag** PGR5710BD[W]	$565		○	◉	◉	○	◑
19	**Jenn-Air** JGS8750AD[W]	1,500		◑	◑	◑	◉	○
20	**Kenmore** (Sears) Elite 7901[2]	1,200		○	◑	◑	○	○
21	**Tappan** TGF363A[W]	550		○	◉	◑	○	○
22	**DCS** RGSC-305	3,700		◑	◑	◑	○	○
23	**Frigidaire** Gallery GLGF377A[S]	800		◑	◉	◑	○	○
24	**KitchenAid** KGRT607H[BS]	1,360		◑	○	◑	◑	◑
25	**Viking** VGSC3064B[SS]	3,890		◑	◑	○	◉	◑
	DUAL-FUEL RANGES							
26	**KitchenAid** KDRP407H[SS]	3,450		○	◑	◉	◑	◑
27	**Jenn-Air** JDS8850AA[S]	2,150		○	◉	◑	◑	◑
28	**Kenmore** (Sears) Elite 4683[3]	1,600		○	◉	◑	◑	◑
29	**Jenn-Air** JDS9860AA[W]	2090		◑	◑	◑	◉	○
30	**Viking** VDSC305B[SS]	3,800		◑	◑	◑	◑	◑
31	**Viking** VDSC3074B	4,000		◑	◉	○	◑	◑
32	**GE Monogram** ZDP30N4D[SS]	3,600		○	◑	◑	◑	◑

See report, page 37. Based on tests published in Consumer Reports in March 2003, with updated prices and availability.

Guide to the Ratings

Under **brand & model,** brackets show a tested model's color code. Similar models have the same high and low burners or elements, oven, and broiler; other details may differ. Overall score includes cooktop speed and simmer performance, oven capacity, baking, broiling, and self-cleaning performance. **Cooktop high** is how quickly the highest-powered burner or element heated 6⅓ quarts of room-temperature water to a near boil. **Low** shows how well the least-powerful burner or element melted and held chocolate without scorching it and whether the most powerful, set to Low, held tomato sauce below a boil. **Oven baking** is baking evenness for cakes and cookies. **Broiling** is searing performance and cooking evenness for a tray of burgers. **Capacity** is usable oven space. **Price** is approximate retail. **Recommendations & notes** list noteworthy features and some minor shortcoming.

Ratings

Recommendations and notes

ALL TESTED MODELS: Are 30 inches wide. Have an oven light, anti-tip hardware, and a self-cleaning oven. **MOST HAVE:** Freestanding construction. Touchpad oven controls. Cooktop rim that holds spills. Two or three oven racks with five positions. A storage drawer. A reasonably clear oven view. **MOST GAS RANGES:** Have sealed burners and cast-iron grates. Can be converted to LP gas.

ELECTRIC SMOOTHTOPS

1 GE JBP80WF[WW] **Excellent performance at a good price.** Has warming element and dual cooktop elements. But only small elements in rear. Discontinued, but similar JBP80WH[] is available.

2 GE JBP82WF[WW] **Excellent performance at a good price.** Has warming element, dual cooktop elements, and bridge element. Discontinued, but similar JBP82WH[] is available.

3 KENMORE (Sears) Elite 9901[2] **Excellent and nicely featured.** Has convection option, dual cooktop elements, warming drawer, warming element, and bridge element.

4 MAYTAG Accellis MER6750AA[W] **Feature-rich and very good, but Maytag has been among the more repair-prone brands of electric ranges.** Has microwave option to speed cooking time. Has numeric-keypad oven controls, dual cooktop elements, and "hot" light indicator for each element.

5 MAYTAG Gemini MER6769BA[W] **A very good model with two ovens, but Maytag has been among the more repair-prone brands of electric ranges.** Has microwave option to speed cooking time. Has numeric-keypad oven controls, dual cooktop elements, and "hot" light indicator for each element.

6 MAYTAG Gemini MER6872BA[W] **A very good model with two ovens, but Maytag has been among the more repair-prone brands of electric ranges.** Small upper oven can toast, bake, and broil. Lower oven mounted very low. Has convection option, dual cooktop elements, warming element, and numeric-keypad oven controls. But only small elements in rear, only one "hot" light for cooktop elements, and no storage drawer.

7 KENMORE (Sears) 9582[2] **Very good overall.** Has warming element, dual cooktop elements, warming drawer, and "hot" light indicator for each element. One of its three oven racks can be split. Discontinued, but may still be available.

8 MAYTAG PER5710BA[W] **Very good, rather basic smoothtop at a reasonable price.** Maytag has been among the more repair-prone brands of electric ranges. Similar: PER5702A[ ], PER5705BA[ ].

9 FRIGIDAIRE FEF366A[S] **A CR Best Buy A good value offering very good performance.** But cooktop has no rim to contain spills. Discontinued, but similar FEF366[C] is available.

10 KITCHENAID KERC500H[WH] **Very good.** Has a warming element and dual cooktop elements, but only one large element. Has "hot" indicator light for each element. Has been among the more repair-prone brands of electric ranges.

11 GE Profile JS968SF[SS] **Cramped controls hamper this very good smoothtop.** Slide-in model; no side panels or backsplash. Has dual cooktop elements, warming element, bridge element, "hot" light for each element, numeric-keypad oven controls, and meat probe with automatic shutoff.

12 JENN-AIR JES8850AA[W] **Very good, but has been among the more repair-prone brands of electric ranges.** Has numeric-keypad oven controls, convection option, dual elements, meat probe for automatic oven shutoff, "hot" light indicator for each element. But cooktop has no rim to contain spills.

13 WHIRLPOOL Polara GR556LRK[P] **A very good smoothtop.** Has a unique feature; a refrigeration mode that allows you to set the range to keep the food cool during the day, then cook it just before you return in the evening. Has convection option, "hot" light for each element and dual cook

GAS RANGES

14 PROFILE JGBP85WEB[WW] **Very good, basic model.** Has warming drawer. Discontinued, but similar Profile JGBP85WEH[] is available.

15 MAYTAG Gemini MGR6772BD[W] **A very good model with two ovens, but Maytag has been among the more repair-prone brands of gas ranges.** Small upper oven can toast, bake, and broil. Lower oven mounted very low. Has numeric-keypad oven controls, and heavy, continuous grates. But no storage drawer, and large pot on rear burner blocked oven controls.

16 MAGIC CHEF CGR3742CD[W] **Very good, fairly basic range at a good price.** Has been among the more repair-prone brands of gas ranges.

17 MAYTAG MGR5880BD[W] **Has convection option, warming drawer, and numeric-keypad oven controls.** But has been among the more repair-prone brands of gas ranges. Similar: MGR5870BD[ ].

Ratings

Recommendations and notes

18 MAYTAG PGR5710BD[W] **Very good, fairly basic range at a good price.** But has been among the more repair-prone brands of gas ranges. Has steel grates. Similar: PGR5705BD[ ].

19 JENN-AIR JGS8750AD[W] **Very good.** Has numeric-keypad oven controls and continuous grates. Rangetop burners automatically reignite. But has been among the more repair-prone brands of gas ranges.

20 KENMORE (Sears) Elite 7901[2] **Very good and feature-filled.** Has convection option, warming drawer, warming element, and glass ceramic cooktop.

21 TAPPAN TGF363A[W] **A very good basic performer and a good value.** Roomy center workspace. Oven door and window hotter than most during self-cleaning.

22 DCS RGSC-305 **A very good pro-style range, but with only mediocre oven space.** Has convection option, heavy continuous grates, and burners that reignite if they go out. Cooktop and oven controls in front. Lacks touchpad and digital display. Only four rack positions. Large fifth burner wasn't the fastest, despite its high heat.

23 FRIGIDAIRE Gallery GLGF377A[S] **Very good overall, but fairly slow cooktop speed.** Has convection option. Discontinued, but similar Gallery GLGF377C[ ] is available.

24 KITCHENAID KGRT607H[BS] **Very good with stainless-steel touches, but has been among the more repair-prone brands of gas ranges.** Has convection option and continuous grates. Numeric keypad oven controls on front panel, but are easy to activate by mistake. Cooktop gets hot during oven and broiler use, and has no rim to contain spills. Similar: KGRT600H[ ].

25 VIKING VGSC3064B[SS] **Good and expensive stainless-steel stove.** Has convection option, continuous grates, and cooktop burners that auto reignite. But unsealed burners and window view not clear. Smallish oven and subpar simmering compromised performance.

DUAL-FUEL RANGES

26 KITCHENAID KDRP407H[SS] **Very good and expensive dual-fuel stainless-steel range with convection option and continuous grates.** Oven dial instead of touchpad controls.

27 JENN-AIR JDS8850AA[S] **A very good dual-fuel range.** Slide-in model; no side panels or backsplash. Burners reignite if they go out. Has convection option, heavy, continuous grates, meat probe with automatic oven shutoff. Door and window less hot than most during self-cleaning.

28 KENMORE (Sears) Elite 4683[3] **A very good dual-fuel model.** Has convection option, glass ceramic cooktop, warming drawer, and warming element, and continuous grates. But oven is somewhat small, cooktop has no rim to contain spills, and only four oven rack positions.

29 JENN-AIR JDS9860AA[W] **Very good.** Dual-fuel range has grill module and downdraft vent, convection option, and meat probe for auto shutoff. But fairly slow cooktop speed. Similar: JDS9860AA[P]

30 VIKING VDSC305B[SS] **Very good albeit very expensive stainless steel dual-fuel range.** Has convection option, heavy continuous grates, and burners that reignite if they go out. But has a smallish oven and unsealed burners, and is among the least effective at self-cleaning.

31 VIKING VDSC3074B **A very good dual-fuel, pro-style range.** Has convection option, heavy continuous grates, and burners that reignite if they go out. Door and window less hot than most during self-cleaning. But smallish oven, and among the least effective at self-cleaning.

32 GE Monogram ZDP30N4D[SS] **Very good albeit very expensive stainless steel dual-fuel stove.** Has convection option and continuous grates. But smallish oven, unsealed burners, and only three oven-rack positions.

Receivers

You can expect very good performance at any price, but connections and features will vary. Spend around $200 and you can get a basic surround-sound (digital) model that can decode Dolby Pro Logic and Pro Logic II, along with Dolby Digital and DTS. The **CR Best Buy** Panasonic SA-HE100, $250, is a very good 5.1 receiver with ample inputs, at a great price. For $300 and up, you can get more features, such as an onscreen display and 6.1-channel decoding, which provides slightly smoother surround sound. The Yamaha RX-V440 and Onkyo TX-SR501, both $300, are very good reasonably priced choices that support three rear-surround speakers. Models priced at $500 and up typically have the most connections and features.

In performance order

Ratings: Excellent ● · Very good ◒ · Good ○ · Fair ◐ · Poor ●

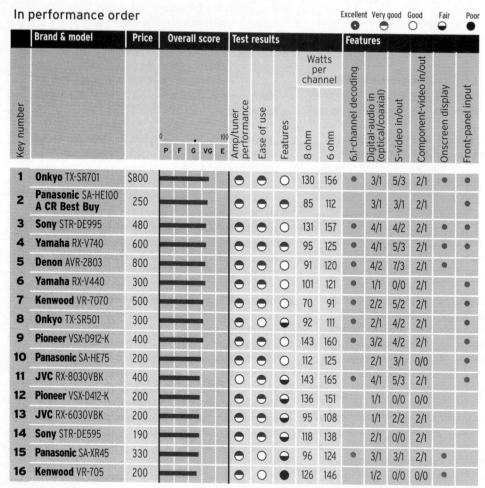

Key number	Brand & model	Price	Overall score (P F G VG E, 0–100)	Amp/tuner performance	Ease of use	Features	Watts per channel 8 ohm	Watts per channel 6 ohm	6.1-channel decoding	Digital-audio in (optical/coaxial)	S-video in/out	Component-video in/out	Onscreen display	Front-panel input
1	**Onkyo** TX-SR701	$800		Very good	Very good	Good	130	156	●	3/1	5/3	2/1	●	●
2	**Panasonic** SA-HE100 A **CR Best Buy**	250		Very good	Very good	Very good	85	112		3/1	3/1	2/1		●
3	**Sony** STR-DE995	480		Very good	Very good	Good	131	157	●	4/1	4/2	2/1	●	●
4	**Yamaha** RX-V740	600		Very good	Very good	Good	95	125	●	4/1	5/3	2/1	●	●
5	**Denon** AVR-2803	800		Very good	Very good	Good	91	120	●	4/2	7/3	2/1	●	
6	**Yamaha** RX-V440	300		Very good	Very good	Good	101	121	●	1/1	0/0	2/1		●
7	**Kenwood** VR-7070	500		Very good	Very good	Good	70	91	●	2/2	5/2	2/1		●
8	**Onkyo** TX-SR501	300		Very good	Good	Very good	92	111	●	2/1	4/2	2/1		●
9	**Pioneer** VSX-D912-K	400		Very good	Very good	Good	143	160	●	3/2	4/2	2/1		●
10	**Panasonic** SA-HE75	200		Very good	Very good	Good	112	125		2/1	3/1	0/0		●
11	**JVC** RX-8030VBK	400		Good	Very good	Very good	143	165	●	4/1	5/3	2/1		●
12	**Pioneer** VSX-D412-K	200		Very good	Very good	Very good	136	151		1/1	0/0	0/0		
13	**JVC** RX-6030VBK	200		Very good	Very good	Very good	95	108		1/1	2/2	2/1		
14	**Sony** STR-DE595	190		Very good	Very good	Very good	118	138		2/1	0/0	2/1		
15	**Panasonic** SA-XR45	330		Very good	Good	Very good	96	124	●	3/1	3/1	2/1	●	
16	**Kenwood** VR-705	200		Very good	Good	Poor	126	146		1/2	0/0	0/0	●	

See report, page 76. Based on tests published in Consumer Reports in November 2003, with updated prices and availability.

Guide to the Ratings

Overall score is based mainly on amplifier and AM/FM tuner performance; ease of use and features also factor in. **Amp/tuner performance** evaluates lack of noise and distortion in the amplifier, plus AM reception (which was good on all tested models) and FM reception (very good on all). **Ease of use** reflects the design of the front panel and remote control. **Features** score reflects the presence or absence of convenience features, including the number of inputs. **Watts per channel** is our measure of power when the receiver is used with 8-ohm and 6-ohm speakers; only three models (2, 5, and 7) were rated for use with 4-ohm speakers. **Price** is approximate retail. Under Features, video outputs listed include one required by TV.

Recommendations and notes

ALL TESTED MODELS: Can decode Dolby Digital, DTS, and Dolby Pro Logic and Pro Logic II surround audio. Can automatically detect which surround format requires decoding. Have a 75-ohm FM-antenna connection, output jack for powered subwoofer. Have other DSP modes besides Dolby Surround. Have test-tone function for setting sound level, remote control that can operate devices of the same brand, and display dimmer. Have an FM tuner that scored very good in our tests, and an AM tuner that scored good. Have at least 30 AM or FM station presets. Lack direct tuning of frequency on console and function to scan preset radio stations for a few seconds. **MOST TESTED MODELS:** Have 5.1 inputs for external decoder, a two-year warranty for parts and labor, sleep-timer function, universal remote control to operate devices from other manufacturers, and one or two switched AC outlets. Lack center-channel preamp output, bass-boost function, phono input, and tape monitor. Dimensions noted below are rounded up to the nearest ¼ inch.

1 ONKYO TX-SR701 **Very good, with reasonable price for a THX-certified model.** Has onscreen display (OSD) and multisource for simultaneous two-room speaker use. Bass boost. Phono input. Center-channel preamp output. 6.75x17.25x17.5 in. (HWD).

2 PANASONIC SA-HE100 **A CR Best Buy Best value among tested models.** FM tuner adjusts in full-channel increments. Radio stations can be tuned directly using remote. Troubleshooting "help" function can advise user of necessary fix. Can be used with 4-ohm speakers. Has tape monitor and phono input. Has DTS-ES (6.1) but cannot decode Dolby Digital EX surround audio. Lacks sleep timer. Warranty only 1 yr. 6.25x17x14.5 in. (HWD).

3 SONY STR-DE995 **Very good.** Has onscreen display (OSD) and multisource for simultaneous two-room speaker use. Can program to show station call letters. Radio stations can be tuned directly using remote. Has phono input. 6.25x17x14.5 in. (HWD). Similar model STR-DE895 lacks multizone capability.

4 YAMAHA RX-V740 **Very good.** Has onscreen display (OSD) and multisource for simultaneous two-room speaker use. FM tuner adjusts in full-channel increments. Has phono input. Center-channel preamp output. Can be used with 4-ohm speakers. 6.75x17.25x15.5 in. (HWD). Similar model RX-V640 permits fewer connections.

5 DENON AVR-2803 **Very good.** Has onscreen display (OSD) and multisource for simultaneous two-room speaker use. FM tuner adjusts in full-channel increments. Has phono input. Center-channel preamp output. Lacks sleep timer. 6.75x18x16.25 in. (HWD).

6 YAMAHA RX-V440 **Very good.** FM tuner adjusts in full-channel increments. Can be used with 4-ohm speakers. 6.5x17.25x15.5 in. (HWD). Similar model RX-V540 permits more connections.

7 KENWOOD VR-7070 **Very good, with very low price for a THX-certified model.** Has multisource for simultaneous two-room speaker use. Has bass boost. Phono input. Center-channel preamp output. Lacks sleep timer. 6.25x17.25x15.5 in. (HWD).

8 ONKYO TX-SR501 **Very good.** 6x17.25x14.75 in. (HWD). Similar model TX-SR601 has multizone capability.

9 PIONEER VSX-D912K **Very good.** Can automatically calibrate sound level. Can program to show station call letters. Radio stations can be tuned directly using remote. Center-channel preamp output. 6.25x16.5x15.25 in. (HWD). Only 1-yr. warranty. Similar model VSX-D812K ($350) permits fewer connections; VSX-D712K has only 5.1 audio decoding.

10 PANASONIC SA-HE75 **Very good.** Troubleshooting "help" function can advise user of necessary fix. FM tuner adjusts in full-channel increments. Radio stations can be tuned directly using remote. Tape monitor. Cannot decode Dolby Digital EX or DTS-ES 6.1 surround audio. Only 1-yr. warranty. Lacks sleep timer. 6.25x17x14.25 in. (HWD).

11 JVC RX-8030VBK **Good.** Has bass boost. Phono input. Center-channel preamp output. Lacks AC outlets. 6.25x17x17.25 in. (HWD). Similar model RX-7030VBK permits fewer connections.

Recommendations and notes

12 PIONEER VSX-D412-K **Good.** Can program to show station call letters. Has tape monitor. Cannot decode Dolby Digital EX or DTS-ES 6.1 surround audio. Only 1-yr. warranty. Lacks sleep timer. 6.25x16.5x16.25 in. (HWD).

13 JVC RX-6030VBK **Good.** Has bass boost. Cannot decode Dolby Digital EX or DTS-ES 6.1 surround audio. Lacks AC outlets. 5.75x18x16 in. (HWD).

14 SONY STR-DE595 **Good.** Radio stations can be tuned directly using remote. Can program to show station call letters. Cannot decode Dolby Digital EX or DTS-ES 6.1 surround audio. Lacks universal remote control, and AC outlets. 5.5x17x11.75 in. (HWD). Similar model STR-DE695 has 6.1 audio decoding.

15 PANASONIC SA-XR45 **Good.** Has onscreen display (OSD) and multisource for simultaneous two-room speaker use. FM tuner adjusts in full-channel increments. Radio stations can be tuned directly using remote. Bass and treble adjustable only via remote. Only 1-yr. warranty. Surround lacks Dolby 3 Stereo mode. Lacks AC outlets. 3x17x15 in. (HWD). Similar model SA-XR25 lacks multizone capability.

16 KENWOOD VR-705 **Good.** Has onscreen display (OSD) and bass boost. Lacks 5.1 inputs for external digital-audio decoders. Cannot decode Dolby Digital EX or DTS-ES 6.1 surround audio. Bass and treble adjustable only via remote. Lacks sleep timer and universal remote control. 5.75x17.25x12 in. (HWD). Similar model VR-707 has 6.1 audio decoding.

Ratings

Refrigerators

Most new refrigerators will keep your milk chilled and your ice cream frozen. We'd stick with those judged very good or excellent for temperature performance. Very good top-freezers with lots of space include the GE Profile PTS22LBN, $980, and the Kenmore 7325, $850. Good midsized choices are the Kenmore 7398, a **CR Best Buy** at $820, and the Frigidaire Gallery GLRT186TA, $500. The Kenmore is quiet, has a filtered internal water dispenser, and makes more ice than most. A very good narrow model at just 28 inches wide is the GE GTS18HBM, $450. A very good bottom-freezer offering the largest capacity of the tested models is the Kenmore Elite Trio 7350, $1,800. Two other bottom-freezers are **CR Best Buys**: the 33-inch-wide Maytag Plus MBB2254GE, $1,000, and the 30-inch-wide Kenmore 7283, $950. Both offer swing-open freezer doors. Side-by-sides judged to be fine, roomy performers and **CR Best Buys** are the GE GSS25JFP, $1,000, and the Kenmore 5350, $800. Three very good true built-ins are the GE Monogram ZIC360NM, $4,000, the Viking DFSB423, $5,300, and the GE Monogram ZISB420DM, $5,200.

In performance order

Ratings key: Excellent / Very good / Good / Fair / Poor

Key number	Brand & model (Similar models, in small type, comparable to tested model. Price shown is for white finish.)	Price	Overall score	Energy efficiency	Temperature performance	Noise	Claimed (cu. ft.)	Usable (cu. ft.)	Touchpad controls	Water dispenser	Stainless finish or lookalike available	HxWxD (in.)
TOP-FREEZERS												
1	**GE** Profile PTS22LBN[WW] D — PTS22LCP[ ]	$980		●	●	●	21.7	16.6	●		●	68x33x32
2	**Kenmore** (Sears) 7398[2] — 7397[ ] **A CR Best Buy**	820		●	●	●	18.8	14.8		●		66x30x32
3	**Kenmore** (Sears) 7325[2]	850		●	●	●	22.1	17.5	●			68x33x32
4	**GE** GTS18KCM[WW] D — GTS18KCP[ ]	650		●	●	○	17.9	14.0				67x30x31
5	**Kenmore** (Sears) 7396[2]	870		●	●	●	19.0	14.5	●			66x30x32
6	**Whirlpool** ET9FTTXL[Q]	750		●	●	○	18.8	14.5		●		67x30x32
7	**Whirlpool** Gold GR9SHKXK[Q]	830		●	●	○	18.8	14.1			●	66x30x32
8	**Frigidaire** Gallery GLRT186TA[W] D — GLRT185TD[ ]	500		●	●	○	18.3	14.3			●	67x30x31
9	**GE** GTS22KCM[WW] D — GTS22KCP[ ]	750		●	●	○	21.7	16.5				68x33x32
10	**Whirlpool** ET1FTTXK[Q]	800		●	●	○	20.8	16.5		●		66x33x31
11	**Whirlpool** Gold GR2SHTXK[Q] — GR2SHKXK[ ]	1,200		●	●	○	21.6	15.9		●	●	66x33x31
12	**GE** GTS18HBM[WW]	450		●	●	○	17.6	12.9				68x28x31
BOTTOM-FREEZERS												
13	**Amana** ARB2217C[W] — ARB2214C[ ], ARB2257C[ ], ARB2259C[ ]	1,250		●	●	○	21.9	16.0			●	70x33x31
14	**LG** LRDC22731[WW]	1,350		●	●	●	22.4	14.7	●			69x33x32
15	**Maytag** Plus MBB2254GE[W] **A CR Best Buy**	1,000		●	●	○	21.9	15.9			●	70x33x31

Ratings

Refrigerators

Key number	Brand & model	Price	Overall score (P F G VG E)	Test results			Capacity		Features			
				Energy efficiency	Temperature performance	Noise	Claimed (cu. ft.)	Usable (cu. ft.)	Touchpad controls	Water dispenser	Stainless finish or lookalike available	HxWxD (in.)
BOTTOM-FREEZERS												
16	**Kenmore** (Sears) Elite Trio 7350[2]	$1,800		●	◉	○	24.8	17.8		●	●	71x36x32
17	**Amana** ARB1914C[W]	1,050		◐	◉	○	18.5	13.2				67x30x31
18	**Kenmore** (Sears) 7221[2]	1,200		◐	◉	○	21.9	16.7				70x33x31
19	**Kenmore** (Sears) 7283[2] **A CR Best Buy**	950		◐	◉	○	18.5	13.8				67x30x31
20	**GE** GBS20KBP[WW]	1,030		○	◉	◐	19.5	13.3				68x30x32
21	**GE** Profile PDS22MCP[WW] PDS22MBP[ ], PDS22SBP[ ], PDS22SCP[ ]	1,400		◐	◉	○	22.3	15.4	●		●	69x33x32
22	**Samsung** RB1855S[W]	750		○	◐	○	18.8	14.2	●		●	70x33x29
SIDE-BY-SIDES												
23	**Kenmore** (Sears) 5365[2] 5366[ ]	1,400		◐	◐	◉	25.4	17.2	●	●		70x36x32
24	**Kenmore** (Sears) 5468[2] 5469[ ]	1,650		◐	◐	◐	25.6	16.2	●	●		70x36x33
25	**GE** GSS25JFP[WW] **A CR Best Buy**	1,000		◐	◉	◐	25	16.9		●		70x36x32
26	**GE** Profile PSS26NGP[WW] PSF26NGP[ ], PSS26SGP[ ]	1,850		◐	◐	◐	25.5	16.2		●		70x36x33
27	**Samsung** RS2555S[W]	1,400		◐	◐	◐	25.2	16.6		●		70x36x33
28	**Kenmore** (Sears) 5350[2] D 5450[ ] **A CR Best Buy**	800		◐	◐	◐	25.3	16.6		●		70x36x32
29	**Whirlpool** ED5VHGXM[Q] ED5FHEXM[ ]	1,000		◐	◐	◐	25.4	15.5		●		70x36x31
30	**Whirlpool** Gold GD5SHAXM[Q]	1,500		◐	◐	○	25.5	16.7		●		70x36x31
31	**Amana** ARSE66ZB[W]	1,150		◐	◐	◐	25.6	16.6		●		71x36x31
32	**Kenmore** (Sears) 5156[2] D 5363[ ]	1,400		○	◐	◐	25.5	16.0		●		70x36x32
33	**Maytag** MSD2456GE[W]	1,350		○	◐	◐	23.6	13.3		●		69x33x32
34	**Hotpoint** HSS25GFP[WW]	800		○	◐	◐	25.0	16.7		●		70x36x32
35	**Frigidaire** Gallery GLRS237ZA[W] D GLRS237ZC[ ]	950		○	○	◐	22.6	14.6		●	●	70x33x33
36	**Maytag** Plus MZD2766GE[W]	1,600		◐	◒	○	26.8	17.7		●	●	71x36x32
37	**GE** GSS20IEM[WW] D GSS20IEP[ ]	950		○	◐	○	19.9	13.3	●	●		68x32x32
BUILT-IN AND CABINET-DEPTH BOTTOM-FREEZERS												
38	**Sub-Zero** 650/F	4,450		◐	◉	○	20.6	15.4	●		●	84x37x26
39	**Amana** ARB8057C[W] (cabinet-depth)	1,900		○	◉	○	19.9	13.5		●	●	70x36x27
40	**GE** Monogram ZIC360NM	4,000		○	◉	◐	20.6	13.6			●	84x37x26
41	**Viking** DFBB363 DDBB363[ ], VCBB363[ ], DTBB363[ ]	4,600		◐	◉	○	20.3	15.0			●	84x36x25

Ratings

Key number	Brand & model	Price	Overall score (0–100; P F G VG E)	Energy efficiency	Temperature performance	Noise	Claimed (cu. ft.)	Usable (cu. ft.)	Touchpad controls	Water dispenser	Stainless finish or lookalike available	HxWxD (in.)
	BUILT-IN AND CABINET-DEPTH SIDE-BY-SIDES											
42	**Viking** DFSB423 DDSB423[ ], VCSB423[ ]	$5,300	▬▬▬▬	◒	◒	◒	24.0	16.6	●		●	83x43x25
43	**GE** Monogram ZISB420DM	5,200	▬▬▬▬	◒	◒	◒	26.1	15.1	●	●	●	84x43x26
44	**Jenn-Air** JS42FWD	6,000	▬▬▬▬	○	●	◒	26.0	14.5	●	●	●	84x42x27
45	**LG** LRSPC2031[W] (cabinet-depth)	1,500	▬▬▬▬	○	●	◒	19.5	12.9	●	●	●	69x36x28
46	**KitchenAid** KSSS42QM[W] KSSO42QM[ ], KSSP42QM[ ], KSSC42QM[ ]	4,900	▬▬▬▬	◒	○	●	25.3	17.7	●	●	●	84x43x26
47	**Sub-Zero** 680	5,500	▬▬▬	◒	◒	○	23.7	16.9	●	●	●	84x43x26
48	**Jenn-Air** JCD2389GE[W] (cabinet-depth)	2,000	▬▬▬	○	◓	◒	23.0	14.7		●	●	71x36x28
49	**Whirlpool** GC5THGXK[Q] (cabinet-depth) D GC5SHGXL[ ]	2,300	▬▬▬	○	◓	◒	24.5	14.8	●	●	●	72x36x28

D Discontinued, but similar model is available. Price is for similar model.

See report, page 41. Based on tests published in Consumer Reports in February 2004.

Guide to the Ratings

Overall score gives most weight to energy efficiency and temperature performance, then to noise. **Convenience** is also factored in; all models were judged at least good for convenience. **Energy efficiency** reflects consumption per the EnergyGuide and usable volume. **Temperature performance** combines outcome of tests at different room temperatures, including high heat; we judge how closely and uniformly recommended settings match our ideal temperatures: Most kept the main space at 37° F and the freezer at 0° F with good uniformity. **Noise** is gauged with compressors running. **Capacity** lists the manufacturer's claimed volume and our measurement of usable volume. Height, width, and depth (without handle) are rounded up to nearest inch. Under **brand & model,** a bracketed letter or number is a color code. Prices for built-ins are for unfinished models; exterior panels cost extra. Stainless-steel and stainless-look finishes (when available) cost about $200 to $400 more for freestanding models, $600 to $1,500 more for built-ins. **Price** is approximate retail, including cost of icemaker if that is not standard. Overall scores may differ slightly from those in previous reports because we have reevaluated our convenience assessment.

Speakers

Most of the speakers we tested are fine performers overall. What distinguishes the best models is accuracy. Because the typical listener is unlikely to notice a difference of less than 8 points in accuracy, even models that aren't at the top of the Ratings are worth considering. Excellent, economical choices for stereo setup or for the front pair in a surround system, and **CR Best Buys,** are the Sony SS-MB35OH, $100, and the Cambridge Soundworks Model Six, $150. Both are bookshelf speakers, but on the large side. If small size is paramount, these five are among the smallest offering fine accuracy and bass handling: the Bose 201 Series V, $220; Pioneer S-DF1-K, $200; Bose 141, $100; KLH 911B, $85; and Bose Acoustimass 3 Series IV, $300.

In performance order

Excellent ● Very good ◔ Good ○ Fair ◖ Poor ●

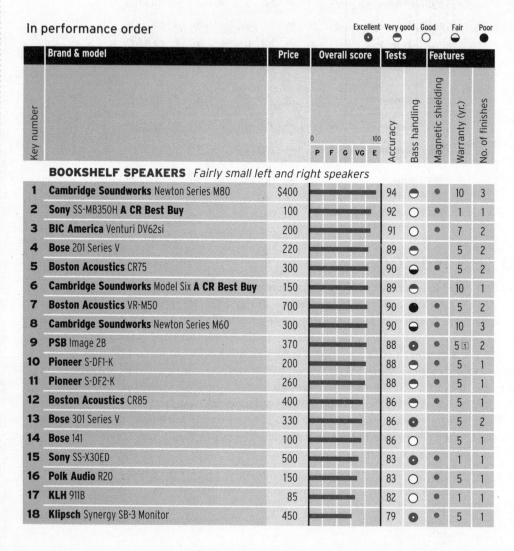

Key number	Brand & model	Price	Overall score (0—100) P F G VG E	Accuracy	Bass handling	Magnetic shielding	Warranty (yr.)	No. of finishes
BOOKSHELF SPEAKERS *Fairly small left and right speakers*								
1	**Cambridge Soundworks** Newton Series M80	$400		94	◖	●	10	3
2	**Sony** SS-MB350H **A CR Best Buy**	100		92	○	●	1	1
3	**BIC America** Venturi DV62si	200		91	○	●	7	2
4	**Bose** 201 Series V	220		89	◖		5	2
5	**Boston Acoustics** CR75	300		90	◕	●	5	2
6	**Cambridge Soundworks** Model Six **A CR Best Buy**	150		89	◖		10	1
7	**Boston Acoustics** VR-M50	700		90	●	●	5	2
8	**Cambridge Soundworks** Newton Series M60	300		90	◕	●	10	3
9	**PSB** Image 2B	370		88	◉	●	5 [1]	2
10	**Pioneer** S-DF1-K	200		88	◖	●	5	1
11	**Pioneer** S-DF2-K	260		88	◖	●	5	1
12	**Boston Acoustics** CR85	400		86	◖	●	5	1
13	**Bose** 301 Series V	330		86	◉		5	2
14	**Bose** 141	100		86	○		5	1
15	**Sony** SS-X30ED	500		83	◉	●	1	1
16	**Polk Audio** R20	150		83	○	●	5	1
17	**KLH** 911B	85		82	○	●	1	1
18	**Klipsch** Synergy SB-3 Monitor	450		79	◉	●	5	1

Ratings

Key number	Brand & model	Price	Overall score (P F G VG E)	Accuracy	Bass handling	Magnetic shielding	Warranty (yr.)	No. of finishes
FLOOR-STANDING SPEAKERS *Fairly bulky left and right speakers*								
19	**Sony** SS-MF750H	$280		91	◉	●	1	1
20	**Cerwin Vega** E-710	300		90	◉		5	1
21	**Polk Audio** R30	300		89	◉	●	5	1
22	**Jensen** Champion Series C-5	180		86	◐	●	5	1
23	**Polk Audio** R50	400		84	◉	●	5	1
24	**Bose** 601 Series IV	600		84	◉		5	2
25	**Bose** 701 Series II	700		82	◐		5	1
THREE-PIECE BOOKSHELF SETS *Two small speakers and a subwoofer*								
26	**Bose** Acoustimass 3 Series IV	300		94	◐	●	5	2
27	**Bose** Acoustimass 5 Series III	600		94	◐	●	5	2

1 *Buyer must mail in completed warranty card to get 5-yr. warranty (1-yr. on subwoofer).*

Key number	Brand & model	Price	Overall score (P F G VG E)	Accuracy	Warranty (yr.)	No. of finishes
CENTER-CHANNEL SPEAKERS *One smallish speaker used near TV*						
28	**NHT** SC1	$300		92	5	1
29	**Boston Acoustics** Bravo Center	200		92	5	1
30	**Boston Acoustics** CRC	250		91	5	1
31	**B&W** VM1	200		87	5	3
32	**Acoustic Research** AR2C	450		86	5	1
33	**Polk Audio** CSi20	165		86	5	1
34	**Polk Audio** CSi30	225		84	5	1
35	**Yamaha** NS-AC40X	150		84	2	1
36	**JBL** Northridge Series N Center II	200		84	5	1
37	**Acoustic Research** AR4C	300		83	5	1
38	**Sony** SS-CNX70ED	$300		83	1	1
39	**Sony** SS-CN550H	100		81	1	1
40	**Jensen** Champion Series C-CS	60		80	5	1
41	**Cambridge Soundworks** CenterStage	200		79	10	1
42	**Cambridge Soundworks** Center Channel Plus	150		77	10	1
43	**Bose** VCS-10	200		73	5	2

Ratings

Key number	Brand & model	Price	Overall score 0 ——— 100 P F G VG E	Test Accuracy	Features Warranty (yr.)	No. of finishes
REAR-SURROUND SPEAKERS *Small left and right satellites*					
44	**Cambridge Soundworks** Newton Series MC100	$140		91	10	2
45	**Infinity** OWS-1	275		87	5	2
46	**Bose** 161	160		84	5	2
47	**NHT** SB1	300		83	5	2
48	**JBL** Northridge Series N24 II	200		82	5	1
49	**B&W** LM1	350		81	5	5
50	**Polk Audio** RTi28	280		79	5	2
SIX-PIECE SURROUND SETS *Five small speakers and a subwoofer*					
51	**Bose** Acoustimass 6 Series III	700		93	5	1
52	**Cambridge Soundworks** Movieworks 208	900		93	10	2
53	**Polk Audio** RM6700 with PSW303 subwoofer	1,000		91	5	3
54	**Cambridge Soundworks** Movieworks 106	400		89	10	2
55	**Cambridge Soundworks** Newton Theater MC100.2	900		89	10	2
56	**Polk Audio** RM6005 with PSW202 subwoofer	500		89	5	2
57	**Bose** Acoustimass 10 Series III	1,000		88	5	2
58	**Cambridge Soundworks** Movieworks II 5.1	650		87	10	2
59	**Atlantic Technology** System T70	1,000		86	5 [1]	1
60	**Sony** SA-VE835ED	1,000		84	1	1

[1] *Buyer must mail in completed warranty card to get 5-yr. warranty (1-yr. on subwoofer).*

See report, page 82. Based on tests published in Consumer Reports in November 2003, with updated prices and availability.

Guide to the Ratings

Overall score is based primarily on the ability to reproduce sound accurately. A score of 100 would be perfect. For bookshelf and floor-standing speakers and for three-piece bookshelf sets, **bass handling** is also factored in, reflecting the ability to play bass-heavy music loudly without buzzing or distortion. Speakers scoring poor or fair for bass handling should be avoided if you enjoy loud bass. You can expect very good or excellent bass handling from the six-piece sets, all of which have separate subwoofers. All center-channel speakers, three-piece sets, and six-piece sets have **magnetic shielding** to prevent video interference when placed near a TV. **Number of finishes** indicates the available choices. Most tested models have a black veneer finish; some are also available in other finishes, such as white, silver, oak, and cherry. **Price** is approximate retail for a pair of bookshelf, floor-standing, or rear-surround speakers; for one center-channel speaker; and for three-piece or six-piece sets.

Ratings

Recommendations and notes

MOST TESTED MODELS HAVE: No included wires.

BOOKSHELF SPEAKERS

1. CAMBRIDGE SOUNDWORKS Newton Series M80 **Excellent, with long (10-yr.) warranty.** Vinyl cabinet.

2. SONY SS-MB350H **A CR Best Buy Excellent and well-priced, but short (1-yr.) warranty.**

3. BIC AMERICA Venturi DV62si **Excellent.**

4. BOSE 201 Series V **Excellent.** Asymmetrical; designed specifically for left or right position. Easy to wall-mount. May cause video interference near a TV.

5. BOSTON ACOUSTICS CR75 **Excellent overall.** But avoid if you play bass-heavy music very loud. Easy to wall-mount.

6. CAMBRIDGE SOUNDWORKS Model Six **A CR Best Buy Well-priced, excellent speakers with long (10-yr.) warranty.** May cause video interference near a TV.

7. BOSTON ACOUSTICS VR-M50 **Excellent but expensive.** Not the best choice if you play bass-heavy music very loud. Easy to wall-mount.

8. CAMBRIDGE SOUNDWORKS Newton Series M60 **Excellent, with long (10-yr.) warranty.** Not the best choice if you play bass-heavy music very loud. Vinyl cabinet.

9. PSB Image 2B **Excellent.** 5-yr. warranty only if card mailed in; otherwise 1-yr.

10. PIONEER S-DF1-K **Very good.**

11. PIONEER S-DF2-K **Very good.**

12. BOSTON ACOUSTICS CR85 **Very good.** Easy to wall-mount.

13. BOSE 301 Series V **Very good.** Easy to wall-mount. Asymmetrical; designed specifically for left or right position. May cause video interference near a TV.

14. BOSE 141 **Very good overall.** Small, light, and well-priced. Compact, gray vinyl cabinet. May cause video interference near a TV.

15. SONY SS-X30ED **Very good.** Short (1-yr.) warranty.

16. POLK AUDIO R20 **Very good.** Easy to wall-mount. Asymmetrical; designed specifically for left or right position.

17. KLH 911B **Very good.** Lightweight speakers at a low price, but short (1-yr.) warranty.

18. KLIPSCH Synergy SB-3 Monitor **Good overall, with excellent bass handling.**

FLOOR-STANDING SPEAKERS

19. SONY SS-MF750H **Excellent, but short (1-yr.) warranty.**

20. CERWIN VEGA E-710 **Excellent,** though may cause video interference near a TV.

21. POLK Audio R30 **Excellent and well-priced.**

22. JENSEN Champion Series C-5 **Very good and well-priced.**

23. POLK AUDIO R50 **Very good.**

24. BOSE 601 Series IV **Very good.** Asymmetrical; designed specifically for left or right position. May cause video interference near a TV.

25. BOSE 701 Series II **Very good.** Has tone controls. Asymmetrical; designed specifically for left or right position. May cause video interference near a TV.

THREE-PIECE BOOKSHELF SETS

26. BOSE Acoustimass 3 Series IV **Excellent.** Vinyl cabinet. Includes speaker wires.

27. BOSE Acoustimass 5 Series III **Excellent.** Vinyl cabinet. Easy to wall-mount satellites.

CENTER-CHANNEL SPEAKERS

28. NHT SC1 **Excellent.**

29. BOSTON ACOUSTICS Bravo Center **Excellent.**

30. BOSTON ACOUSTICS CRC **Excellent.**

31. B&W VM1 **Very good.**

32. ACOUSTIC RESEARCH AR2C **Very good.** Has tone controls.

33. POLK AUDIO CSi20 **Very good.**

34. POLK AUDIO CSi30 **Very good.**

35. YAMAHA NS-AC40X **Very good, but short (2-yr.) warranty.** Has tone controls.

36. JBL Northridge Series N Center II **Very good.**

Ratings

Recommendations and notes

37. ACOUSTIC RESEARCH AR4C **Very good.** Easy to wall-mount.

38. SONY SS-CNX70ED **Very good, but short (1-yr.) warranty.**

39. SONY SS-CN550H **Very good, well-priced, and more compact than most.** Short (1-yr.) warranty.

40. JENSEN Champion Series C-CS **Very good and well-priced.**

41. CAMBRIDGE SOUNDWORKS CenterStage **Good.** Long (10-yr.) warranty.

42. CAMBRIDGE SOUNDWORKS Center Channel Plus **Good.** Long (10-yr.) warranty.

43. BOSE VCS-10 **Good.** But there are better choices.

REAR-SURROUND SPEAKERS

44. CAMBRIDGE SOUNDWORKS Newton Series, MC100 **Excellent and lightweight.** Long (10-yr.) warranty.

45. INFINITY OWS-1 **Very good, but larger than most.** Not stable on a horizontal surface.

46. BOSE 161 **Very good and lightweight.** Not stable on a horizontal surface.

47. NHT SB1 **Very good, but may cause video interference near a TV.**

48. JBL Northridge Series N24 II **Very good.**

49. B&W LM1 **Very good.**

50. POLK AUDIO RTi28 **Good.**

SIX-PIECE SURROUND SYSTEMS

51. BOSE Acoustimass 6 Series III **Excellent.** Vinyl cabinets. Has tone controls.

52. CAMBRIDGE SOUNDWORKS Movieworks 208 **Excellent, with long (10-yr.) warranty.** Vinyl cabinets. Has tone controls.

53. POLK AUDIO RM6700 with PSW303 subwoofer **Excellent.** Vinyl cabinets. Has tone controls.

54. CAMBRIDGE SOUNDWORKS Movieworks 106 **Excellent and well-priced.** Long (10-yr.) warranty. Vinyl cabinets. Has tone controls.

55. CAMBRIDGE SOUNDWORKS Newton Theater MC100.2 **Excellent.** Long (10-yr.) warranty. Vinyl cabinets. Has tone controls.

56. POLK AUDIO RM6005 with PSW202 sub-woofer. **Excellent and well-priced.** Vinyl cabinets. Has tone controls.

57. BOSE Acoustimass 10 Series III **Very good.** Vinyl cabinets. Has tone controls.

58. CAMBRIDGE SOUNDWORKS Movieworks II 5.1 **Very good.** Long (10-yr.) warranty. Has tone controls.

59. ATLANTIC TECHNOLOGY System T70 **Very good, but expensive.** Rear speakers differ in design from front pair.

60. SONY SA-VE835ED **Very good, but expensive.** Short (1-yr.) warranty. Metal cabinets. Has tone controls.

Ratings

Stains, exterior

Opaque (solid-color) stains generally offer more years of protection and better value than semitransparent stains. Stains we test begin to differ markedly in appearance after the equivalent of three years of exposure. Latex formulations have a slight edge over oil-based stains in appearance. Overall, the best brands in any color are Sherwin-Williams Woodscapes and Olympic Premium. Among white stains, the Sherwin-Williams Woodscapes (latex) is the standout. It's the only white stain that resists cracking and color change. For green stains, the Sherwin-Williams Woodscapes (latex) is a standout; it's resistant to dirt buildup, mildew, cracking, and color change. Red stains tend to be the most resistant to dirt. The best choices are the Olympic Premium (latex) and Behr Plus 10 (alkyd). Both do a good job of resisting dirt buildup, color change, mildew, and cracking. The Behr, sold at Home Depot, is the best oil-based stain, and it cleans up with water.

In performance order

Rating key: ● Excellent ◖ Very good ○ Good ◔ Fair ● Poor

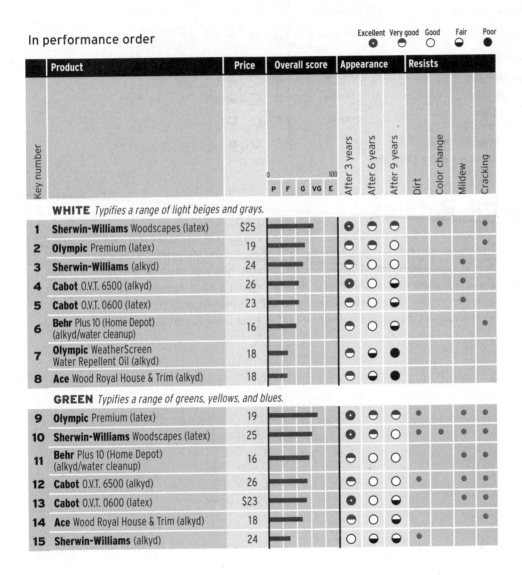

Key number	Product	Price	Overall score	Appearance: After 3 years	After 6 years	After 9 years	Resists: Dirt	Color change	Mildew	Cracking
	WHITE *Typifies a range of light beiges and grays.*									
1	**Sherwin-Williams** Woodscapes (latex)	$25		●	◖	◖		•		•
2	**Olympic** Premium (latex)	19		◖	◖	○				•
3	**Sherwin-Williams** (alkyd)	24		◖	○	○			•	
4	**Cabot** O.V.T. 6500 (alkyd)	26		●	○	◔			•	
5	**Cabot** O.V.T. 0600 (latex)	23		◖	○	◔			•	
6	**Behr** Plus 10 (Home Depot) (alkyd/water cleanup)	16		◖	○	◖				•
7	**Olympic** WeatherScreen Water Repellent Oil (alkyd)	18		◖	◔	●				
8	**Ace** Wood Royal House & Trim (alkyd)	18		◔	◔	●				
	GREEN *Typifies a range of greens, yellows, and blues.*									
9	**Olympic** Premium (latex)	19		●	◖	◖	•		•	•
10	**Sherwin-Williams** Woodscapes (latex)	25		●	◖	○	•	•	•	•
11	**Behr** Plus 10 (Home Depot) (alkyd/water cleanup)	16		◖	○	○			•	•
12	**Cabot** O.V.T. 6500 (alkyd)	26		◖	○	○			•	•
13	**Cabot** O.V.T. 0600 (latex)	$23		●	○	◖		•		•
14	**Ace** Wood Royal House & Trim (alkyd)	18		◖	○	◖				•
15	**Sherwin-Williams** (alkyd)	24		○	◖	◖	•			

Ratings

Key number	Product	Price	Overall score (P F G VG E, 0–100)	Appearance — After 3 years	Appearance — After 6 years	Appearance — After 9 years	Resists — Dirt	Resists — Color change	Resists — Mildew	Resists — Cracking

RED *Typifies a range of browns, reds, and other earth tones.*

Key number	Product	Price	Overall score	After 3 years	After 6 years	After 9 years	Dirt	Color change	Mildew	Cracking
16	**Olympic** Premium (latex)	19	▬▬▬	◒	◒	◒	•	•	•	•
17	**Sherwin-Williams** Woodscapes (latex)	25	▬▬▬	◒	◒	◒	•	•	•	•
18	**Behr** Plus 10 (Home Depot) (alkyd/water cleanup)	16	▬▬	◒	◒	◒	•	•	•	•
19	**Cabot** O.V.T. 6500 (alkyd)	26	▬▬	◒	○	◓	•		•	•
20	**Cabot** O.V.T. 0600 (latex)	23	▬▬	◒	○	◒	•		•	
21	**Sherwin-Williams** (alkyd)	24	▬▬	◒	○	◑	•			•
22	**Olympic** WeatherScreen Water Repellent Oil (alkyd)	18	▬	◒	○	◒				
23	**Ace** Wood Royal House & Trim (alkyd)	18	▬	○	●	◑				

Based on tests published in Consumer Reports in August 2003.

Guide to the Ratings

Overall score reflects a weighted average of the stains' appearance in three years of testing. **Appearance** scores summarize our long-term testing. One year of our tests is comparable to three years in real life, so we can say how well a stain should do after about three years, six years, and nine years. Specific attributes help you choose models that match your needs. **Resists dirt** shows which stains are better than most at preventing dirt buildup. **Resists color change** shows which change the least from the original color. **Resists mildew** shows which do the best job of preventing mildew growth. **Resists cracking** shows which provide the best protection for the siding. **Price** is the approximate retail.

Ratings

Toilets

Toilets are available in three main types: gravity flush, vacuum assist, and pressure assisted. Gravity-flush models, the traditional type, cost least but are least effective. The Kohler Wellworth 3422, $150, and American Standard Cadet 2798.012, $170, are both good performers for the type. The pricier Toto Carlyle MS874114SG, $460, offers a more stylized one-piece design with a plastic trapway. The top-rated Briggs Vacuity 4200, $190, is a very good choice, but may be difficult to find. The pressure-assisted models we tested performed reliably, but they are all noisy.

In performance order

Rating key: Excellent / Very good / Good / Fair / Poor

Key number	Brand & model	Price	Overall Score (0–100, P F G VG E)	Type	Solid waste	Wash down	Draining	Dilution	Noise
1	**Briggs** Vacuity 4200	$190		Vacuum	Very good	Excellent	Excellent	Excellent	Very good
2	**American Standard** Cadet PA 2333.100	450		Pressure	Very good	Very good	Excellent	Excellent	Good
3	**Gerber** Ultra Flush 21-302	280		Pressure	Excellent	Very good	Excellent	Excellent	Good
4	**Crane** Vacuum Induced Power FlushVIP 3999	250		Vacuum	Very good	Excellent	Very good	Very good	Excellent
5	**Gerber** Ultra Flush 21-312	300		Pressure	Excellent	Very good	Excellent	Excellent	Good
6	**Kohler** San Raphael Power Lite K-3398	600		Pressure	Excellent	Very good	Very good	Excellent	Good
7	**Crane** Economiser 3834	200		Pressure	Very good	Very good	Good	Very good	Good
8	**Toto** Carlyle MS874114SG	460		Gravity	Very good	Good	Very good	Excellent	Very good
9	**Kohler** Wellworth 3422	150		Gravity	Very good	Good	Excellent	Excellent	Excellent
10	**American Standard** Cadet 2798.012	170		Gravity	Good	Very good	Very good	Very good	Very good
11	**Eljer** Aqua Saver 091-7025	420		Pressure	Very good	Fair	Very good	Excellent	Fair
12	**Kohler** Wellworth K-3423	120		Gravity	Good	Good	Very good	Very good	Very good
13	**Eljer** Canterbury 081-1625	505		Gravity	Good	Good	Very good	Very good	Very good
14	**Eljer** Patriot 091-2125	185		Gravity	Very good	Good	Excellent	Poor	Very good
15	**Eljer** Patriot 091-2175 17"	285		Gravity	Good	Fair	Excellent	Good	Very good
16	**American Standard** Cadet 2898.012	210		Gravity	Fair	Very good	Excellent	Excellent	Excellent
17	**American Standard** Colony 2399.012	170		Gravity	Fair	Good	Very good	Excellent	Very good
18	**Eljer** Patriot 091-2120	160		Gravity	Fair	Good	Excellent	Good	Very good
19	**Toto** Ultramax MS853113S3	360		Gravity	Fair	Good	Excellent	Very good	Fair
20	**Universal-Rundle** Atlas 4191	240		Gravity	Fair	Good	Very good	Very good	Very good

Ratings

Key number	Brand & model	Price	Overall Score	Type	Solid waste	Wash down	Draining	Dilution	Noise
			P F G VG E						
21	**Crane** Galaxy Elite II 3792	100	▬	Gravity	●	◐	●	●	◐
22	**American Standard** Antiquity 2464.019	370	▬	Gravity	●	○	○	○	◉
23	**Gerber** Aqua Saver 21-702	100	▬	Gravity	●	○	○	●	●
24	**Kohler** Gabrielle Comfort Height K-3322	400	▬	Gravity	●	○	◐	◐	◉
25	**American Standard** Cadet One Piece 2100.016	400	▬	Gravity	●	○	●	●	◉
26	**Kohler** Portrait K-3591	300	▬	Gravity	●	●	●	●	●
27	**Gerber** Aqua Saver 21-712	140	▬	Gravity	●	○	○	●	◐

See report, page 180. Based on tests published in Consumer Reports in October 2002, with updated prices and availability.

Guide to the Ratings

Overall score is based on performance with water pressure of 35 pounds per square inch (psi). **Solid waste** includes how well each model moved sponges, plastic balls, latex cylinders, and baby wipes through the bowl and trap. This test carried by far the greatest weight. **Wash down** is a measure of how well the toilets cleaned the sides of the bowl with each flush. **Draining** shows how well each toilet could move solid material through a drainline. **Dilution** shows how well the toilets flushed liquid waste. **Noise** characterizes how loudly the toilets flush, with the lid up. **Price** is the estimated average.

Recommendations and notes

Models listed as similar should offer performance comparable to the tested model's, although features may differ.
Most of these toilets: Have an elongated bowl and are two-piece designs. Require 12 inches of clearance from the wall to the center of the drain hole. Have rim that's 14 to 15 inches from floor. Complete a flush cycle in 75 seconds or less. Work with water pressure of 20 to 80 psi. Have a basic warranty of one to five years, some have a lifetime warranty on china.

1 BRIGGS Vacuity 4200 **Very good overall.**

2 AMERICAN STANDARD Cadet PA 2333.100 **Very good overall.** Mold and mildew can grow in stagnant water below pressure-assist tank. Very good at minimizing soil and odor in bowl.

3 GERBER Ultra Flush 21-302 **Very good overall.** Mold and mildew cangrow in stagnant water below pressure-assist tank. Round-front bowl. Very good at minimizing soil and odor in bowl.

4 CRANE Vacuum Induced Power FlushVIP 3999 **Very good overall.** Taller than most; designed for the elderly and disabled. Very good at minimizing soil and odor in bowl.

5 GERBER Ultra Flush 21-312 **Very good overall.** Mold and mildew can grow in stagnant water below pressure-assist tank.

6 KOHLER San Raphael Power Lite K-3398 **Very good overall.** One-piece design. Seat included. Uses electric pump.

7 CRANE Economiser 3834 **Very good overall.** Mold and mildew can grow in stagnant water below pressure-assist tank. Round-front bowl.

8 TOTO Carlyle MS874114SG **Very good overall.** One-piece design. Seat included. Similar: MS874114S.

9 KOHLER Wellworth 3422 **Very good overall.** As received, used more than 2 gal. per flush. Similar: 3438, 3448, 3479, 3480.

10 AMERICAN STANDARD Cadet 2798.012 **Very good overall.** Round-front bowl. Very good at minimizing soil and odor in bowl. Similar: 2319.015, 2321.018.

Ratings

Recommendations and notes

11 ELJER Aqua Saver 091-7025 **Good overall.** Mold and mildew can grow in stagnant water below pressure-assist tank. Poor at minimizing soil and odor in bowl.

12 KOHLER Wellworth K-3423 **Good overall.** As received, used more than 2 gal. per flush. Round-front bowl. Similar: 3449, 3480, 3433.

13 ELJER Canterbury 081-1625 **Good overall.** One-piece design. Seat included.

14 ELJER Patriot 091 **Good overall.** Poor at minimizing soil and odor in bowl. Similar: 2125 091-2195, 091-2127, 091-2135, 091-2155, 091-0225, 091-0228, 091-0227, 091-0245, Preserver II 091-4835, 091-2136.

15 ELJER Patriot 091-2175 17" **Good overall.** Taller than most. Designed for the elderly and disabled. Poor at minimizing soil and odor in bowl. Similar: Laguna 17" ER 091-3385.

16 AMERICAN STANDARD Cadet 2898. 012 **Good overall.** Similar: 2898.014, 2316.019, 2323.011, 2898.010.

17 AMERICAN STANDARD Colony 2399.012 **Good overall.** Similar: 2399.010, 2399.014.

18 ELJER Patriot 091-2120 **Good overall.** Round-front bowl. Similar: Preserver II 091-4830, 091-2150, 091-2190, 091-0220, 091-0240, 091-2130, 091-0223, 091-2122.

19 TOTO Ultramax MS853113S **Good overall.** Round-front bowl. One piece. Seat included.

20 UNIVERSAL-RUNDLE Atlas 4191 **Good overall.** Round-front bowl. Similar: 4190, 4192, 4193, 4290.

21 CRANE Galaxy Elite II 3792 **Fair overall.** Similar: Radcliffe II 3852, 3793, 3972, Galaxy II 3790.

22 AMERICAN STANDARD Antiquity 2464.019 **Fair overall.** Similar: 2483.019.

23 GERBER Aqua Saver 21-702 **Fair overall.** Round-front bowl.

24 KOHLER Gabrielle Comfort Height K-3322 **Fair overall.** Seat included. Taller than most; designed for the elderly and disabled. One- piece design.

25 AMERICAN STANDARD Cadet One Piece 2100.016 **Fair overall.** Seat included.

26 KOHLER Portrait K-3591 **Fair overall.** Poor at minimizing soil and odor in bowl.

27 GERBER Aqua Saver 21-712 **Fair overall.**

Ratings

TVs, direct-view

Shopping for a TV requires balancing the space the set occupies, features you want, and price. Our tests turned up very good choices in each size category. For a 27-inch analog set, consider the flat-screen Toshiba Cinema Series 27AF53, $450. Among the 32-inch analog sets, the standout is the Toshiba FST Black 32A43, which offers fine performance for $480. Among the 32-inch flat-screen models, the Sharp F630 Series 32F631, $600, offers very good performance at a good price. For a 36-inch analog set, consider the very good Toshiba FST Black 36A43, $750. If you want an HD-ready set, the 36-inch Sony, $1,800, was the best of all the TVs tested and offers excellent HD performance, while the 32-inch Sanyo, $700, combines very good performance with a low cost.

In performance order

Ratings legend: Excellent ● / Very good ◕ / Good ◑ / Fair ◔ / Poor ○

Key number	Brand & model	Price	Overall score (P F G VG E)	Antenna/cable input	S-video input	Sound quality	Ease of use	Flat screen	Dual-tuner PIP	Composite-video	S-video	Component-video	Front-panel A/V inputs
27-INCH CONVENTIONAL SETS													
1	**Toshiba** Cinema Series 27AF53	$450		◑	●	◑	◑	•		2	1	1	•
2	**JVC** l'Art AV-27FA44	430		◑	●	◑	○	•		2	1	1	•
3	**Sony** FD Trinitron Wega KV-27FS210	550		○	◑	◑	◑		•	2	1	2	•
4	**Toshiba** FST Black 27A43	330		○	◑	◑	◑			2	1	1	•
5	**JVC** D-Series AV-27D104	280		○	◑	◑	◑			2	1	1	•
6	**Sanyo** DS27930 (Wal-Mart)	300		○	◑	◑	◑	•		2	2	1	
7	**Panasonic** E Series CT-27E13	280		○	◑	◑	◑			2	1	1	•
8	**Philips** Designer Series 27PT643R	370		○	◑	◔	◑			2	1	1	•
9	**Apex Digital** AT2708S	200		◔	○	○	○			3	1		•
32-INCH CONVENTIONAL SETS													
10	**Toshiba** FST Black 32A43	480		◑	●	●	◑			2	1	1	•
11	**Sony** FD Trinitron Wega KV-32FV310	900		◔	●	●	○	•	•	2	1	2	•
12	**JVC** D-Series AV-32D104 AV-32D304	440		○	◑	◑	○			2	1	1	•
13	**JVC** l'Art AV-32FA44 AV-32FA54	700		○	◑	◑	○	•		2	1	1	•
14	**Sharp** F630 Series 32F631	600		○	◑	◑	○			2	1	1	•
15	**Panasonic** Tau Pureflat CT-32SL13	650		○	◑	◑	◑			2	1	1	•
16	**Sony** FD Trinitron Wega KV-32FS210	800		○	◑	◑	◑	•	•	2	1	2	•
17	**Philips** Designer Series 32PT563S	450		○	◑	◑	◔			2	1	1	•

32-INCH CONVENTIONAL SETS

Key number	Brand & model	Price	Overall score (P F G VG E)	Picture quality — Antenna/cable input	S-video input	Sound quality	Ease of use	Flat screen	Dual-tuner PIP	Composite-video	S-video	Component-video	Front-panel A/V inputs
18	**Philips** Designer Series 32PT663R	$700		○	◐	◐	◑			2	1	1	●
19	**Panasonic** E Series CT-32E13	450		◑	◐	◐	○			2	1	1	●
20	**Apex Digital** AT3208S	330		◑	○	○	○			3	1		●

36-INCH CONVENTIONAL SETS

Key number	Brand & model	Price	Overall score (P F G VG E)	Picture quality — Antenna/cable input	S-video input	Sound quality	Ease of use	Flat screen	Dual-tuner PIP	Composite-video	S-video	Component-video	Front-panel A/V inputs
21	**Toshiba** FST Black 36A43	750		◐	◐	◐	◐			2	1	1	●
22	**JVC** D-Series AV-36D104	700		○	◐	○	○			2	1	1	●
23	**Sony** FD Trinitron Wega KV-36FS210	1,100		○	◐	○	○	●	●	2	1	2	●

HDTVs

Key number	Brand & model	Price	Overall score (P F G VG E)	HD performance	Antenna/cable input	S-video input	Sound quality	Ease of use	Flat screen	Dual-tuner PIP	Composite-video	S-video	Component-video	Front-panel A/V inputs
24	**Sony** FD Trinitron Wega KV-36HS510 (36 in.)	$1,800		●	○	●	●	◑	●	●	3	2	2	●
25	**Panasonic** Tau Pureflat CT-32HL43 (32 in.)	1,200		◑	◐	◐	●	◐	●	●	3	2	2	●
26	**Panasonic** Tau Pureflat CT-36HL43 (36 in.)	1,500		◐	◐	◐	◐	◐	●	●	3	2	2	●
27	**Philips** HD Series 30PW850H (30 in. wide-screen)	1,000		○	●	●	●	○	●		2	1	2	●
28	**Sanyo** DS32830H (32 in.)	700		○	◐	◐	◐	◐		●	2	2	1	
29	**Philips** Matchline Series 34PW9819 (34 in. wide-screen)	2,500		◑	●	●	●	○	●	●	2	1	3	●

See report, page 84. Based on tests published in Consumer Reports in December 2003.

Ratings

Guide to the Ratings

Overall score is based primarily on picture quality; sound quality and ease of use are also figured in. Expert panelists evaluated **picture quality** based on clarity and color accuracy. **Sound quality** is for the built-in speakers. **Ease of use** assesses the remote control, on-screen menus, labeling of the rear-jack panel, and useful features. **Price** is approximate retail. **Most tested models:** Have at least one component-video input on the rear panel, adjustable color temperature, virtual surround sound, channel block-out, clock, alarm ("on") timer, universal remote. 12-month warranty on labor and parts (with 24-month warranty on picture tube).

All HD models: Are HD-ready units that require the use of an external tuner to receive HD programming. **Most HD-ready models:** Have picture-in-picture (PIP) or picture-out-of-picture (POP), at least two component-video inputs, motion compensation, automatic volume leverler, and Digital Visual Interface (DVI) input for potential use with copy-protected HD content.

Recommendations and notes

27-INCH CONVENTIONAL SETS

1. TOSHIBA Cinema Series 27AF53 **Very good, with excellent S-video picture.** Has headphone jack, automatic volume leveler, customizable channel labels, and auto power-off. Remote control easy to use in low light. Front A/V inputs include S-video. Lacks PIP and auto clock-set. Rear jacks are poorly labeled. Short (3-month) labor warranty.

2. JVC I'Art AV-27FA44 **Very good, with excellent S-video picture.** Has auto power-off, auto clock-set, and front-panel lock feature. Lacks PIP. Similar: AV-27FA54.

3. SONY FD Trinitron Wega KV-27FS210 **Very good.** Has customizable channel labels. Lacks channel block-out. Short (3-month) labor warranty. Rear jacks are poorly labeled.

4. TOSHIBA FST Black 27A43 **Very good.** Has automatic volume leveler, customizable channel labels, and auto power-off. Lacks adjustable color temperature. Rear jacks are poorly labeled. Short (3-month) labor warranty.

5. JVC D-Series AV-27D104 **Good.** Has auto power-off, auto clock-set, and front-panel lock feature. Rear jacks are poorly labeled. Lacks adjustable color temperature. Similar: AV-27D304.

6 SANYO DS27930 **Good.** Has auto flesh-tone correction and auto clock-set. Automatically displays active program's rating. Remote control easy to use in low light. Lacks channel block-out and alarm ("on") timer. Short (12-month) warranty on CRT.

7. PANASONIC E Series CT-27E13 **Good.** Has headphone jack, automatic volume leveler, and customizable channel labels. Automatically displays active program's rating. Short (3-month) labor warranty.

8. PHILIPS Designer Series 27PT643R **Good, but harder to use than most other sets tested.** Has headphone jack, automatic volume leveler, and switchable video-noise reduction. Excellent on-screen menu. Front A/V inputs located on side. Lacks virtual surround sound, clock, and alarm ("on") timer. Remote control difficult to use in low light. Rear jacks are poorly labeled. Short (3-month) labor warranty.

9 APEX Digital AT2708S **There are better choices; no component-video input, and lackluster display via RF input.** Lacks adjustable color temperature and channel block-out. Remote control is not universal. Short CRT (12-month) and labor (3-month) warranties.

32-INCH CONVENTIONAL SETS

10. TOSHIBA FST Black 32A43 **Very good, with excellent S-video picture and excellent sound from built-in speakers.** Very good remote control, and excellent on-screen menu. Lacks clock and alarm ("on") timer. Rear jacks are poorly labeled.

11. SONY FD Trinitron Wega KV-32FV310 **Very good, with excellent S-video picture and excellent sound from built-in speakers.** Has automatic volume leveler and customizable channel labels. Front A/V inputs include S-video. Lacks channel block-out. Rear jacks are poorly labeled. Short (3-month) labor warranty.

12. JVC D-Series AV-32D104 **Very good.** Has auto power-off, auto clock-set, and front-panel lock feature. Lacks adjustable color temperature. Similar: AV-32D304.

13. JVC I'Art AV-32FA44 **Very good.** Has auto power-off, auto clock-set, and front-panel lock feature. Lacks dual-tuner PIP and a second component-video input. Similar: AV-32FA54.

Ratings

Recommendations and notes

14. SHARP F630 Series 32F631 **Very good.** Has automatic volume leveler and customizable channel labels. Lacks channel block-out, clock, and alarm ("on") timer. Rear jacks are poorly labeled.

15. PANASONIC Tau Pureflat CT-32SL13 **Good.** Has headphone jack, automatic volume leveler, and customizable channel labels. Automatically displays active program's rating. Front A/V inputs include S-video. Rear jacks are poorly labeled.

16. SONY FD Trinitron Wega KV-32FS210 **Good.** Has customizable channel labels. Lacks channel block-out. Rear jacks are poorly labeled. Short (3-month) labor warranty.

17. PHILIPS Designer Series 32PT563S **Good, but harder to use than most other sets tested.** Has headphone jack, automatic volume leveler, and switchable video-noise reduction. Front A/V inputs located on side. Lacks clock, and alarm ("on") timer. Remote control difficult to use in low light. Rear jacks are poorly labeled. Short (3-month) labor warranty.

18. PHILIPS Designer Series 32PT663R **Good, but harder to use than most other sets tested.** Has headphone jack, automatic volume leveler, and switchable video-noise reduction. Excellent on-screen menu, but remote control difficult to use in low light. Front A/V inputs located on side. Lacks display, clock, and alarm ("on") timer. Rear jacks are poorly labeled. Short (3-month) labor warranty.

19. PANASONIC E Series CT-32E13 **Good, but lackluster display via RF input.** Has headphone jack, automatic volume leveler, and customizable channel labels. Automatically displays active program's rating.

20. APEX Digital AT3208S **There are better choices; no component-video input, and lackluster display via RF input.** Automatically displays active program's rating. Lacks channel block-out. Short CRT (12-month) and labor (3-month) warranties.

36-INCH CONVENTIONAL SETS

21. TOSHIBA FST Black 36A43 **Very good across the board.** Has auto power-off. Excellent on-screen menu and very good remote control. Lacks clock, and alarm ("on") timer. Rear jacks are poorly labeled.

22. JVC D-Series AV-36D104 **Good.** Has auto power-off, auto clock-set, and front-panel lock feature. Lacks adjustable color temperature. Similar: AV-36D304.

23. SONY FD Trinitron Wega KV-36FS210 **Good.** Has customizable channel labels. Lacks channel block-out. Rear jacks are poorly labeled. Short (3-month) labor warranty.

HD-READY SETS

24. SONY FD Trinitron Wega KV-36HS510 (36 in.) **Very good, with excellent HD performance, excellent S-video picture, and excellent sound from built-in speakers.** Has customizable channel labels and scrolling channel preview. Front A/V inputs include S-video. Rear jacks are well labeled. Lacks channel block-out. Short (3-month) labor warranty.

25. PANASONIC Tau Pureflat CT-32HL43 (32 in.) **Very good, with excellent sound from built-in speakers.** Has switchable video-noise reduction, customizable channel labels, scrolling channel preview, and auto flesh-tone correction. Front A/V inputs include S-video. Automatically displays active program's rating. Lacks channel block-out. Rear jacks are poorly labeled.

26. PANASONIC Tau Pureflat CT-36HL43 (36 in.) **Very good, with excellent sound from built-in speakers.** Has switchable video-noise reduction, customizable channel labels, scrolling channel preview, and auto flesh-tone correction. Front A/V inputs include S-video. Automatically displays active program's rating. Lacks channel block-out. Rear jacks are poorly labeled.

27. PHILIPS HD Series 30PW850H (30-in. wide screen) **Very good, with excellent picture quality from antenna/cable and S-video inputs, and excellent sound from built-in speakers.** Single rear S-video input may limit connections. Has customizable channel labels, and auto clock-set. Excellent on-screen menu. Front A/V inputs, located on side, include S-video. Lacks DVI and motion compensation. Rear jacks are poorly labeled. Short (3-month) labor warranty.

28. SANYO DS32830H (32 in.) **Very good, but single component-video input limits connections.** Has auto clock-set. Automatically displays active program's rating. But lacks channel block-out, alarm ("on") timer, automatic volume leveler, and DVI. Short (12-month) warranty on CRT.

29. PHILIPS Matchline Series 34PW9819 (34-in. wide screen) **Good, with excellent picture quality from antenna/cable and S-video inputs, and excellent sound from built-in speakers.** But HD performance only fair. Single S-video input may limit connections. Has switchable video-noise reduction and auto clock-set. Front A/V inputs, located on side, include S-video. Lacks motion compensation. Rear jacks are poorly labeled. Short (3-month) labor warranty.

Ratings

TVs, LCD

Prices are creeping downward, but inch for inch, LCD TVs still cost much more than bulkier sets with picture tubes. And with all but the most-expensive HD sets, the picture quality doesn't measure up to what a conventional set can deliver. For good picture quality under $1,000, consider the 15-inch Sony LCD Wega KLV-15SR1 or 17-inch Panasonic TC-17LA1. If you want to spend more, the Sony LCD Wega KLV-30XBR900, $5,000, is a very good set for HD and standard-definition picture quality. Its 30-inch screen makes it suitable as a primary set.

In performance order

Ratings key: Excellent ◉ Very good ◖ Good ○ Fair ◗ Poor ●

Key number	Brand & model	Price	Overall score	HD performance	Antenna/cable input	S-video input	Sound quality	Ease of use	Composite-video	S-video	Component-video	Control unit
STANDARD-DEFINITION MODELS — All tested models are 4:3 (squarish).												
1	**Sharp** Aquos LC-20E1U (20 in.)	$1,300		-	○	○	◖	○	2	1	1	
2	**Sony** LCD Wega KLV-15SR1 (15 in.)	900		-	○	◖	○	◖	1	1	1	
3	**Panasonic** TC-20LA1 (20 in.)	1,300		-	○	○	○	○	2	2		
4	**Panasonic** TC-17LA1 (17 in.)	900		-	○	○	○	○	2	2		
5	**Panasonic** TC-14LA1 (14 in.)	600		-	◐	○	◐	○	2	2		
6	**Toshiba** 14VL43U (14 in.)	650		-	◐	◖	◐	◖	2	2	1	
7	**Toshiba** 20VL43U (20 in.)	1,300		-	◖	◖	○	◖	2	2	1	
8	**Sharp** Aquos LC-15E1U (15 in.)	700		-	◐	◖	◐	○	2	1	1	
HD-READY MODELS — All tested models are 16:9 (wide-screen).												
9	**Sony** LCD Wega KLV-30XBR900 (30 in.)	5,000		◖	◖	◖	◉	○	3	3	2	●
10	**Sony** LCD Wega KLV-23HR1 (23 in.)	2,300		○	◖	◖	◉	◖	1	1	1	
11	**Sharp** Aquos LC-30HV4U (30 in.)	4,000		○	○	◖	◉	◖	4	4	2	●

See report, page 84. Based on tests published in Consumer Reports in December 2003.

Guide to the Ratings

Overall score is based primarily on picture quality; sound quality and ease of use are also figured in. Experts evaluated **picture quality** based on clarity and color accuracy. **Sound quality** is for built-in speakers. **Ease of use** assesses the remote control, on-screen menus, labeling of inputs, and useful features. **Price** is approximate retail. **All tested models:** Have sleep ("off") timer and 12-month warranty on parts and labor. Display closed-caption data. Measure 2.5 to 3.75 inches in depth (excluding base). Can't receive Extended Data Services (XDS) program information. Standard-definition models have a 4:3 aspect ratio; HD-ready models are wide-screen with a 16:9 ratio; they require an external HD tuner to receive HD programming.

Vacuum cleaners

You can get a very good vacuum cleaner for $150 to $300 or so; paying more doesn't buy better performance. Some of the priciest models are middling performers and come with relatively few features. Still, many of the least-expensive models compromise performance and convenience. Our tests also reveal that some otherwise-impressive machines don't excel in airflow through the hose, which means they have limited suction or they're more likely to lose suction as their bags or bins fill with dust. Two standout values, which are solid performers at superb prices, are the Eureka Boss Smart Vac Ultra 4870, $140 (upright), a **CR Best Buy,** and the Samsung Quiet Jet VAC-9069G, $200 (canister).

In performance order

Ratings key: Excellent ◉ Very good ◕ Good ○ Fair ◔ Poor ●

Key number	Brand & model	Price	Overall score	Carpet	Bare floor	Tools	Ease of use	Noise	Emissions	Bag	Brush on/off	Easy on/off	Manual pile adjust
	UPRIGHTS												
1	**Hoover** WindTunnel Self Propelled Ultra U6439-900	$300		◉	◉	◉	○	◕	◉	•	•	•	•
2	**Kenmore** (Sears) Progressive with Direct Drive 31912	330		◕	◉	◕	◕	○	◉	•	•	•	•
3	**Eureka** Boss Smart Vac Ultra 4870 **A CR Best Buy**	140		◉	◉	○	○	○	○	•	•		•
4	**Hoover** WindTunnel U6630-900	400		◕	◉	○	○	◕	◉	•	•	•	•
5	**Eureka** Ultra Whirlwind 4885	250		◕	◉	◕	○	○	◉	•	•	•	•
6	**Hoover** WindTunnel Bagless U5750-900	200		◉	◉	◕	◕	◕	◕		•	•	•
7	**Dirt Devil** Platinum Force 091210	120		◉	◉	◕	◔	◕	◔	•		•	•
8	**Oreck** XL21-600 [1]	700		◕	◉	N/A	◕	○	◕	•			•
9	**Panasonic** Dual Sweep MC-V7522	150		◕	◉	◕	○	◕	◕	•	•		•
10	**Kenmore** (Sears) Progressive 33912	300		◕	◉	○	○	◕	◕	•	•		•
11	**Kenmore** (Sears) Progressive 34612	190		◕	◉	◕	○	◕	◕	•	•	•	•
12	**Kirby** Ultimate G7D	1,300		◕	◉	◕	○	◕	◕	•		•	•
13	**Bissell** ProLite 3560-2 [1]	200		◕	◉	N/A	◕	◕	◕	•		•	
14	**Dyson** DC07	400		○	◉	◕	◔	◕	◕		•		
15	**Panasonic** Dual Sweep Bagless MC-V7582	$180		◕	◉	○	○	◕	◔		•		
16	**Aerus** Lux 3000	700		○	◉	◔	○	◔	◕	•			
17	**Dirt Devil** Featherlite Plus 085560	$60		◕	◉	◔	◕	●	◕	•		•	
18	**Dirt Devil** Scorpion 088100	80		◉	◉	○	○	●	◔	•		•	
19	**GE** (Wal-Mart) 106585	120		○	◕	○	○	○	◉				•

Key number	Brand & model	Price	Overall score	Cleaning			Other results			Features			
			P F G VG E	Carpet	Bare floor	Tools	Ease of use	Noise	Emissions	Bag	Brush on/off	Easy on/off	Manual pile adjust
UPRIGHTS													
20	**Hoover** Fold Away U5162-900	$110		◐	◐	◑	○	◐	●				•
21	**Oreck** XL-2 [1]	370		○	●	N/A	◐	●	◐			•	
22	**Kenmore** (Sears) Progressive 32734	260		○	◐	◐	◐	◐	●	•	•	•	
23	**Eureka** Whirlwind Plus 4684	150		○	◐	○	◐	◐	●				
24	**Sharp** Multi Floor EC-T5180A	160		○	◐	○	○	◐	●		•	•	
25	**Bosch** Turbo Jet BUH11700UC	300		◐	◐	◐	◐	◐	○	•	•	•	
26	**Bissell** Powerforce 3522-1	50		◐	◐	○	◐	◐	◐				•
27	**Euro-Pro** Shark UV204	100		◑	◐	◐	◐	◐	◐				•
28	**Kenmore** (Sears) Quick Clean 33720	100		◐	◐	○	◐	◐	●			•	•
29	**Fantom** Twister FM740 (300SE)	160		◑	◐	○	◐	◐	●				
30	**Bissell** Cleanview Power Trak 3593-1	100		○	◐	◐	◐	◐	●		•		
31	**Bissell** Cleanview Bagless 8975	80		○	◐	○	○	●	●				
CANISTERS													
32	**Kenmore** (Sears) Progressive 22612	380		◐	◐	◐	◐	◑	●	•			
33	**Samsung** Quiet Jet VAC-9069G	200		◐	◐	◐	◐	◐	●		•		
34	**GE** (Wal-Mart) 106766	150		◐	◐	◑	○	◐	◐		•		
35	**Miele** Plus S251	450		○	◐	◐	◐	◐	◐	•			
36	**Eureka** Home Cleaning System 6984	300		○	◐	◐	○	◐	●	•		•	
37	**Aerus** Lux 7000	$750		◐	◐	◑	◐	○	◐	•		•	
38	**Hoover** WindTunnel Bagless S3765-040	500		◐	◐	○	○	◑	○		•		
39	**Hoover** WindTunnel Plus S3639	350		◐	◐	◐	◐	◐	○	•			
40	**Miele** Solaris Electro Plus S514	700		○	◐	○	◐	◐	●	•	•		
41	**Kenmore** (Sears) eVo 22822	380		○	◐	○	◐	◑	◐	•	•		
42	**Oreck** Dutch Tech DTX1300C	900		◑	◐	◐	◐	◐	◐	•		•	
43	**Fantom** Falcon FC251	190		◑	◐	●	◐	◑	◐	•		•	
44	**Sanyo** High Power SC-800P	300		○	◐	◐	◐	◐	◐	•			
45	**Hoover** PowerMax Runabout S3614	200		◐	◐	○	◐	◑	●	•	•		
46	**Kenmore** (Sears) Magic Blue DX 23295	180		○	◐	◑	◐	◑	◐	•	•	•	•
47	**Rainbow** e-Series E-2	1,800		○	◐	◐	◐	◐	○		•		•

[1] Comes with minicanister for cleaning with tools. Performance was fair for (13); poor for (8) and (21).

See report, page 136. Based on tests published in Consumer Reports in November 2003, with updated prices and availability.

Guide to the Ratings

Overall score mainly reflects cleaning performance, ease of use, and emissions. Under **cleaning, carpet** denotes how much embedded talc and sand the vacuum lifted from a medium-pile carpet. **Bare floor** shows how well the model vacuumed sand without dispersing it. **Tools** relates to tool use and reflects airflow with increasing amounts of dust-simulating wood "flour"; a higher score means the vac provides more airflow and maintains airflow better as dirt accumulates. **Ease of use** denotes how easy the machine is to push, pull, carry, and use beneath furniture as well as the dust bag's or bin's capacity. **Noise** denotes results using a decibel meter. **Emissions** is our measure of how much wood flour is released while vacuuming. **Features** notes whether the model has a **bag** (as opposed to being bagless), allows you to turn off the **brush** when not needed, has an **on/off switch** that is easy to access, and has manual pile-height adjustment, which can improve cleaning. **Price** is approximate retail; bag/filter prices are per unit. **Recommendations & notes** lists noteworthy features and some minor shortcomings.

Recommendations and notes

UPRIGHT VACUUMS

1. **HOOVER** WindTunnel Self Propelled Ultra U6439-900 **Excelled at cleaning, but noisy.** May not fit on some stairs. Bag: $2. Filter: $5. Similar: U6433-900, U6436-900, U6437-900.

2. **KENMORE** (Sears) Progressive with Direct Drive 31912 **Very good all around.** Bag: $4 to $5. HEPA filter: $21. Similar: 31913.

3. **EUREKA** Boss Smart Vac 4870 **A CR Best Buy Highest performance for the dollar.** Excelled at most cleaning, but hard to pull. Bag: $2.30. HEPA filter: $20.

4. **HOOVER** WindTunnel U6630-900 **Very good, but noisy, heavy, and tippy on stairs.** HEPA filter: $20. Similar: U6607-900, U6616-900, U6617-900, U6632-900, U6660-900.

5. **EUREKA** Ultra Whirlwind 4885 **A very good bagless vac, but small capacity.** HEPA filter: $20. Similar: 4880.

6. **HOOVER** WindTunnel Bagless U5750-900 **Very good.** Bagless model with excellent performance on carpets. Less prone to tipping when hose is fully extended. Small rotating brush for stairs. HEPA filter: $30 (Replace every 3 years). Similar: U5722-900, U5751-900, U5752-900, U5758-900, U5759-900.

7. **DIRT DEVIL** Platinum Force 091210 **Excelled at most cleaning, but noisy and tippy on stairs.** Bagless. Hose longer than most. Hard to push and pull. HEPA filter: $25.

8. **ORECK** XL21-600 **Very good, but no overload protection.** Filter on tested models wasn't a HEPA, despite label. Bag: $3.

9. **PANASONIC** Dual Sweep MC-V7522 **Very good overall but has a power cord shorter than most.** Also relatively noisy. Bag: $1.65. Filter: $12.

10. **KENMORE** (Sears) Progressive 33912 **Very good, full-featured machine.** Bagless. Exhaust filter: $14; chamber filter: $20. Similar: 33913.

11. **KENMORE** (Sears) Progressive 34612 **Very good, with lots of features.** Bag: $3.50. Exhaust filter: $14. Similar: 34613.

12. **KIRBY** Ultimate G7D **Very good, though ultra-expensive.** Retro design. For the money, you get a body of aluminum, instead of the more-common plastic, and better-than-average reliability. This machine also has some extra attachments, including a sprayer for shampooing carpet (not tested). Kirbys are usually sold door-to-door. Relatively heavy: 24 lbs. Bag: $3.17.

13. **BISSELL** ProLite 3560-2 **Very good, but noisy and awkward to carry.** No overload protection. Bag: $2.

14. **DYSON** DC07 **A very good bagless vac, but has confusing controls.** Hose longer than most. Noisy. Hard to push and pull. No headlamp. HEPA filter (washable): $17.50.

15. **PANASONIC** Dual Sweep MC-V7582 **Very good overall.** But relatively noisy. Filter: $25. Similar: MC-V7572.

16. **AERUS** Lux 3000 **Good, but pricey and noisy.** Tippy with hose extended. Unstable on stairs. Tools don't stow onboard. Bag: 12 for $18.

17. **DIRT DEVIL** Featherlite Plus 085560 **Good.** No overload protection or upholstery tool. Hose and cord shorter than most. Standard bag: $1. Microfilter bag: $3.30.

18. **DIRT DEVIL** Scorpion 088100 **Good performance for the money, especially on carpet.** Relatively light: 13 lbs. But noisier, with more emissions than most. Bagless. Exhaust filter: $10; HEPA filter: $25.

Recommendations and notes

19. GE 106585 **A good bagless vac, but small capacity and poor furniture clearance.** HEPA filter: $16. Wal-Mart only.

20. HOOVER Fold Away U5162-900 **Good, somewhat spartan upright.** Suction for cleaning with tools not as effective as most. Unique design enables user to fold down the handle for easier storage. But we found the handle harder to grip while vacuuming. Bagless. Primary filter: $13; final filter $4. Similar: U5161-900, U5163-900, U5167-900.

21. ORECK XL-2 **Good performer, though very noisy.** Comes with minicanister for cleaning with tools; we found the performance of that machine to be poor. Bag: $2.50.

22. KENMORE (Sears) Progressive 32734 **Good bagless model, with a number of attractive features.** Exhaust filter: $14, chamber filter: $20. Similar: 32735.

23. EUREKA Whirlwind Plus 4684 **A good bagless vac, but noisy.** Tippy on stairs and with hose extended. Small capacity. Cord shorter than most. HEPA filter: $20.

24. SHARP Multi Floor EC-T5180A **Good performer, but poor on emissions.** HEPA filter: $10.

25. BOSCH Turbo Jet BUH 11700 UC **Good overall, though just so-so on emissions.** Curvy design includes front-mounted hose that we found awkward to remove. Bag: $4. Filter: $25.

26. BISSELL Powerforce 3522-1 **Good, but noisy.** Tippy with hose extended and unstable on stairs. Hard to push. Hose and power cord shorter than most. No overload protection. Bag: $3. Filter: $3.

27. EURO-PRO Shark UV204 **Good performance overall, though worse than most on carpet.** Also relatively noisy. Accessory pack, $5, includes 4 bags and 2 carbon pre-motor filters. HEPA filter: $13.

28. KENMORE (Sears) Quick Clean 33720 **A good bagless vac, but noisy.** Tippy on stairs and with hose extended. Hose and cord shorter than most. No upholstery tool. Tower filter: $20. Exhaust filter: $14. Similar: 33721.

29. FANTOM Twister Bagless FM740 (300SE) **Good overall, but with few amenities.** Performance on carpet worse than average. Relatively noisy. Fantom uprights ranked among the most repair-prone brands. Bagless. HEPA filter: $10.

30. BISSELL Cleanview Power Trak 3593-1 **A good bagless vac, but noisy.** Tippy with hose extended and unstable on stairs. Hard to push. No upholstery tool. HEPA filter: $10.

31. BISSELL Cleanview Bagless 8975 **There are better choices.** Upper-tank filter: $4. Premotor filter: $1.50. Postmotor filter: $3.

CANISTER VACUUMS

32. KENMORE (Sears) Progressive 22612 **Very good, but noisy and heavy.** Hose longer than most. Bag: $4. HEPA filter: $21. This model has been discontinued. Similar: 22613.

33. SAMSUNG Quiet Jet VAC-9069G **Very good, and quieter than most, but hard to push.** No overload protection. Bag: $2. Limited availability.

34. GE (Wal-Mart) 106766 **Very good, well-priced canister, with better-than-average performance on carpet.** Also relatively light: 11 lbs. On the downside, its suction for cleaning with tools was less effective than most. Available only at Wal-Mart. Bag: $1.97.

35. MIELE Plus S251 **Very good.** Less bulky and heavy than most. Cord shorter than most. Bag: $2.60.

36. EUREKA 6984 **Very good, but among the more repair-prone canister brands.** Hose longer than most. Cord shorter than most. Bag: $1.70. HEPA filter: $20.39.

37. AERUS Lux 7000 **Fine for most cleaning, but tippy on stairs.** Cord shorter than most. Bag: $2. Filter: two for $7.

38. HOOVER WindTunnel Bagless S3765-040 **A very good canister vac, with better cleaning than most on carpet.** But relatively noisy, and released dust when we emptied the bin. Dirt cup filter: $14.25. HEPA: $9.45. Similar: S3755.

39. HOOVER WindTunnel Plus S3639 **A very good, well-rounded vac.** Bag: $2.

40. MIELE Solaris Electro Plus S514 **Very good, and quieter than most, but hard to push and pull.** Cord and hose shorter than most. Filters and five-bag set: $12.

41. KENMORE (Sears) eVo 22822 **A very good bagless vac, but noisy and heavy.** Unstable on stairs. Hose longer than most. HEPA filter: $15.50.

Ratings

Recommendations and notes

42. ORECK DutchTech DTX1300C **Very good, but hard to push and pull.** Quieter than most. Bag: $2.80. HEPA filter: $40.

43. FANTOM Falcon FC251 **Good overall, with better-than-average cleaning on carpet.** But disconnecting the powerhead and wiring to change tools was very difficult. Vac also was relatively noisy, and released dust when bin was emptied. HEPA filter: $30.

44. SANYO High Power SC-800P **Good, but spartan for the price.** Noisy. No overload protection. Cord shorter than most. Bag: $4. Electrostatic micron filter: $9.95.

45. HOOVER PowerMAX Runabout S3614 **A good, inexpensive canister for most cleaning, but high emissions.** Noisy. No overload protection. Standard bag: $1.30. Allergen filtration bag: $2.90.

46. KENMORE (Sears) Magic Blue DX 23295 **Good overall, with lots of features.** But worse-than-average suction for cleaning with tools, and noisier than most. Bag: $1.25.

47. RAINBOW e-Series E-2 **Extremely high price not justified by performance.** Among the worst on bare floors, and relatively noisy. Unusual design utilizes water to retain dust and dirt that's been picked up; that makes the machine very heavy (32 lbs.) when filled with water. Special features include the ability to pick up wet spills (not tested), an inflator for toys and a dusting brush for plants and animals. Rainbow ranks among the more reliable brands.

Ratings

Wall ovens

Based on our tests, it's hard to choose a bad wall oven; nearly all performed a variety of cooking tasks at least adequately. The best models for most, with capable cooking at a relatively low price, are the GE JTP20WF at $850 and the Frigidaire Gallery GLEB30S8C at $700. The GE lacks a convection mode, but delivers as much space and performs nearly as well as the Thermador SC301T, $1,700, for less. The Frigidaire excelled at baking, but its small capacity could be a problem if you have a large family or entertain often. If you broil lots of steak, the Thermador is a good bet.

In performance order

Rating key: Excellent ● / Very good ◕ / Good ○ / Fair ◔ / Poor ⬤

Key number	Product (Similar models, in small type, comparable to tested model.)	Price	Overall score	Capacity	Bake	Broil	Covered element	Meat probe	Convection cooking
1	**Thermador** SC301T[W] SC301Z[ ]	$1,700		Very good	Very good	Excellent			●
2	**Kenmore** Elite 4904[2]	1,650		Good	Very good	Very good	●		●
3	**GE** Profile JT915WF[WW]	1,500		Very good	Very good	Very good	●	●	●
4	**GE** JTP20WF[WW]	850		Very good	Good	Very good			
5	**Frigidaire** Gallery GLEB30S8C[S] PLEB30S8C[ ]	700		Very good	Excellent	Good			●
6	**Whirlpool** Gold GBS307PD[Q]	1,220		Very good	Very good	Very good		●	●
7	**Bosch** HBL74[2] ①	1,600		Very good	Good	Good	●		●

Overall score scale: 0 — P F G VG E — 100

① Tested model comes with stainless, typically $300 extra on others.

See report, page 37. Based on tests published in Consumer Reports in September 2003, with updated prices and availability.

Guide to the Ratings

Overall score includes capacity as well as baking and broiling performance. **Capacity** is usable space; all could hold a 20-pound turkey. **Bake** shows baking evenness for cakes and cookies. **Broil** shows cooking evenness and searing for a tray of burgers. We also test the self-cleaning mode. **Price** is approximate retail. Under **Product,** brackets show a tested model's color code. Similar wall ovens have the same broiler; other details may differ. **All have:** Timed cooking. Self-cleaning. Delay start. **Most have:** Convection. Less capacity than range ovens. Five or more rack positions. Two lights. One timer. Temperature display. A one-year full warranty. Child lockout.

Washing machines

Most of the washing machines we tested did a very good or excellent job. Paying more within a category may get you fancier styling, more settings, and a porcelain top. For very good performance at a modest price, a top-loader should fill the bill. If you prefer to spend more for the best performance overall and the largest capacity, get a front-loader. An outstanding and reasonably-priced choice is the Whirlpool Duet GHW9100L[Q], $1,100. If space is tight, the efficient and quiet Asko W6021 delivers excellent washing.

In performance order

Rating key: ● Excellent ◕ Very good ○ Good ◔ Fair ⬤ Poor

Key number	Brand & model	Price	Overall score (0–100: P F G VG E)	Washing performance	Energy efficiency	Water efficiency	Capacity	Gentleness	Noise	Auto temp. control	Auto dispensers	Stainless-steel tub	Cycle time (min.)
TOP-LOADING MODELS													
1	**Kenmore** (Sears) Elite Calypso 2206[2]	$1,000	▬▬▬▬	●	◕	◕	●	◕	●	•	•	•	70
2	**Fisher & Paykel** GWL11	600	▬▬▬	◕	◕	○	○	◕	◕			•	50
3	**GE** Profile WPRB9220C[WW]	725	▬▬▬	◕	◔	◕	●	○	◕	•		•	50
4	**Maytag** SAV5701A[WW]	600	▬▬▬	◕	○	◕	◕	○	○	•			50
5	**Kenmore** (Sears) 2493[2]	520	▬▬▬	●	◔	◕	◕	○	◕	•			45
6	**Hotpoint** VWSR4150B[WW]	390	▬▬▬	◕	◔	○	◕	◕	○				45
7	**Maytag** Atlantis MAV9501E[WW]	750	▬▬▬	●	○	◕	◕	◕	◕	•		•	60
8	**Whirlpool** Gold GSW9650[W]	500	▬▬▬	◕	◔	◕	◕	○	○	•	•		50
FRONT-LOADING MODELS													
9	**Whirlpool** Duet HT GHW9200L[W]	1,300	▬▬▬▬	●	◔	●	●	●	●	•	•	•	60
10	**Whirlpool** Duet GHW9100L[Q]	1,100	▬▬▬▬	●	◔	●	●	●	●	•	•	•	70
11	**LG** WM2032HW	1,000	▬▬▬▬	●	◕	●	●	○	◕	•	•	•	80
12	**Kenmore** (Sears) 4304[2]	800	▬▬▬	●	◕	●	●	◕	◕	•	•	•	60
13	**Maytag** Neptune MAH6500A[WW]	1,200	▬▬▬	●	○	◕	○	○	○	•	•	•	70

Ratings

Key number	Brand & model	Price	Overall score P F G VG E	Washing performance	Energy efficiency	Water efficiency	Capacity	Gentleness	Noise	Auto temp. control	Auto dispensers	Stainless-steel tub	Cycle time (min.)
	COMPACT MODELS												
14	**Bosch** Axxis+ WFR2460UC	1,100	▬▬▬▬	○	◉	◉	●	◉	◉	•	•	•	60
15	**Asko** W6021	1,000	▬▬▬	◉	◉	◉	●	◒	◒	•	•	•	95
16	**Bosch** Axxis WFL2060UC	930	▬▬▬	○	◉	◉	●	◉	◉	•	•	•	60
17	**Miele** Novotronic W1966	1,500	▬▬▬	◉	◒	◒	●	◒	◉	•	•	•	55

See report, page 47. Based on tests published in Consumer Reports in August 2003, with updated prices and availability.

Guide to the Ratings

Overall score is based mostly on performance, capacity, energy efficiency, and noise. Water efficiency and gentleness are also considered. **Washing performance** indicates how well each machine removed soil in the most-aggressive normal cycle. All washers of the same type used the same detergent. **Energy efficiency** is based on the electricity needed to run the washer and to heat the water for a warm wash, and the amount of water extracted in the final spin cycle (which lessens time in the dryer). **Water efficiency** reflects how much water per pound of laundry it took to do an 8-pound load and each machine's maximum load. **Capacity** measures how large a load each machine could handle effectively. Models that earned lower scores for **gentleness** are more likely to treat your clothes roughly, causing wear and tear. Panelists gauged **noise** during the fill, agitation, drain, and spin cycles. **Cycle time** is for the normal cycle, rounded to the nearest 5 minutes. **Price** is approximate retail. Under **brand & model,** bracketed letters or numbers are color codes. Ratings may differ from earlier reports because of changes to scoring.

Recommendations and notes

TOP-LOADING MODELS

1 KENMORE (Sears) Elite Calypso 2206[2] **An excellent, efficient washer with an especially large capacity.** Gentle on clothes. Because this is a newer model with a unique design, the Brand Repair History for top-loading Kenmores may not apply to this model. Similar model: 2408[ ].

2 FISHER & Paykel GWL11 **A very good washer that's gentler and more energy-efficient than most top-loaders.** Among the best at extracting water from clothes. Has selectable automatic water level. Fairly quiet.

3 GE Profile WPRB9220C[WW] **A very good washer with very large capacity.** Fairly quiet. Handles unbalanced loads better than most. Programmable favorites/custom keys.

4 MAYTAG SAV5701A[WW] **A very good washer with continuously variable water level.**

5 KENMORE (Sears) 2493[2] **A very good washer with very large capacity.** Similar: 2492[ ], 2490[ ].

6 HOTPOINT VWSR4150B[WW] **Very good.** A fine, basic performer.

7 MAYTAG Atlantis MAV9501E[WW] **A very good washer with selectable wash/spin speed combinations.** Has continuously variable water level. More aggressive than most in gentleness tests. Similar: MAV9750A[ ].

8 WHIRLPOOL Gold GSW9650[W] **A good washer with continuously variable water level.** Lacks selectable spin speeds.

Recommendations and notes

FRONT-LOADING MODELS

9 WHIRLPOOL Duet HT GHW9200L[W] **Strong performer with handy two-direction dial controls.**

10 WHIRLPOOL Duet GHW9100L[Q] **Much like the Whirlpool Duet HT GHW9200L, but has lower price and fewer features.**

11 LG WM2032HW **An excellent washer with very large capacity.** Inner tub is angled up for easier access. Among the best at extracting water from clothes. Handles unbalanced loads better than most. Has internal water heater.

12 KENMORE (Sears) 4304[2] **A very good washer that's among the best at extracting water from clothes.** Very frugal with water and energy usage. Similar: 4314[ ], 4305[ ].

13 MAYTAG Neptune MAH6500A[WW] **A very good washer with inner tub angled up for easier access.** Has internal water heater. Remembers last cycle on Start. Maytag front-loaders have been more repair-prone than other brands. Similar: MAH5500B[ ].

COMPACT MODELS

14 BOSCH Axxis+ WFR2460UC **Very good.** Extremely thrifty with water and energy. Gentle on clothes. Can provide high temperature wash cycles using internal water heater. Requires 240 volt electrical outlet.

15 ASKO W6021 **Very good compact model; extremely thrifty with water and energy.** Has internal water heater. Requires 240-volt electrical outlet.

16 BOSCH Axxis WFL2060UC **Very good.** Extremely thrifty with water and energy. Gentle on clothes. Can provide high temperature wash cycles using internal water heater. Requires 240 volt electrical outlet.

17 MIELE Novotronic W1966 **A very good compact washer.** Among the best at extracting water from clothes. Has spin hold feature and internal water heater. Requires 240-volt electrical outlet. Similar: W1986.

Ratings

Water filters

Carafes and faucet-mounted filters are a simple solution but installed models provide more water with less effort. Among carafes, the Brita Classic, 0B01, $20, was best at removing off-tastes. The undersink Kenmore 38460, $80, is an excellent choice and a **CR Best Buy.**

In performance order

Ratings legend: Excellent ● · Very good ◕ · Good ○ · Fair ◔ · Poor ◑

Key number	Brand & model	Price	Overall score (P F G VG E)	Off-tastes	Lead	Chloroform	Flow rate	Annual cost (Cartridge model)
CARAFES *(Filter cartridges last 2 months)*							
1	**Pur** Advantage CR-1500R	$18	▬▬▬	○	◕	●	●	$54 (CRF-1550)
2	**Brita** Classic 0B01	20	▬▬▬	◕	●	◕	◑	48 (0B03)
3	**Pur** Ultimate Small CR-800	23	▬▬▬	◑	●	●	●	72 (CRF-950)
4	**GE** SmartWater XPL03D	19	▬▬	◑	○	◑	○	108 (FXPL3D)
FAUCET-MOUNTED MODELS *(Filter cartridges last 2 to 3 months)*							
5	**GE** SmartWater GXFM03C	22	▬▬▬	●	◕	●	○	52 (FXMLC)
6	**Pur** Ultimate Horizontal FM-4700L	43	▬▬▬	●	●	●	●	80-120 (RF4050L)
UNDERSINK MODELS *(Filter cartridges last 6 months, except where noted)*							
7	**Kenmore** 38460 **A CR Best Buy**	80	▬▬▬▬	●	●	●	◕	54 (34370; 34377)
8	**Omni** CBF-20	170	▬▬▬	●	●	●	○	120 (CB20)
9	**Culligan** SY-2500	180	▬▬▬	●	●	●	○	44 (D-25)
10	**Omni** OT32	150	▬▬▬	●	●	●	○	168 (RS2; CB3)
11	**Kenmore** 38465	150	▬▬▬	◑	●	●	◕	90 (38466)
12	**Culligan** SY-1000	55	▬▬▬	◕	◕	●	○	45 (1000R)
13	**Kenmore** 38455	100	▬▬▬	●	◕	●	●	54 (38456)
REVERSE-OSMOSIS MODELS *(Filter cartridges last 6 months)*							
14	**Kenmore** 38470	230	▬▬▬	●	●	◕	●	44 (34370; 34373)
15	**GE** SmartWater GXRV10ABL01	240	▬▬	●	●	●	●	80 (FX12PA; FX12M)
WHOLE-HOUSE (POINT-OF-ENTRY) MODELS *(Filter cartridges last at least 3 months)*							
16	**Kenmore** 38440	35	▬▬	◕	●	◑	◕	14-21 (34370)
17	**Omni** U-25	55	▬	●	●	○	◕	52 (T01SS)

See report, page 200. Based on tests published in Consumer Reports in January 2003, with updated prices and availability.

Ratings

Guide to the Ratings

Overall score is based mainly on the cartridges' effectiveness in removing chloroform, lead, and off-tastes, as well as flow rate and resistance to clogging. Panelists judged removal of **off-tastes**. To test **lead** and **chloroform** we measured chloroform and lead levels in water entering and leaving the filters. Except as noted, filters are National Sanitation Foundation International (NSF) certified for parasite and chlorine removal. **Flow rate** measures performance of filters with a new filter cartridge. It typically slows with continued use. **Annual cost** is based on the number of cartridges required per year and their cost as estimated by the manufacturers. **Cartridge model** is the replacement cartridge. **Price** is approximate retail.

Recommendations and notes

"Other metals" means other than lead and mercury; "organics" refers to a variety of organic compounds; "VOCs" means volatile organic compounds. MTBE (methyl tert-butyl ether) is a gasoline additive.

CARAFES

1 PUR Advantage CR-1500R **Very good.** Fills quickly. Life indicator. But no covered spout. Doesn't remove cysts. Two quarts. Certified for mercury, lindane/atrazine, 0.5-1 micron particles, organics.

2 BRITA Classic OB01 **Economical, but relatively slow.** Doesn't remove cysts. Two quarts. Certified for mercury, 0.5-1 micron particles, organics, other metals. **1**

3 PUR Ultimate Small CR-800 **Very good, but slow.** Filter tends to clog. Two quarts. Life indicator. Certified for lindane/atrazine, mercury, 0.5-1 micron particles, organics, MTBE, other metals, cysts.

4 GE SmartWater XPL03D **A good choice.** Fills quickly. Two quarts. Doesn't remove cysts. Certified for mercury, other metals.

FAUCET-MOUNTED MODELS

5 GE SmartWater GXFM03C **Very good, but processed water lever must be reset with each use.** Certified for 0.5-1 micron particles, sediment, cysts.

6 PUR Ultimate Horizontal FM-4700L **A good choice.** But clogged prematurely. Life indicator. Certified for lindane/atrazine, mercury, asbestos, 0.5-1 micron particles, organics, MTBE, cysts.

UNDERSINK MODELS

7 KENMORE 38460 **A CR Best Buy An excellent choice.** Less likely than others to clog. Filter is hard to change. Certified for 0.5-1 micron particles, sediments, cysts.

8 OMNI CBF-20 **Excellent performer.** Less likely than others to clog. Includes tools. But hard to change filter. Certified for lindane/atrazine, mercury, asbestos, MTBE, VOCs, cysts.

9 CULLIGAN SY-2500 **Excellent, with long-lasting (12 mos.) double-filter set.** Life indicator. Includes tools. Certified for lindane/atrazine, mercury, asbestos, 0.5-1 micron particles, sediment, organics, cysts.

10 OMNI OT32 **Very good double-filter model.** Includes tools. But hard to change filter. Clogging worse than most. Certified for 0.5-1 micron particles, sediment, cysts. Cartridges last 3 and 4 months.

11 KENMORE 38465 **Very good double-filter model, but falters removing off-tastes.** Hard to change filter even with tools. Life indicator. Certified for lindane/atrazine, asbestos, MTBE, organics, VOCs, cysts.

12 CULLIGAN SY-1000 **A very good choice.** No filter housing. Certified for lindane/atrazine, 0.5-1 micron particles, sediment, cysts.

13 KENMORE 38455 **Very good against contaminants, but poor at removing off-tastes.** Hard to change filter, even with tools. Life indicator. Certified for lindane/atrazine, asbestos, organics, MTBE, cysts.

REVERSE-OSMOSIS MODELS

14 KENMORE 38470 **Excellent filtering, but slow.** Hard to change filter. Certified for sediment, total dissolved solids. Does not claim to remove lead. Doesn't remove parasites.

15 GE SmartWater GXRV10ABL01 **Excellent filtering, but slow.** Less likely than others to clog. Hard to change filters, even with provided tools. Certified for mercury, 0.5-1 micron particles, sediment, total dissolved solids, other metals, cysts.

WHOLE-HOUSE (POINT-OF-ENTRY) MODELS

16 KENMORE 38440 **A very good choice, except for chloroform removal.** Hard to change filter. Certified only for sediment. Doesn't remove parasites.

17 OMNI U-25 **Not a good choice.** Poor at removing off-tastes. Doesn't remove parasites. Includes tools.

Finding
Reliable Brands

In general, products today are pretty reliable. But CONSUMER REPORTS surveys have found that some brands have been more reliable than others. By buying the brands that have been the most reliable, you can improve your chances of getting a less repair-prone product. We know about trends in product reliability because, every year, CONSUMER REPORTS asks its readers to report on repairs and problems they encounter with household products. From responses to the Annual Questionnaire, we are able to derive the percentage of each brand's products that have been repaired or suffered a serious problem.

Products with complicated mechanisms typically need more repairs than simpler devices. Gas ranges break down more than electric ranges. Self-propelled lawn mowers fail more often than push models. The presence of an icemaker or a water dispenser in a refrigerator increases the chance of needing a repair.

These reliability findings can shed light on the dilemma that you face when a product breaks. Should you fix it or replace it? Two factors conspire to make obtaining repairs difficult. Prices are plummeting for many products, notably electronics and computers, often making repair the more expensive option. Also, repairs may be harder to obtain—parts and repairers may be scarce, their fees are high, and repair times are long.

Many people decide to get a model with new features when a product breaks. And you can sometimes get a lot more for less. Electronics products are the best example. For instance, a typical 27-inch TV set currently costs about $350 and has more features than did TVs that cost $500 five years ago. With appliances, you might reap cost savings due to newer models' greater efficiency. Appliances are more efficient today, especially refrigerators and washers. The most frugal cost the most, but the energy savings may make replacing a broken older model worthwhile.

Should you repair it?

Here's a way to assess whether or not to repair something. Consider its original cost, repair cost, and the technology velocity—the speed of improvement and innovation. Thus, replacing a broken product may be worthwhile if a new model brings major new technology and if the cost of repair is high. With many electronic products, a repair often involves replacing an entire circuit board—a costly proposition. Complexity and proprietary parts can be a disincentive to fixing a laptop computer, for example.

You should probably fix nearly anything in its first year—especially if it's under warranty. Items such as pro-style ranges, lawn tractors, and projection TVs are usually worth repairing long into their lives because new ones are so expensive. Otherwise consider replacing products if their repair cost exceeds 50 percent of replacement.

When something breaks, a few simple steps can help make the repair process easier. First, determine if you can fix it yourself. Most owners' manuals have a troubleshooting section, and manufacturers' Web sites sometimes include repair instructions.

If the item is still not working, you may have to call the manufacturer. This can be frustrating: In a reader survey, about one quarter of those who tried had difficulty getting through, and almost half found the assistance wanting. Persistence can sometimes pay: Nearly 10 percent of those who called the manufacturer got an offer to fix or replace an out-of-warranty item for free.

Manufacturers generally train authorized service technicians on the latest equipment and hold them to certain standards—but repairs by these technicians may cost more. Independent repairers can be a viable choice, especially for products out of warranty. Ask if the repairer belongs to a trade association such as the Professional Service Association or the International Society of Certified Electronics Technicians (ISCET). While membership doesn't guarantee integrity, it may mean repairers have had special training.

If you feel victimized by a repairer, you can file a complaint with your local community-affairs department, the Better Business Bureau *(www.bbb.org)*, or your state's attorney general's office. You can also take the repairer to small-claims court. Keep all receipts and records. And ask to keep any parts that are replaced.

If you replace it

Disposing of broken products may make economic sense for the individual consumer, but the environmental costs for communities include burdening landfills and the risk that hazardous materials will enter the waste stream. Examples of dangerous waste include lead in circuit boards and picture tubes; mercury in laptops and digital cameras; and cadmium in some rechargeable batteries. Repositories for batteries and other potentially hazardous products are available.

Reliability

Brand
Repair Histories

To help you gauge reliability, the graphs that follow give brand repair rates for 14 product categories. CONSUMER REPORTS has been asking about brands' reliability for more than 30 years. The findings have been quite consistent, though they are not infallible predictors. A brand's repair history includes data on many models, some of which may have been more or less reliable than others. And surveys of past products can't anticipate design or manufacturing changes in new products. Product categories include appliances such as refrigerators and vacuum cleaners, electronic products such as TV sets and camcorders, as well as lawn mowers and tractors. Histories for different kinds of products aren't directly comparable because they cover products of different ages, and older products tend to break more often than newer ones.

Reliability

Camcorders

Camcorders are used an average of only 12 hours per year, which may influence their repair rate. We found that people use digitals for more hours than analogs, however. Among digital camcorders, Canon MiniDV and JVC MiniDV were the most repair-prone brands; for analog cameras there were small differences among leading brands. Differences of 3 or more points are meaningful.

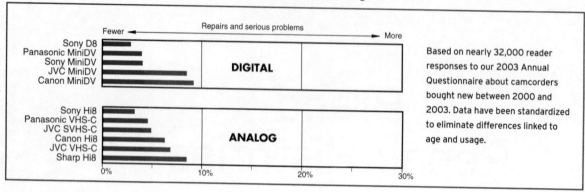

Based on nearly 32,000 reader responses to our 2003 Annual Questionnaire about camcorders bought new between 2000 and 2003. Data have been standardized to eliminate differences linked to age and usage.

Dishwashers

Asko has been the most repair-prone of these 12 brands. Bosch has also been among the more repair-prone brands. Differences of 4 or more points are meaningful.

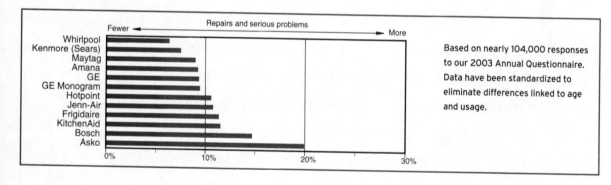

Based on nearly 104,000 responses to our 2003 Annual Questionnaire. Data have been standardized to eliminate differences linked to age and usage.

Reliability

Dryers

Gas and electric dryers have been equally reliable, with small differences among leading brands. Differences of 3 or more points are meaningful.

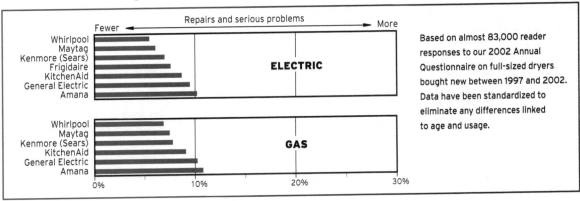

Based on almost 83,000 reader responses to our 2002 Annual Questionnaire on full-sized dryers bought new between 1997 and 2002. Data have been standardized to eliminate any differences linked to age and usage.

Lawn mowers (Push and self-propelled)

Among push models, Lawn-Boy was the most repair-prone brand; Snapper was among the more repair-prone brands of the self-propelled mowers. Differences of 5 or more points are meaningful.

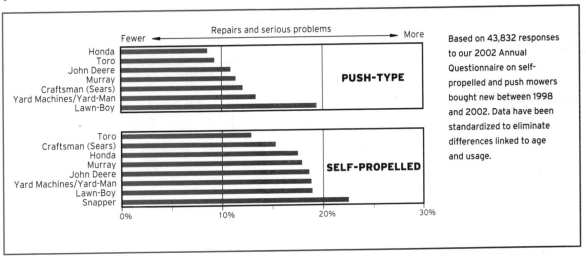

Based on 43,832 responses to our 2002 Annual Questionnaire on self-propelled and push mowers bought new between 1998 and 2002. Data have been standardized to eliminate differences linked to age and usage.

Reliability

Lawn tractors and riding mowers

Cub Cadet was among the more repair-prone brands of lawn tractors. Among riding mowers, Murray (whose repair rate may in part reflect a 2002 fuel-tank recall) and Snapper were among the more repair-prone brands. Differences of 6 or more points are meaningful.

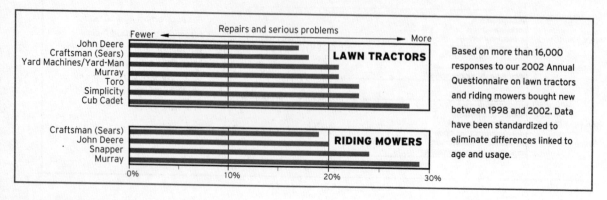

Based on more than 16,000 responses to our 2002 Annual Questionnaire on lawn tractors and riding mowers bought new between 1998 and 2002. Data have been standardized to eliminate differences linked to age and usage.

Microwave ovens

Major brands of nonconvection countertop microwave ovens generally have been quite reliable: They had repair rates of 6 percent or less, with no meaningful differences.

Sharp has been one of the more repair-prone brands of over-the-range models (listed below). Kenmore, KitchenAid, and Whirlpool are not included in the chart; certain models from these brands were recalled in 2002, resulting in high repair rates of 35 to 48 percent for those brands. Differences of 4 or more points are meaningful.

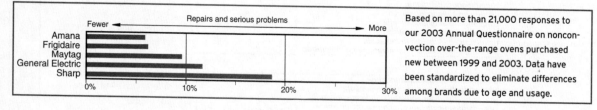

Based on more than 21,000 responses to our 2003 Annual Questionnaire on nonconvection over-the-range ovens purchased new between 1999 and 2003. Data have been standardized to eliminate differences among brands due to age and usage.

Ranges (Electric models)

In general, electric ranges have required fewer repairs than gas models. Smoothtop models have been about as reliable as conventional coil-burner models. Jenn-Air, Amana, KitchenAid, and Maytag have been among the more repair-prone brands. Differences of 3 or more points are meaningful.

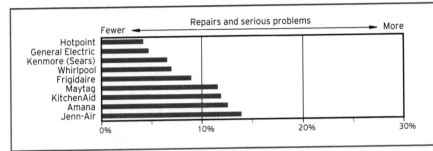

Based on more than 50,000 responses to our 2002 Annual Questionnaire covering electric ranges purchased new between 1997 and 2002. Data have been standardized to eliminate differences linked to age.

Ranges (Gas models)

Gas ranges have generally required more repairs than electric ranges. Amana was the most repair-prone brand followed by Jenn-Air, Maytag, KitchenAid, and Magic Chef. Differences of 4 or more points are meaningful.

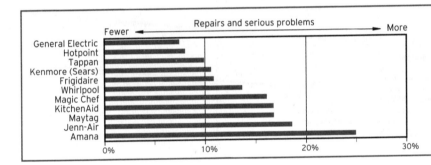

Based on more than 27,000 responses to our 2002 Annual Questionnaire covering gas ranges purchased between 1997 and 2002. Data have been standardized to eliminate differences linked to age.

Reliability

Refrigerators

Built-ins appear to have higher repair rates than freestanding fridges. We have enough data to include only Sub-Zero built-ins in our graphs. Sub-Zero bottom-freezers with icemakers were more repair-prone than all other top- and bottom-freezer brands analyzed. In side-by-sides, Frigidaire and Sub-Zero were among the more repair-prone brands, and Maytag was the most repair-prone. We lack enough data to place Jenn-Air freestanding side-by-sides in the graphs, but the data we have give us concern. Differences of 5 or more points are meaningful.

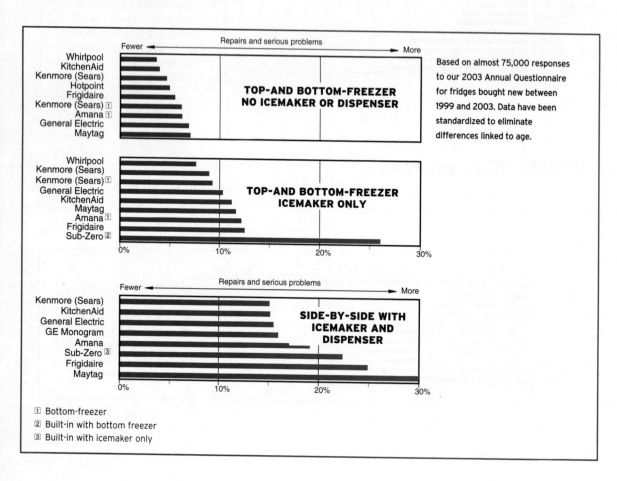

Based on almost 75,000 responses to our 2003 Annual Questionnaire for fridges bought new between 1999 and 2003. Data have been standardized to eliminate differences linked to age.

1 Bottom-freezer
2 Built-in with bottom freezer
3 Built-in with icemaker only

Reliability

TV sets (25 to 27 inches)

RCA and General Electric were among the more repair-prone brands. Differences of 3 or more points are meaningful.

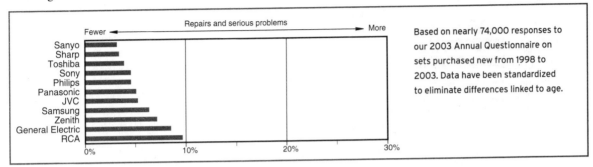

Based on nearly 74,000 responses to our 2003 Annual Questionnaire on sets purchased new from 1998 to 2003. Data have been standardized to eliminate differences linked to age.

TV sets (30- to 36-inches)

Among 30- to 32-inch models, Zenith was among the more repair-prone brands. In both the 30- to 32-inch and 34- to 36-inch categories, RCA was the most repair-prone brand. Included in the charts are both HD-capable and standard sets. The two types showed no significant difference in reliability, but HD-capable sets are much newer than analog models, so we will monitor their repair record closely in the years to come. Data do not apply to LCD TVs. Differences of 3 or more points are meaningful.

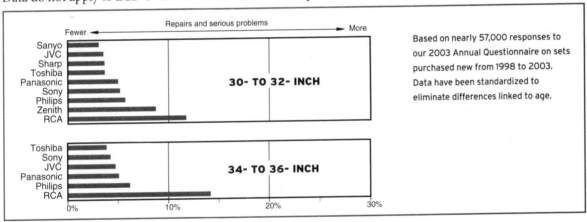

Based on nearly 57,000 responses to our 2003 Annual Questionnaire on sets purchased new from 1998 to 2003. Data have been standardized to eliminate differences linked to age.

TV sets (Projection)

Data include both HD-capable and standard sets, which showed no difference in reliability. Differences of 3 or more points are meaningful.

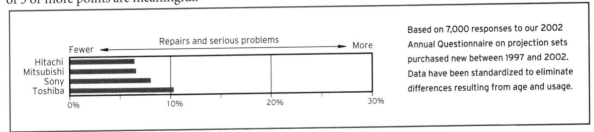

Based on 7,000 responses to our 2002 Annual Questionnaire on projection sets purchased new between 1997 and 2002. Data have been standardized to eliminate differences resulting from age and usage.

Reliability

Vacuum cleaners

Fantom uprights and Eureka canisters were the most repair-prone brands. The results shown here don't include broken belts—a frequent though usually inexpensive problem that was more common for uprights and for Eureka and Hoover among canister brands. Differences of 4 or more points are meaningful.

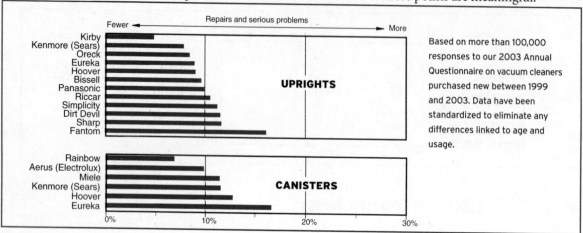

Based on more than 100,000 responses to our 2003 Annual Questionnaire on vacuum cleaners purchased new between 1999 and 2003. Data have been standardized to eliminate any differences linked to age and usage.

Washing machines

Maytag front-loaders were more repair-prone than all other brands of washers. Differences of 4 or more points are meaningful.

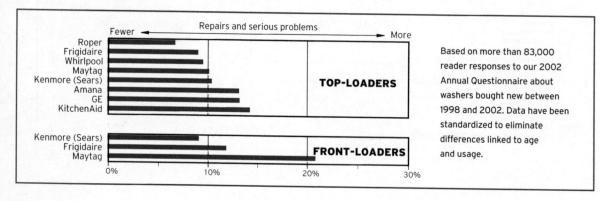

Based on more than 83,000 reader responses to our 2002 Annual Questionnaire about washers bought new between 1998 and 2002. Data have been standardized to eliminate differences linked to age and usage.

Reliability

Brand Locator

Phone numbers and Web addresses of selected manufacturers.

A

Acoustic Research	800 225-9847	www.acoustic-research.com
Admiral	800 688-9900	www.maytag.com
Aerus (Electrolux)	800 243-9078	www.aerusonline.com
AGFA	888 988-2432	www.AGFA.com
Aiwa	800 289-2492	www.aiwa.com
Akai	888 697-2247	www.akaiusa.com
Amana	800 843-0304	www.amana.com
Apex	866 427-3946	www.apexdigitalinc.com
Ariens	800 678-5443	www.ariens.com
Asko	800 898-1879	www.askousa.com
Aspire Digital	310 856-0630	www.aspiredigital.com
AT&T	800 222-3111	www.att.com
Audiovox	800 229-1235	www.audiovox.com

B

B&W	800 370-3740	www.bwspeakers.com
B.I.C.	888 461-4628	www.bicamerica.com
Bionaire	800 253-2764	www.bionaire.com
Bissell	800 237-7691	www.bissell.com
Black & Decker	800 544-6986	www.blackanddecker.com
Bosch	800 944-2904	www.boschappliances.com
Bose	800 444-2673	www.bose.com
Boston Acoustics	800 246-7767	www.bostonacoustics.com
Braun	800 272-8622	www.braun.com
Broilmaster	800 255-0403	www.broilmaster.com
Brother	800 276-7746	www.brother.com

C

Cambridge Soundworks	800 367-4434	www.cambridgesoundworks.com
Canon	800 652-2666	www.usa.canon.com
Carrier	800 227-7437	www.carrier.com
Casio	800 962-2746	www.casio.com
Cerwin Vega	805 584-5300	www.cerwinvega.com
Char-Broil	800 241-7548	www.charbroil.com
Coleman	800 356-3612	www.bbqhq.com
Compaq	800 345-1518	www.compaq.com
Craftsman	Call local Sears store	www.sears.com
Creative Labs	800 998-5227	www.creative.com
Cub Cadet	877 282-8684	www.cubcadet.com
Cuisinart	800 726-0190	www.cuisinart.com

D

Dacor	800 793-0093	www.dacor.com
Daewoo	888 643-2396	www.daewoous.com
Dell	800 879-3355	www.dell.com
DeLonghi	800 322-3848	www.delonghiusa.com
Denon	973 396-0810	www.usa.denon.com
DeWalt	800 433-9258	www.dewalt.com
DirecTV	800 347-3288	www.direcTV.com
Dirt Devil	800 321-1134	www.dirtdevil.com
Dish Network (EchoStar)	800 333-3474	www.dishnetwork.com
Ducane	800 382-2637	www.ducane.com
Dynamic Cooking Systems (DCS)	800 433-8466	www.dcsappliances.com
Dyson	866 693-9766	www.dyson.com

E

Echo	800 673-1558	www.echo-usa.com
Electrolux	800 243-9078	www.electroluxusa.com
Emerson	800 898-9020	www.emersonradio.com
Envision	888 838-6388	www.envisionmonitor.com
Epson	800 463-7766	www.epson.com
Ericsson	800 374-2776	www.ericsson.com
Eureka	800 282-2886	www.eureka.com

F

Fantom	800 668-9600	www.fantom.com
Fedders	217 342-3901	www.fedders.com
Fiesta	800 396-3838	www.fiestabbq.com
Fisher	818 998-7322	www.fisherav.com
Fisher & Paykel	888 936-7872	www.fisherpaykel.com
Franklin	800 266-5626	www.franklin.com
Friedrich	800 541-6645	www.friedrich.com
Frigidaire	800 374-4432	www.frigidaire.com
Fujifilm	800 800-3854	www.fujifilm.com

G

GE (appliances)	800 626-2000	www.geappliances.com
GE (electronics)	800 447-1700	www.home-electronics.net
Gibson	888 203-1389	www.frigidaire.com
Goldstar	800 243-0000	www.lgeus.com
Great Outdoors Grill Company	888 869-5454	www.gogrills.com
Grizzly	570 546-9663	www.grizzly.com

H

Haier	888 764-2437	www.haier.com
Hamilton Beach	800 851-8900	www.hambeach.com
Handspring	888 565-9393	www.handspring.com
Harman/Kardon	800 422-8027	www.harmankardon.com
Haier	877 337-3639	www.haieramerica.com
Hitachi	800 448-2244	www.hitachi.com
Holland	800 880-9766	www.hollandgrill.com
Holmes	800 546-5637	www.holmesproducts.com
Homelite	800 242-4672	www.homelite.com
Honda	800 426-7701	www.hondapowerequipment.com
Hoover	800 944-9200	www.hoover.com
Hotpoint	800 626-2000	www.hotpoint.com
Hughes	800 274-8995	www.hns-usa.com
Husqvarna	800 487-5962	www.husqvarna.com

I

Infinity	516 674-4463	www.infinitysystems.com

J

JBL	516 255-4525	www.jbl.com
Jenn-Air	800 688-1100	www.jennair.com
Jensen	800 732-6866	www.recoton.com
John Deere	800 537-8233	www.deere.com
Jonsered	877 693-7729	www.usa.jonsered.com
JVC	800 252-5722	www.jvc.com

K

KDS	800 237-9988	www.kdsusa.com
Kenmore	Call a local Sears store	www.sears.com
Kenwood	800 536-9663	www.kenwoodusa.com
Kia	800 333-4542	www.kia.com
Kirby	800 437-7170	www.kirby.com
KitchenAid	800 422-1230	www.kitchenaid.com
KLH	818 767-2843	www.klhaudio.com
Klipsch	800 554-7724	www.klipsch.com
Kodak	800 235-6325	www.kodak.com
Konica	800-285-6422	www.konica.com
Kyocera	800 349-4188	www.qualcomm.com

Locator

L

Land Rover	800 346-3493	www.landrover.com
Lawn-Boy	800 526-6937	www.lawnboy.com
Lexmark	800 539-6275	www.lexmark.com
LG	800 243-0000	www.lgeus.com

M

Magic Chef	800 688-1120	www.maytag.com
Magnovox	800 531-0039	www.philipsusa.com
Makita	800 462-5482	www.makita.com
Maxim	800 233-9054	www.salton-maxim.com
Maytag	800 688-9900	www.maytag.com
McCulloch	800 521-8559	www.mccullochpower.com
Microsoft	800 426-9400	www.microsoft.com/actimates
Microtek	310 687-5940	www.microtekusa.com
Miele	800 289-6435	www.mieleusa.com
Milwaukee	877 279-7819	www.mil-electric-tool.com
Minolta	800 808-4888	www.minoltausa.com
Mintek	866 709-9500	www.mintekdigital.com
Mitsubishi	800 332-2119	www.mitsubishi.com
Motorola	800 331-6456	www.motorola.com
MTD	800 800-7310	www.mtdproducts.com
Murray	800 224-8940	www.murrayinc.com

N

NEC	800 338-9549	www.necus.com
Nikon	800 645-6687	www.nikonusa.com
Nokia	888 665-4228	www.nokia.com

O

Oki	800 654-3282	www.okidata.com
Olympus	800 622-6372	www.olympusamerica.com
Onkyo	201 785-2600	www.onkyousa.com
Optimus	Call local RadioShack	www.radioshack.com
Oreck	800 989-3535	www.oreck.com
Oster	800 597-5978	www.sunbeam.com

P

Panasonic	800 211-7262	www.panasonic.com
Pentax	800 877-0155	www.pentax.com
Philips	800 531-0039	www.philipsusa.com
Pioneer	800 421-1404	www.pioneerelectronics.com
Polaroid	800 432-5355	www.polaroid.com
Polk Audio	800 377-7655	www.polkaudio.com
Porter-Cable	800 487-8665	www.porter-cable.com
Poulan	800 238-9333	www.poulan.com
Precor	800 477-3267	www.precor.com
Precisionaire	800 347-2220	www.precisionaire.com

Proctor-Silex .... 800 851-8900 .... www.proctorsilex.com
PSB .... 888 772-0000 .... www.psbspeakers.com

Q

Quasar .... 800 211-7262 .... www.panasonic.com

R

RadioShack .... 800 843-7422 .... www.radioshack.com
RCA .... 800 336-1900 .... www.rca.com
Regal .... 262 626-2121 .... www.regalware.com
Regina .... 228 867-8507 .... www.reginavac.com
Remington .... 616 791-7325 .... www.remingtonchainsaw.com
Research Products .... 800 545-2219 .... www.resprod.com
Rival .... 800 557-4825 .... www.rivalproducts.com
Roper .... 800 447-6737 .... www.roperappliances.com
Rowenta .... 781 396-0600 .... www.rowentausa.com
Royal .... 800 321-1134 .... wwww.dirtdevil.com
Ryobi .... 800 345-8746 .... www.ryobi.com

S

Sabre by John Deere .... 800 537-8233 .... www.deere.com
Salton .... 800 233-9054 .... www.salton-maxim.com
Sampo .... 800 203-4429 .... www.sampoamericas.com
Samsung .... 800 726-7864 .... www.samsungusa.com
Sanyo .... 818 998-7322 .... www.sanyo.com
Sharp .... 800 237-4277 .... www.sharp-usa.com
Siemens .... 888 777-0211 .... www.icm.siemens.com
Simplicity (yard equipment) .... 262 284-8669 .... www.simplicitymfg.com
Simplicity (vacuum cleaners) .... 888 974-6759 .... www.simplicityvac.com
Skil .... 877 754 5999 .... www.skiltools.com
Snapper .... 800 762-7737 .... www.snapper.com
Solo .... 800 765-6462 .... www.solousa.com
Sony .... 800 222-7669 .... www.sony.com
Southwestern Bell .... 800 366-0937 .... www.southwesternbell.com
Stanley .... 800 788-7766 .... www.stanleylawnmowers.com
Stihl .... 800 467-8445 .... www.stihl.com
Sub-Zero .... 800 222-7820 .... www.subzero.com
Sunbeam .... 800 458-8407 .... www.sunbeam.com

T

Tappan .... 800 537-5530 .... www.frigidaire.com
TEC .... 800 331-0097 .... www.tecgasgrills.com
Technics .... 800 211-7262 .... www.panasonic.com
T-Fal .... 800 395-8325 .... www.t-falusa.com
Thermador .... 800 735-4328 .... www.thermador.com
Toastmaster .... 800 947-3744 .... www.toastmaster.com
Toro .... 800 348-2424 .... www.toro.com
Toshiba .... 800 631-3811 .... www.toshiba.com
Tripp Lite .... 773 869-1234 .... www.tripplite.com

Trion . . . . 800 338-7466 . . . . www.fedders.com
Troy-Bilt . . . . 866 840-6483 . . . . www.troybilt.com

U

Umax . . . . 214 342-9799 . . . . www.umax.com
Uniden . . . . 800 297-1023 . . . . www.uniden.com

V

ViewSonic . . . . 800 688-6688 . . . . www.viewsonic.com
Viking . . . . 800 467-2643 . . . . www.vikingrange.com
Visioneer . . . . 925 251-6398 . . . . www.visioneer.com
Vivitar . . . . 805 498-7008 . . . . www.vivitar.com
VTech . . . . 800 624-5688 . . . . www.vtech.com

W

Walker . . . . 800 843-7422 . . . . www.radioshack.com
Waring . . . . 800 492-7464 . . . . www.waringproducts.com
Weber . . . . 800 446-1071 . . . . www.weber.com
Weed Eater . . . . 800 554-6723 . . . . www.weedeater.com
West Bend . . . . 800 367-0111 . . . . www.westbend.com
Whirlpool . . . . 800 253-1301 . . . . www.whirlpool.com
White Outdoor . . . . 800 949-4483 . . . . www.whiteoutdoor.com
White-Westinghouse . . . . 800 245-0600 . . . . www.frigidaire.com

X

Xerox . . . . 800 832-6979 . . . . www.xerox.com

Y

Yamaha . . . . 800 492-6242 . . . . www.yamaha.com
Yard Machines by MTD . . . . 800 800-7310 . . . . www.mtdproducts.com
Yashica . . . . 800 526-0266 . . . . www.yashica.com

Z

Zenith . . . . 256 772-1515 . . . . www.zenith.com

Index

Index